DATE DUE

DEC 000			

DEMCO 38-296

IDEAS OF SOCIAL ORDER IN THE ANCIENT WORLD

Recent Titles in
Contributions in Political Science

The Leviathan in the State Theory of Thomas Hobbes: Meaning and
Failure of a Symbol
Carl Schmitt
Translated by George Schwab and Erna Hilfstein

On Ruins of Empire: Ethnicity and Nationalism in the Former Soviet Union
George Mirsky

Ethnoregional Conflict in Democracies: Mostly Ballots, Rarely Bullets
Saul Newman

Neocolonialism American Style, 1960–2000
William H. Blanchard

Government Structures in the U.S.A. and the Sovereign States of the Former U.S.S.R.:
Power Allocation Among Central, Regional, and Local Governments
James E. Hickey, Jr. and Alexej Ugrinsky, editors

Roman Catholicism and Political Form
Carl Schmitt
Translated and annotated by G. L. Ulmen

International Theory: To the Brink and Beyond
Andrew P. Dunne

To Sheathe the Sword: Civil-Military Relations in the Quest for Democracy
John P. Lovell and David E. Albright, editors

President Reagan and the World
Eric J. Schmertz, Natalie Datlof, and Alexej Ugrinsky, editors

Ronald Reagan's America
Eric J. Schmertz, Natalie Datlof, and Alexej Ugrinsky, editors

Germany for the Germans? The Political Effects of International Migration
Wesley D. Chapin

Out of Russian Orbit: Hungary Gravitates to the West
Andrew Felkay

IDEAS OF SOCIAL ORDER IN THE ANCIENT WORLD

Vilho Harle

Contributions in Political Science, Number 383

GREENWOOD PRESS
Westport, Connecticut • London

Library of Congress Cataloging-in-Publication Data

Harle, Vilho.
    Ideas of social order in the ancient world / Vilho Harle.
       p.   cm.—(Contributions in political science, ISSN 0147–1066
; no. 383)
    Includes bibliographical references and index.
    ISBN 0–313–30582–X (alk. paper)
    1. Social control—History. 2. Social institutions—History.
3. International organization—History. 4. Civilization, Ancient.
I. Title. II. Series.
HM271.H297 1998
303.3′3′09—dc21   97–33962

British Library Cataloguing in Publication Data is available.

Library of Congress Catalog Card Number: 97–33962
ISBN: 0–313–30582–X
ISSN: 0147–1066

First published in 1998

Greenwood Press, 88 Post Road West, Westport, CT 06881
An imprint of Greenwood Publishing Group, Inc.

Printed in the United States of America

The paper used in this book complies with the
Permanent Paper Standard issued by the National
Information Standards Organization (Z39.48–1984).

10 9 8 7 6 5 4 3 2

Contents

Foreword

Johan Galtung

The scope opened up by the author of this important book is breath-taking and will no doubt generate some scepticism in readers unaccustomed to such vistas. His theme is well known to any scholar in political science, international relations, and peace studies: How do various schools/thinkers understand social order and its negation, chaos? What are the factors, actors, and forces behind these phenomena and more particularly: How would a transition from chaos to order be possible? The questions are very close to the core of political science, and—if we read "chaos" as "violence," and "order" as "peace"—also to the core of peace studies.

Enter Professor Harle. He could have done what countless authors have done—written one more Western (from Machiavelli to Morgenthau) book, certainly via Hobbes. Or he could have written his own book, the Harle view of chaos and order (there are some modest indications in the present book). Instead he opens our time horizon back to the Golden Age, the magic fifth (or so) century B.C.E., and he opens our space horizon well beyond the Occident, into India and China. As a Norwegian I know one reason why: coming from a minor culture in Europe it is easier to be a cosmopolitan in time and space than for those encased in their own presumably major culture.

But that is a minor reason. I can see a number of other reasons for welcoming this audacious exercise; some of them, not all, mentioned by the author.

We live in a globalizing world. International relations are global relations, not only the foreign policy of a major country or regional relations. How can anyone dare draw upon theory developed in only one region? What kind of provincialism sustains that type of intellectual laziness?

Then, Harle brings us back to the classics. Some may be surprised to find Jesus among them, and yet he evidently had a theory of both chaos and order. Together with Jesus, figure Confucius, Kautilya, Plato, Aristotle, Cicero, Livy and Virgil, and the concrete persons behind such schools as (Chinese) Legalism, Mohism, Daoism, ancient Indian thought, Buddhism, Zoroastrianism, ancient Hebrew thought, Judaism, early Christians and Church.

There are two rather heavy arguments in favor of the classics. First, they have stood the test of time. There must be some reason aside cultural inertia why this is so. One reason is very clear when the reader devotes some time to the classics: they have said much, maybe most, not quite all, and perhaps better than most contemporaries. Admittedly, they have the upper hand there. They set some discourses two, two- and a half millennia ago, and these discourses are still with us.

Objection: But isn't that a good reason to liberate ourselves? Oh yes, but liberation by ignoring the classics is the way of totalitarianism. The way of democracy is to give them a voice through intertemporal dialogue. Harle does that for us; he poses questions, they answer across millennia.

Second, they are not only commenting on chaos and order, these people and schools. They gave us our codes, and one hundred or so generations later we are still under the sway of those codes. As Harle shows, much of contemporary politics can be understood by knowing the codes deeply rooted in us all. Thus, Mao Zedong's Cultural Revolution is a latter-day version of the struggle of the Legalists against the Confucians, so it is useful to know the worldviews of these schools.

Harle has his seventeen classics well distributed over the Occident-Orient dimension, and he has seventeen subdivisions (including the images of chaos in Chapter 2, also repeated in the Conclusions)—a fascination with the number 17? In short, he had 289 jobs to do. He must have applied a considerable quantity of Finnish *sisu* to these formidable tasks. The result fits neatly into Table 1. The reader might like to consult it at the beginning rather than the end of the reading.

Very important in the understanding of the images of chaos is the distinction between immanent and transcendent ideas of reality, very closely related to Occident-Orient. Very important in the understanding of social order is the distinction between moral and coercive power. I will not reveal how these two distinctions seem to relate to each other; the reader either knows, has guessed, or should be kept in suspense as with an excellent play. Let me only say that few relations seem more basic in the contemporary world, and these particular syndromes have been with us for a very long time. Reading Harle may empower us to do something about it.

Personally, I miss Islam and I miss Shinto. I know why—they were late-comers. Islam, although often mentioned for instance in connection with Zoroastrianism) is only 1,300+ years old. State Shinto, the early Meiji construction, is more like one hundred years old. Given Harle's framework, the reader will have to work them on his or her own and may speculate on the worldviews of African, Amerindian, and Pacific peoples.

The book will, as mentioned, cause some raised eyebrows. There will be enough to discuss. Perhaps the reader should focus on the basic interrelations in Table 1, in Conclusions, and on the column and row totals. Also, Harle should be read twice. I for one, did not grasp his rich thoughts on the first reading of this truly global (in an age of globalization on Western premisses) book, which brings us back to our civilizational roots.

Lillehammer, Norway, September 1997

Preface and Acknowledgments

This book calls attention to the age-old and ever present issue of social order, defined as the opposite of chaos, nothingness. In social order, everything has its place and name, and everybody knows what life is about. In social order, *cosmos*, life has full meaning and content, it is a good life. Such a good life is only possible in society, and for the members of society. In social order this constitution of a meaningful and good life covers, naturally, all social relations as a totality: between individuals, between social groups, between the states, and between all of these levels.

The idea of social order does not exclude change. On the contrary, social order is never given or permanent; it is constituted socially by human beings. Chaos and nothingness continuously threat human beings who must work hard to find a new solid basis for their life, especially during rapid social and political changes when real dangers threaten their lives and values, but especially when they experience—for many reasons—the basis of their spiritual and social life collapsing. It is not an exaggeration to say that the greatest ideas humankind has invented are answers to the problem of social order. Those answers are presented in great religious, literary, and philosophical works, which actually have constituted and defined the civilizations in which they were born.

The present comparative analysis of ideas concerning social order in classical Chinese political philosophy, the Indian epic and political literature, Zoroastrianism, Judaism, classical Greek and Roman political thought, and early Christianity suggests that there are two major approaches to establishing and maintaining social order in social relations: *moral principles* and *political power*. This book discusses culturally important religious, philosophical, and literary works which suggest alternative, often contending, approaches to social order along this basic division.

Studies in the history of peace ideas and international (political) theory have almost totally neglected this fundamental source of ideas, mainly due to two intertwined reasons. First, scholars have been interested almost exclusively in European ideas. Second, scholars' interests in those European ideas are mainly related to the modern states system born since the fifteenth century. Therefore, this book tries to fill a gap in the literature of peace and international studies, justified by the reemergence of the issue of social order in the turbulent post-Cold War world, where the age-old issue of social order must be reexamined. Without the idea of social order, all phenomena—like war—remain isolated and therefore impossible to explain or understand. All single events should be explained instead by asking how they are related to social order—because that is why people are willing to undertake them. It is obvious, however, that narrow conceptions of international order or simplistic definitions of order in various applications of law and order are insufficient in delineating the basic issues at hand. Social order must be a wide and comprehensive concept; it must cover all social life and all social relations, not just relations between states.

The idea of social order is impossible to define briefly. Instead, we must examine what has been said about social order when humankind has introduced its basic approach to establish and maintain social order. In fact, various approaches give various definitions to social order. These approaches are actually attempts to define social order, which never exists as an objective fact because it is always constituted socially by the mutual interaction of human beings. This book concentrates on one source of this debate—fundamental religious, political, and literary texts written in the genesis of important civilizations. However, it is important to note that these texts still are read and highly respected in the civilizations where they were created. Even if an original civilization has disappeared, the ideas born within it often have a strong influence on later, modern ideas. Therefore, the discussion of such basic texts hopefully helps us to understand social and political thought in the respective contemporary civilizations.

This is important in at least two respects. First, due to increasing contacts between various civilizations, we have time to reject Eurocentric and any civilization-bound ideas and learn about social and political thinking in other civilizations. Second, in order to find alternatives to statecentric models of international relations, it is time to reject the narrow conception of international order typical to mainstream studies of international relations—social and political life is a whole. The normal tendency to call attention to inter-state relations gives nothing more than a partial picture of social and political complex, a picture which is actually becoming more and more inaccurate all the time. It is time to see that we cannot go beyond the nation state by simply repeating over and over again that the time of the nation state is past—we need a picture of social and political relations, where the nation state has no exclusive role, if any.

I launched this book a rather long time ago. I have perhaps spent more time on this project than is usually thought reasonable. However, I do not think that I have lost a single day in vain. On the contrary, close contact with the greatest ideas of humankind has been both challenging and motivating, and it has been a solid basis for my other activities as both a researcher and teacher in political science and international relations. I have fully enjoyed the perspectives I gained during the research process, especially when I have been able to share many of the ideas.

I am indebted to a number of colleagues, all of whom are impossible to list here. Some of them, however, must be mentioned. I must extend my thanks to the two

intellectual fathers of this book. First, Johan Galtung whose excellent paper "Social Cosmology and the Concept of Peace" (1981) called my attention to this important but neglected area of ancient ideas. Second, James A. Aho whose groundbreaking *Religious Mythology and the Art of War* (1981) proved such a study by a social scientist fully justified. Naturally, my approach has been different from these two innovators. I would like to extend my warmest thanks to Johan for his foreword, and I have been delighted to have both prominent teachers to encourage me to complete this book. Reijo Raivola and Heikki Räisänen have provided concrete advice which helped me in the effort. Stephen Chan, Michael W. Doyle and Pete Furia, and Gershon Weiler gave me detailed comments. I must also mention a number of more formal referees who had more indirect influence on my work: Esko Antola, Harto Hakovirta, Kalevi J. Holsti, Lauri Karvonen, Zeev Maoz, Nikolaj Petersen, and Klaus Törnudd. It is certain that all their explicit and implicit comments have improved my production, and forced me to think about what I have been doing and why. On the other hand, all weaknesses and misunderstandings remain fully my responsibility.

I have written this book in three innovative, scholarly communities: Tampere Peace Research Institute (1985–1993), the University of Jyväskylä (1992–1993), and the Centre for International Studies of the London School of Economics and Political Science (1996–1997). All three communities have been invaluable, but the Centre for International Studies and its former chairman, Professor John Mayall, deserve the warmest thanks for arranging, fully in accordance with the best English social and academic traditions, the splendid isolation of undisturbed work that made the completion of this project possible. Finally, I must extend my warmest thanks to the Academy of Finland for its financial support for my project on Otherness, Identity & Politics, to which this book is one of my personal contributions.

Hämeenlinna, London, and Rovaniemi, November 1997

Introduction

The comparative analysis of ideas concerning social order in classical Chinese political philosophy, the Indian epic and political literature, Zoroastrianism, Judaism, classical Greek and Roman political thought, and early Christianity suggests that there are two major approaches to establishing and maintaining social order in human relations, both between individuals and within and between various social groups: *moral principles* and *political power*. According to the first approach, if and when people follow strict moral principles, the relations between them will be orderly and harmonious. According to the second approach, orderly relations can only be based on the application of power by the ruler over the ruled.

The first approach gives an exclusive role to individual human beings, who are presupposed to govern themselves by simply following the moral principles—orderly human relations and subtle forms of societies become possible without any political structures. The second approach does not believe in voluntary arrangements, but requires humankind to be organized in a group or groups in order to establish a feasible political government, without which no order is possible. To apply a convenient expression to the suggested distinction between "self-government by men over themselves in the light of moral principles" and "the use of power by the ruler over the ruled," I shall hereafter refer to *principle-oriented* and *power-oriented* patterns of social order.

The suggested basic distinction between principle-oriented and power-oriented patterns can be found in an analogous form within the latter group. According to some views, all politics must be based on and strictly follow moral principles, while other views exclude moral norms from politics. This debate concerning the nature of politics is so fundamental that it seems to include the suggested distinction of the principle-oriented and the power-oriented patterns. However, I wish to emphasize the possibility of social order without any political organization and to distinguish between two types of moral rule (one excluding politics and the other trying to make politics moral). On the other hand, I am fully aware that my distinctions are analytical. Politics as "power over" can be found anywhere, including the historical (or real) applications of the principle-oriented patterns.

Civilizational thought, under my investigation, represents well-known cultures of the ancient world. The ideas were born and grew to full maturity in about a thousand years between the sixth century B.C.E. and the fifth century C.E. Therefore, this book looks like a study in ancient history or ancient religions. Why does a scholar in peace and international studies, a political scientist, write such a book? Why should another social scientist or anybody interested in post-Cold War international affairs read it?

The questions might be justified only if the present work is defined as a study of ancient history and religions. The point is, however, that this book neither can nor must be categorized as a study of ancient history and ancient religions, but as a modest interdisciplinary contribution to peace and international studies, that is, as a work in international political theory. In fact, all the basic texts discussed are still in existence and recognized as basic works in contemporary civilizations. Furthermore, all the discussed civilizations either still exist—Confucian, Hindu, and Western civilizations; Buddhism, Judaism, and Christianity—or have had considerable influence and impact others, including Islam. That is, the relevant modern civilizations still respect or at least indirectly share the basic values of the ancient texts. Indeed, the long life span of civilizations makes the distinction between the past and the present irrelevant. Materials born in the genesis of the civilizations are still fully present in current thought. On the other hand, this is not a study of contemporary civilizational values, but it is based on works written or composed about two thousand years ago. Therefore, some justifications for this book must be made explicit.

First, according to recent popular claims civilizational values and traditions have become increasingly relevant in post-Cold War international politics (e.g., *The Economist*, November 9, 1996). Samuel P. Huntington's (1993, 1996) well-known thesis about the clash of civilizations is the best known of such visions. Huntington's thesis represents a widely shared conventional wisdom, not likely to be dismissed by an extensive academic criticism (cf. Ajami 1993; Halliday 1995 and 1996). There is also an increasing number of academic works that claim ancient traditions have a striking, if undeniably complex, role in contemporary, international politics. For example, Dorraj presents a systematic investigation into ancient Iranian and Islamist traditions and their role in the Iranian revolution of 1989 (Dorraj 1990: 5, 32; cf. Lewis 1994: 157; Taheri 1985: 120–21). Similarly, Sicker and others have discussed the case of modern Israel in light of the continuity of the Judaic tradition and historical experiences of external threats (Sicker 1992; cf. Dossa 1988, 1990; Gorny 1994; Weiler 1990). Among other civilizations, the continuity between the past and the present is the most conspicuous in China. This was illustrated, for example, by a debate on Confucianism and Legalism during the Cultural Revolution and the current emphasis on the unification of China (cf. Chen 1991). Concerning India, Nalini Kant Jha (1989), in his systematic investigation into the cultural roots of India's foreign policy has suggested that India's foreign policy is determined by the interplay of a large number of factors, which include the cultural-philosophical values and traditions of the country.

What Huntington *says* may be right or wrong in the empirical sense, but what he *does* is a striking example of the continuity of the tradition of the politics of exclusion, a basic pattern of social order discussed in detail in Chapter 13 of this book. However, cultural factors, including the ancient traditions, do not have an independent role— beyond contemporary political interests and power struggles—but help to understand Huntington's political act in introducing his thesis. The same applies to many instances of contemporary international and political activities.

A gap in the study of the history of peace thought provides a basis for the second justification. The gap concerns the ancient era which has been either ignored or given minor treatment as a prehistory of modern ideas. Indeed, the history of peace ideas has been described in rather Eurocentric terms as an aspect of the modern states system in major classical works of the field (Constantinescu-Bagdat 1924, 1925; Lange 1919; Lange and Schou 1954; Raumer 1953; Russell 1972; Schou 1963; Stawell 1936; Ter Meulen 1917, 1929, 1940). The same holds true in the case of more recent investigations (Archibugi 1989; Brock 1968, 1970, 1972; Gallie 1978; Horowitz 1973; Kende 1989, 1990; Knutsen 1992; Parkinson 1977) .

Scholars of ancient history, religions, and political thought have paid more attention to the ancient world, but they have not been much interested in peace ideas or international thought in general. While there are exceptions like John Ferguson (1977), the rules of academic professionalism have prevented attempts in the comparative study of peace thought or other types of generalized knowledge. Therefore, the specialized study of the ancient world has remained less relevant to peace or international studies.

When the history of international thought leaves the student of peace and international studies without prehistory, and the professional history of the ancient world gives him or her mere details of international thought without comparisons and generalizations, the situation becomes unbearable in the contemporary world of globalization and the encounter of various civilizations. In order to contribute to the current needs of intercivilizational communication and understanding, peace and international studies must break out of the jail of conventional academic borders and pay more attention to ancient and non-European worlds (Chan 1996; Radhakrishnan and Raju 1960). This requires, among other things, an attempt to deal with ancient—but still relevant— texts and ideas in order to make them familiar and relevant to social and political scientists as well as anybody interested in civilizational political thought in various cultures.

Recognizing the growing need for intercivilizational understanding, and encouraged by Johan Galtung's (1981) "Social Cosmology and the Concept of Peace," among other works by Galtung, and by James A. Aho's *Religious Mythology and the Art of War* (1981), I ventured into fields less familiar to me as a social scientist. Understandably, my work cannot claim originality on all the issues and material discussed in this book. Any potential originality concerns the suggested generalization and the system of comparison as well as the insights derived from it. I am fully aware of the fact that some of my decisions are controversial and that some arguments require better documented and more convincingly argued justifications. The reader is welcome to contribute to such efforts, if he or she finds the present work innovative and promising enough. While this effort is not written for historians and religious scholars, I sincerely hope it encourages them to carry out comparative studies in topics relevant to social and political scientists. But my message is dedicated to the students of peace and international studies in order to help them discuss and understand the issues of social order in the broader perspective of history, instead of the more limited world of international order in the contemporary world.

Third, as already implied by the preceding claim, a comparative study of ideas is justified as an academic approach to the study of ideas, but also as a unconventional vision concerning intercivilizational relations. A comparative approach is more or less typical to a social scientist who has no possibilities to collect new data and present details typical to professionals in various fields of ancient history. Because extensive comparative work has been almost totally neglected by the experts, the comparison of ideas seemed to be a challenging task, and I soon discovered that the comparison of ideas coming from different cultures was even more so. Academically, I believe that an elaboration of the comparative approach to the study of ideas—and cultures—is a challenging and sufficient goal for this project. I hope it is both a full justification for the work and simultaneously its major achievement.

However, this book is also a potential contribution to debates concerning relationships between civilizations. While Huntington and other scholars perceive cultural encounters as hostile or problematic, claiming that civilizations are separated from each other by civilizational fault lines, this book strongly maintains that civilizations have much in common. Instead of conventional images of cultures that define their unique features, I claim that various cultures have many similar features and ideas. Furthermore, differences *within* a civilization can be much wider than those *between* civilizations. This is not usually recognized in the Western, Eurocentric, academic world, which has been trained to ignore contributions from the non-western, "primitive" world. I do not maintain that there is a universal civilization of the same basic values, but that there is a common cultural heritage to which various civilizations have contributed, and where both collaboration and rivalry of ideas are as likely between different civilizations as within different civilizations.

Fourth, in reading the ancient texts I found that the issue of chaos and cosmos (i.e., the ways of establishing order in social life and human relations) was a central theme. I maintain that this is and should be the case now—and in the future—as well. When I launched this project at the beginning of the 1980s it was not clear that such a theme was relevant for the modern world. The Cold War had stabilized both political and international structures for decades. Therefore, the issues of political and international order appeared permanently solved by the states, and the orderly relations between them everywhere in the world. Nuclear war was understood as a major danger to humanity, but the arms race and even wars were seen as intentional contributions to international order.

However, the case of disintegrating Lebanon, while not actually the first case of chaos in the Cold War world, revealed that the state and society are based on a very delicate social balance, that is surprisingly easy to collapse. Not unexpectedly, scholars tried to explain Lebanonization away by making Lebanon an exception by suggesting various religious, ethnic, economic, and world-system explanations, or by making

Israel's invasion of Lebanon responsible for social and political chaos. However, Lebanon did not remain the last example of its kind. Since the end of the 1980s chaotic and violent turbulence has been typical to some African (Ethiopia, Somalia, Rwanda) and European countries (Bosnia, Georgia-Abkhazia, Russia-Chechenia). The post-Cold War conflicts have become chaotic, extremely violent, and almost unaccessible to control and international mediation because they are examples of the collapse of social order, not the traditional conflict of interests.

This conclusion is justified by the fact that it is not violence as such which is at stake here. The basic questions concern the basis of social order in an increasing number of well-established societies. In addition to the violent clashes, we have also experienced the peaceful division of Czechoslovakia into two independent states. In 1995 Quebec was close to quitting Canada. Forces of disintegration have been recognizable in various forms and phases in many other countries from the United States and the United Kingdom to Italy, Belgium, and China. In more homogenous nation-states—if there are any—like Finland, the integrity of the state is not in imminent danger, but regional and social divisions are not difficult to find. Both violent and peaceful cases of disintegration reveal that political and international order based on nation-states has become too unstable to justify ignoring the problem of social order. It is obvious that Aho's (1981) classical sociological views are right in emphasizing that society is permanently afraid of chaos, and that human beings are and must be working toward establishing and maintaining shields against the terror of disorder. Because social order is never permanent and must be carefully cultivated and elaborated even during times of order and peace, the student of peace and international studies has a duty to contribute knowledge concerning the basis and nature of social order.

As a part of the process of which violent and peaceful disintegration of societies are an example, an additional factor demands the reconsideration of social order: the uncertainty of the postmodernist condition. While many postmodernist scholars can afford to enjoy postmodernist uncertainties as a positive challenge that promises full freedom for individuals, most people perceive the postmodernist condition as chaotic and destructive. Therefore, many individuals prefer to resort to violence and hate towards the Other—as the cases of ethnic conflicts, racism, neo-Nazism, and antisemitism reveal—in order to find a new social reality. In this situation the basic question is: Are there alternatives to such formidable constructions of social reality? As we know, there are—otherwise human beings would never have been able to live together. This book, hopefully, contributes to knowledge about such alternatives.

There is a danger that my present claim can be misunderstood as a position of historical impurism, implying that history can be used to show how to change the present into a better future (Boucher 1985: 59–80; Skinner 1978/1980; Tully 1984). I do not subscribe to such a position. Concrete problems and issues are always unique to each period and place, therefore, ways of solving such problems demand original answers. However, I maintain that we can learn to ask some important questions. For example, social scientists have too often forgotten and ignored fundamental questions and limited their attention and analysis to current issues which often disappear before the answers have been found. In order to avoid such irrelevance in academic work, it would be wise to recognize some basic questions that look perennial at a higher level of abstraction. The problem of social order is likely to be one of these questions.

Fifth, continuing with the idea of alternatives, it must be pointed out that knowledge of traditions is a prerequisite to any critical study. While this book implies that ancient ideas and traditions play a key role in the contemporary world, I do not suggest that traditions justify hostility and violence between contemporary civilizations. Unlike Huntington, or politicians in general, the scholar of peace and international studies must have some knowledge of traditions in order to present criticism against the (mis)use of tradition in contemporary politics and political rhetoric. Then it must be recognized that the scholar participates in age-old debates which continue in both politics and the study of politics. The scholar has his or her own preferences and therefore must explore all issues in an open and self-critical way.

As to the content of my investigation I introduce the foundations of my work in Part I. In Chapter 1 I discuss international theory and suggest how this book is connected to it. In Chapter 2 I introduce the cases and my approach comparing them. Parts II and III contain detailed discussions of the ideas of social order. Part II includes the principle-oriented patterns of social order. Part III contains the power-oriented patterns. Finally, the Conclusions present typologies which can be derived from the current study, in addition to the basic one imbedded in the structure of the work.

PART I

Research Design

CHAPTER 1

International Theory and Social Order in Civilizational Thought

The purpose of this book is to delineate and compare basic approaches to social order, or social cosmos, in some selected cultures of the ancient world. I introduce a concept of social order as a point of departure, but it must be kept in mind that all of the patterns discussed represent various approaches to understanding and defining social order. This book is an analysis of the definitions of and approaches to social order in the selected schools of thought. In addition to the clarification of the concept of social order, the study of ancient thought must be justified as an approach to the study of international theory.

As McKinlay and Little (1986: 1–3) correctly note, order is frequently applied in the study and practice of international relations. However, this concept has remained ambiguous, simplistic, and elusive. Furthermore, the idea of order has often indicated an adherence to the status quo, and even worse, been applied to justify violence or maintain injustice by uncritically implying an undisputed value for law and order. This concept has acquired so many connotations that it becomes arbitrary to select a particular way of denoting order. Even so, the particular meaning of social order applied in this book must be suggested as a working definition.

We can ignore simplistic proposals typical to a number of definitions (Banks 1973: 189, 192, 194; Bull 1977a: 3–4; James 1973: viii, 63; Lyon 1973: 24; McKinlay and Little 1986: 1–4, 21; Stern 1973: 133). Among these definitions the best one is suggested by Bull, who maintains that certain social goals stand out as *elementary* (because otherwise a social association could hardly be called a society at all; *primary* (because other goals a society may set for itself presuppose the realization of these goals in some degree); and *universal* (because all actual societies appear to take account of them). Bull suggests three such goals: *life, truth,* and *property*. All societies seek to ensure that: (1) life will be in some measure secure against violence resulting in death or bodily harm (cf. Northedge 1973); (2) promises, once made, will be kept; and (3) the possession of things will remain stable to some degree and will not be subject to challenges that are constant and without limit. Against these presumptions, order in social life for Bull means a pattern of human activity that sustains the elementary, primary, or universal goals of life, truth, and property. Bull maintains that men attach value to order for they value the greater predictability of human behavior that comes as the consequence of conformity to the elementary or primary goals of coexistence (Bull 1977a: 1–8).

There is much value in Bull's understanding of social order, as we shall see in discussing the images of chaos and the suggested approaches to end chaos and establish a new order in its stead. However, Bull's definition ignores the fact that life, truth, and property, among other values, are often sacrificed in the very name of order. If the existing order is not perceived as right or is perceived as chaos, individuals and groups are willing to give their life and property, and even lie if and when they think that a new, better, order would follow. As James A. Aho (1981: 3–4; cf. Bull 1977a: 3; McKinlay and Little 1986: 3) puts it, every society takes elaborate pains to preserve social order from threats to its integrity, therefore, even war—sacred warfare—has often been applied to end chaos. To understand this is to understand what social order is.

The ultimate and universal purpose of sacred combat has been to sustain social order and sanity, to preserve *nomos* in the face of *anomos*. Killing and dying, particularly when done well, in the name of an ethical principle, are among man's most convincing witnesses to the solidity of social order. In the sacrifice of the warrior, the reality of society is symbolically cleansed of any taint of chaos and its members are persuaded of its immortality.

This fundamental nature of social order, social cosmos, can be understood when we understand that, in Aho's words, social order is a "shield against terror," a shield against *nothingness, anomos*. In other words, we can speak of social order only where a group of people share a given social reality, when they perceive such a social reality as meaningful, or better, full of meaning, as a situation of non-contested *nomos*. In this sense, people do not always experience social order when life, truth, and property appear to be safe. They often need something much more and look for meaning and content in their lives. The patterns of social order presented in this book are approaches to establish such meaningful, rich, social worlds (Berger and Luckmann 1966; cf. Manning 1962: 174, Banks 1973: 206–9).

Bull's definition and the more fundamental and broad understanding of the meaning of social life are not exclusive of one another, they represent the two ends of the same continuum. It is practically impossible to imagine any social order—in the fundamental sense—in which Bull's definition might be totally irrelevant. However, life, truth, and property do not define or establish social order, but become possible only through or by social order. If there is no social order, life, truth, and property as well as other values simply lose their sense. Because social constructions are not existing, objective, facts but things of shared, intersubjective imagination, the true meaning of social order can and must be intuitively understood. Social order can never be fully defined by listing things like life, truth, and property.

The conception of social order adopted in this book is a way of repeating the classical question of political philosophy: How is human association possible in a world where uncertainty, unpredictability, conflicts of interest, and strong affections prevail in human relations? My purpose is to expand the classical question by asking how social cosmos, or order and meaningfulness of social existence can be maximized?

While there are strong reasons to understand the role of war in establishing and maintaining social cosmos, it is interesting to know if there are other approaches to create social order and meaning in addition, or instead of war, what shields against terror have been suggested in various cultures and contexts, and what is the role of war among those shields? In other words, what are the various patterns of social cosmos suggested by the texts, schools, and thinkers perused for this book.

By making social order the basic object of study the texts, schools, and thinkers discussed make an explicit assumption of the preference of order and predictability to chaos and unpredictability in human relations. It might actually be impossible to find social life based on a preference for chaos. However, I maintain that the preference of order and predictability does not exclude the possibility and acceptability of social change. Social change is a fact of social life, its prevention or control often causes chaos rather than order. However, a new social order must always be promised and legitimized in the process of change. This implies a preference for an orderly change. The ideas of social order in this book do not prefer *status quo* but rather are willing to maximize the potential of an orderly change, when change is inevitably caused by social and economic development and ever shifting constellations of power in human relations.

This book concerns selected philosophical or religious schools and thinkers in ancient China, India, Iran, Israel, Greece, Rome, Judaism, and early Christianity. The idea is to cover historically important cultures, which have had a direct or indirect influence on worldviews in contemporary civilizations. Attention is concentrated on the periods when such major religions and political or philosophical schools experienced their Golden Age, that is, mainly from around 600 B.C.E. to around 400 C.E. While I deal with ancient political, religious, or philosophical ideas, this book is a modest contribution to international theory as a field of international studies. International theory has become rather well-known and accepted among scholars in international studies, but requires some introduction to other readers. Simultaneously, I ponder the relationship between international thought and ideas discussed in the present work.

While political theory perceives the study of ideas as a legitimate field where Plato, Aristotle, Sartre, Habermas, and many other ancient, medieval, and modern authors have equally undisputed status, this is not inevitably so in international studies. Some recent references to certain ancient figures, for instance, or perhaps above all, to the Greek Thucydides (Alker 1987; Patomäki 1992) are still first and show marginal signs of change. With the exception of the so-called British school, international studies neglected the history of international thought as an instance of traditionalism during the 1950s and 1960s, when behavioral and quantitative approaches dominated the study of international relations. The first change in the attitude towards the study of international thought, or political ideas in general, made itself felt during the 1960s with a growing interest in the history of international relations (Carroll 1969). However, while increased attention to the history of ideas has been paid by some scholars since the mid-1970s, the basic situation has not changed much during the postbehavioral revolution. In general, it is still a widely shared notion that international studies deals with contemporary issues—or, as it has been often put, with contemporary international politics. Contemporary issues have been seen such as crisis, conflicts, foreign policy, arms control, the arms race, or the Third World problems. Indeed, the study of international thought is perceived to lie outside the field, or to occupy nothing more than a marginal area within the field. As if to prove this, scholars often make short, formal references to famous expressions by well-known figures (e.g., Clausewitz), in order to show academic knowledge and intelligence rather than to suggest that the past should be taken and studied seriously. Prominent historians and political thinkers such as Thucydides, Machiavelli, Burke, and Schmitt are not usually perceived as students of international politics; the questions suggested and discussed by them are often seen as irrelevant in the study of contemporary international politics. In the final analysis, this exclusion has implied, that the study of political ideas does not belong to international studies.

In 1977 Parkinson (cf. Gallie 1978: 2) maintained that numerous works on the theory of international relations still lacked historical depth, and that "no comprehensive text exists on the philosophy of international relations, and only fragments on the history of thought in that field." Corroborating this picture, Galtung (1981: 183) pointed out that "earlier times present us with gold mines of peace thinking," but added in the same sentence that "whereas in earlier ages the greatest spirits of humankind were working on problems of peace, in our age there is certainly a dearth" of such efforts. In the case of more empirical subfields of international studies it may be granted that scholars have "learnt from past mistakes," that is, they have abstained from "grandiose peace architectonics," and dedicated themselves to "the less glamorous, more laborious work of elaborating the details of a viable peace" (Galtung 1981: 183). Unfortunately, this emphasis on the scientific study of international relations (Harle 1987a) has ignored the study of international thought. Its uncritical acceptance has eliminated a fruitful source of theories, explanations, and hypotheses required in any empirical study of contemporary politics (cf. Germino 1975: 231).

Consequently, most international events and phenomena—including the collapse of the Soviet Union, for instance—are perceived to be like car accidents or earthquakes, that is natural but not social and political or, in general, intentional issues (cf. Halliday 1994). For example, researchers have collected an enormous amount of data on wars, producing a number of often conflicting findings and statistical coefficients, without any understanding of the social and political nature of war (Gurr 1980; Zinnes 1980; cf. Harle 1987c). Therefore, it is not surprising to find out that important, and highly relevant contributions to the study of war have been published outside international studies. For one, Aho (1981: xiii) pointedly suggests that "the way in which man does violence to man in warfare is as much a philosophical, or better a spiritual problem, as it is a problem of technology and political economy."

International thought as an area of study was introduced by Martin Wight, who also coined the term international theory (Wight 1966, 1991; Bull 1976, 1977b).[1] To understand the term, one must remember that international theory has a thousand faces. Theories can sometimes be formulated as empirical theories, and put to empirical or statistical tests. Sometimes theories are formulated in a traditional way and discussed qualitatively without any rigorous scientific procedure. But, in addition to these academic theories there are similar theories and assumptions supported by decision makers and the general public. In this latter group theories remain implicit examples of political wisdom reflecting fundamental cultural and political values, or *Weltanschauung* in general. The study of international thought must cover all such cases, especially traditional academic thinking and practical political and social thought.

Wight not only suggests the term but also shows what international theory is all about (cf. Herz 1951; Horowitz 1973; Waltz 1970). As Bull (1976: 103–4) has suggested there are three central elements characterizing Wight's international theory. First, it is a study in the main traditions of thought about international relations. Second, it aims to discuss all that had been said and thought on the subject throughout the ages. Third, the outcome of such studies is an account of the debate among contending theories and doctrines, to which no resolution must be expected. The idea is to delineate all potential types of international thought in order to describe and understand them without any attempts to evaluate which one is right or wrong.

Wight's famous categorization of international thought (Wight 1991; Bull 1976, 1977b) includes three groups of thinkers: the Machiavellians (the Realists); the Grotians (the Rationalists); and the Kantians (the Revolutionists). In some versions of his lectures Wight suggested a fourth category called the Inverted Revolutionists, representing the pacifist stream of thought. Wight traced the distinctive doctrines that each of them put forward concerning war, diplomacy, power, national interest, the obligation of treaties, the obligation of an individual to bear arms, the conduct of foreign policy, and the relations between civilized states and so-called barbarians.

For the Machiavellians—which includes Hobbes, Hegel, Frederick the Great, Clemenceau, and twentieth century Realists Carr and Morgenthau—international politics represents a relationship of pure conflict among sovereign states. In such anarchy, each state must pursue its own interest. The Grotians—which includes the classical international lawyers, as well as Locke, Burke, Castlereagh, Gladstone, Franklin Roosevelt, and Churchill—saw international politics as international intercourse, chiefly among states, consisting of both conflict and cooperation. In other words, states form an anarchical international society observable in institutions such as diplomacy, international law, and the balance of power. States in their dealings with one another are not free of moral and legal restraints, but wish to maintain the rules of this international society in order to limit the role of military force and threats in international relations.

For the Kantians, international politics is not a matter of relations among states but relations among human beings of whom states are composed. The ultimate reality is the community of mankind. Human relations are controlled by morality that consists of the revolutionary imperatives that require men to work for brotherhood. In the Kantian doctrine the world is divided between the elect, who are faithful to this vision of the community of mankind, and the damned, the heretics, who stand in its way. The Kantian pattern of thought is embodied in Revolutionist and Counter-Revolutionist ideologies: the Protestant Reformation, the French Revolution, and the Communist Revolution on the one hand, and the Counter-Reformation, International Legitimism, and Dullesian Anti-Communism on the other hand.

Wight's categorization—or the others suggested (e.g., Waltz 1970; cf. Herz 1951)—seems to offer a point of departure for further research. His approach suggests a way to categorize and appraise the basic theoretical and value assumptions concerning international order. However, there are strong reasons to criticize Wight's categorization. Here I should like to emphasize just a single point, the fact that Wight's categorization is conspicuously Eurocentric. This bias was fully recognized by Bull in his Wight memorial lecture, where he witnessed that Wight did not have any "deep understanding of non-Western culture" but rather displayed "insensitivity about non-Western peoples and their aspirations today" (Bull 1976: 115).

Wight is not alone with his Eurocentric bias. In fact, all the works on the history of peace ideas listed in the preface share the very same feature. They represent attempts to rediscover, assemble, and categorize international thought mainly in the domain of the modern Western tradition. This can no longer be enough. The Eurocentric tradition has become so widely and convincingly criticized (cf. Smith 1978: 295–96) that it would look ridiculous to uncritically adopt Wight's categorization, which openly justified the history and glorious memories of British colonialism.

Ours is a global world, not the world of the Europeans or Occidentals. The history of ideas cannot remain exclusively the history of the Western, Occidental world. Disregarding the belief that modern Western political language has a monopolistic right to express and reflect the truth suggests that some knowledge of various cultures is relevant in the current debate. One must go beyond modern (mainly Western) politics towards systematic and explicit comparisons of international thought not only across time, but also across different social and cultural contexts. This strongly implies the use of the comparative approach to collect data and systematize discussion in different cultural contexts including the Western context "among other things" (Nederveen Pieterse 1994; cf. Armer and Marsh 1982; Fitzgerald 1980: vii; Galtung 1981: 183).

Wight is not only Eurocentric but bound to the modern states system. Therefore, Wight's categorization is *inapplicable outside modern Western culture*, that is, in Western culture before modern states were born. This is because international relations mean intrerstate relations. Wight's conception of international theory is strictly bound to this image.

For example, while it is possible to suggest that there are some interesting similarities between the Realists and the classical Chinese Legalist school, the Rationalists and the Confucian school, and the Inverted Revolutionists and Daoism (I do not know if Wight suggested these same similarities), this would lead to a serious misunderstanding of Chinese traditions. It is impossible to discuss Chinese traditions without referring to the domestic issues, the debates concerning political life within certain geographical areas. The same holds true for ancient traditions, including ancient and medieval Western traditions. Bull (1976: 15) witnesses that Wight possessed "a mastery of Western culture, ancient and medieval no less than modern," but Wight himself lists Hobbes and Grotius as the earliest international thinkers. Machiavelli is only implied in the title of the categorization. Similarly, Wight praises Thucydides but ignores Plato, Aristotle, and many other Greco-Roman figures (Wight 1966).

We must note that Wight's approach to international theory makes sense only after the genesis of the modern states system. Before its emergence no tradition of thought embodied a description of the nature of international politics or a set of prescriptions as to how men should conduct themselves in international issues. In fact, there was no radical difference between political thought and international thought in classical Chinese, Indian, or any other ancient philosophy. Similarly, international thought was equivalent to political thought in Western culture up to, at least, the eighteenth century.

Interestingly enough, Wight's Revolutionists deny the role of the state in the organization of humankind, but this obvious challenge to the international remains ignored. The distinction between the state-oriented theory and the humankind-oriented theory is not suggested by Wight, or Bull, as a theoretically interesting issue. On the contrary, the humankind-oriented category is moved into the background, to the field of political and ideological movements. The point is that only the state-oriented theories are suggested to be realistic and represent the truth, while the Kantian views are suggested to represent ideological activism. Indeed, international studies has remained exclusively statecentric, in spite of many verbal challenges to the statecentric model during the past two decades. The political spheres of domestic and international have been combined (surprisingly late) only as a perception of the comprehensive nature of post-Cold War politics (Halliday 1994). Consequently, the relevance of thought preceding the modern state and the states system has remained ignored as far as the international is concerned.

International thought should not be limited to the modern conception of international but should include other political areas as well, without undue distinctions between them. This has become an undeniable fact, once again, as it was before the modern state was born. The collapse of the post-Cold War political and international order demands us to think about the bases of orderly human associations. The process has revealed that international and domestic factors have been strongly intertwined in political transformation. This suggests that something is fundamentally wrong in the distinction between domestic and international politics (expressed in the academic world in divisions between political science and international studies).

Furthermore, my claim can be further justified by the challenge to "the logic of *raison d'état*" suggested by Neumann and Welsh (1991) who introduce "the logic of culture" as an alternative view. The "logic of *raison d'état*" suggest that the states interact with one each other like billiard balls, with power politics as their mechanical, given dynamic. The "logic of culture" refers to the fact that order among states can be generated by agreement on international values as well as domestic values of a social and cultural nature. While the realist logic is unique to the interactions between sovereign states, the cultural logic is common to all forms of human interaction. I suggest that in the ancient world it is such forms of human interaction which must be considered a totality.

Therefore, a conventional wisdom in international theory must be challenged. This is a generally shared wisdom by some British scholars like Wight that the political theorists in the past—nobody outside the Greco-Roman world is implied here—have only little to say about international relations (Donelan 1978: 75; cf. Russell 1972; Stawell 1936). It has been suggested that the Greek political theorists, and by implication the other political theories before and after them, paid attention exclusively to politics, that is, the individual, the *polis*, and the relationship between the individual and the *polis* (Donelan 1978). Therefore, Purnell (1978: 19–21) has maintained that Greco-Roman thinkers did not develop "a more or less comprehensive theory" of international relations. Corroborating this image Stawell (1936: 15) emphasizes that "Aristotle does not even envisage the question how the peace is to be kept between his tiny State and the many who must surround it," or that "the organization of Plato's 'Fair City' involves the organization of the fighting men, and peace has no part in his bright vision."

This image implies that there has been practically no international theory, either as part of ancient political theory or independently, or at least the existing pieces of international theory were not expressed explicitly as the body of international theory. It is maintained uncritically that political theorists have become interested, if only to a limited degree—Machiavelli and Burke are the only figures deserving mention here—in international theory as a consequence of the genesis and growth of modern political theory and sovereign states, and the emergence of their political relations in the Golden Age of Balance-of-Power politics. If there were some figures, like Thucydides, preceding the stage of modern states, they were not political theorists but historians (Wight 1966).

Those maintaining the thesis of the non-existence of international theory in the past explicitly say that "international relations in terms of coexisting multiple sovereign units was . . . transcended" in the Greco-Roman world (Purnell 1978: 19–21). As this argument openly reveals, the suggestion is based on the modern image of sovereign actors as central units of international relations. Instead of accepting the jail of such anachronisms, it must be fully recognized that ancient international thought is part of political theory: ancient thinkers were discussing international issues without using this term. Nobody mentioned international relations in the ancient past, because there was *no distinction between political and international*. This distinction only emerged after the genesis of the modern state. On the other hand, there was something international in the very beginning, even in the modern sense of the word such as questions of relations between different nations or distinctive groups of human beings. Those relations were not organized as relations between nation-states, they were organized in other ways due to different political constellations and different units of relations.

Therefore, in order to understand the ancient conceptions of international, and to learn something relevant from them, one must remember a decisive fact: the ancient thinkers had another kind of international dimension in their mind. The existence of such an element is indirectly recognized. For example, Purnell (1978: 21) has suggested that in the Greco-Roman world there persisted "visions of a genuine world order, embracing in theory the whole of human society." It is well-known that cosmopolis became the leading idea in the Greco-Roman world, and consequently, emphasis was moved on the conception of a more or less unified world order. This concept of a world order "envisaged a kind of world-city, coexistensive with the human race itself, and of which, as a natural consequence, individual men were citizens" (pp. 20–21). Therefore, it is understandable that international thought in the Roman world gave only a minor part to actors outside the Roman imperium, while being much interested in peace and order within Rome.

As a minor point it must be added that the language of modern political thought, especially the term international, is extremely problematic in periods preceding the modern states system. International, inevitably, reproduces the modern image of sovereign actors. Therefore, when applying international we indirectly or unconsciously share the state-actor definition of the term. Due to the linguistic connection between the modern state and international relations there could be no international relations, in the modern sense of the word, before the modern states were born. Therefore, there could not be a theory on international relations either. In order to avoid such a conclusion, the linguistic problem must be overcome by some explicit agreements. We must agree that the term international be given a wider meaning in the present study (cf. Rosenau 1990: 4). In short, I minimize the use of the term and due to the reasons discussed earlier, I speak of social order instead of international order and use international thought where appropriate, synonymously with peace thought, political thought, and religious thought. This is a practical solution, and does not imply any acceptance of problematic distinctions such as international vs. domestic, peace vs. war thought, political vs. religious, and so forth (cf. Bederman 1991: 4; Willms 1991).

NOTE

1. However, Frank M. Russell (1972) applied international theory in his book originally published in 1936, and F. Meriam Stawell (1936, originally published in 1929) wrote of international thought well before Wight.

CHAPTER 2

Comparison of Civilizational Thought: The Cases and the Method

Considering a well-justified claim that in any comparative study the comparison should concern total ensembles rather than isolated motifs (Smith 1978: ix; cf. Smith 1982: 34), a conventional point of departure might seem well justified. Actually, it would be expected that in the case of several cultures or civilizations, the cultures should be compared with each other. This is perceived as nonproblematic both in the everyday usage of the term civilizations (Huntington 1996) as well as in the more academic study of world religions (Aho 1981; Ferguson 1977).

The conventional assumption concerning the uniqueness of cultures would make comparisons senseless. If civilizations have no common features, there would be no point in comparing them. But my claim is that this assumption holds true at a general level, only as far as its phenotype—language, key texts, eminent figures, specific historical issues and events, and the like—is concerned. However, all such features are rather unimportant; other cultures are not as familiar as our own culture primarily because we have been taught mainly local and national facts in school.

If we take a closer look at civilizations, we soon recognize similar elements in many of them. We see that political, philosophical, or religious schools within each culture are not always similar with or close to each other; in fact, intracivilizational differences between them can be striking. Therefore, it is also likely that the substantive messages of these schools may have conspicuous similarities with schools in *other* cultures. Therefore, culture as a unit may give a basis for textbook-like presentations of peace thinking in a given civilization (Ferguson 1977), but surely not for a comparative study of international thought.

Therefore, I break cultures into specific texts written or composed by prominent individual writers, an authoritative body of a school, or other promoters of certain ideas. Due to the prominence of the individual or collective authors and the central role of the texts in a civilization, these specific texts can be called civilizational thought—they represent, to both members and non-members of a given civilization, that specific civilization, not just their authors. Neither do such texts represent either national or universal thought. Even when they are perceived as the common cultural heritage of humankind, their civilizational origin is well recognized, but only due to systematic learning processes typical to all civilizations.

In explicit terms, this book discusses the following cases:

1. Classical Chinese political philosophy
   - Confucianism
   - Legalism
   - Mohism
   - Daoism

2. India
   - Ancient Indian political thought
   - Kautilya
   - Buddhism

3. Iran
   - Zoroastrianism

4. Israel
   - Ancient Hebrew thought
   - Judaism

5. Christianity
   - Jesus's teachings
   - The early church

6. Greece
   - Plato
   - Aristotle

7. Roman Stoicism
   - Cicero
   - Livy
   - Virgil

In each case my discussion deals with the quest for and approaches to social order (including orderly social change). In this chapter I describe the cases and summarize their main claims. Finally, I discuss the comparative study of international thought and introduce the approach I am using in this book.

THE CASES AS APPROACHES TO SOCIAL ORDER

It would be important to know what kind of practical and theoretical problems the selected cases were formulated as answers. This contextual element might be found both in the practical historical context in which the texts were written and in the images of chaos in which the context was abstracted and described in the texts. It is obvious that the texts and ideas to be discussed in this book were born and formulated in times of deep social and political changes and, therefore, it was often understood that the existing chaos had to end and new social order established instead (Aho 1981; Allen 1957: xv, 132, 272, 367, 515; Berger and Luckmann 1966; Boucher 1985: 78; Chernus 1991; Cohn 1993; Eliade 1959; Tully 1984: 506).

However, it is well known that the question of historical context is rather problematic in the case of ancient texts. It is not always known when the texts were written for the first time, and their authors are often unknown or mythical. The works represent, as I have stated, civilizational thought to which many persons have contributed, and which have survived much beyond the practical historical context in which they originated. I do not have any panacea to such problems, but I have, however, tried to carefully consider historical contexts in attempting to understand what kinds of problems were prominent during the times the texts were written or compiled. I do not claim that my historical understanding is either profound or uncontroversial, but I have the duty to make my choices explicit. How I interpret history will at least explain some of my interpretations concerning the ideas of social order I have read from the texts under study.

Ancient China

The gradual disintegration of the Zhou dynasty (c. 1122 to 221 B.C.E.) led to continuous wars and struggles for power in the Spring and Autumn (771–481 B.C.E.), and especially in the period of the Warring States (481–221 B.C.E.). At the beginning of the Warring States period the number of individual small states—originally more than one hundred—had been reduced to no more than fourteen significant states. During this period the number was further reduced to six states, until finally, one of the six, Qin, was able to conquer the others and force the unification of China in 221 B.C.E.

The Qin dynasty did not reestablish the original unity of the Zhou dynasty. The Qin had a much larger geographical area, its power structure was more hierarchical and unified, and finally, it applied totally new foundations of political power—the religious basis had been replaced by that of rewards and punishments as well as a strong military force. The classical Chinese political philosophy contributed to this process by finding new legitimation for political power. New approaches to legitimization were required, and after the collapse of the Western Zhou dynasty it was necessary to build a unified political structure for China.

There emerged a myriad of ideas (Fung 1983; Watson 1967), but it is justified to concentrate on the four major schools of classical Chinese philosophy: Confucianism, Legalism, Mohism, and Daoism. The major division between them concerns the centralized and decentralized structure of political power. Due to practical economical needs and the awareness of common culture and togetherness, there was a clear-cut tendency for answers to emphasize a single power center in China, or in the *tien-hsia*— "all under the heaven." In general, it was agreed that a central government was required in order to guarantee peace and order in the community of all people between "the four seas." The answers and politics based on (or justified through) them were directed against the centrifugal forces and feudalism, which was the major reason behind the collapse of the Western Zhou dynasty. Chaos had been caused by the division of society into individual states; therefore, these states had to be replaced by a strong central government. Consequently, the outstanding characteristic of the Warring States period was the gradual collapse of the feudal system.

Both Confucianism and Legalism accepted the idea of the unification of China, but suggested two opposing ideas to create a central government. The Confucian school suggested the return of the original religious basis of political power in the sense of a comprehensive code of rituals, or proper manners and five basic social relations (*li*). It was suggested that man would follow these rules voluntarily, thus preserving peace and order. Furthermore, it was promised to the ruler that if he followed the rules, all peoples would voluntarily submit themselves to his power.

The Legalist school had serious doubts about persuasion and the goodness of human nature. The Legalists suggested instead that peace and order—within society—had to be brought about by force, with heavy punishments and mild rewards. The Legalists thought that it was dangerous to trust in the goodness of human nature. Human nature consisted of selfishness and, therefore, selfishness had to be applied in the production of social order through punishments and rewards. The Legalist idea was based on the conceptions of coercive and deterrent power. Similarly, the Legalists maintained that the leading state (Qin) had to conquer all others in order to end wars between individual states.

While Mohism and Daoism participated in the same debate, they rejected the need to unify China. Furthermore, they represented a pacifist mode of thinking, much more so than Confucianism, which cherished some pacifist ideas, too. More importantly both Mohism and Daoism put forward neither questions nor answers similar to either Confucianism or Legalism. Mohism and Daoism suggested alternative ideas about political power, order, and peace.

Mohism suggested the idea of sovereign states, within and between which peace and order was to be preserved through universal love and the example of the ruler. Daoism maintained that no man-made, planned order is possible or permanent, whatever its basis. Peace and order become possible if individuals have high morals and are willing to follow Dao without any compromises; that is, if they reject the conventional power struggle. These alternatives were not accepted by the majority of the Chinese. They were either annihilated by those in power—as was the case with Mohism—or given the opportunity of withdrawing voluntarily from the power struggle—as was the case with Daoism.

The Legalist doctrine of power politics was victorious in raising new forces to power during the transition period and in uniting China. However, military force was unable to keep new rulers in power. For politics and administration subtler means were required. With the help of neo-Confucianism, the Han dynasty and neo-Confucianism conserved the unification of China, building the basis of its power on political ideas derived from the Zhou dynasty—disregarding some original elements but adding others from the philosophical debate of the classical schools. The Confucians' final victory materialized by the middle of the Han dynasty, when the new political and social order gradually became stabilized, and in the sphere of economics the people became accustomed to the changed conditions.

Ancient India

After the fall of the highly developed Indus Civilization (c. 2550–1400 B.C.E.), the Vedic Aryans arrived in the Indus valley around 1200 B.C.E. The Aryans were followed in 511–485 by another foreign master, the Persian Darius (521–485), who conquered northwestern India and made the river Indus the border of the Persian empire. Towards the late seventh century B.C.E., some small Indian states were able to establish their hegemony over others, and during the fifth century Kosala and Magadha aimed for victory over their neighbors and for the annexation of their territory. Magadha was able to win the power struggle with its rival and establish the first Indian empire. Magadha lost some areas to the Macedonians in 327–325, but otherwise survived. Chandragupta Maurya, who usurped the throne of Magadha in 320, defeated the last of the Macedonians in 305 B.C.E.

The glorious Magadha empire, however, remained a mere episode in Indian history. The Maurya dynasty came to its end in 185 B.C.E. The following dynasties remained both limited geographically and short-lived politically. After the fall of Magadha, India experienced the dark age of five centuries, when foreign invaders fought each other for short-lived and ephemeral supremacy over Northern India. A new Indian empire, the Gupta dynasty, was established by Chandragupta I in 320 C.E., but that empire fell in 540, followed by the age of regional kingdoms in Central India, and later by a succession of foreign conquerors finally ending in colonial British rule (Kulke and Rothermund 1986; cf. Dutt 1991; Hirakawa 1990; Kinsley 1982; Parpola 1994).

While we can speak of a common cultural background in a very wide sense, there was no common language or even a script accessible to all, like in China. It is, therefore, impossible to imagine that the major part of the population could have had a developed idea of national unity and sovereignty in ancient or more modern India. In fact, no empire—including the Magadha and Gupta dynasties—covered all Indian areas. The history of India was primarily North Indian history (Basham 1982: 95, 121–23; Kulke and Rothermund 1986: 63, 96, 109; Mookerji 1957: 74; Russell 1972: 38).

Instead of the idea of all-Indian unity, decentralism was the leading theme in Indian political development. Decentralism was the ideal, or the existing model practically taken anywhere in political life (Drekmeier 1962: 22; Kulke and Rothermund 1986: 29–30, 44, 49, 57).

In clear contrast to the Chinese or Iranian cases, ancient Indian thought did not give direct or indirect justification to state- or empire-building. A lot of attention was paid to the duties of the king, but this did not require or imply the political unity of India. The norms applied to tribal or regional kingdoms. For example, the horse sacrifice seemed to imply a world government, but in practice must have covered a rather limited geographical area. Furthermore, the legitimation of royal power by religious ceremonies contributed to the emergence of small territorial kingdoms, and even then encouraged internal divisions giving a major role to the Brahmin priests and divine ceremonies (Kulke and Rothermund 1986: 44, 54, 56, 58–59, 64, 69–71).

Instead of political and military expansion, religious and philosophical thought in India turned towards individual salvation and moral conduct. Attention was paid to the fundamental tension between supporting or renouncing the world. The orthodox religious thought, Brahmanism, either preferred the first element or tried to adopt both. Buddhism and Jainism challenged the orthodox approach to supporting the world (castes and the role of Brahmins) by preferring the latter (Drekmeier 1962: 176; Hirakawa 1990; Kinsley 1982).

In short, the achievement of political unity, especially the all-Indian one, was *not* understood to be the most important task. The idea of a united political state remained for obvious reasons a *subordinate idea*. The state and state-politics were conspicuously volatile and therefore could not be given an exclusive role in establishing and maintaining order in human relations, the civil society had to do that. Pressures on orderly social relations were enormous, the task was actually too challenging for the continuously disintegrating state to fulfill. There were three unique types of social relations to be managed: (1) relations between Aryan tribes; (2) relations between Aryans and indigenous peoples; and later on (3) between Indians and the continuous waves of new foreigners. The territorial state was a way of stopping conflicts between the Aryan tribes, but another type of mechanism—the caste system—was required to make possible the coexistence and mutual assimilation of the Aryans and the indigenous peoples, as well as later that of Indians and immigrating foreigners (Basham 1982: 34; Ghoshal 1959: 157; Radhakrishnan 1929: 478; Raju 1960: 220).

Therefore, in ancient Indian political thought social order was claimed possible either without the state or with the help of the wise king fully respecting the basis of social order: *dharma*. Without *dharma* no social life was thought possible—the moral basis had to maintain the castes and their strict responsibilities. The king's duty was to maintain civil society and its moral basis, he was not supposed to replace the civil society by establishing a system of political power instead.

Buddhism challenged the orthodox position of the castes and the role of Brahmins by renouncing the world. Kautilya's *Arthashastra* was another step away from the orthodox doctrine, but in the opposite direction. Kautilya's major emphasis was on conventional state-politics and the application of force for establishing social order. However, even he shared the idea of the moral basis of social order. The establishment of the empire was Kautilya's approach to guarantee *dharma*.

Ancient Iran

In Iran empire-building started when Media in the northwest and Persia in southwest became major regional powers in the seventh century B.C.E. The empire was established in 549 when the Persians, led by Cyrus the Great, defeated the Medes. The Achaemenian dynasty survived until 331, when Iran was conquered by Alexander the Great. His generals established the Seleucid dynasty, which was overthrown in 141 B.C.E. by the Parthian Arsacid dynasty. Their successors, the Sasanians, came to power in 226 C.E., declaring themselves the direct heirs of the Achaemenian kings and claiming that both the Seleucids and the Arsacids had been foreigners. The Sasanians ruled the empire for about 400 years until the rise of the new power, the Islamic Arabia in 652 (*Cambridge History of Iran*, Vol. 2, hereafter referred to as CHI 2: 1, 10, 110).

The well-known history of the successive empires is only a part of the Iranian story, religion forms the other part. The political center of the country was—with the exception of the Parthians—in the south or west; religion came from the north and east. The religion was founded by Zoroaster (Zarathustra) who lived sometime between 1700 and 1200 B.C.E. on the South Russian steppes. Zoroastrian teachings were brought to Iran by Indo-Iranian or Aryan tribes who invaded the Iranian plateau in successive waves in the first half of the second millennium B.C.E. Zoroastrianism spread slowly, meeting with hostility from members of the original hereditary western Iranian priesthood, the magi, who are not likely to have welcomed a new teaching and a new scripture. However, the magi of Raga, the capital of Media, became the first converts perhaps as early as the eighth century B.C.E. It is possible that the last Median kings became Zoroastrians; the Achaemenids, in the early sixth century B.C.E., publicly declared their allegiance to Zoroastrianism. Cyrus the Great may have been a Zoroastrian, although there is no evidence that Zoroastrianism became a state religion before the time of Darius the First. However, it was the Sasanian dynasty that consolidated Zoroastrianism as an authoritarian state church: the Sasanian clergy taught that the kingdom and the true religion were twins. Furthermore, the Sasanians recreated ancient Iranian history along the Zoroastrian view of the world (Boyce 1984; Boyce 1987: 2; CHI 2: 41–49, 141, 217, 416; *Cambridge History of Iran*, Vol. 3, hereafter referred to as CHI 3/1: xvii, 7, 342, 367; CHI 3/2: 687, 689, 866; *Cambridge History of Judaism*, Vol. 1, hereafter referred to as CHJu 1: 279–308; Sharif 1963: 56–57).

While the connection between the political empire and the Zoroastrian religion is conspicuous, it does not prove that wars for the expansion of the empire were carried out in the name of the religion or its god. Zoroastrianism became regarded as the religion of the Iranian people alone. Instead of violent conversions, non-Iranians, the *anarya*, were left to follow whatever religion they pleased as long as it was peaceable; sometimes the Persian rulers themselves accepted foreign gods. Religious tolerance was a remarkable feature of Persian rule. Cyrus the Great encouraged, for example, the return of the Jews to Palestine in order to reestablish their religion and temple (Boyce 1987: 47; CHJu 1: 279ff.; CHI 2: 288, 412; Ferguson 1977: 21–22). Therefore, Zoroastrianism's social and political functions must be found elsewhere.

I claim that Zoroastrianism represented originally a society-building process, and only later contributed to an empire-building process. While Zoroastrianism served the interests of a power struggle within the expanding empire, the political function of the religion can be found in the domestic power struggles, because foreign enemies were too weak to be a real danger until Alexander the Great, who became the incarnation of the evil. Therefore, I emphasize the ethical and social elements of Zoroastrianism and give a minor role to its theory of the violent exclusion of the other. That is, it was not the latter element but the original ethical theory which has had a tremendous influence on the doctrines of exclusion in Judaism, Christianity, and Islam (Boyce 1987: 30–31, 78; CHI 2: 416; CHI 3/1: xxxii–xxxv; CHJu 1: 214).

To understand the basic message of Zoroastrianism, it must be recognized that it was born to serve the demand for social order in a rapidly changing and expanding society. Around 1700 B.C.E. the steppe-dwellers began to learn the use of bronze and develop a new economy in which the horse-drawn war chariot came to play a large part. Heroic warriors, the chariot-standers, began to form a new and dominant group in Iranian society, challenging the property and security of pastoralists who used to herd their cattle on foot. Zoroastrianism was unable to stop social change or reverse it, but it did attempt to harness the warriors—and promise the weak some security in the new religion—by suggesting a doctrine where immoral and violent men were declared servants of the Evil Spirit (Boyce 1984: 8–9).

Zoroaster introduced unique, a full-fledged explanation of the existence of conflicts and evil. He specified the meaning of evil and why suffering exists. The point of his doctrine is that a good Ahura cannot be responsible for evil. Imperfection and suffering are original and inherent in the nature of things, and remain permanent (Mills 1887: xix, 26; cf. Darmesteter, 1880: lvii; Darmesteter 1883: 92).

According to Zoroastrianism, there are two primal spirits who have a fundamental and permanent cosmic conflict between them. The good one is called Ahura Mazda, and the evil adversary is called Angra Mainyu (Hostile or Evil Spirit). They never accept or share the adversary's thought, word, or act. Ahura Mazda lives in the "Endless Light," but Angra Mainyu is in "Endless Darkness." There is no connection between the two spirits, between them there is only "emptiness" (Yasna 30 and 45 in Boyce 1984: 35–36, 45–46; cf. Gershevitch 1959: 45–47; Mills 1887: 31; Sharif 1963: 59, 67–68, 73).[1]

The antagonism of the two spirits rages through space and time. Everything in the world is engaged in the conflict. Whatever works for the good of man or for his harm, for the wider spread of life or against it, comes from, and strives for, either Ahura Mazda or Angra Mainyu, respectively (Darmesteter 1880: lxii, lxxii; Boyce 1984: 35, 51; Mills 1887: 123).

In other words, the history of the world is the history of the Great Conflict. That historical conflict is both unavoidable and predetermined: there is no history outside the process—where Angra Mainyu invades and spoils the world of Ahura Mazda, where the basic conflict goes on, and where the Evil Spirit is finally expelled from the existence, from the world of meaning (Darmesteter, 1880: lvi; cf. Boyce 1984: 20–21, 46–49).

Consequently, life is a battleground between the two powers. Man has a specific role in the conflict between good and evil. The myth states it that the two spirits cannot beat each other in a simple duel. The transcendent entities can struggle, win, and lose, only through their incarnations in the visible world. It is in the terrestrial, visible, and tangible world only that the battle against the powers of evil can be fought and won. The struggle must be carried out with their allies. Both spirits—even the omnipotent Ahura Mazda—need both gods and men for help. Man is Ahura Mazda's special creation, and among men, Zoroaster is his first assistant. The Evil Mind has a servant, *Aeshma*, the impersonation of invasion and rapine, the chief scourge of the Zoroastrians, and an evil angel, *Drug*, who personifies deceit. Among men, the *daeva*-worshippers constitute representatives of the Evil Spirit (Ferguson 1977: 21; Darmesteter 1880: lxi; Mills 1887: xix; Sharif 1963: 71).

In conclusion, a clear preference was given to the service of the Good Spirit. Everybody had to respect the law of nature, called *asha* (corresponding to the Indo-

Aryan *rta*), which ensured not only physical order but governed human conduct as well. This principle was expressed as the duty to respect the contract, keep the promise, and maintain social order. To keep the promise was to follow Ahura Mazda, to break the promise was to cause chaos and worship the Evil Spirit and his representatives (Boyce 1984: 8–11; Boyce 1987: 9–10; CHI 1: 411; CHJu 1: 283; Parpola 1994: 147–49; Sharif 1963).

Ancient Hebrew Thought and Judaism

The Hebrews arrived in Egypt from the northeast, but had to leave Egypt around 1447 B.C.E. They penetrated into Canaan through the Sinai, where they destroyed a number of city-states and their inhabitants. The military campaigns made the Israelites establish a common kingly leadership under Saul (1025–1012), who represented the Nordic tribes. After Saul's death, power went to David (c. 1012– 972), who represented the southern tribes, the House of Judah. David conquered Jerusalem and made it his capital. David's kingdom included both Canaan and part of Syria. Soon, however, the hostility between the northern and southern tribes increased until the Nordic ones formed a kingdom of their own under the name of Israel around 930. In 721, Israel was overrun by the army of Assyria and the inhabitants were driven into exile. The southern kingdom, Judah, remained a vassal state to Assyria, excluding a short period of independence under Josiah (639–609). However, Babylonia under Nebuchadnezzar occupied Judea and destroyed Jerusalem and the first Temple in 587 B.C.E.

When Persia conquered Babylonia, Cyrus the Great let the Jews[2] return to Judea and rebuild the Temple. However, the Macedonians (the Seleucids) became the new masters during the reign of Alexander the Great. Under the Seleucids, the Jews became divided into contending and hostile parties. The Hellenistic-oriented internationalists were strongly hostile towards nationalistic and religious conservatives—all had to become world citizens. Struggles between the Jews justified the last Seleucid ruler, Antiochus Epiphanes, to destroy Jerusalem and change its religious center to the temple of Zeus in 168 B.C.E.

Consequently, the civil war between the Jews turned into a campaign against the Seleucids. The nationalists achieved glorious victories. In 166–160 B.C.E. Judas Maccabees conquered Jerusalem and reconsecrated the Temple, but the Jewish state degenerated gradually into a Roman vassal. After some internal conflicts in Judea, Rome formally conquered Jerusalem in 63 B.C.E. Hyrcanus and his followers became client rulers, autonomic within Judea. This status was not sufficient for the more nationalistic Jews, who rebelled against Rome in 66–73 and 132–135 C.E. These rebellions ended tragically, Jerusalem and its Temple were destroyed during the first rebellion, and the Jews were forced to leave the Land of Zion after the second rebellion (CHJu 1–2).

A well-known narrative has been derived from the suggested Jewish history. In this narrative, a small wandering nation is eager to stop living among other peoples and wishes to establish a state of its own. It is successful in conquering a fertile land for that purpose. This does not create unity among the population and furthermore the divided nation is located in a strategically central area where powerful empires struggle for power. Consequently, the nation is too weak to stop continuous invasions by surrounding empires. A more positive side of this constant turmoil is the fact that the nation has a strong cultural basis of its own, and is able to take advantage of the cross-fertilization of a number of advanced cultures, as well as assorted social and political ideas. However, continuous and conscious efforts were required in order to find and maintain a national identity. New challenges to national unity and identity emerge, and new answers had to be formulated. While the religious tradition is the basis of the analysis and answers, new inventions had to be made.

Concerning ideas of social order, a fundamental point in the narrative must be recognized: we have several cases at our hands. Indeed, Judaism is a rather elusive concept. Instead of one civilization or religion, there are several Judaisms. They have been categorized in literature in different and contending ways (Boccaccini 1991: 10–19; cf. Batho 1945; Blau 1966; Lumb 1937; Maynard 1928; Silver and Martin 1974; Welch 1935).[3]

A detailed picture of various Judaisms is unnecessary for this book. The contending categorizations try to capture theological nuances and partly reflect contemporary scholarly disputes between religious experts. This book deals with patterns of social order; therefore, the decisive question is: are there one or more patterns to be delineated from various Judaisms? I maintain that there are two patterns. The first is a power-oriented pattern evolving around the definite geographic center, the Land of Israel, on which a state or a temple-state must be established in order to have social order. The second is a principle-oriented version evolving around the divine principle called *torah* (law, teaching, direction) that gives a specific identity to the people following it. The latter pattern is representative of mainstream Judaism. The power-oriented pattern, in my opinion, represents a minority view.

It is not simple to find appropriate names for the two Judaisms but I call the first pattern "ancient Hebrew thought" (cf. Weber 1952; Aho 1981), and the second "Judaism." These patterns overlap and contend with one another from the earliest times to the present, but there perhaps is a historical development from the original power-oriented pattern to the later principle-oriented approach. The decisive points are: (1) the invasion into Canaan and the establishment of the kingdom; and (2) the captivity in Babylonia and the following Diaspora.

During the occupation of Canaan by the Israelites, the wandering nomads settled in a specific geographical area and conquered it for themselves. Ancient Hebrew thought, especially as later expressed in the *Hexateuch*, justified both the settlement of wandering Hebrew nomads and the consequent use of extreme violence against those who had earlier occupied the same area. It was maintained that social order can be established within a specific geographical area, the Land of Israel. This land was given to the Israelites by the deity for men to establish it through rituals and win it by conquest. It was a strategic hamlet walled against the demonic forces of evil and chaos (Smith 1978: 110–12). The idea did not die with Israel and Judea, but was much cherished in Judaism born in the captivity of Babylon. It did not fully disappear later, but has remained a powerful, if minority, view among Judaism.

Simultaneously, the captivity in Babylon and especially the Diaspora after it gave birth to Judaism (CHJu 1: v). This Judaism puts the emphasis on the maintenance of the national and religious identity of Jews living in a foreign land or among foreigners. The leaders of the Jews in Babylon concentrated on the problem of national survival and regaining the lost sovereignty. They emphasized that the distinctiveness of the Jews had always rested on religion. God's law got the task of uniting the people and giving an historical duty to them. *Torah* denoted the body of doctrine, written and oral, which had come down from the ancient past. These relics of the former national life constituted the only rock upon which the exiled Jews could stand in a gentile environment. Jews had to have a religion which would not only distinguish them from the heathens, but would likewise be a constant reminder to that they were members of the Jewish faith. Jews were to be demarcated from their neighbors not merely by a creed, but by a mode of living. With the help of the religious doctrine the exiles would remember that though in Babylon they were not of Babylon, and the sacred obligation rested upon them to remain a people apart (Cohen 1975: xiv–xvii; Moore 1954 1: 83–93).

Jesus and Early Christians

The historical Jesus, as well as the authentic content of his teachings and activities remain highly contested issues, but it looks like Jesus, a Jewish peasant, challenged all the earlier conventional Jewish positions concerning temple-state and the relationship between Jews and foreigners. Jesus seems to be closer to the Essenes (the Qumran sect), deviating more clearly from both the collaborators (the Sadducees), the nationalists (the Pharisees), and the national resistance movement (the Zealots), and even more importantly, from conventional politics in general (Adeney 1965: 3; Borg 1991: 86–91; Brown 1984; Crossan 1994: 103; Farmer 1956: 186–91, 197–98; Sanders 1993).

For Jesus, both conventional politics and the strict letter of religion had incorrectly structured society by creating distinctions instead of unity. He returned to a partly forgotten idea of the old Israelite prophets: a peaceful, orderly human association, the Kingdom of God, structured exclusively on the basis of God's word. Jesus maintained that the Kingdom of God was people under divine rule (Crossan 1994: 55).

Jesus challenged political power—both Roman and Jewish—by ignoring it. However, this challenge did not remain a simple renunciation of the world. Jesus suggested a radically new way of life, which became extremely political. It remains open if this application of the politics of the weak was intentional or a practical consequence of Jesus's position as an "underdog" as Crossan calls him. In any case, the radically new way of life became the central form of politics when Jesus not only discussed the Kingdom of God but enacted it and instructed others to do so as well. This established a radically subversive and socially revolutionary movement, which openly challenged all conventional social and political structures from a single family to the privileged classes in the Jewish community. The new order was based on open commensality and free healing—both generally shared Mediterranean hierarchies. Jesus's new community was open to anybody: outcasts, women, the poor, tax-collectors, and soldiers (Borg 1991: 131; Crossan 1994: 93, 103, 105, 181).

There is no need to speculate if Jesus had some knowledge of the ideas of Cynicism (cf. Crossan 1994; Farmer 1956: 188 192, 200–201). However, his ideas likely looked familiar, but were much more accessible to his less educated and pragmatic audience. In addition, his ideas were open to anybody to join. Jesus's message was therefore soon understood anywhere where conventional structures of politics and society had lost their ability to maintain social order. This was the case all over the Mediterranean world, where rapidly expanding exchanges of goods, peoples, and ideas were becoming retarded by national, social, and class distinctions. When Jesus had been a Jew among other Jews and contributed to their debates, Christianity was formulated by people who perceived the national distinctions outlived by the deep, rapid, and complex social change in the Roman empire. Distinction between original and foreign populations was disappearing everywhere (Räisänen 1990: 114).

In the cosmopolitan context, there was a quest for doctrines transcending the old distinctions, to make orderly social life possible among men of different nationalities and social positions. Judaism had developed a doctrine for human associations at the domestic level between individual Jews. Christians put the goal into a much a wider perspective, recognizing the need to transcend a number of *new* divisions. There was an urgent need to feel that everybody, anywhere, had something in common. While there were alternatives, like philosophical schools and religions (Mithraism), Christianity the creation of peasants, was open to the masses. In this light, it was claimed that all became "filled with the Holy Ghost" (Acts 2:4, 8–11; Col. 3:11; Rom. 1:14; cf. Dossa 1987).

I maintain that Jesus's doctrine, more or less combined with other relevant ideas such as Cynicism and Stoicism was adopted by an increasing number of different people in the Roman world, and soon was applied by them as a justification for new political struggles and structures. This was the divisive factor between two contending Jewish sects: those wishing to modify Judaism to the post-fall Diaspora, and those wishing to extend the power of the new Christian church. Judaism remained—due to the total collapse of the state—a specific application of the politics of the weak, while the Christians, by opening the Kingdom of God to non-Jews, became so numerous and powerful that the original element of the politics of the weak degenerated into an asset in challenging the Roman state from within and below. Unfortunately, this change leaves us the eternal problem of the historical Jesus and his teachings. Jesus and his teachings have almost disappeared from the stage, practically all that remains served the interests of the Christian expansion. The original message was not totally ignored, but was made an asset for the expansion of the early Church (Crossan 1994; Farmer 1956; Ferguson 1977; Mack 1993; Meyer 1992; *Gospel of Thomas*; Pagels 1995).

Ancient Greece

By the third millennium B.C.E. most of the Greek sites had been settled. On Crete the Minoan culture flourished in 2000–1400, but in 1400–1200 the Mycenaean culture moved the focus to the mainland. The Mycenaean culture was declining throughout

the thirteenth century, and was finally destroyed shortly after 1200 by invaders—
or rebellious local peasants—called the Dorians (Starr 1974: 104–10, 186).

The political administration of the Mycenaean world belonged to local kings.
According to Homeric tradition, one of the kings was a suzerain served by the other
kings (Starr 1974: 191–92). When the system collapsed, the Greek Dark Ages followed.
During this time, the inevitable dispersion of people to small, geographically distinct
units provided the basis for new political and social structures in the century following
750 B.C.E.: the *polis* or the city-state (Starr 1974: 205–7). Within the *polis* the society
was strongly divided into higher and lower classes; and relations between the city-states
became hostile. Homer describes this dramatic change in his two epics: in the *Iliad*,
he shows how the original unity collapses when the suzerain (Agamemnon) offended
the rights of the ruled (Achilles); in the *Odyssey* he further elaborates the social
consequences of individuality by showing that in the divided world the hero will
encounter only monsters and strangers whom he must cheat and even be ready to
struggle for power when back home.

The expanding Persia formed a serious threat for the city-states. However, Athens
and Sparta never agreed upon the existence of threat. Therefore, hostility and rivalry
between the city-states continued after the Persian wars, culminating (but not ending)
in the Peloponnesian War between Athens and Sparta from 432 to 404, which Athens
lost. Sparta's hegemony (404–371) became even less popular than Athenian imperialism.
By 362, the Greeks found the era of the city-state over.

The idea of the city-state was first challenged by the ideal of pan-Hellenic unity
supported by some writers and orators, among which the Athenian Isocrates (436–
338) became a leading proponent with his Panegyrics of 380 suggesting a Greek holy
war against Persia. However, only the rise of Macedonia made the realization of pan-
Hellenic unity possible. The Macedonian king Philip II and his son Alexander defeated
the Athenian troops in 338. After this victory, Philip convened the Greek states at
the isthmus of Corinth and formed a league. However, Macedonian power soon was
challenged by Rome. Macedonia allied with Carthage against Rome (217 B.C.E.),
but Rome won the struggle for Mediterranean hegemony.

The thousand-year cycle from original, or more likely mythical, unity through chaotic
and warring city-states, to the Hellenistic unity established by Macedonia is a fascinating
story that reveals tension between pan-Hellenistic unity and the city-state model. It
is, however, clear that the idea of unity was never shared by all Greeks. To the very
end, the Greeks were inclined to prefer individual freedom for tyranny, even if the
negative consequences of individualism turned out to fulfill all the predictions of
Homer.

Still, the debate was always present, even if in less open terms. Unlike conventional
wisdom (cf. Donelan 1978; Saunders 1984a: 19), I maintain that all classical Greek
works practically taken represent the two competitive approaches to the fundamental
issue of social order. Authors representing the majority view demanded that in order
to have peace, the human being had to become a social animal, live in a human
community, and create associations with other human beings over their selfishness
and individual interests. Consequently, intercity relations were likely and sure to remain
peaceful and orderly. According to this model, Greek society did not require an all-

encompassing pan-Hellenic unity; there was space for an infinite number of city-states, living in peace and harmony with each other (Sinclair 1984: 18; Stawell 1936: 11; cf. Plato's *Apology* 28c–d, 32e–33a, 38, 39b, 40a–41e, 42a; *Critias* 108c; *Gorgias* 492–493a–d; *Laws* 31d–e; *Letters* VIII.321, 325).

I also claim that explicitly participating in the debate Plato gave the clearest expression for the city-state pattern of social order. He saw the solution in the educated and balanced individual, ideal structure of the *polis*, and the right relation between the *good individual* and the *good state*. This reflected the view that the roots of the problems were not found between the states but within the states. International agreement or other international arrangements were to become relevant only through the moral development of the individual and the *polis*.

However, another answer to the same problem was also suggested: the return to the domination of a suzerain over all Greeks. By referring to historical experience and practical evidence, supporters of the pan-Hellenic ideal were able to say that no city-states system would ever end the war. Instead, the unity of the whole Greek was required to end the war. This unity would be achieved by a voluntary association of all Greek-speaking men. If the voluntary system failed, as was anticipated based on earlier historical experiences, the use of military power by the wise king to end war was recommended. This kind of war became the just war, the only acceptable war. This was Aristotle's and the old Isocrates' message, later developed fully in Roman Stoicism.

Rome

Rome grew from an Etruscan base (800–575 B.C.E.) to one of the strongest centers in Western Italy, and finally to a powerful Mediterranean empire by 133 B.C.E. when Carthage and other rivals lost the hegemonic wars.

According to a conventional image, Rome expanded its power not by an explicit design but an impersonal strategy, as one move of preventive action led to another. The process was an unplanned result of pragmatic military skill (Jackson Knight 1985: 11; Russell 1972; cf. Ogilvie 1982: 20–21). However, this picture must be inherently wrong: the Romans purposefully applied their military talents in order to promote their economic and political interests. This expansion required a solid theoretical basis of political and international ideas. This basis remained rather implicit, but towards the end of the expansion process the ideas had to become more and more explicit.

Indeed, successful wars had an important consequence for the Roman mind—Romans became conscious of their qualities and role in the world (Ogilvie 1982: 24). That conscience gave birth to poetical and historical mythologies: philosophers, historians, poets, and others wished to prove that there had been, since the very beginning, some meaning or knowledge of the coming Roman destiny to rule the world.

Furthermore, the continuous wars between 133 and 43 B.C.E. had become a major problem in the new empire. By definition, they had become civil wars. War was no longer a heroic opportunity to expand Roman hegemony, but an internal affair of the imperium. All wars—excluding less important clashes with other civilizations—became civil wars threatening the new cosmopolitan society of economic and cultural interaction. Therefore, it was not unexpected that war became a concrete civil war within Rome itself. The Roman Republic collapsed as a political system and fell in the civil wars of 49–45 B.C.E. Caesar became dictator in 46 for 10 years and in February of 44 for life. However, Caesar was murdered in 44.

The solution had to be found within Rome, and so it was done. Chaos of the civil war of 44–43 was stopped by Octavius, later called Augustus, who took power and held it until 14 C.E. Octavius-Augustus brought the longed-for end to the revolutions, civil wars, and chaos which had beset Rome since the preceding century. The new system of government by the single ruler over Rome and its imperium gave a long period of peace to Rome and the Mediterranean world.

This was fully recognized in theoretical and political debates that legitimized the ideas of cosmopolis, the universal state. World government as the basis of peace and order required the birth of the wise heroic leader. The philosopher-sage was not enough, the leader was to be the warrior. Only after peace and order were established in the world, including Rome, would there be space for the warrior to become the wise king. It was understood that the emergence of the world power and its government under one individual were intertwined processes. As Rome won its rivals in the Punic Wars, Octavius won his rivals in the Civil War. Consequently, military and economic dominion over foreign countries grew into the idea of the world government justified by the promise of coming peace and order at both international and domestic levels. Roman Stoicism formulated the required theory. Concerning this theory, I have concentrated on three prominent figures—Cicero (106–43 B.C.E.), the politician; Virgil (70–19 B.C.E.), the poet; and Livy (64/59 B.C.E.–17 AD), the historian—who contributed to the formulation of such justifications.

Cicero's contribution to the debate appears at the time where the Republic appeared to be on the point of breaking down forever. Revolutionary tribunes had been superseded by the far more dangerous phenomenon of great warlords, who not only felt a total disrespect for the senate, but commanded sufficient force to intimidate its members. Two of these men, Pompeii and Caesar, came to blows in the Civil War of 49 B.C. Cicero tried to stop this development. He suggested that wise and morally good men would be able to save the Republic. But the Republic was not able to survive, and it collapsed in the Civil War. Therefore, in order to find a new basis for order and a way of preventing a new civil war, people looked back on their rich moral inheritance and became increasingly interested in the origins of Rome and in the Roman myth, which was both life-giving and poetically true (Jackson Knight 1985: 11; MacFarlane 1991; Panayiotou 1984).

While Cicero gave the best expression to the Stoic idea of the cosmopolis, it was for others to develop it into the final idea of the world government. In this process, the mythical history was interpreted in a purposeful way: to show the role of important individuals, the leaders, in the Roman success and in its internal social order. Historians and poets emerged to prove that capable and wise leaders had guaranteed military success and, consequently, order and peace in society. Major parts of Roman literature can be read in this light, but this perspective justifies us in concentrating on two persons—Virgil and Livy. Both Virgil and Livy contributed to the process and especially to the effort to legitimize new leadership. Virgil, by appealing to Rome's mythical destiny; Livy, by recording Rome's past achievements (Jackson Knight 1985: 11–12, 15, 23; Ogilvie 1982: 7–8, 14–15, 23; Livy I.19.3, IV.20.7, XXXIV.4.8.).

Cicero and the two later figures are found on opposite sides of the battle. Cicero actually lost his life for preferring the Republican rule for the rising power of Octavius. Virgil and Livy chose the latter, the winner. But we must note that the debate, after the collapse of the Republican rule, concentrated on the question of the best ruler, and it is clear that philosophical debates had a prominent influence on Roman political thought and practice. Cicero tried to apply his suggestions for saving the Republic, but, in effect, contributed indirectly to the emergence of the wise king. In other words, Cicero's emphasis on the cosmopolis and Virgil's and Livy's emphasis on the controlled government over it were intertwined.

The Images of Chaos

Direct and practical historical experience was often expressed in more general images of chaos. I did not, however, find any one-to-one relation between a given image of chaos and a given approach to social order, somewhat against earlier findings (Aho 1981; Cohn 1993; Waltz 1970), but this was mainly because I did not carry out the required case studies. Case studies would have taken attention away from the ideas of social order, which are under investigation in the present work. Therefore, I briefly list five different but partly overlapping images of chaos found in the selected texts. This brief presentation justifies the conclusion that even unique historical experiences have common features over civilizations.

The first image can be called immanentist-cosmological, coined by Aho (1981: 11). This image perceives all human suffering, from individual to social problems, as disruptions of cosmological order and symptoms of chaos. Chaos is the direct consequence of mankind's failures to adhere to the cosmic order called *dao* or *dharma*. This image of chaos is found in Chinese Confucianism, Daoism, Mohism, and ancient Hindu thought.

In the second image, called transcendent-historical, chaos is viewed as a disruption of the historical order (Aho 1981: 11). Chaos is caused by men who break God's Law, that is, those who cause injustice. Such men are defined as absolute evil. Ancient Hebrew thought, Judaism, and early Christianity represent such an image, which can be found in several places in the *Old Testament*, the apocryphal texts, and the Qumran scrolls.

The third image, called dualism, represents a religious mythology outside Aho's (1981) dichotomization of the immanentist-cosmological and the transcendent-historical types. This image, formulated by Zoroastrianism, has connections to both, but is closer to the latter due to mutual influences. This image perceives chaos both as an interruption of the cosmological order and as a disruption of the historical one.

The three religious mythologies do not cover all the cases in our investigation. The fourth and fifth images, called individualist and societal, call attention to individual immorality and social decline, respectively. The individualist image finds the causes of chaos in the nature of man, and the societal image in the corruption of society. Typically to all variations in these political images of chaos, the problems of order,

and the existence of chaos, is supposed to be caused by the fact that individual morality
has become spoiled. Furthermore, because man is corrupted, the society of men is,
consequently, even more so.

All this does not deviate much from the religious images of chaos. Perhaps the
only difference is that the religious images speak of social chaos more or less as a
consequence of the collapse of the sacred system. However, at the social level the
images become similar both in religious mythologies and political theory. Similarly,
it is possible to find a religious basis behind any political theory. For example, Fustel
de Coulanges (1920/1955) speaks of the ancient Greco-Roman religions, which gave
the basis for the city-states, and undeniably influenced Plato's and Aristotle's political
thinking.

While the immorality of the individual and general social decline are intertwined,
we can speak of them as two distinct cases, the first case emphasizes the nature of
man, the second case focuses on the nature of society. The first includes Plato, Cicero,
and Livy, while the second includes Plato, Aristotle, Virgil, and the Chinese Legalists.

THE COMPARATIVE STUDY OF IDEAS AND *TERTIUM COMPARATIONIS*

A comparative study of international thought has remained underdeveloped. Attention
has been paid to making comparative studies, without stopping for methodological
elaborations. This is not unique to the study of international thought. While the process
of comparison is a fundamental characteristic of human intelligence, deeper questions
of method and the underlying philosophical implications of comparison have been
almost ignored in all comparative disciplines (Smith 1978: 240; cf. Alestalo 1992;
Niessen et al. 1984; Przeworski and Teune 1985; Ragin 1987, 1991; Raivola 1984;
Tilly 1984).[4] Therefore, I did not find a single earlier study to use as a basis or model
for this book. As a political scientist I first consulted a number of major works in
comparative politics (Eckstein and Apter 1965; Merritt and Rokkan 1966; Rokkan
1968; Sartori 1994; cf. Hayashi et al. 1992) but found them less relevant for the study
of ideas. In comparative politics the data is quantitative, and furthermore, the empiricist,
nomothetic approach that applies empirical data to hypothesis testing in order to find
all-encompassing laws of social behavior is not feasible in the study of ideas (cf.
Smith 1982: 25 ff.). The idiographic comparative style used to comprehend particular
features is more appropriate in the present case where data cannot be quantified without
a great loss of the substantive information for which ideas are studied in the first place
(Ishida 1969: 134; Nadel 1967; Roberts 1967; Spiro and d'Andrade 1967; Whiting
1967).

Among the fields dealing with texts, political theory, or the history of political ideas,
was the natural first choice in my efforts to locate relevant works. However, this
was not the case at all. While so-called revisionists have made a remarkable contribution
to the methodological discussion in the study of the history of political thought, problems
of comparison have failed to draw any attention (cf. Liu 1988; Maitra 1951; Tang
1951). For example, in his comprehensive study of the methodological debate, Boucher
(1985) mentions comparison not more than three times! However, the issue of com-

parison, while totally ignored as an explicit problem, is omnipresent in the debate about the study of ideas, which is all about various modes of comparison.

Consulting a number of other areas, including, for example, comparative literature (Shaffer 1981, 1984), I found Jonathan Z. Smith's (1978: 241–44) methodological discussions on religious studies of high general value. However, I adopted the practical solution from comparative education.

The success of comparison has been considerable in many fields of study and research. Therefore, it has been introduced and perceived as *the* scientific method of true scholarship, that is, a substitute for controlled experimentation. Therefore, in the developed fields of comparative studies the goal has been ambitious. The major proposition has suggested that there is a common origin or teleological goal of development. There was no point in adopting such a view in this book—the image of the scientific development is impossible to accept in the study of ideas, where a comparative approach is more likely to imply a taxonomic enterprise more indicative of natural history than science (Alestalo 1992; Ford 1977; Smith 1978: ix, 241, 244). In other words, the aim cannot be to find some eternal laws but to understand and make *interpretations*. The findings cannot be independent of the scholar, they must be unique to the scholar suggesting them. However, other scholars and readers can apply various criteria to evaluate the validity, relevance, and interest of the product. Among those criteria, some kind of truth must be included as correspondence between interpretation and the texts, as well as correspondence between the suggested interpretation and earlier knowledge. In addition, originality and innovativeness may be at least as important.

There is still another general goal to be excluded from the comparative study of international thought. As far as the study of ideas is concerned, a major aim has been to apply the comparative approach to document a thinker's influence on another thinker. This has been applied in the study of international thought as well. It is interesting to reveal influences and thus explain and describe the genesis and development of ideas inevitably occurring in intellectual history. However, the presence of an influence is impossible to ascertain, and too much emphasis on influence analysis would exclude interesting cross-historical and intercultural comparisons. Indeed, the most interesting comparisons between figures in different cultures—for instance, Plato and Meng Zi (Mencius) or Aristotle and Kong Zi (Confucius) on political education, or Machiavelli and Han Fei Zi on political realism—would become totally irrelevant because any suggestions of an influence-relation would lead to highly controversial debates on the original unity of humankind and lost connections between distant geographical areas (Bernal 1987, 1991; Boucher 1985; Burress 1988; Chydenius 1985; Jha 1983; Wu 1978).

Excluding the common origin and the study of influence (the latter, however, can be applied in feasible cases as a suggestive approach) seems to leave the comparative study of international thought groundless. This is not necessarily true. It is possible to suggest some less ambitious functions, sufficiently challenging and interesting from the point of the study of international thought, for comparative analysis to fulfill.

A comparative approach goes beyond simple descriptions and summaries of peace ideas. Second, a comparative approach is helpful in theory construction or paving the way for further analyses. Third, comparative analysis can be applied to test a hypothesis or a framework. Fourth, a comparative approach increases understanding or expands the scope of central concepts in international thought. Fifth, comparative data can provide a solid basis for criticism, and can help to avoid an ethnocentric bias, and give necessary stimulus to critical self-reflection in the study of international thought. Sixth, a comparative approach can suggest new questions and answers which are appropriate beyond a given period of time and a given culture (e.g., Aho 1981: 3–11; Archibugi 1989; Eckhardt 1972; Ferguson 1977: 15, 156; Galtung 1981: 183; Gallie 1978: 3; Harle 1987c; Horowitz 1973: 193; Hoffmann 1970; Ishida 1969; Levine 1963; Meinecke 1984: 21; McKinlay and Little 1986; Parekh and Pantham 1987; Raju 1960: 23–24; Wight 1991).

All the suggested goals of a comparative study of peace ideas are more or less academic. Nevertheless it might be possible to envisage normative goals, such as promoting international understanding. The task is similar to that in world philosophy, which surveys "the planet-wide turmoil" not with "the aim of justifying and protecting any prerogatives for the particular economy, political framework, moral ideals, or religion" but with "the aim of understanding the place and constructive role of each in relation to their living alternatives" (Burtt 1951). Thus, the purpose is to learn lessons from each other, share diverse ideals, and achieve an appreciation of what each has to offer in the presence of definite issues. World philosophy is thought to contribute directly to the elimination of conflicts by showing that the philosophies of two or more civilizations rest on basically different assumptions, both of which are true, that is, by showing that certain modes of thinking are different but compatible (Northrop 1951). A comparative study of international thought can well enhance this process. An increasing knowledge of political, social, and religious thinking in various cultures is required in order to increase mutual understanding.

If we look at earlier applications in the comparative study of international thought, a typical and all too often applied approach in international theory consists of a simple description or summary of a thinker's ideas. Most available works on the history of international thought fall in this category (Russell 1972). This does not mean that the works have been irrelevant. On the contrary, many descriptive efforts have produced interesting results, which have greatly increased our understanding of ideas and concepts of various cultures (cf. Basu 1983; Ferguson 1977; Gallie 1978; Hyslop 1984; Ishida 1969; Khanna 1983; Nargolkar 1981; Singh 1986; Srivastava 1982; Tandon 1980).

However, studies dealing with the historical development of conceptions are a step towards more genuinely comparative efforts (Boucher 1985: 51; Maurseth 1964; Skinner 1978/1980; Smith 1978: 262–64; Vagts and Vagts 1979). In the final analysis, a comparative study of ideas goes beyond description to classification and therefore results in a typology of ideas. Wight has presented one of the best known (Wight 1991; cf. Archibugi 1989; Herz 1951; Levine 1963; Hoffmann 1970).

There are at least three approaches to construct a typology of ideas. First, one can apply "pigeon-holing," i.e., arranging ideas in a single, often evolutionary, scheme (Collingwood 1980; cf. Airas 1978; Meinecke 1984; Parkinson 1977: 8). In an interesting methodological solution Gallie turns this approach upside down by looking not for similarities but for differences. His thinkers do not form a school, or even a clear succession or progression of thought about peace and war. Gallie (1978: 1–3) suggests, however, that "their arguments and conclusions, so differently motivated and so different in personal style and spirit, can be seen by us today to supplement one another to a degree which neither of their authors could possibly have appreciated."

Second, the scholar can derive hypotheses or questions from a general framework (very likely suggested by himself) in order to direct the analysis of texts to specific questions (Aho 1981; Waltz 1970; McKinlay and Little 1986). Third, one can suggest the existence of the basic tale, of which specific stories are a manifestation. This idea was originally introduced by Joseph Campbell (1988). He suggested the basic myth of the adventure of the hero, and applied it to an enormous number of tales, all of them being, in his opinion, manifestations of the basic story (cf. Alker 1987; Lakoff 1991; Smith 1978: 57–60).

While a typology of ideas is methodologically interesting and substantively informative, there are some problems. A typology is based on one crucial presupposition that there is a certain economy that appears fitting, and an understandable uniformity. Consequently, there can only be a relatively limited number of systems or archetypes, though there may be an infinite number of manifestations. One may only compare within the system, or between the pattern and a particular manifestation (Smith 1978: 259). It is difficult to say if all this holds true in the complicated and changing world of ideas, but in any case I have found "the pattern and its particular manifestation" the single possible and practical approach in this book. However, my application, which I call *tertium comparationis*, remains a rather heuristic device, mainly due to the lack of one or more common denominators required for a systematic comparative effort.

Concerning international thought, the major methodological problem arises from the fact that there is no shared or clear common denominator to provide criteria for evaluating similarities or differences, and to make the objects of study analytically comparable (cf. Ishida 1969; Galtung 1981; Burress 1988; Nargolkar 1981; Singh 1986; Tandon 1980; Wallach 1986; Targ 1974; Srivastava 1982; Khanna 1983). The problem of a common denominator is aggravated by the fact that most of the suggested ones are contested concepts. This is the case especially with the concept of peace. As Ishida (1969) and Galtung (1981) have shown, there are too many (and even mutually conflicting) variations of this concept and furthermore, we may remember the complexities involved in the all-encompassing ideas of positive peace. Security might be a better candidate, especially due to Buzan's (1984, 1991) contribution to its conceptual clarification. However, this alternative is likely to lead to problems similar to those encountered with peace. Airas's (1978) idea of the process of valuing is a more likely unifying factor, that is universally applicable in different contexts.

In fact, the problem of comparability can never be settled definitively—if something is really unique, it is incomparable by definition. As Jonathan Z. Smith (1978: 242–43) put it, unique is a negative term signifying what is mentally nonapprehensible; that is, the absolutely unique is by definition indescribable. The first thing the intellect does with an object is to class it along with something else. But any object that is infinitely important to us and awakens our devotion feels as if it must be *sui generis*, unique. Tension between the subjects' sense of the unique and the methodological requirement of the analogous generates both the excitement and the problems of comparative research (Smith 1978: 242–43). Therefore, one must presuppose a balance between "completely strange" and "nothing strange" (cf. Butchvarov 1966: 5–8). This assumption always remains a matter of taste.

Furthermore, in constructing typologies in international thought, and quite likely in other fields of comparison as well (cf. Boucher 1985: 139), we encounter a practical problem in making classifications: particular schools and thinkers in many cases straddle the suggested categories (cf. Bull 1976: 106). In evaluating, for instance, Wight's approach, one may wonder whether the traditions tend to overlap. There might be some similarities between elements of the three or four traditions. This, in fact, was suggested by Wight himself (Bull 1976: 106).

In the final analysis, the role of imagination becomes a central feature in the study of international thought. There are texts which can be used for the study of international thought, but there is no body of international theory (Wight 1966; cf. Smith 1982: xi). International theory is solely the creation of the scholar's study, just like political theory or history are: "The past in history is a creation of historians. Therefore, the past world of politics considered historically is the product and not the object of the historian's studies. In other words, we create it" (Boucher 1985: 105).

Indeed, international theory is created for the scholar's analytic purposes by his imaginative acts of comparison and generalization; it has no independent existence apart from the academy. This does not make the effort fruitless, and the basic message here is, in the final analysis, methodological. Smith does not suggest that there are no religions in the world, neither can we say that there is no international thought. Rather, the study of these phenomena is an academic industry, and as such is based on imagining the object of the study.

Therefore, considering the current process of transformation of the nation-states system, we should be aware of the Eurocentric bias. The transformation process, including especially intellectual elements related or even contributing to it, must not remain Eurocentric in the sense of being biased towards the uncritical truth of nation-state and the states system of international relations (cf. Bull 1977a). It is inevitable that all elements in cultural traditions are equally discussed, and it is required that all voices be heard and become understandable to all others (Chan 1996). From this perspective, humankind has many voices, each contributing to a common debate.

As an answer to these problems (cf. Smith 1978: 2–3) I suggest a practical solution: because it seems impossible to find a common denominator, the basis of comparison must be expressed in general, abstract terms. In other words, to make a comparison a *tertium comparationis* is required. The *tertium comparationis* is, to use the behavioral jargon, an imagined variable or factor against which cases under comparison are discussed or classified (Ulich 1967; Bereday 1966, 1969; Edwards 1970).[5] It may be that the cases under comparison share the quality expressed by a *tertium comparationis*, or, on the other hand, they do not share it. The basis of the comparison of the cases in this book is the quest for social order (including orderly social change). This quest can be described and discussed by a number of *tertium comparationis* variables, which were derived from the material under study by recognizing what the texts, schools, and thinkers were discussing.

The classification of the cases along the *tertium comparationis* variables makes it possible to solve the problem of straddling. In order to minimize this problem, I discuss various elements of a text, school, or thinker's production within more than one *tertium comparationis* variable, if required. My decision is not only a technical solution to the problem of classification, but represents a conscious methodological consideration. I challenge the coherence of a given text, school, or thinker. Because most of them contribute to or suggest more than one pattern of social order, incoherency must be seen as an essential feature of the texts. I have no right or duty to imagine coherency where it does not exist, sometimes against the will of the original writer(s).

Tertium comparationis has not been used in international relations vocabulary, but the idea is not new in the study of international thought. The approach has been used before, for instance, by Wight (1991), and by McKinlay and Little (1986). The main difference between my work and theirs is rather slight. The above mentioned works apply a given typology, they compare the ideal types over more or less theoretical issues, of which not all are derived from the data. In this book I compare concrete texts, schools, or thinkers with the aim of establishing a typology on the basis of their relation to the *tertius comparationis* variables, which were, I must repeat, derived from the data.

As I suggested in the Introduction, I soon found that the variables I was using could be divided into two groups. The first group consists of a general moral rule for individuals to follow, and when they do, peace and order prevail. The second group requires some kind of political government: power must be used to get individuals to live in peace within their community and have orderly relations between the communities, if there are several of them. Therefore, there are basically two answers to the quest for social order: the individual's duty to follow a moral principle or the existence of a political government regulating individuals' behavior. The first approach believes that an individual is able to follow the demanding moral responsibility voluntarily; the latter believes only in the use of power in establishing social order. I call the first case the principle-oriented pattern and the second the power-oriented pattern—noting that both basic patterns appear in several versions. This suggestion is reminiscent of earlier distinctions of, for example, compassion and compulsion (Eckhardt 1972), or idealism and realism (Carr 1981; Herz 1951). Such similarities will become even more obvious in the Conclusions, where I discuss more detailed typologies derived from the findings in Parts II and III.

NOTES

1. I refer to the Zoroastrian texts either in the *Zend-Avesta*, published in the *Sacred Books of the East* or in Boyce 1984. I use Gershevitch's (1959) translation of the *Avestan Hymn to Mithra*.

2. The development of Judaism is a long process, which began by at least 1200 B.C.E. and has continued to the present day. The first period in the development is called the Biblical era (1200–400 B.C.E.) documented in the *Old Testament*. During that period the term Hebrew, meaning a member of an ethnic group, gave way to Israelite, members of a nation united with each other through God's law. When the first five books of the *Old Testament* (i.e., the *Torah*) were published by Ezra as a guide to the conduct of life, those who accepted it as God's law

and worshipped at Jerusalem were called Jews and their faith Judaism. To be exact, therefore, we should speak of the Hebrews down to 1200 B.C.E., the Israelites around 1200–500, and the Jews since then (cf. Starr 1974: 144–45, 147, 158, 581).

3. However, it is usually in the specific sense of Rabbinic Judaism that "Judaism" is normally used (Neusner 1975: ix, and 3). According to Neusner, this type of Judaism came into existence in three distinct stages. During the first century C.E. the foundations of Judaism were formed by events in Judea and the system and thought of the Pharisees; Judaism came into full expression between 70 and 130. The second stage began in the aftermath of the Bar Kokhba War, 132–135, and reached its climax with the publication of the *Mishnah*, c. 200 C.E. Finally, the third and final stage started in the Mishnaic period and reached its full statements in the *Talmud* of the Land of Israel, c. 400 C.E. and in the *Talmud* of Babylonia (Neusner 1985: 1).

4. I have published a systematic review of comparative studies of peace ideas elsewhere (Harle 1989b). Therefore, in the present discussion I have given only some examples.

5. I thank Professor Reijo Raivola for calling my attention to this idea (cf. Raivola 1984: 74, 150–55).

PART II

Principle-Oriented Patterns
of Social Order

The principle-oriented pattern of social order maintains that social order can and must be exclusively based on moral norms or principles. This claim appears in two versions. The first suggests that the principle alone is necessary and sufficient to order (Chapter 3). The second maintains that an additional factor is required (Chapters 4–6). This factor is a set of social norms or rules derived from the basic principle and which, simultaneously, support the basic principle.

The supporting elements, whatever they may be, form a kind of civil society, an alternative to the state. In some cases, such a civil society is expressed in the texts with the conventional vocabulary of the state, the king, and so on. Furthermore, the supporting elements and the state are often so close to each other that it looks less justified to claim that the models discussed in Chapters 4 through 6 belong to the principle-oriented pattern instead of the power-oriented pattern of order. While the distinction between the pure principle-oriented model (Chapter 3) and the power-oriented model is rather clear, the less pure applications of the principle-oriented version are undeniably problematic to categorize (cf. Conclusions). In fact, some of the ideas to be discussed in this section of the book should be (and sometimes will be) discussed in the third part, as the logic of the *tertium comparationis* design demands and makes it possible.

While my basic categorization is controversial in light of some earlier works (Drekmeier, 1962; Neusner 1992), it is justified by the fact that in the present section all the models are based on explicit moral principles: *dao/dharma* and the Kingdom of God in the pure model, and *dharma*, *asha*, and *torah* in the models supported by some social structures.

In reporting my findings, I give exclusive emphasis on description. There are some brief comparative remarks, but the comparison is imbedded in the structure of the *tertium comparationis* variables. I describe one or more schools, texts, or thinkers who share the given variable. If there many cases sharing the variable, the implication is that they are telling the same story in other words, but the stories must be retold because they are unique in their expressions. If a case does not share the given *tertium comparationis* variable, it is not mentioned at all; and this is the case quite often. Furthermore, the *tertium comparationis* variables are theoretical constructions, or ideal types. Together they form a framework imbedded in the structure of this book. This structure is both a major finding of my investigation and a way of comparing the cases. In this sense, discussions within a chapter are illustrations of both the general theory and the respective variable.

In short, the comparative element in the first section maintains that some cases represent the principle-oriented pattern of social order, while others do not. The cases representing the principle-oriented pattern can be divided into pure and applied cases. Each of the latter cases are magnificent and unique suggestions, but simultaneously, they repeat the same basic idea.

CHAPTER 3

Moral Principles as the Basis
of Social Order

The idea of the moral basis of human associations is typical to all principle-oriented patterns of order; it also appears as a subordinated idea among several power-oriented patterns. This moral basis alone is claimed sufficient by the present pattern, which suggests that peace and order can and *must* be achieved without conventional power structures. The existing social and political systems are ignored or openly challenged. The conventional social order and politics are actually criticized for destroying orderly human associations, which might achieve a natural harmony on the basis of the given moral principle. All this implies a fundamental reconsideration of human relations and social values.

In the strict sense, the present pattern can be found in Daoism,[1] Jesus's teachings, and Buddhism. However, concerning Jesus's teachings, we have no written document of his original words. The *New Testament* (hereafter referred to as NT) Gospels were written to justify the Early Church as the ideal organization of humanity (Section 7.3.). While I use some general principles stated in the NT Gospels to illustrate the present pattern,[2] the discussion is based on recent studies of the historical Jesus (Crossan 1994), "The Lost Gospel" or Q Gospel,[3] and the *Gospel of Thomas* (hereafter referred to as GT), of which about one third have parallels in Q, especially in its first layer, Q1 (Meyer 1992: 10, 181).

For practical reasons I do not give much space to Buddhism, which at least partly belongs to the present pattern. The Buddhist doctrine emphasizes spiritual life instead of social life, and therefore does not present a systematic discussion of social points. Buddhism would deserve a more extensive discussion where religions are concerned, but for this book it remains, in its major substance, distant.

THE PRINCIPLE: *DAO*, THE KINGDOM OF GOD, AND *DHARMA*

Daoism does not suggest any definition of *dao*. On the contrary, it explicitly denies the possibility of definition (Lao Tzu I.1). The well-known translation in Western languages—the Way—does not divulge much. It is better to say that *dao* is the moral principle governing all human and material existence. The message is: to accept and follow *dao* is to have and maintain order; any deviation from it means disorder and chaos. It is also feasible to say that *dao* equals life in *all* varieties. To respect all existing variations of life, without compromises, is to respect and follow *dao*. In other words, the precepts of following *dao* are similar to the modern liberal principle of live and let live, but gives it a fundamental, uncompromising, and comprehensive meaning.

In Jesus's teachings, the key program and principle was expressed as the Kingdom of God. The fundamental idea was to promise orderly human associations created in the name of God: "where two or three are gathered together in my name, there am I in the midst of them" (Mat. 18: 20; cf. GT 23, 30). Indeed, God had to be the basis of human associations: "Thou shalt love the Lord thy God with all thy heart, and with all thy soul, and with all thy mind." With God's will, this love will be extended to human associations: "Thou shalt love thy neighbor as thyself" (Mat. 22: 37–40).

The Kingdom of God was a great mystery to Jesus's original audience. The idea was so new and original that it took a rather long time to reject existing social conventions of hierarchical power and order (cf. GT 46). The Kingdom of God represents power and rule in a specific sense. When the Kingdom of God prevails, people are not ruled by somebody above them, they are ruled by themselves when they follow the moral principle. Because the moral principle comes from God, people who submit themselves to it are under God's direct dominion. The Kingdom of God involves the question of meaning in life. Life alone does not have the same intrinsic value as in Daoism (GT 3; Crossan 1994: 55, 58; Mack 1993: 111; Meyer 1992: 10).

In ancient Indian thought[4] the moral principle giving order to everything was called *dharma* which denotes "law, moral law, a spiritual law of righteousness, the eternal law of the Universe, Truth." In the golden age (*satya*, or truthfulness) *dharma* had four legs established by the principles of austerities, cleanliness, mercy, and truthfulness (Mascaró 1987: 9, 27).

The principle of *dharma* was of supreme importance in Buddhism, too. In Buddhism, *dharma* was used to denote moral laws prescribed by the Buddha. Subsequently, the term came to be used in various senses such as nature, duty, truth, justice, virtue, laws, quality, and predicate. In Buddhism these senses are clearly expressions of a basic moral principle similar to the other two approaches discussed here (Bhattacharyya 1990: 52–53). However, unlike in the cases of Daoism and Jesus's teachings, the social consequences of the key principle remain indirect.

Buddhism is, in its essence, a system of self-restraint. It represents a serious effort to end human suffering by living a holy life, free from passions and desires. Concerning the two main trends of Indian ethical tradition—the maintenance of the social good or the importance of the householder's state of life here and now on the one hand, and the furtherance of individual spiritual development or keen attention upon the ultimate end of life, on the other—Buddhism preferred the latter.[5] Buddhism is a world-renouncing religion. The basic moral principles of Buddhism are spiritual, that is, oriented to the perfection of the individual; no explicit discussion of human associations are presented. The Buddhist ethic is self-centered, a disciple is expected to follow his own salvation rather than the needs of others. He will seek to serve others because this is part of his own effort or his own path to salvation, it is not simply a matter of love. For example, the actual basis for the acceptance of non-violence as a moral norm was not, originally, social. Non-violence is considered a necessary norm for the sake of the spiritual development of the acting individual himself. According to the doctrine of *karma*, each good or evil deed has spiritual consequences for the doer, it was important for the acting subject to abandon an evil or impure will (Dutt 1991 I: 342; Ferguson 1977: 42; Tahtinen 1979: 53–54).

Consequently, in Buddhism, *dharma* is related to *nirvana*, the ultimate goal of all Buddhist endeavors. *Nirvana* implies or demands the extinction of craving and separate selfhood, a life which has gone beyond death. Following a more general use of the term to denote liberation, salvation, emancipation, the highest good, or absolute bliss (*moksha*), *nirvana* is described as the free state of consciousness, the tranquil state of one's internal nature and the highest emotional state of spirituality and blessedness. Therefore, *nirvana* means the annihilation of passion, hatred, and delusion. *Nirvana* is the cessation of suffering, not the extinction of existence, but the extinction of misery and rebirth. The real nature of *nirvana* can only be grasped intuitively, it cannot be described in terms of ordinary experience (Bhattacharyya 1990: 102, 110; *Buddhist Scriptures* 1982: 247).

On the other hand, the Buddhists thought that fulfillment of moral duty leads to social good, because Buddhism stresses the service of others in this world to help them escape suffering. The Buddha's own activity was directed to spiritual assistance to everybody. According to the legend, Buddha was given the chance to go straight to *nirvana*, but rejected it as a mere temptation. He saw men whose sight was darkened and required help and enlightenment. Therefore he wandered about India for forty-five years proclaiming his doctrines.

Moral responsibility has social implications. The search for *nirvana* alone makes social order, and the association between good people, possible. The religious goal of individual Buddhists is to realize enlightenment and live a life that is in agreement with and contributes to their religious objectives. Only such individuals are able to assemble and live together peacefully and harmoniously (Bhattacharyya 1990: 139; Ferguson 1977: 41–45; Hirakawa 1990: 60; Tahtinen 1983: 31).

THE REJECTION OF POLITICS

Daoism was directed against both the Legalist and Confucian ideas of social order. The Daoists state that there can be no laws or other permanent rules without quarrel about their meaning and content. The basic problem is not, however, caused by written language and its linguistic obscurities—the comprehensive code of rituals suggested by the Confucian school is disregarded as well (cf. Pocock 1973, 42–79). Any rules—whether written or not—are partial and incomplete. The laws and edicts cause disagreements, suspicions and quarrels, and cause rather than prevent crimes (Lao Tzu XXXVIII.82, LVII.132; Chuang Tzu: 108).

Daoism was not interested in questions like How to govern? or How to govern in order to unify China? No answers to these questions were formulated, and, in fact, no meaning was seen in them. The Daoist sage preferred not to discuss the extension of good government to the *tien-hsia*, but disappeared in the forests in order to avoid answering such useless questions (Chuang Tzu: 272).

According to Daoist philosophy, all problems had been produced by the very act of the foundation of the political society. The conventional social order, that is, political power, was responsible for making it impossible for individuals to follow *dao*. The Daoist ideal was to live in harmony with oneself and nature.

However, while Daoist questions and answers are unconventional, this does not imply indifference towards social responsibilities. Daoism is interested in alternative social order and its approach is unconventional. It is not action but non-action that gives birth to order. Therefore, if a Daoist philosopher was willing to answer the question of How to govern?, he recommended abstention from all conscious action. That is, the Daoists found it impossible to arrange any type of conscious governance, with any type of government. One could only avoid conscious action, the government over the others, and therefore have peace and order. Since any conscious action leads to disasters, it is better to do nothing (Lao Tzu III.10, LXVI.154a). The Daoist logic suggests a paradox. But there is nothing paradoxical to say that one must deal with a problem before it emerges while it is still small, and to keep things in order before disorder sets in. It is better to have peace than to make a peace treaty after the war.

Therefore, the Daoist saw the fundamental issues not in the question of government but somewhere else. The Daoist question is something like this: Is it possible to have order and survival without conventional social and political power structures? Or, Are there any alternatives to conventional social order as a shield against terror? (cf. Aho 1981). If there is an alternative, there is no sense in thinking about the relations between states—there could be no states in the first place. There might be an un-organized humankind where its members are just individuals without any kind of human government—neither a state nor a world government—above them. This alternative implies that harmony will be achieved and maintained without any use of power and violence.

Daoism sometimes appears to be speaking for the good government or the wise ruler. In addition to precepts for individuals, the Daoist model suggests some societal approaches to solve and eliminate conflicts and social problems. There are some precepts directed to the ruler; those precepts seem to define the Daoist ideal of good government.

But this, actually, is not the case at all. It must be emphasized that the Daoist ruler (if there ever is one) would not be indifferent towards his people. On the contrary, he would always be concerned about their lives and their survival; he would do the impossible in order to save his people, and would never abandon anyone. However, the Daoist ruler would have no action in these efforts because any activity would lead to disaster instead of saving people. Things should be spontaneous; people should think that it all happened naturally (Lao Tzu XXVII.61, XVII.41).

In other words, the Daoist idea of the ruler and government is actually about the non-ruler and non-government. Because all action produces ruin and disaster, it is not possible to direct the flow of events. All directing or governing of activities bounces back like a boomerang with disasters. Therefore, it is difficult to imagine that there ever will be a Daoist ruler (Lau 1983a: 32). That is why Zhuang Zi (Chuang Tzu) is fond of telling stories about sages who were not willing to accept the post of ruler:

the sage always knows that it is impossible to govern. This is expressed in an ironic tone in the *Dao De Jing*, where an ideal ruler is defined as a person who prefers his body to domination over the empire (Lao Tzu XIII.31).

The Daoist doctrine states that there will be nobody to accept domination over the empire simultaneously fulfilling the criterion of valuing his body more than domination over the empire. Therefore, evil caused by government must be removed altogether. When all are interested in preserving their body and life, no one is interested in damaging others through government in order to pursue political power. Then all conflicts and violence will disappear. In this sense, the ideal Daoist ruler is not a ruler over others, he is ruler over *himself*. To govern an empire is nothing, but to have full sovereignty over himself represents all that is important.

Jesus did not support conventional political power, but referred to the existence of a more important, divine ruler as well as the full reality of the Kingdom of God. Jesus saw that man was able to transcend conventional distinctions and become one with other human beings (Mat. 16: 24). Thus, Jesus set out to challenge the conventional order within society as well as the legitimacy of the Jewish temple-state and the Roman Empire.

From a religious point of view, the old order must be removed because man can have just one master—for Jesus it was the Kingdom of God, for the NT Gospels it was the church. This must be done in order to unconditionally serve God. If someone loves his father or mother, son or daughter, more than God, he is not worthy of Jesus (Mat. 10: 21–23, 34–39; Q1 in Mack 1994: 75). The family structure had to be abolished in order to give everybody—including wife and child—freedom to serve God, but even more importantly, freedom from conventional social hierarchies (GT 16, 55; Q1 in Mack 1993: 79).

In fact, it was not a simple question of the religious role of God, but an issue in the social dimension, where the old order—the distinctions between the father and the child, between the master and the servant, between the male and the female— had to be destroyed. The old order was the opposite of true human associations. The old order was divisive; the new one was to be associative: all had to become one. From the social point of view, Jesus challenged existing and accepted inequality and structures that maintained it. The Kingdom of God was a challenge to groupism, based on kinship and gender (GT 22; Crossan 1994: 58–60).

The challenges to family, kinship, and gender were examples derived from the idea of a nondiscriminating society. According to Crossan, the challenge concerned the most basic inclination to draw lines, invoke boundaries, establish hierarchies, and maintain discriminations. It did not invite a political revolution but envisaged a social revolution. The distinctions between Gentile and Jew, female and male, slave and free man, poor and rich were simply but dramatically ignored (Crossan 1994: 196; cf. GT 64).

According to Crossan, such a program clashed fundamentally with honor and shame, the basic values of ancient Mediterranean culture and society. It pursued the absolute equality of people, where the master and the host must become both the servant and the female. In the miniature society of open commensality, especially at the Last Supper table, Jesus is not served, but "Jesus himself serves, like any housewife, the same meal to all, including himself" (Crossan 1994: 70–74, 181).

While Jesus clearly concentrated on the immediate social associations, his message had direct and challenging implications to the political power structures of his time—the temple-state and the Roman Empire, both of which were based on and maintained by the social structures criticized by Jesus. The challenge was implicit but well understood by both the Jesus movement and its enemies. Occasionally the challenge was presented in explicit terms.

According to Crossan, the Kingdom of God consisted of radical egalitarianism: the equal sharing of spiritual and material gifts, free healing, and eating. The Kingdom of God is a community of unbrokered equality in which individuals are in direct contact with one another and with God, unmediated by the priests or the Temple. It is clear that Jesus at least symbolically destroyed the Temple's legitimate brokerage function in the name of the unbrokered Kingdom of God (Crossan 1994: 101, 107–9, 133, 195–96).

There is nothing related to the Roman Empire among Jesus's original sayings. However, Crossan is likely right in perceiving some connections to the nationalistic traditions of his time, especially in baptism, which symbolized the ancient and archetypal passage from imperial bondage to national freedom (Crossan 1994: 195; Mack 1993; Meyer 1992). Due to this influence, Jesus perhaps first shared the end of the world vision of the Baptist movement (cf. GT 10–11), but left it rather soon. Crossan suggests that Jesus thought it futile to wait for the divine destruction of the Roman Empire, and that the death of John the Baptist revealed that no God was going to destroy the political leaders, no matter what they do. Therefore, he found that the weak can and must challenge the state's overwhelming power by pursuing a radical, egalitarian life-style (Crossan 1994: 197–98).

In Buddhism no explicit rejection of politics is made, at least in the ways suggested by the other two approaches. The rejection, however, exists in a controversial form. It is expressed in the legend of the Buddha, with conspicuous similarities to the Jesus narratives in the NT Gospels. According to legend, a sage saw that a king's child—who later became the Buddha—had only two paths open to him: (1) as participant in economic and political activities, he was to become king and unite the world as a universal ruler; and (2) as a hermit, he was to become a Buddha. After recognizing the existing social evils of old age, sickness, and death, the boy chose the latter option and abandoned the kingship (Campbell 1986: 252–55; *Buddhist Scriptures* 1982: 34–66; Hirakawa 1990: 21).

However, as the later tradition and history reveals, neither the Buddha nor his followers defined politics as absolutely evil, rather it became the question of who is the ruler, and especially, if the ruler is the wise ruler with the full Buddhist mind and morality. This is best revealed by the example of both Ashoka's kingship and one of his edicts where he promised "to pay this debt due to my people" and "render them as happy as possible here below" (Dutt 1991 II: 9). Furthermore, as the Buddha legend reveals, one can leave the world only after tasting the pleasures of life and fulfilling social responsibilities, among them, having a son.

Another, more explicit challenge contained similar aspects of a political power struggle. Buddhism rejected the castes system. Unlike orthodox thought, in Buddhism *dharma* was not applied to justify this system (cf. Chapter 4). It is claimed that the Buddha respected the brahmin for his virtue and learning, not for his caste. Indeed, he ignored castes by claiming that a man's distinguishing mark was his work, not his birth (Dutt 1991 I: 349).

Buddha's position has an interesting historical background. The historical Buddha was born into the Gautama clan. It was a small kshatriya tribe, which did not appear to have been divided into four castes. The government was an oligarchy, within which all equal members (called *raja* or king) alternated as head of the tribe. It is even possible to say that this group of equal members was similar to the Athenian democracy—within the clan or clans all men, called kings, belonged to a collective body or assembly, called *samgha*. The Buddha lived and spread his message among such clans. In fact, he made his order rather similar—those who wished to enter the Buddhist *samgha* were admitted without regard to social position but had to accept the wise rule within the monastic order (Hirakawa 1990: 21, 66; Law 1987).

However, the Buddhist alternative to conventional politics and social structures remained rather weak, it was not made a central expressed element in the doctrine of spiritual development. Furthermore, the Buddha's position concerning castes remained controversial. The historical context strongly suggests that the Buddhist texts contributed to the power struggle between brahmins and kshatriyas; and that they believed the kshatriya to be superior to the brahmin, that is, they preferred the state's power over the old religious power of the priests (Dhawan 1990: 131).

NON-RESISTANCE

The duty to follow the moral principle, as the challenge to conventional politics and violence, leads to the problem of resistance. To suggest a comprehensive moral principle and the duty to follow it without compromise implies that one cannot apply violence against anybody, however evil or violent. But the challenge to conventional politics implies something more: that one cannot oppose conventional politics by conventional politics, by just replacing those in power. To challenge conventional politics and political structures is to say that peace and order can and must be maintained without them. Therefore, the alternative must be based on the strict principle of non-resistance. Non-resistance can be applied as a powerful force of declared non-violence, as Gandhi did, but also as an alternative program without a direct face-to-face encounter between the weak and the oppressor. Such covert resistance is extremely political (Crossan 1994), while overt acts of non-violence may remain rather conventional politics, especially if they lack the alternative program. In the worst case, non-violent action can be used to struggle for power.

The Daoist texts condemn all wars from offensive to defensive, from just wars to any violence, and the condemnation is often presented explicitly. It is not possible to assist the ruler by the use of weapons because arms are an ill omen and because a military victory is not a matter of joy but of mourning (Lao Tzu XXX. 69a, and XXXI.72).

In general, the condemnation of war is based on moral precepts, but it is not impossible to find some Mohist-like economic arguments as well. Daoist thought maintained that a mighty army can cause bad harvests; only in peacetime do horses plow the fields which during war are destroyed or remain unplowed (Lao Tzu XLVI.104). Such arguments are, however, less important than moral ones.

There are no justifications for war because nobody is able to carry out the tasks of heaven in punishing culprits or tyrants. If anyone tries to kill on behalf of the executioner (heaven), few escape hurting themselves instead (Lao Tzu LXXIV. 180). On the face of it, Lao Zi (Lao Tzu) accepts the use of arms as a desperate remedy, if there is "no choice" (XXX.69; cf. Lau 1983a: 30). However, Lao Zi never imagines that there wouldn't be a choice: non-contention, submission, and negation of conflict *are* always available and strongly recommended by him. The choice is available when it is understood that action, and its correlates—values, language, and knowledge—cause rather than prevent or solve social and human problems. Conscious effort should be avoided, everything should be allowed to proceed spontaneously.

The dismissal of conscious effort implies the idea of total non-resistance. During chaos, conflicts, and war an individual should give up all kinds of resistance—both violent and non-violent—and be submissive. The *Dao De Jing* makes several references to the demand for avoidance of contention, resistance, and struggle. Contention leads to defeat and death sooner or later (Lao Tzu XLII.97). Therefore, Lao Zi speaks about the virtue of non-contention. This virtue promises absolute success, where the word "victory" must be understood rather paradoxically. The weak do not contend, and therefore never suffer defeat. In other words, when one avoids contention, one wins by surviving (Lau 1983a: 55 29; Lao Tzu LXVI.162, LXVIII. 166a).

What is even more important in the virtue of non-contention is the negation of conflict. This precept is based on the assumption of a non-reality of conflicts: conflicts and contention do not really exist (Chuang Tzu: 27). Therefore, no one should sacrifice his or her life because of conflicts and contention in the futile effort to overcome the adversary. This attitude, also typical of some Western religious sects and sectarian pacifists, does not deny the possibility of losing one's life, no matter how submissive an individual is. But losing one's life is not so important in the final analysis. One should not be afraid of dying because then they cannot be frightened by threats and therefore forced to fight (Lao Tzu LXXXIV.180).

Indeed, the *Dao De Jing* abounds in expressions praising submission and non-resistance. For example, nothing is more submissive or weaker than water, but there is nothing that can surpass it for attacking that which is hard and strong. Therefore, the weak can overcome the strong, and the submissive can overcome the hard. A living creature is pliant and weak when living, but hard and stiff when dead. Therefore, an uncompromising submission, when required for survival, is called true strength (Lao Tzu LXXVIII.186, LXXXVI.182, LII. 119).

In the extreme, this attitude leads the Daoists to praise deformity—physical, moral, and mental. For example, a hunchback, who can avoid a conscription and public works, receives more donations of grain and firewood than anybody else (Chuang Tzu: 54).

The virtue of non-contention is supplemented by the precept of recognizing limits, of knowing when to stop. It is better to stop in time to avoid bringing calamity upon oneself. The precepts of non-contention and stopping in time are interrelated. Both entail contentment with what one has, then one will always have enough (Lao Tzu IX.23, XXXII.72, XLVI.105a).

According to Daoism, it is forbidden to control and govern others. One must be able to know and govern oneself. Therefore, the Daoist ideal is not to withdraw from moral and social responsibilities. An individual must apply these responsibilities to oneself. An individual can overcome others by using mere force, but he or she can overcome oneself by using "true strength" (Lao Tzu XXXIII.74).

Non-contention, submission, and self-discipline have positive consequences: they lead to enduring victories. When an individual does not attempt to be great, he or she succeeds in becoming great (Lao Tzu XXXIV.76b). This can be understood in light of the Daoist paradox: there is nothing more important than to survive in a violent world, therefore, non-contention, submission, and self-discipline are the most efficient—the only—ways of attaining this precious goal.

In Jesus's teachings the world is perceived as dangerous, especially for Jesus's believers. They are sent out as "lambs among wolves" (Q1 in Mack 1994: 76; GT 21). Therefore, it is clear that non-resistance is a demanding choice, not a consequence of an idealistically imagined world of harmony (Q1 in Mack 1993: 73–74).[6]

Some of Jesus's sayings disclose an everyday wisdom familiar from other documents in the Jewish scriptures and elsewhere. Other sayings suggest a more provocative and radical wisdom that might be called counterculture wisdom (Meyer 1992: 11). As Crossan has recognized, Jesus located the borderline between covert and overt arts of resistance. It was not as open as the acts of protesters and prophets, but still more explicit than waiting for and imagining revenge in the end of the world. Free eating and healing hovered around the line between private and public, never resisting state-politics or the priests' power openly. Such an indirect resistance ignored them, not remaining a theoretical idea, but becoming a purposefully enacted practice (Crossan 1994: 93, 105).

In Buddhism[7] non-resistance in the sense of non-violence (*ahimsa*) was made the absolute moral norm. *Ahimsa* has been translated by various writers as non-killing, non-injury, non-hatred, harmlessness, inoffensiveness, non-cruelty, non-aggression, tenderness, innocence, good-will, and love. *Ahimsa* was a multidimensional concept (Tahtinen 1976: 10).

Sometimes one sees non-violence interpreted narrowly as non-killing. Specifically, the non-killing of animals for religious purposes. This is justified, for instance, by Ashoka's edicts demanding that individuals "not . . . kill any living animal by immolating it, not for the purpose of feasts," and to respect the life of living beings (Dutt 1991 II: 6–7).

However, *ahimsa* has a much broader meaning, it implied comprehensive physical non-injury rather than simple non-killing. Apart from death, physical damage and bodily aches and pains were symptoms of violence. *Ahimsa* forbade killing or physical damage to a living or feeling being, to a person or an animal. In addition to physical damages, violence by word or thought was also considered morally wrong. Thus, non-violence was to be observed in thought, word, and deed. There was spiritual, verbal, and physical non-violence. One of the five precepts[8] given by the Buddha to all human beings demanded that they abstain from taking a life. This precept forbade the murder of anything that lives, by both action and speech (*Buddhist Scriptures* 1982: 70–71; *Dhammapada* 14: 183–85; Tahtinen 1976: 2; Tahtinen 1979: 53). In short, non-violence means that one should not harm others, avoid exploitation for furthering one's own interests, and behave with others as one would wish them to behave. One should take only what one needs, control one's desires, and not be jealous of the success of others.

PEACE

The Daoist model suggests a utopia of eternal peace, a world where no wars exist and no weapons are used (Lao Tzu LXXX.193a). This utopia is feasible to achieve through reducing the size and population of the state, in fact, until there are only individuals and the state no longer exists. If the state does exist, the need for its expansion should be minimized or eliminated altogether. When people are reluctant to move to distant places and are content in their homes, there is no need to expand or even to interact with neighbors (Lao Tzu LXXXX.193c).[9]

Jesus's teachings place a great value on peace: if two individuals make peace with each other they will be able to move mountains (GT 48). But, it must be emphasized, Jesus's teachings do not recognize the existence of the state. If violence occurs, it occurs, by definition, between individuals, not between the states. Consequently, peace must be applicable to relations between individuals.

Therefore, debates on the idea of peace in the NT Gospels are irrelevant.[10] It is meaningless to maintain that there is no explicit discussion of international peace or war in the Gospels, to claim that Jesus only spoke of human associations between the Jews. It is true that he did, but he did so without making the modern distinction between domestic and international. Jesus did not speak of the world of states but of the Kingdom of God, i.e., peaceful and orderly associations between all human beings.

With this in mind, we can return to the fact that the concept of peace (*shalom*), extensively[11] applied in the Scriptures and by early Christian writers, sees peace as an orderly association between individuals. Such a conception of peace emphasizes non-selfishness and distance from the temporary world, man's unconditional submission of himself and his conventional values to God's grace. It gives the major role to high ethical values in human associations, and peace as well. The Lord's Sermon on the Mount[12] declares that "blessed are the peacemakers: for they shall be called the children of God" (Mat. 5: 9).

In interactions between individuals, both positive and negative instructions help to maintain peace. The positive instructions tell us to do something: "love your brother like your soul, protect that person like the pupil of your eye" (GT 25; cf. Mat 7: 12; Q1 in Mack 1993: 73–74).[13] It is especially important to love one's enemies, not only those who love you (Q1 in Mack 1993: 73–74; cf. GT 24). Some other instructions are even more explicit: "whosoever is angry with his brother without a cause shall be in danger of the judgement." In other words, "no one should bring a gift to the altar, if he remembers that his brother has something against him. Instead, one must leave there the gift before the altar, and go to reconcile the brother, before coming back" (Mat. 5: 22–25).[14]

The negative instructions advise us to avoid something. For example, not to murder,[15] commit adultery, steal, or bear false witness (Mat. 19: 18; cf. Q1 in Mack 1993: 73–74). Similarly, one must not speak evil of one another because by doing so, by judging someone, one speaks evil of the law and judges the law, therefore setting himself above the law instead of submitting to it (Jam. 4: 11; Mat. 7: 1; cf. Jam. 5: 9). Instead of criticism towards others, one should take care of himself (Mat. 7: 3), and one must "not lie, and do not do what you hate" (GT 6).

In general, the Buddhist contributes to peaceful and orderly human associations in two ways, through non-violence, and, indirectly, by recommending *nirvana*. In Buddhism, peace means peace of mind, the achievement of *nirvana*. Such a great achievement, the ultimate goal of the individual, it is maintained, has social consequences when peace of mind has been achieved by a higher number of men. Only then can social relations become orderly. Wise men who have attained knowledge do not cause any injury to living beings (*Dhammapada* 1: 6).

Furthermore, peace is praised in explicit terms. For example, a poem or verse that speaks of peace is better than a thousand useless words. Peace can only be achieved by peaceful means, "hate is conquered by love" (*Dhammapada* 8: 100–102, 1: 5). It is correct to maintain that the saying "enmity is not eliminated by enmity; only when enmity is abandoned, is it eliminated" is an unchanging and eternal truth, the basic *dharma* (Hirakawa 1990: 45).

According to Ferguson, Buddhist pacifism is stated the most unequivocally in the *Brahmajala-sutra*. The work insists that the children of Buddha may take no part of any kind in war, they must avoid lethal weapons. They may not participate in revolts, rebellions, or uprisings, nor even watch a battle (Ferguson 1977: 50).

On the other hand, the case of Buddhism is somewhat controversial because it is believed that Buddha in one of his former lives killed heretic brahmins in order to protect his doctrine and save the heretics themselves from the consequences of continuing their attacks against good. It is, therefore, said that if Buddhist doctrine is in danger, when it becomes impossible to pursue due to chaos, the five precepts —including the prohibition on taking life—may then be ignored. Furthermore, there were other justifications for killing. First, it was good to kill one in order to save two. Second, due to the illusory nature of existence, no one is really killed (cf. *Bhagavad Gita*). Third, it is better to kill another than to allow him to kill. Fourth, because destiny is predetermined, it can not be a sin to put someone to death, if the person who kills acts out of compassion and charity, or thoughtlessly so that inner peace is not disturbed (Ferguson 1977: 55–56). However, all such justifications are rather far away from the core principles, and similar reservations are not difficult to find in the cases of Daoism and Jesus's teachings, when the followers use the original doctrines to justify their power struggles.

ALTERNATIVE VALUES

The moral principles in present applications, as the alternative to conventional social and political order, strongly imply that there is an alternative system of values as well. Indeed, Daoism emphasizes the absolute value of life, as does Buddhism. Life obtains first place in the hierarchy of values and is preferred to any other values. In Buddhism, one reason for the insistence on *ahimsa* was the metaphysical concept that all life was one and that even the meanest insect was a manifestation of the divine essence (Bhattacharyya 1990: 10). Concerning Jesus's teachings we have no explicit sayings on the matter, but the sayings related to non-resistance (as well as to loving enemies) may be interpreted as such. In any case, the similarities of the three approaches become even more so when other values are added to the picture.

According to Daoism, one should never cherish his achievements or boast (Lao Tzu II.7–7a, XXII.50b, XXX.69b). Thus, one must not value one's conventional, material possessions (Lao Tzu III.8). Similarly, Jesus pointed out that conventional values cannot be kept safe. There will always be somebody stronger than the strongest armed man. Everyone will lose the contest one day, and the new winner will take his property (Luke 11: 21–22). Therefore, it is better to sell all that one has, and distribute the money to the poor in order to have "treasure in heaven" (Luke 18: 22).

Jesus's own alternative was more permanent and powerful: "lay for yourselves treasures in heaven, where moth and rust doth corrupt, and where thieves do not break through nor steal" (Mat. 6: 20; cf. Mat. 6: 19). One had to become weak in order to survive and enter the Kingdom of God (Mat. 18: 3–4). Indeed, one cannot achieve conventional values or make them permanent: "And seek not ye what ye shall eat, or what ye shall drink," but "rather seek ye the kingdom of God; and all these things shall be added unto you" (Luke 12: 29–31). Faith became more powerful than weapons. Faith and love became the strongest breastplate and the hope of salvation an unbreakable helmet (1 Thess. 5: 8). Therefore, there was no need to be afraid of those who can kill the body but not the soul (Q1 in Mack 1993: 77, 80).

In order to put the sayings into context, we must observe that the values Jesus suggested were not conventional. Jesus told his audience not to care much of the world, life is more than food, and the body more than clothing (GT 27; Q1 in Mack 1993: 75–76; cf. Crossan 1994: 196). The world had to be ignored in order to find the Kingdom of God, but the message was not only religious, it represented a social position.

It is correct to note that Jesus's stance of social critique was a call for individuals to go against conventional norms, not a program offered for the reform of society's ills. Simultaneously alternative values challenged conventional values: wealth, learning, possessions, secrets, rank, and power (Mack 1993: 46, 111; GT 48, 54; cf. Mack 1993: 9). The challenge was part of a more fundamental pattern. As Crossan maintains, Jesus declared the destitute blessed because "the only ones who are innocent or blessed are those squeezed out deliberately as human junk from the system's own evil operations" (Crossan 1994: 62, 195).

The message and its context seem to reflect some ideas which were rather well-known in the Mediterranean world. Mack (1993: 43) and Crossan (1994: 115–16, 122) emphasize that the life style called for in Q was much closer to patterns of behavior characteristic of Cynics in the Hellenistic tradition of popular philosophy than to Christian charismatic prophets.[16] They may be right or wrong. In any case it is impossible to prove the existence of Cynicism's influence on Jesus's thought. It may be that Jesus's words were written down in a vocabulary more or less familiar to the authors and their audiences. In any case, the alternative values of the weak expressed in Jesus's teachings can also be found elsewhere, not only in Cynicism.

In the Vedic tradition there were only three values: ethical (*dharma*), economic (*artha*), and psychological (*kama*). The fourth value, *moksha* or the spiritual value, was later added. It was suggested that uncontrolled satisfaction of a sensual desire does not pacify the desire but rather makes the man desire repeatedly and more avidly than before. The final result is bound to be frustration because unlimited desires cannot be satisfied. Therefore, it was believed that ignorance, action, and thirst are the causes of *samsara*, the intrinsic disvalue, the opposite of *moksha. Samsara* and *moksha* are "conceptually intertwined and are like two discs of the same coin" (Tahtinen 1976: 12; Tahtinen 1983: 13, 52).

The Buddhist system suggests a totally new set of alternative values, which are exclusively spiritual. The Buddha taught all is transient, all is sorrow. Everybody will become old, sick, and die. Therefore, it is meaningless to cling to the transient, to things that pass away, thus forgetting the spiritual values of the uncorrupted mind available to everybody (Mascaró 1987: 22). It is *nirvana* alone that represents the single true value, the alternative to earthly wealth (*Dhammapada* 5: 75, 8:103–5).

CONCLUSION

The ideas of true, orderly, and peaceful human associations on the basis of radical equality is often understood as an escape from social realities and responsibilities. In the case of Daoism, Jesus's teachings, and Buddhism this is not true—all were responses to social problems and took social responsibility seriously. However, criticism is right in asking us to think about the consequences of any doctrine. Social responsibility can be a central element in all three doctrines, but they have often, at least indirectly, justified politics, which they originally criticized.

The Confucians, the Legalists, and the Mohists devoted their ideas and recommendations to the ruler, while the Daoists were more worried about the common man. The morality of Daoism deviates from the conventional morality of the other schools, but one cannot deny that following Daoist—or Jesus's—principles presupposes higher individual morality than any other schools. This is seen in the fact that the Daoist is not indifferent towards his fellow beings. The Daoist can achieve happiness only by pursuing the happiness of others (Lau 1983a: 39). One must forget about private ends in order to accomplish them (Lao Tzu VII.192).

Similarly, Jesus's teachings suggested a high moral duty for everybody. Jesus spoke to and for the common people, the poor, and the destitute. In order to find the meaning of life for them by making them fully accepted members of society, he also encouraged the weak by revealing the powerlessness of the state and of death. In short, Jesus saw the problems of his time and contributed to their elimination in both theory and practice.

Buddha's doctrine served more clearly the powerful and the rich. His doctrine even suggested escape from the social world and its responsibilities. This clearly differentiates Buddha from the Daoist sage and Jesus, but even he believed peace of mind was available to anybody and everybody.

On the other hand, as political philosophy the present pattern of order supports the idea of authoritarian rule, or centralized political power. Sometimes this support is almost direct, as in the case of the Daoist criticism of knowledge that gives the ruler the duty to keep the ruled innocent of all knowledge (Lao Tzu III.9). More often, however, justification is more indirect. The moral principles can be used to justify *any* politics. Confucianism, Legalism, Mohism, Stoicism, the early Christians, and especially the early Church have proved this theory. Furthermore, while Daoism, Jesus's teachings, and Buddhism positively reject or even ignore the idea of centralized political power, this often implies in practice that no alternatives to the existing power structures are available. The potential opposition is atomized into individuals, who then will be governed by an authoritarian ruler without any far-reaching efforts. The atomized mass of individuals minimizes the energy required in governing them.[17] It is likely that Jesus's teachings and activities are the least vulnerable to such criticism, due to the politics of the weak present in his doctrine.

NOTES

1. I have discussed Daoism (Harle 1995), and both Daoism and Mohism (1987b) in earlier versions.

2. The point is not to claim that the NT Gospels support the present pattern, a number of recent studies have shown that they do not. The Gospels challenge conventional politics and the state, but not the politics and politicking by the Church. But they are able to fulfill such a function because they likely repeat the more original ideals declared by Jesus and his close followers. Furthermore, in the present chapter I use sayings similar to those claimed to come directly from Jesus (Crossan 1994; Mack 1993; Meyer 1992).

3. "The Lost Gospel," usually referred to as Q Gospel, is claimed to be the primary source (Q comes from the German word "Quelle" for "source") of Jesus's original words used by the NT Gospel authors. Q Gospel consists, according to Mack, of three layers (Q1, Q2, and Q3). The first layer, he insists, is closest to Jesus's original sayings. The references will be to "The Lost Gospel" reconstructed by Mack (1993).

4. I discuss *dharma* of the epic literature in the next chapter as an element of ancient Indian political thought. My discussion—Brahmanism/Hinduism rather than Buddhism (or Jainism). In any case, we can note that differences between Indian religious schools have been usually overemphasized, whereas the basic unity of the key terminology has been ignored (Bhattacharyya 1990: xvi, 105). There are substantive religious differences, e.g., the Buddhist conception of *nairatmya* (the denial of *atman*) but such nuances do not concern us in this book.

5. The two traditions did not exclude each other absolutely. The epic literature, including the *Bhagavad Gita*, attempts to integrate the society-directedness of the Vedic orthodoxy with the *moksha*-orientedness of the ascetic movements (Tahtinen 1976: 12–13).

6. The NT pacifism represents a purposeful reconciliation after the Jewish war, when Christians represented themselves as not hostile to Romans. This denies the fact that many persons and movements have been willing to follow these principles quite strictly. Among them are many sectarian pacifists and figures like Tolstoy and Gandhi. For all of them the Kingdom of God had a strong pacifist meaning, forbidding even the resistance of evil.

7. The doctrine of non-violence was a basic element in Buddhism and Jainism, but its ideals are also appreciated and upheld in Brahmanism where, as in Buddhism, the king (kshatriya) had the exclusive licence and duty to kill in order to save the other castes and *dharma*.

8. The other precepts demanded that everybody abstain from taking what is not given, from sensuous misconduct, from false speech, and from intoxicants tending to cloud the mind (*Buddhist Scriptures* 1981: 70). Furthermore, the eightfold path to the noble truth about suffering, its origin, and its destruction consists of: (1) right understanding, (2) right thought, (3) right speech, (4) right action (including "not to kill"), (5) right vocation, (6) right effort, (7) right mindfulness, and (8) right concentration (Ferguson 1977: 42–44).

9. Plato and Aristotle suggest similar views, but accept the establishment and role of their ideal state.

10. Summarizing the debate, Räisänen (1984) maintains that the topic of war and peace (i.e.,the international dimension) is not specifically addressed in the *New Testament*.

11. In many places "peace" is a polite and pious way of wishing good luck, or to say that "I" am "your" friend (Mat. 10: 13; Luke 2: 14).

12. The NT Gospel sayings such as "ye love one another, as I have loved you" (John 15: 12–19); "honor thy father and thy mother" and "thou shalt love thy neighbor as thyself" (Mat. 19: 19), as well as similar sayings in the Jewish texts suggest that it was generally thought important to have peace in relations between individuals.

13. There is no need to repeat the continuing debate on the doctrine expressed in the Lord's Sermon on the Mount. I prefer to share the views of those who say that it applies to relations between the Jews (Räisänen 1984), but I also share the view that this interpretation does not exclude applications at the international level. Concerning the interpretations, St. Augustine's (*The Lord's Sermon on the Mount*; cf. Gregory of Nyassa) is one of the most interesting. He maintains that the ethical content of the sermon as a moral code is not limited for a select few but uncompromisingly binds every Christian.

14. When the NT Gospels and the early Christian writers speak of orderly human associations we must remember that this was said in order to prevent or correct internal disputes within the new community. In the case of Jesus's teachings, there was not such a closed community and his program was dealing with human associations in any place.

15. Expert scholars agree that the 5th Commandment refers to the murder of a member of the society.

16. For Crossan, Cynicism did not mean belief in nothing or doubt about everything; Cynicism as a philosophical orientation represented theoretical disbelief and the practical negation of ordinary cultural values and civilized presuppositions (Crossan 1994: 115–16).

17. Actually, Chinese Legalism soon adopted these Daoist ideas, as if to prove my argument. Furthermore, I must emphasize that the so-called Daoist rulers in China have been unexceptionally hated tyrants. All of them have followed the Legalist mode of government instead of the Daoist ideals. Something similar has often happened in the Western world, where Christian ideals have been unquestionably used for the justification of tyrannies and wars.

CHAPTER 4

Dharma and Caste as the Basis of Social Order

Like Daoism, Jesus's teachings, and Judaism, ancient Indian thought maintains that social order must be based on moral norms called *dharma*. However, the principle of *dharma* alone is not sufficient to maintain order. An additional factor is required: the system of four castes. This system makes a division of labor, or, the division of roles within society, the basic element of social order. This factor, on the other hand, is not independent of the basic principle and the castes without *dharma* might be a weak shadow of the principle-oriented pattern of social order. The castes are a consequence of the moral principle, they are an expression of it and they support *dharma*.

Ancient Indian thought is unique in providing a major emphasis on the caste system. The caste system represents a case of civil society suggesting an alternative to conventional state-politics. In Indian thought the political, the state, and the king (kshatriya) are not independent of or above *dharma*, but submit to *dharma* and the caste system. State-politics does not direct the castes, but the castes, representing civil society, define the nature of politics and set the specific boundaries. Consequently, political struggle is not related to the question of who will rule the state, but how the caste system—that is, the society—is maintained. The society is maintained by *dharma,* not by politics or the use of power.

In other words, there is no real role for the state. The functions of the state can be fully served by the caste system, which contains some elements of conventional political structures. Indeed, the *Mahabharata* (hereafter referred to as MAH), the *Bhagavad Gita* (hereafter referred to as BG), as well as many other ancient Indian works often speak of kings (i.e., the state) and war. Such views would certainly deserve discussion in the relevant chapters of the power-oriented patterns, however, the same material can and has been used for documenting both the principle-oriented and power-oriented patterns. I do so myself by emphasizing a major point from the present chapter: the principle-oriented and power-oriented patterns are not independent, they overlap with one another in the Indian example. Therefore, in order to document *dharma* as the center of social order, I present and discuss material concerning the wise king and the heroic king in ancient Indian thought.

DHARMA

The Hindu religious tradition clusters around two concepts; *dharma* and *moksha* (Kinsley 1982: 85, 88–89). At the heart of the tradition lies a paradoxical assertion. In order to fulfill one's human destiny, *dharma* states that it is necessary to uphold human society, and in order to find ultimate release from the world, *moksha* demands individuals to renounce society (Kinsley 1982: 82). This tension between supporting or renouncing the world is a central theme in Indian thought. There are several solutions to the problem (Kinsley 1982: 16), but it is obvious that social responsibility is never ignored in the epic literature.

Dharma represents the temporal perspective, the social dimension, which had an important role in ancient Indian thought since the earliest times. Health, wealth, sons, and a long life were the chief concerns of the Vedic religion. These blessings were insured by performing appropriate sacred rituals aimed at maintaining an overarching cosmic order. By the time of the *Bhagavad Gita* and the *Mahabharata* (c. the third century B.C.E.) all human actions, not just specific rituals, were believed to contribute to the maintenance of cosmic and social order. The support of the world captured the heart of the *dharma* tradition. Each person, no matter how low born or how menial a social task he or she inherited according to caste birth, had a fundamental obligation to perform his or her ascribed social function for the welfare of society as a whole. Therefore, *dharma* referred both to the orderliness of human society and to each person's duty to uphold that order through every action.[1] In other words, *dharma* acquired two related interpretations: virtue, the moral duty vs. the performance of caste function, the social duty (Drekmeier 1962: 8; Kinsley 1982: 83).

Dharma replaced the earlier Vedic term *rita* (*rta*), which refers to the principle of the universe that established the patterns and processes that regulate all things. Consequently, *dharma* is something that maintains or supports. *Dharma* undergirds and sustains the universe.[2] It is the force that holds things together in unity, the center that must hold if all is to go well (Drekmeier 1962: 8–9; Easwaran 1986: 215–16). In order to try to capture the word in English one might say "God's law" or the "eternal truth." Thus, *dharma* comes close to *dao*, the Kingdom of God or God's Word, and *torah*.[3]

Dharma is one of the most pregnant words in Indian thought.[4] *Dharma*'s basic meaning is repeated in many ways justifying the expression "the complex word *dharma*" as Easwaran (1986: 215–16) puts it. *Dharma* is, by definition, the opposite of *adharma*, caused by those who break their *dharma*. *Adharma* means evil, injustice, or chaos. In this sense, *dharma* is a "sense of unity," while *adharma*, chaos, applies to a "society plunged into chaos" (BG l.40–45). If *dharma* disappears, the strong suppress the weak and chaos damage the weak and endanger social life (Ghosal 1966: 22).

Dharma is basically a moral norm. It requires that one respect ethical rules, as well as conventional customs shared by men. *Dharma* is a divine gift, it is the moral and religious duty (MAH: 145). *Dharma* is the basis of duties, justice, laws, virtues, and values, that is, all things related to social order. Law is based only on *dharma* (Ghosal 1966: 35, 103; Ghoshal 1959: 19, 43, 529).

Dharma implies the existence of cosmic and social laws. *Dharma* demands that one take these laws into consideration and work accordingly. In this sense *dharma* makes behavior rational. Consequently, *dharma* represents truth and justice. *Dharma* implies the duty to do the thing right. An act becomes right if it follows the Vedas, and fulfills the religious basis of existence. This gives the basis for correct social behavior as well (Basham 1982: 113; Ghoshal 1959: 292; Raju 1960: 212, 218). The Purusa-Sukta (*Rig Veda* 10.90. v.19 in O'Flaherty 1984) speaks of "the sacrifice the gods sacrificed to the sacrifice," saying that "these were the first ritual laws (*dharma*)." Therefore, *dharma* designates the archetypal patterns of behavior established during this first sacrifice to serve as the model for all future sacrifices. *Dharma* guarantees the salvation (*moksha*) of the individual, as well as peace and happiness on earth (O'Flaherty 1984: 32; Radhakrishnan 1929: 505). In the final analysis, *dharma* and *karma* are intertwined. One must follow *dharma* because it will effect the form one will take when reborn (*Rig Veda* 10.16.v.3 in O'Flaherty 1984: 51).

Dharma is the basis of life, it supports life. Life is supported as long as it is not in conflict with its own basis, *dharma*. Therefore, *dharma* means, more specifically, the law of life. Existence is based on that law, and if the law is broken existence becomes non-existence (Raju 1960: 26). This basic function of *dharma* is expressed in the *Bhagavad Gita* (4.6–8) as Krishna, who will be continuously reborn to protect good and reestablish *dharma*. Therefore, in the same work Arjuna defines Krishna as the supreme, ultimate reality, as the guardian of eternal *dharma* (BG 11.18). Indeed, while the *Bhagavad Gita* is called the Song of the Lord, it should be called, more specifically, the Song of *dharma*.

An individual is responsible for his or her own *dharma*. It is emphasized that one must perform one's own duties even imperfectly rather than master the duties of another, otherwise competition would breed fear and insecurity (BG 3.35). Furthermore, no one should abandon his or her duties, even if he or she sees defects in them (BG 18.47–48).

Dharma concerns all people. *Dharma* is something's inner nature, and no one can avoid his or her inner nature. According to Krishna, one cannot egoistically skip the fundamental battle fought in the name of social order. This type of resolve will be useless: one must and will finally do anything *dharma* demands, even when one would prefer not to carry it out. Therefore, as exemplified by Arjuna's hesitation before the great war, it is nothing but a delusion to object to the duties of one's *dharma* (BG 18.59–60).

Devotion to *dharma* guarantees both individual and social goals—the individual's spiritual perfection and social order within society. At the individual level the fulfillment of one's duty is a tribute to the creator, to the omnipresent cosmic spirit (BG 18: 45–46). At the social level, everyone must contribute to the common productivity and efficiency. The *Bhagavad Gita* (3: 20–24) teaches that above all each individual must work for preserving the world from anarchy. Regardless of the caste into which a person is born, each person must adhere religiously to *dharma* (Aho 1981: 73). There are nine duties common to the four castes. Everyone must control anger and avoid quarrels;

pursue truthfulness, justice, purity, forgiveness, and simplicity; have lawful children, and look after dependents (MAH: 307).

However, proper actions are relative. Certain types of actions may be forbidden for one caste and permitted for another (Kinsley 1982: 128), because *dharma* is specific to certain castes and persons (BG 18.40–41). It must be noted that moral duties concern the brahmin and kshatriya castes, not the vaishya and shudra castes. A brahmin is born to high personal virtues, wisdom, and faith. The qualities of a kshatriya are related to courage and political or military leadership. The *Bhagavad Gita* does not list any moral qualities specific to the vaishyas or shudras, but it does speak of occupations suitable for a vaishya and proper work for a shudra (BG 18.42–44).

CASTE SYSTEM

Because chaos is caused by mankind's failure to adhere to the cosmic principle (*dharma*), it follows that for one's own inner peace, as well as for the sake of reality as a whole, individuals must conform to *dharma* particular to his or her position in the cosmos. In order to define this position in the cosmos, each caste (*varna*) provides the required social coordinates. Therefore, the *dharma* tradition focuses on the maintenance of the caste system (Dhar and Mehta 1991: 89; Dhawan 1990: 17; Kinsley 1982: 85).

It is impossible to say when and why the caste system was established. The stories of mythological origin appear for the first time as part of a creation myth, the Purusa-Sukta (*Rig Veda* 10.90.v.12 in O'Flaherty 1984). The Purusa-Sukta tells how the gods created the world by dismembering the cosmic giant, Purusa, the primeval male victim in a Vedic sacrifice. Purusa's mouth became the brahmin, his arms were made into the kshatriya, his thighs became the vaishya, and from his feet the shudras were born. Thus, mankind was classified under four *varnas* or orders, with reference to their occupations, reflecting the division of labor between the four castes.[5] The historical origin of the castes, however remains, unclear. For example, according to O'Flaherty (1984: 29–30) the Purusa-Sukta is part of an Indo-European corpus of myths of dismemberment, and the underlying concept is quite ancient. However, it is one of the latest hymns in the *Rig Veda*.[6]

Legend is repeated in the *Laws of Manu* (hereafter referred to as Manu I.87). Indeed, underlying all law books in ancient India is the strong Hindu affirmation that an orderly, refined, stable society is to be cherished. Order, stability, and refinement have primarily to do with the proper functioning of the various castes and the proper observance of interaction among castes and among members of the same castes.

Brahmins had the duty to teach and study the Veda, sacrifice for their own benefit and for others, and give and accept alms. Kshatriyas had the duty to protect the people, bestow gifts, offer sacrifices, study the Veda, and abstain from sensual pleasures. Vaishyas were commanded to tend cattle, bestow gifts, offer sacrifices, study the Veda, cultivate land, and lend money (Manu I.88–91). Shudras were entitled to serve meekly those who were born twice, that is, the members of the other castes. According to another source, they had the right to cultivate land, trade, raise cattle, and work as artisans and court singers (Kautilya I.3).

It is not difficult to recognize that in Hindu writings concerned with *dharma*, the ideal human society is described as hierarchically arranged according to caste. The social system has as its primary aim the support of brahmins, who undertake Vedic rituals to maintain and renew the cosmic forces that periodically must be refreshed in order to keep the world bounteous and habitable. Beneath the brahmins are the kshatriyas and vaishyas. These three castes are called twice-born, and these castes alone are qualified to study the Vedas and undertake Vedic rituals. The Shudras must support the higher castes by performing services for them. Beneath the Shudras are the untouchables, whose occupations are considered highly polluting or who are so classed because they belong to tribal groups that are not yet acculturated (Kinsley 1982: 84, 169).

The suggested hierarchical system was not, however, referred as permanent and eternal. The division of roles was permanent but individuals were able to move from one position to another. Movement was not only possible but inevitable. This movement must be understood in religious terms. While it was assumed that rank and hierarchy were intrinsic to human relations, it was believed that people were continually reborn according to their actions in the past. *Karma*, the moral law of cause and effects by which one reaps what one sows, and *samsara*, rebirth, combine to teach an individual that the particular caste into which he or she is born is determined by his or her past actions and that the caste that he or she will be born into in the future is determined in the present by how he or she acts. Finally, class restrictions had not completely hardened even in Gupta times. The *Mahabharata* often differentiated between the poor and the wealthy within the same caste. In fact, because the caste system was a religious innovation, it was not, therefore, so rigid that it prevented social movement. The origin of the Maurya dynasty proves that it was possible for a shudra to become a ruler. In the *Mahabharata* the caste system was equated with character not birth. While no one can be sure of his or her own caste's purity, character is the only thing that is certain (Aho 1981: 157; Drekmeier, 1962: 69–70; Kinsley 1982: 84).

Furthermore, ancient Indian sources only rarely refer to *jati*, a concept that more closely approximates the term caste as it is used nowadays. Kinsley suggests that the *varna* system of the Vedic religion and the *jati* system found at the village level are different, though they are seen as complementary in the Hindu tradition. It is a fact that the books of law in India divided society formally into four castes, but the system was less rigid than the *jati* system of the indigenous peoples with closed, endogamous groups based on occupational specialization (Drekmeier 1962: 69–70; Kinsley 1982: 122–25).

In analytical terms the caste system was aimed at maintaining social order in Indian society without accepting any other divisions within the society. Only the role of family, as the basic unit of human associations, was given a similarly central role. However, the function of the family was to strengthen, not challenge the caste system. The state or its status above all castes, was rejected. Therefore, it is not difficult to understand the role of caste and *dharma* as the basis of peace of mind and social order. The caste system gives structure and meaning to social life. The place or status of man is defined by his caste. His social role, or duties, are derived from this status and expressed as *dharma*.

Indeed, the caste system had a great function to fulfill. The caste system did not suggest the division of labor as its ultimate goal or as a means to obtain economic prosperity, but as a means to achieve social order. The castes were created, Manu states (I.87) "in order to protect this universe." The caste system created unity, stability, and strong predictability by dividing men into specific castes, each of them extending over mankind and beyond national and other boundaries. It does not matter that in practice, just like in the Chinese and the Western cases of world government, this universe remained more or less limited. Thus, while the horse sacrifice (*asvamedha*) reassures society the king will enjoy supreme power over the earth, in practice it can only apply to a small regional power, not a big nation-state or global power (Aho 1981: 63; Basham 1982: 85; Ghosal 1966: 77; MAH: 77, 331; Russell 1972: 37).

The caste system likely had another, more specific function, according to both historical and linguistic evidence. In early Vedic times a distinction was made between the ordinary free members of Aryan tribes and the warrior nobility, from among whom the tribal chieftain was elected. The brahmins, as priests, were also mentioned as a distinct social group. When the Aryans settled down they established close relations with the indigenous people. In such a situation social conflicts between the Aryan and indigenous tribes, as well as within them, had to be managed in order to establish the new orderly society. The caste system was then applied as the method of integration and justification. It served as the badge of distinction between the free Aryans and the subjugated indigenous people, who were made to work for them as laborers or artisans. In addition, and partly to justify the suggested historical interpretation, it has been suggested that the caste system is related to complexion—according to this explanation, *varna* means "color" not class, like *jati* does. This theory maintains that the system was created to make the division between the light Aryans and the dark natives. The first three castes were exclusively reserved for the Aryans, the last one was for the natives (Kulke and Rothermund 1986: 40–41; Radhakrishnan 1929: 111).

Indeed, it is not wrong to maintain that the castes system did produce social order. The castes system maintained orderly pluralism and diversity. There is, however, no reason to praise the system uncritically. It is an exaggeration and a rationalization to say that with the caste system India "became the happy home of many races, cults, and cultures, coexisting in concord, without seeking overlordship or mutual exter-mination" Mookerji 1957: 98). The caste system, especially if it was created in order to distinguish the Aryans from the native populations, justified the use of power by the Aryans over the natives. This was far from idealized harmony, nor did the system prevent conflicts and power struggles between and within the castes. But the system of managing conflicts and establishing social order were both unique and efficient in its task (Aho 1981: 60–61; Drekmeier, 1962: 69–70).

THE KING

In ideal terms, *dharma* gives the society its structure and basis. Neither the brahmin (priest) nor the kshatriya (king) is above *dharma*, both are the fountain of law. The kshatriya had two important roles: (1) the protection of the people in battle; and (2) the acquisition of wealth. But the brahmin had the more fundamental task—to lead a life of renunciation, live on the barest subsistence allowance, and occupy the most honored position in the social hierarchy. He, like the others, was to find real satisfaction with his own place and work in society. It was emphasized within the caste that those who seek a higher place will lead a life of simplicity and self-denial.

However, an ideal combination of roles (the exemplar: Yudhishthira) produced the philosopher king, whose words are considered the highest codes of rationality and morality. In traditional, orthodox thought the brahmin was above the kshatriya. The leader of the Pandava brothers was brahmin (Yudhishthira) not kshatriya (Arjuna). In fact, Karna, the oldest brother, the greatest of the warriors, was never accepted among the Pandavas (Dhawan 1990: 125–26; Drekmeier 1962: 49).

While I discuss the king and war in this light, it cannot be denied that the opposite interpretation—that the king or the state was above civil society—might be justified. There was an open power struggle going on between brahmins and kshatriyas. Indeed, a central theme of Indian political speculation is the relationship between brahmin legitimation and kshatriya authority, that is, religious authority vs. the guardian of the secular power. While the latter function was properly recognized, an unbounded authority was perceived as the greatest evil and danger. Therefore, the ruler who abused the power of sanction and coercion (*danda*) was warned that he might find himself its first victim. In this light, the *Mahabharata* is a manifesto on behalf of the strong monarch, but the monarch does not rule arbitrarily. He must govern in accordance with the sacred authority represented by brahmins, and he knows that the eternal duties of kings are to make their subjects happy, observe truth, and act sincerely. Even more openly, the *Bhagavad Gita* and the philosophical currents it contains are an attempt to civilize the knight and turn his energies toward the larger goals of the community. The *Bhagavad Gita* is about "the taming of the heroic ideal" (Drekmeier 1962: 6, 10, 146, 157).

The accomplishment of one's duty was an individual's highest achievement, but the preservation of *dharma* was simultaneously the major obligation of the state. *Dharma* expresses individual caste obligations, and the state, in committing itself to the maintenance of *dharma*, is thus only indirectly concerned with the achievement of a unifying common purpose. Law is ultimately divine and removed from popular interpretation and appeal. The priests were its custodians. *Dharma* stood above the king, and his failure to preserve it must accordingly have disastrous consequences (Drekmeier 1962: 9–10). The king is not an independent element; he is not above the castes. If the state, or the king and his power, exists it appears subservient to the castes. The king does not challenge *dharma* and the castes, he maintains them. This is revealed by the origin and nature of the state.

The state has either divine origin or is based on social contract. Both appear simultaneously in literature. Divine origin is suggested by the creation of the castes, while division of labor implies the existence of a social contract. In both cases, the state is required to end chaos. Without established order no social life possible. The family and the caste cannot survive without the existence of order, and in its absence the big fish eat the smaller ones. Without the king's use of punishment, without his embarkation on campaigns of righteous conquest first to establish and then to maintain sacred law, and without his fighting justly against the enemies of order, men would become corrupt. They would fall from *dharma*; caste lines would become confused. The horror of anomie, *matsyanyaya* (the way of the fishes), would replace the world of structure and psychological security (Aho 1981: 73; Basham 1982: 81–83; Ghoshal 1959: 103, 296). Even Kautilya's *Arthashastra* shares this view that seems to make the state an independent unit, something above the castes, but actually sees it as a means to safeguard the religion and duties of the castes and as a means to obtain peace of mind through undisturbed religious ceremonies.

The *Mahabharata* contains a myth which maintains that there was an idyllic harmony in the state of nature. It was not based on divine powers, but human beings following high moral duties. The degeneration of morality made the life of the gods dangerous; no sacrifices were made for them any more. Therefore, the gods created the *arthashastras* (political wisdom). The king respected the political wisdom, but his successors lost the ability to follow the wisdom. Finally, the sixth king became a tyrant. The people killed and sacrificed him, and in the process the hand of the killed tyrant became the true king (Ghoshal 1959: 194–96).

The divine origin of the king did not justify or expand his power. Everyone and everything else had the same origin. Instead, there were limits to the king's power, specifically the duty to defend and guarantee the life of the individual. Therefore, the king remains accountable for his actions to the ruled, which have the right to abolish his power or even kill him. Furthermore, *dharma* does not justify uncontrolled power. On the contrary, *dharma* makes the king a servant to his people, and the state remains nothing more than a subordinated element in the caste system (Basham 1982: 86; Edwardes 1961: 87; Ghoshal 1959: 207, 540).

The *dharma* of the king (*rajadharma*) defines and gives a social task to the king. Relations between the king and his people are based on the king's *dharma*. The king's power is strictly regulated; it is submitted into *dharma*. In practice this implies that a kshatriya, without the direction of a brahmin, is nothing "but an elephant without a driver" (MAH: 144). *Rajadharma* exists as the guarantor of the whole social structure. *Danda* is the means, *dharma* is the end. Political power must ensure each man the broad opportunity to fulfill his religious duties and ceremonies without interference (Drekmeier 1962: 10).

The king has no power over the subjects, only duties towards them. The king is a servant, not the master. The king must respect his *dharma* as a service paid by his subjects in taxes. The subjects pay the salary to maintain the king. As a reward, the king guarantees the security of the subjects. The highest duty of a kshatriya is to protect his subjects, for the king who enjoys the rewards is bound to duty (Manu VII.144; Ghoshal 1959: 24, 104, 536).

Instead of the use of power and force, the king provides an example for the subjects. When the king follows his *dharma*, all others follow their *dharma*. Similar to Mo Zi's theory of the king as the teacher of universal love, Kautilya writes: "If a king is energetic, his subjects will be equally energetic. If he is reckless, they will not only be reckless likewise, but also eat into his works" (Kautilya I.XIX.37). Another explanation related to the origin of the king states that he has been formed with particles of the god, therefore he has supernatural powers and his *dharma* is above all others (Manu VII.5–7; Ghoshal 1959: 24, 104, 536).

It is important to emphasize that the king's *dharma* submits him to the servant of the interests of the individuals. The king must not only please himself, but he must please his subjects. Therefore, we find no traces of *Staatsräson* (the reason of the state). The existence of moral order is based on the existence of the state, but not without the utilitaristic consequences of the king's behavior. The king is evaluated by his success, and success is defined in terms of utilitaristic production. The power is not the goal but a means to the goal. The strength, welfare, or security of the state is not the goal. The goal is the good life of the individual. The state must make it possible for an individual to become perfect and free. Consequently, the individual's morality and the morality of the state are not distinct but the same thing (Kautilya I.XIX; Ghoshal 1959: 500).

In the *arthashastras* the state is given a more independent role. They suggest the theory of the seven elements of the kingship. The theory is shared by Kautilya who speaks of the king, the minister, the country, the fortress, the treasury, the army, and the ally. The elements are discussed and contending theories of their preferences are suggested. It is concluded that the king and the treasury are the most important elements (Kautilya II.8.65–66; Ghoshal 1959: 125).

However, not even *arthashastras* make the state the central unit. The ruled must be wealthy in order to pay their taxes, and there must be a harmonic relationship between the ruler and the ruled. The state must be free of famine and sickness, internal problems, and disloyalty. The state also must be able to defend the population against enemy attacks. In brief, instead of the power of the state and the king, the society and the rights of the people are emphasized by ancient Indian thought (Ghoshal 1959: 291).

In conclusion, early Indian kingship was broadly contractual and therefore subject to popular approval. Most important, the king was subject to higher law and other restraints, normative and practical. The institution was basically secular, an extension of the civil society, not a Leviathan above society (cf. Drekmeier 1962: 25).

WAR

In addition to the king, war also was submitted to *dharma*. War is not an end, nor a means, but a part of *dharma*. As part of *dharma* war is a duty to be fulfilled. There are two justifications to this interpretation: the law of *karma* and the religious nature of war.

Karma, the law of cause and effect, is a major preventative against war. Because a human being can influence the form of his next life, it is preferable to make good and help those in need. In general, this means helping those who have been less lucky in their reincarnation. Furthermore, man has to live in harmony with the human and material environment. There is no good life without respect towards truth and the pursuit of piety (Radhakrishan 1929: 131–32, 215, 244–49).

Similarly, the religious nature of war sets limits (cf. Aho 1981). One must act in concordance with *dharma* concerning war as well as any other activity. Political power is not the aim of the battle. War is nothing more than a temporary consequence of the fulfillment of *dharma*, and *dharma* is much more than mere political or collective morality. In the *Bhagavad Gita*, Arjuna ignores his doubts and sorrows and begins a war not to win a kingdom but to follow the law of life. He understands Krishna's message that says war is related to the law of death and is a means to control death. Uncontrolled, death was a fire threatening to consume all living creatures at once. Birth and death are integral parts of the cosmic process. Men must die in order to make life possible—if there is no death, men cannot survive. Death must be put under control, and is achieved by maintaining it as a continuous process concerning individuals, not the total and abrupt destruction of the human race. Controlled death appears under several disguises—war, sickness, and accident—in order to guarantee equilibrium between birth and death. Death is the basis of existence, a way of making existence possible. Consequently, no one is born, so no one ever dies. In other words, one does not die when the body dies. In the final analysis, "death is inevitable for the living; birth is inevitable for the dead" (BG 2.20–21, 2.27). In this sense, the *Mahabharata* (p. 64; cf. p. 66) speaks of the eternal succession of long historical cycles (*yuga*) and claims that everything dead will be reborn and live again and again before it attains *nirvana*. It is in this light that we understand Krishna's magnificent role as immortality, time, death, and the destroyer of the worlds. This is also why he tells Arjuna to kill those that have already been killed (BG 9.19, 10.34, 11.32, 11.34).

Therefore, it is not wise to show impatience towards death or mourn for those who die. The wise grieve neither for the living nor for the dead, they are not deluded by temporary changes, for experiences come and go. The ultimate reality lies only in the eternal (BG 2.11–8; MAH: 9).

Both the *Bhagavad Gita* and the *Mahabharata* should be read in the suggested interpretation, even if their message is not easy to see. Indeed, considering the role of war in the *Mahabharata* and the first chapter in the *Bhagavad Gita*, the issues of war and force represent a major bone of contention in the interpretations of both works.

The first chapter of the *Bhagavad Gita* has caused a great deal of debate, largely because of the verses about the morality of war. According to the orthodox Hindu viewpoint, the book condones war for the warrior class. It is the *dharma*, the moral duty, of soldiers to fight for a good cause as part of an elaborate and highly chivalrous code prescribing the just rules of war. According to this view, the lessons of the *Mahabharata* and the *Gita* are that although war is evil, it is an evil that cannot be avoided—an evil both tragic and honorable for the warrior. Due to this belief, Yudhishthira and his noble brothers find their peace in the next world when they have finished their duty on earth (Aho 1981; Morrison 1986: 50).

But it is clear that no *Staatsräson* logic is supported by the *Bhagavad Gita*. It speaks for moral values, in the sense of individual morality, that is, morality shared by men, not that which is monopolized by the state. Yudhishthira's outstanding qualities and Duryodhana's corruption decide the issue explicitly from the moral point of view. It is only for Duryodhana that conflict must be resolved on the battlefield. Otherwise he could not achieve the kingdom. Duryodhana alone supports *Staatsräson* logic and therefore loses the campaign. This makes it a moral duty for Yudhishthira and his brothers to accept the challenge and fight against immorality (cf. Morrison 1986: 49).

In fact, the *Bhagavad Gita* does not glorify war but *dharma*. War is never glorified as such, nor is it accepted for purely material aims (MAH: 233, 303). One has the right to work, but never to the fruits of work. The fruits of work are enjoyed in *nirvana* when man is no more reborn (BG 2.47–48; MAH: 214). Therefore, Krishna prefers collective morality to individual morality—one must fulfill his duty, not for himself but for the community. According to Krishna, Arjuna's sorrow is unmanly because such unjustified sorrow leads to chaos rather than the order of *dharma* (MAH: 213). Work is superior to inaction because it maintains *dharma* and *dharma* maintains order. Without activity the world crumbles and all beings perish (BG 3.24).Therefore, Arjuna must work—to fight like a kshatriya—in order to serve the welfare of the world (BG 3.19), but he must fight selflessly, without efforts at personal glory, for mankind and the obligation of selfless service can never be separated from one another (BG 3.8–10).

In the *Bhagavad Gita* (2.39–44) activity is related to religious aims, to the principles of *yoga*. Krishna says that by practicing these one can break through the bonds of *karma*. If the aim of one's activities is pleasure and power, the fruit of one's action is continual rebirth.

Men must be born again in order to be rid of the chain of rebirth. If all people live forever, they continue to degenerate due to *karma*. Therefore, Krishna has determined that the material body of the unchanging, eternal living creature, *atman*, will disappear (BG II.26–8). Consequently, war does not represent violence. Animals killed in sacrifices will obtain human shape and be rid of rebirth; kshatriyas killed in war reach *nirvana* (MAH: 114).

The good of the game is peace of mind. Peace of mind is the absolute precondition for wisdom, meditation, peace, and joy. The mind is restless, turbulent, powerful, violent, and hard to tame. Still, peace of mind is possible because man is free to renounce selfish desires and jail "I," "me," and "mine." Man is able to unite with the divine principle, *atman*, and pass from death to immortality (BG 2.66, 6.33–34, 2.71).

Therefore, it is not chance that Arjuna makes Krishna his first choice among the allies. Arjuna rejects "the strength of a hundred million soldiers" and instead takes Krishna, who must never use military weapons, on the battlefield. Arjuna prefers Krishna, who cannot fight but guarantees social order, *dharma*, without which any military victory would be meaningless. Arjuna submits himself to *dharma*, even if it would make it impossible to beat his adversaries. Arjuna is not simply a warrior and military hero but an instrument in reestablishing social order. Therefore, Krishna's instructions are not required for the achievement of a military victory but for the fulfillment of *dharma* (MAH: 194). The role of the *Bhagavad Gita*, otherwise an independent work of moral instructions, is to control war and submit it to *dharma*.

Consequently, there are reasons for giving the *Bhagavad Gita* an interpretation Morrison calls the mystics' point of view. According to this perspective the battle is an allegory, a cosmic struggle between good and evil. Krishna has revealed himself on earth in order to reestablish spiritual well-being, and he asks Arjuna to engage in a spiritual struggle, not a worldly one. Arjuna is asked not to fight his kin but his own lower self. According to Morrison's interpretation, the *Bhagavad Gita* (1.1.) calls Kurukshetra "the field of *dharma*," *dharma-kshetre*, hinting that the battle is to be an allegorical one, a fight of *dharma*, justice, against *adharma*, evil (Morrison 1986: 50, 215).

The mystics' point of view is fully acceptable, but one of its implications must be initially rejected—the implication that the interpretation justifies historical struggles between good and evil. This implication seems to be rather logical. It is possible, due to the common origin, that the Vedic myths about the battle between good and evil share some basic elements with Zoroastrianism. Arjuna's enemies are responsible for evil, wrong, and sin. They have destructed social order, and therefore deserve to be destroyed. The sinners cause chaos, the cosmic process is deviated into the wrong direction. Therefore, the god obtains a human incarnation in order to correct the cosmic process. To refuse to kill the sinners is to refuse to redirect the cosmic process into the right direction (Aho 1981: 62).

But while ancient Indian thought shares the original Zoroastrian view that this battle takes place between principles (*dharma* and *adharma*) not between human beings, it does not share the Zoroastrian idea that the cosmic battle is repeated in the historical world. In the *Mahabharata* it is not clear who is good and who is evil. In fact, there are several features that blur the distinction between good and evil *persons*. The good are able to win only by breaking the moral rules of warfare. On both sides of the battle there are indisputably good men, and in the final analysis all participants will reach heaven, *nirvana*. Not all will reach *nirvana* immediately until *karma* accomplishes its work and ends the rebirth process (Radhakrishnan 1929: 109–10, 242–43; cf. Ghoshal 1959: 191).

Therefore, it is logical to find that the *Bhagavad Gita* has become the major justification for *ahimsa*, non-violence, rather than a text legitimizing the struggle between friends and enemies. For example, Mahatma Gandhi based his daily life on the *Gita*; he felt it would be impossible to live the kind of life taught in the *Gita* and still engage in violence (Morrison 1986: 50–51).

In conclusion, the importance of *dharma* and the non-importance of war is the reason why the *Mahabharata* (or the *Bhagavad Gita*) can not be interpreted as glorification of war. Both the Pandavas and the Kauravas are fulfilling their *dharma*. This is reflected especially by the great heroes that join Dhritarashtra's—and Duryodhana's—side. For example, Bhishma, the heroic military teacher and educator of both sides, a respected elder statesman, knows what he must do in order to respect his own teachings on *dharma*. As Dhritarashtra's advisor of many years, he considers it his duty to stand by his king and try to protect him from his weaknesses and bad decisions (MAH: 206; Morrison 1986: 49).

The *Mahabharata* and the *Bhagavad Gita* give no independent value to war. On the contrary, war remains a duty. It is connected to *dharma*, the practical duty to maintain order. In the *Mahabharata* (p. 193), Yudhishthira says: "War is not our object. Peace is." This is because reconciliation and compassion provide better and more permanent results of peace. War does not guarantee any permanent peace, because in war one beats his adversary but sooner or later the losers win and the victors lose (MAH: 278).

NOTES

1. Kinsley (1962: 53–55) has eloquently and correctly summarized one of the final stories of the *Mahabharata* (17.2–3) in order to illustrate the importance and comprehensiveness of the moral principle.

2. Aho (1981: 73; cf. Easwaran 1986: 223) gives some etymological references to *dhri* (to support or hold up) and *ma* (cosmos).

3. In the *Mahabharata* (p. 81), *Dharma*, the god of justice, is called "the best of the celestials."

4. Bhattacharyya (1990: 52–53) documents the use of the concept in all major schools of Indian thought. The present discussion is mainly based on the *Mahabharata* and the *Bhagavad Gita*. I claim that all contending religious views were actually inserted into the great epics.

5. Megasthenes speaks of seven castes (Edwardes 1961: 54), and concerning the modern caste-system Smith (1984: 61) writes: "It consists essentially in the division of Hindu mankind into about 3,000 hereditary groups, each internally bound together by rules of ceremonial purity, and externally separated by the same rules from all other groups."

6. To make the conclusion even more elusive, it is suggested that the Aryans originally had no caste system. Everybody had the right to be a priest, a soldier, a tradesman, and a peasant.

CHAPTER 5

Asha and Contract as the Basis of Social Order

In Zoroastrianism, order is based on keeping the contract or promise, which includes all types of contract extending from the first one made by Ahura Mazda to all those represented by human associations; from written to oral and from explicit to given contracts (e.g., the father-son relationship). Therefore, while the ethical principle of *asha* (truth) has a divine origin and religious meaning, its extension is social, presupposing that *all* social relations are contracts. Therefore, to keep the contract is to maintain orderly human associations.

Zoroastrianism recognizes, however, that not all men keep their promises. Such men remain outside the commonwealth of those who respect the contract. In other words, they remain outside true society. The ordered society of men who keep contracts represents the Good Spirit, Ahura Mazda, in the historical world. Those who break contracts and remain outside society represent the Evil Spirit, Angra Mainyu. The two groups of men together cover *all* men who keep or who break their promises, respectively. The ordered society may or may not correspond with a state, because the distinction between the two groups is moral, not national.

In short, the Zoroastrian order is based on both the ethical rule of keeping the contract and the dualism of the two contending groups of men. It is logical to envisage a permanent war between the two worlds: good and evil. In this chapter I emphasize the principles and concentrate on the ethical rule and dualistic division of the world. It is not difficult to anticipate a violent relation between the two worlds, but such a case belongs to a power-oriented pattern, the politics of exclusion (Chapter 13). I break Zoroastrianism into two patterns, which are logically and highly intertwined: early and late Zoroastrianism. This is based on the assumption that the principle-oriented element represents a religious and ethically-oriented Zoroastrianism, whereas the power-oriented element (the violent exclusion of the Other) represents a mature, state-oriented, Zoroastrianism. This analytical distinction, a separation of principle-oriented elements and the more politically-oriented elements in Zoroastrianism, is not something that can be documented in the historical development of religion—and politics—in ancient Persia.[1]

Ancient Hebrew doctrine is similar to Zoroastrianism in its emphasis on the covenant, but the Hebrew doctrine the emphasizes the covenant between God and the Israelites. Such a covenant has social applications in human relations, but social relations as such are not seen as the covenant. Furthermore, the Hebrew doctrine geographically limits the society to those who live within the Holy Land and respect the covenant. Some later religious doctrines or movements (the Essenes, the Jewish nationalists, the Jesus movement, and the early Christians) also share parts of the dualistic doctrine, but they also subscribe to the politics of exclusion. The Roman tradition of keeping promise is surprisingly close to Zoroastrian doctrine, which partly explains the popularity of Mithraism in Rome. However, in Rome the idea is a mere detail, however important, that is partly outside the framework of my present investigation and the present chapter.[2]

THE ETHICAL RULE AND ITS SOCIAL EXPRESSION: THE CONTRACT

Zoroastrianism demanded men follow strict moral rules derived from priestly acts of worship. For these acts of worship to be acceptable to the divine beings three things were required: the right intention, truly spoken words, and correctly performed rituals. This produced the threefold ethic of good thought, good word, and good act (Boyce 1984: 15).

Zoroaster (Zarathustra, Zartusht), is praised for the fact that he first "thought what is good, who first spoke what is good, who first did what is good." It is said that Zoroaster was the first to take possession of the "word" and show and recommend obedience to it. He was the first "bearer of the law." Zoroaster "thought according to the Law, spoke according to the Law, and did according to the Law" (Farvardin Yasht 24.88–90 in the *Zend-Avesta*, published in the *Sacred Books of the East*, hereafter referred to as ZA/SBE 23; Zamyad Yasht 13.79 in ZA/SBE 23).[3]

The law of Mazda is not, however, just an abstract moral principle, it must be interpreted in a social, as well as religious, context. The law of Mazda can then be expressed by the duty to keep the contract, also called the promise. This ethical principle represents a contract between Ahura Mazda and man, as well as between men themselves.

Zoroastrianism speaks of all forms of contracts that exist in society, including involuntary relationships, such as that between brothers, or father and son. The major emphasis seems to be on explicit agreements, mainly between individuals.[4] This suggests that the question was mainly related to domestic order, that is, social relations within the community. But there are also contracts that have a more international connotation. These contracts vary from the contract between two friends, called "twentyfold"; to between two countries, called "thousandfold," to the contract of the Zoroastrian religion, called "ten-thousandfold" (*The Avestan Hymn to Mithra*, hereafter referred to as Mithra 29.116–17; Gershevitch 1959: 26).

Zoroastrianism's point of departure is that everything goes on in a "serene and mighty order" due to a law fixed by the god (Darmesteter 1880: lvii). Natural processes are regarded as unending so long as men do their part by offering regularly required sacrifices to the gods.

Against this background, the contract is a sacred expression of *asha,* a universal principle translated as truth, order, and righteousness. This principle should govern everything from the workings of nature to human laws and all human conduct. It has been received from Ahura Mazda, who is called the Father of Order. Zoroaster himself perceived *asha* as an ethical divinity, who gave to each what morally he or she deserved (Boyce 1984: 34, 38).

In short, Zoroaster's idea was to give contracts a divine basis. One must keep the contract because it is required by the ethical rule and the will of the god. Failure to keep one's promise is a lie and therefore absolutely forbidden.

In addition to the fact that ethical rules and religious duties always connect men with their god, the ethical rule has positive consequences to (or actually appears) in orderly relationships (order, security, and peace) among righteous human beings. The divine aspect has a strong social and practical function: Zoroastrianism gives the contract a special meaning by emphasizing its moral nature. One must keep the promise because breaking it might break the *moral* basis of social order and predictability required by all human associations (cf. Koskenniemi 1989; Golding 1989).

This suggested principle demands high, uncompromising morality in all and any situations. One must be good—to keep the promise—to the just man, that is, to the partner in the contract, whoever he or she is, whether or not he or she is a Zoroastrian. Indeed, one is never allowed to break a covenant, it must be kept uncompromisingly even if the situation in which it was made changes. It does not matter if the partner worships truth (*asha*) or falsehood (*drug*). It does not count if the partner keeps or breaks the promise, it must be kept anyway (Mithra 1.2; cf. Boyce 1984: 28).

DUALISTIC CONFLICT

The most unique feature of Zoroastrianism is that the moral duty does not imply a comprehensive moral society like in Daoism or Jesus's teachings. The moral principle, due to its social interpretation and social function, divides men into two groups—those who respect the contract and those who break the contract. This division obtains a central place in the doctrine which instead of monotheism develops toward dualism (Yasna 33 in Boyce 1984: 36–39).

Zoroaster's theory of conflict gives meaning to social life, it creates names and order to things which otherwise might look chaotic. But it is not enough to have an explanation for conflict and a consequent guide to the good and bad participants. One must also know what is expected due to the definition of the situation.

In the conflict between the gods and fiends man is to be active on the basis of the duty laid before him in the law revealed by Ahura Mazda to Zoroaster. But even so, man has free will and he can, and must, choose sides. It is hoped and recommended that man act wisely and make the right choice (Yasna 30.3 in ZA/SBE 31; Darmesteter, 1880: lxviii, lvi).

This choice repeats the choice originally made by the two spirits (Yasna 30 in Boyce 1984: 35). The same choice was also repeated by *fravahrs* (souls or angels). According to the Greater Bundahishn (Ch. 3 in Boyce 1984; cf. Sharif 1963: 65), Ahura Mazda asked the *fravahrs* whether they preferred to remain untouched by, and protected from, every danger in the invisible world, or whether they were ready to incarnate themselves in the visible world in order to struggle with the Evil Spirit. The *fravahrs* correctly chose the latter option.

The choice is real. It is a choice between two, therefore some men do not choose correctly. But men do not choose evil because of human nature or some selfish needs. On the contrary, man is fundamentally good—a good deity cannot create an evil man! The evilness comes from Angra Mainyu, who chose evil while Ahura Mazda chose good. Evilness is delivered to men by *daevas*,[5] who had not chosen correctly because Angra Mainyu seduced them (Yasna 30 in Boyce 1984: 35). The *daevas* for their part seduced some men, who then became *daeva*-worshippers. The *daeva*-worshippers propagated their evil creed to an expanding number of victims, and thus, "destroyed the hopes of mankind for a happy life upon earth, and for Immortality in heaven" (Mills, 1887: 54; cf. Boyce 1984: 36, 51).

MITHRA

The idea of the contract was born among a chiefly agriculturalist population. As their land and cattle represented their most valuable property, whatever threatened them was the thing most dreaded. Accordingly rapine and the raid were regarded as "the most terrible of visitations" (Mills 1887: xxi). While the keeping of contracts hopefully limited external threats or at least united the society for defense against them, the weak population had few ways of assuring that contracts and treaties would be kept by the stronger members of society.

Indeed, Zoroaster was fully aware that men do not always follow the moral law of Ahura Mazda. Zoroaster knew that men did not always keep their promises, but often deceive and oppress their fellow human beings in order to win material goods or other advantages. Therefore, Zoroaster's system had to have mechanisms for the control and verification of the contract, including both positive and negative sanctions.

As in similar cases religious mythologies came to help. Men had to create a god to make sure that the contract was not broken. In Zoroastrianism such a divine assistant is called Mithra.[6] Mithra represents a moral approach and solution to the problem of verifying contracts. When the community grew larger and stronger, it was able to take care of more practical measures against the contract-breakers. Concrete violence and war is discussed in the context of later, mature Zoroastrianism (Chapter 13).

Mithra functions as the guardian of the contract. His spies sit as watchers of the contract and recognize a contract-breaker immediately just at the point he is planning to do so (Mithra 2.7, 6.24, 10.45; Boyce 1984: 29).

Gershevitch (1959: 26–32) has suggested that Mithra's epithet as "director of (boundary) lines" pertains to his role in international contracts. Mithra contributes to treaty-abiding behavior in international relations in two ways. First, Mithra's care for the nations' welfare and prosperity creates conditions of internal stability, and therefore increases the willingness of the contractors and their progeny to carry out the required obligations. Second, Mithra gives the inevitable verification to agreements[7] (Mithra 26.103, 27.104).

There are four major reasons to keep the contract. The first is purely religious: when a just man follows Ahura Mazda's high principles, he imitates and adopts the goodness of his god, who always thinks good thoughts, speaks good words, and does good deeds (Mithra 27.106).

Second, there are positive sanctions promised to those who keep the contract. Some promises are religious and spiritual, such as Mithra helping an individual to follow the law of Mazda, thereby protecting him or her from evil. In addition, practical and concrete rewards are available for those who follow the contract. These individuals will get material rewards—like fast horses, the straightest path to their destinations, peaceful and comfortable dwellings, and wide pastures where their cattle and men wander freely and safely. Mithra will give the followers of treaties assistance, spaciousness, support, mercy, therapy, the ability to defeat opponents, a comfortable existence, and truth. In the case of war between two countries, Mithra will support the country that first reveals its allegiance to him, that is, proves that it will keep the promise. Mithra will lead such a country to superior strength and vigor (Mithra 1.3–5, 2.9, 2.96, 7.26, 22.93; cf. Boyce 1987: 27–29, 71).

Third, there is a threat of negative sanctions. Mithra protects the countries that respect him and destroys the countries that break their contract. Defiance on the part of a country earns Mithra's implacable revenge. Some sanctions look rather symbolic: being false to the treaty "wrecks the whole country," because the deception hits "the Truth-owners as hard as would a hundred obscurantists" (Mithra, 1.2, 3.20, 6.23, 11.48; Boyce 1984: 28).

Fourth, the law of Mazda is not sufficient (and neither are positive and negative sanctions) if it remains abstract and spiritual. These religious sanctions might be sufficient in the case of Zoroaster and his devoted followers, the just men, but a majority of individuals still require stronger reasons for keeping the contract. Only the threat and application of real violence, that is, war, can make the evil men, the *daeva*-worshippers, adhere to the rules. Therefore, Mithra takes an active part in punishing the treaty-breaker. If an agreement is broken, Mithra will become enraged and provoked and smash all who break the contract, from individuals to countries (Mithra 3.18). This final way of sanctioning the contract is discussed in more details in Chapter 13.

PACIFISM IN ZOROASTRIANISM

The conception of the dualistic struggle between good and evil, and the practical duty for men to participate in the struggle, makes the doctrine look like justification for war and violence. This is undeniably true, but not the whole truth. As an example of the principle-oriented patterns of order, the law of Mazda requires that a supporter be a just man, "murderers and whores" are not allowed to "take of these offerings." Otherwise the punishment falls on the wrong-doing individuals or members of the good society, *not* upon the Others (Tir Yasht 59–61 in ZA/SBE 23; Zamyad Yasht 7.34 in ZA/SBE 23).

Zoroastrianism, as discussed in this chapter, represents a conspicuously pacifistic mode of thought. The texts make several explicit allusions to peace, such as: "Peace, whose breath is friendly, and who is more powerful to destroy than all other creatures." As I already stated, peace is among the most important social needs of Zoroastrians: "Let everything be as friendly to us as anything can be: may we go smoothly along the roads, find good pathways in the mountains, run easily through the forests, and cross happily the rivers" (Sirozah I.2, II in ZA/SBE 23; Din Yasht in ZA/SBE 23).

The suggested principles—the contract and dualism—are pacifist by nature. It is true that in the conflict between Ahura Mazda and Angra Mainyu man is active, but he or she carries out this activity exclusively in the sacrifice. In fact, the sacrifice is more than an act of worship, it is "an act of assistance to the gods." It was thought that gods, like men, need drink and food to be strong, as well as praise and encouragement. Without this kind of human help, the gods might be helpless before their foes (Darmesteter, 1880: lxviii).

One may note the Zoroastrians' moral earnestness in their determination to avoid rapine, even when tempted by a desire for retaliation (Mills, 1887: xxi). The ethical rule required individuals to do good deeds " both toward the wicked and the righteous, as well as toward those who are both" (Yasna 33.1 in ZA/SBE 31).

Ethical ideals are the most efficient weapons against evil. Zoroaster's greatest weapon is neither the thunder-stones he hurls, nor the glory with which he is surrounded, it is the word of truth. Truth (*asha*) is "the best of all fiend-smiters." When Zoroaster asked Ahura Mazda for advice to make the world free from lies (*drug*), he was advised to do nothing but invoke "the good law of Mazda!" (Srosh Yasht 1.3 in ZA/SBE 23; Fargard 19.12–15 in ZA/SBE 4; cf. Ohrmazd Yasht 1–5 in ZA/SBE 23; Ram Yasht in ZA/SBE 23).

Truth, that is the law of Mazda, cannot be overcome by weapons. Neither can the Evil Spirit deliver Ahura Mazda's representatives unto death. According to a parallel expression of that conviction, nobody can forcibly seize glory or the blessings of Ahura Mazda (Tir Yasht 12.44 in ZA/SBE 23; Zamyad Yasht 8.49, 9.56 in ZA/SBE 23).

In conclusion, the pacifistic nature of the moral order is expressed in its sanctions, both positive and negative. On the positive side, *asha* leads to goodness in spirit and material existence (Sharif 1963: 67; Yasna Haptanhaiti in Boyce 1984: 53–55; Farvardin Yasht 1.18 in ZA/SBE 23). The negative sanctions are similarly abstract and mythological. "A long life of darkness, foul food, the crying of woe" are promised as a punishment for him or her who promotes power for a wicked man of evil actions (Yasna 31 in Boyce 1984: 39; cf. Mills 1887: 31).

NOTES

1. Early Zoroastrianism was introduced by Moulton. He suggests (1913: x) that Angra Mainyu, Enemy Spirit is a casual epithet occurring only once in the Gathas. Furthermore, he claims that Mithra himself was probably a *daeva* in Zoroaster's own system. Such "Magian ideas" were, according to Moulton, added to the system by the Magi who were an indigenous tribe of priests, the leaders of the non-Aryan population of Media.

2. The value of the contract and the need to respect it, as well as the need to verify the implementation of contracts, was not an exclusively Zoroastrian idea, but rather typical to Mediterranean and Middle Eastern cultures in general. For example, it is interesting to see that Livy gives Jupiter similar functions in controlling and verifying agreements (Livy VIII.6–7).

3. In addition to the old translations of the *Zend-Avesta* in the *Sacred Books of the East* (SBE), I will use Boyce's (1984) more modern translations. *The Avestan Hymn to Mithra* is Gershevitch's (1959) translation. Later, I consulted a good, modern translation of the Gathas by Humbach (1991).

4. Contracts, both domestic and international, were made orally (word-contracts) or by shaking hands (hand-contracts). As to their objects, they are sheep-contracts, ox-contracts, man-contracts, or field-contracts. No contract can be made void by the will of one party alone. He who breaks a contract is obliged to pay the value of the contracts next higher in value (the value of a contract is expressed in money). In criminal law, the family and next of kin must fulfill the contract. Assaults are of seven degrees: menaces, assaults, blows, sore wounds, wounds causing blood to flow, broken bones, and manslaughter. The gravity of the guilt depends on the gravity of the deed and its frequency. A crime amounts, by being repeated without having been atoned for, to the crime that immediately follows on the scale (e.g., menace seven times equals manslaughter), and every crime makes the guilty man liable to two penalties, one "here below," and another in "the next world" (Darmesteter 1880: xcv– ci; Fargard 4 in ZA/SBE 4).

5. According to Boyce (1984) *dev, daeva,* or *deva* was the amoral god of war, but in Zoroaster's doctrine that god became the demon. According to Sharif (1963: 58), Zoroaster, possibly utilizing a pre-existing naturalistic sky-god (Varuna), created a new monotheism, so strong that the name of the old gods (*daevas*) came to signify demons.

6. Mithra was worshipped by Indo-Iranian tribes before Zoroaster. In Western Asia, Mithra appears in a list of five gods by whom a treaty was sworn in the early fourteenth century B.C.E. (Gershevitch 1959: 3). However, the *Avestan Hymn to Mithra* was transcribed much later.

7. The Avestan common noun "mithra" means "contract." Gershevitch has carefully documented the fact that Mithra's association with the contract represents a (or the) primary function of the god (Gershevitch 1959: 28 ff., cf. 4–7; cf. also Boyce 1984: 29–30, 61–64).

CHAPTER 6

Torah and National Identity as the Basis of Social Order

When the Jews lost the divine centers of their Holy Land and the Temple as well as their state (Sicker 1992: 35), Judaism found the basis of social order in the moral principle of *torah*, that is God's law, with a major emphasis on the national identity of the members of the covenant community. *Torah* connected individuals living in distant countries to each other. It created a community and order between individuals sharing a national identity and its religious or cultural symbols not with the people among which they were living but with brothers and sisters of the nationality of their own. The importance of national identity is the major difference between the present and the preceding principle-oriented patterns.

The following discussion of the present pattern is problematic and controversial for two reasons. First, "Judaism" in this chapter is a construction that somewhat deviates from more conventional usages of the term. Judaism mainly refers to the development of the doctrine from the Babylonian captivity down to the Talmudic Rabbinism of Babylonia of the sixth century C.E. (Lightstone 1988),[1] but the present pattern does not include all of that development. On the other hand, the present chapter is partly based on elements from both before the Babylonian captivity and after the sixth century C. E. Furthermore, some features of Judaism (cf. Neusner 1992: ix–x) must be discussed in the context of power-oriented patterns of social order, especially as the politics of exclusion.

Second, due to the amount and nature of the authoritative Jewish texts, it was impossible to use them as primary sources in this book. After time consuming consultations with the major texts, I found it more practical to use less extensive, popular introductions to Judaism and earlier studies dealing more directly with social and political issues relevant to this book. This is not, however, too problematic because the full pattern has been developing continuously from early history to the present day. Therefore, the delineation and understanding of the present pattern requires the inclusion of the historical developments, or the interpretations concerning the historical development of the doctrine and the nation.[2]

TORAH

Judaism succeeded in achieving a unity of belief and observance among Jews in their wide dispersion. In fact, the fundamental principles of the Jewish religion had a central role in achieving this unity. The moral order in the history of the world was identified with the will and purpose of God—God himself was made the basis of human relations (Moore 1954 I: 110–11, 115).

Indeed, all order and meaning comes from God. He is the basis of natural and social order. Without God no material, and certainly no social life, would be possible. God "forms light and creates darkness, makes peace and creates all things" (Cohen 1975: 1). The conception of God is monotheistic in the strictest degree. There was a definite line never to be crossed: rebellion against God by worshipping other gods threatened to destroy the very basis of the society. Otherwise, the image of God was left open, impossible for the human mind to understand. Too clear a picture might have divided the believers. God had to be acceptable to all and everybody had to have an opportunity to believe in God (Moore 1954 I: 223; Silver and Martin 1974: 24).

The primary image of God is that of a king who has laid down certain laws for his subjects to obey. *Torah*, the revelation of God, is a conglomeration of rules from various sources and periods unified only by the post-exilic assumption that every phrase had been revealed by God to Moses (Alexander 1984: 6, 11, 68, 75; Cohen 1975: 125; Silver and Martin 1974: 27). Before discussing the content of that *torah*, its letter must be recognized as a key element of the doctrine: the authoritative and strictly defined *torah*—both written and oral tradition—is the point of departure for social order.

Torah was not always written. It became a written document in and after the Babylonian captivity. In the pre-exilic times, there were the *torot*, the divine laws, but no *torah*, the single inclusive statement of the will of God. Only by the third century B.C.E. were the five books of Moses accepted as a faithful record of the revelation at Sinai, and consequently as the substance of the covenant between God and Israel. The need for the official text was underscored by the interminable and bitter debate between the Judeans and the Samaritans during and after the return from the Babylonian captivity (Alexander 1984: 1; Silver and Martin 1974: 147, 215–16).

According to Neusner, Pharisees and Scribes gave *torah* its special status. Scribes especially perceived that Moses's law was binding for everybody and therefore had to be authoritatively interpreted and applied to daily affairs. Later on, Rabbinism found earlier Scribism highly congenial to its ideal. The ideal of the study of *torah*, rather than the piety of the cult and the replication of that cultic piety in one's own home, was central to Rabbinism too (Neusner 1975: 66, 69; cf. Blau 1966: 119).

Torah was not presented in written form only. It was accompanied by the oral *torah*. According to Neusner, the written revelation to Moses at Sinai existed for the cult to be used in the holy place, the oral tradition applied better to the world outside the cult in the realm of the ordinary and profane (Neusner 1975: 32–33). The comprehensive tradition is expressed in a number of works, especially in the *Mishnah*, completed around the year 200 C.E. (Neusner 1993b: 14–15; Neusner 1981: 45).[3] In addition, the *Talmud*, or better, two *Talmuds*, define Mishnaic Judaism. One presents the teachings of various Galilean academics between the publishing of the *Mishnah* and the end of organized Jewish life in Galilee (c. 480) and is called the *Palestinian* (or *Jerusalem) Talmud*. The *Babylonian Talmud*, which is another version that became authoritative, was compiled between 200 and 640 (Silver and Martin 1974: 279).

In a sense, the Jewish doctrine seems to share a general idea of contract as the basis of social relations. However, clearly deviating from Zoroaster's doctrine, the contract between man and God was put in the very center of Jewish doctrine. For the Jews *torah* is a covenant between Jews and God. The covenant detailed in specific terms not only what Israel could expect from God but what God could expect from Israel (Silver and Martin 1974: 26).

According to Moore, *torah* must not be interpreted in the restricted sense of legislation, *torah* includes the whole of revelation—all that God has made known of his nature, character, and purpose, and of what he would have man be and do. Furthermore, this broad conception of *torah* was identified with wisdom. Consequently, *torah*, in connection of with learning and virtue, define the world view, way of life, and theory of social order that maintains the world view and realizes it in its shared existence. The land, the Exodus, the covenant all depend upon *torah* (Moore 1954 I: 263; Neusner 1993a I: 7; Neusner 1993a III: 48).

To emphasize the importance of *torah*, it was thought to be older than the world. Therefore, *torah* was said to be unchangeable. The law that was fully revealed to Moses existed before the world was created and will remain the same as long as the world exists (Moore 1954 I: 266–69). In other words, the world was created solely for the sake of *torah:* the world must have been made with a religious plan. Since *torah* existed before the world, the world must have been made to correspond to *torah*. Therefore, the unity of the moral order in the history of the world, identified with the will and purpose of God, on the basis of which the world and history will end one day. Following this logic, it might be suggested that if there had been no nation to accept the Revelation, the purpose of creation would have failed (Moore 1954 I: 115, 268; Moore 1954 II: 268, 323; Cohen 1975: 61).

SOCIAL RELATIONS UNDER *TORAH* AND SYMBOLS

Lightstone (1988: ix–x) contends that the consistent patterns that characterize the cultures of ancient Judaic groups encode meaning and thereby make statements about how the world is, the location of the group in that world, and the nature of the interaction within and among human beings and social groups. In other words, *torah* provided the immutable, official map of things. Indeed, *torah* gave the basis for nothing less than the establishment of solid and orderly human associations, a completely *torah*-based society (Sicker 1992: 19; Tractate Avot, 3: 2 in Neusner 1993a III).[4]

The relationship that exists between the creator and his creatures is conceived under the image of father and children. When one loves God, one also loves his or her fellowmen, and even strangers. This represents the relationship of the individual to God, not in isolation but in the fellowship of the religious community of all Jewish people: "Not alone the synagogue but the entire communal life—even what we should call the secular life—knit together by these peculiar beliefs, laws, and observances was the expression and the bond of this fellowship" (Cohen 1975: 20; cf. Moore 1954 I: 116, 121).

Torah gave the basis of social order, but the community only developed gradually under its instructions. Furthermore, the community did not always remain the same, both the doctrine and human associations had to be adopted to new situations. In the process, developments in the Babylonian captivity, and the Diaspora after that, including the destruction of the second Temple are decisive.[5] While all changes in the basis and the nature of the community should be documented in details, it is not possible here without expanding the present chapter too much. Furthermore, a full picture of these changes is available from literature (Batho 1945: 63; Moore 1954 I: 113; Silver and Martin 1974: 257–58; Welch 1935: 304–6). I, however, claim that not only *torah* but historical situations contributed to the specific nature of the community of the Jews—social relations between the dispersed Jews were established on the basis of their traditions, that is, *torah* and its interpretation, under the challenges of the time. The fall of Jerusalem in 70 C.E. has been given a prominent role among these challenges. This fall forced modern Judaism out of the jail of time and place.

However, the age of the Temple and the temple-state was over before the destruction of the Temple. According to Neusner the basic question confronted by the Jews after the destruction of the Temple and in 70 C.E. was social and religious, not a matter of government or politics in the conventional sense. The Temple had already been rejected by some Jewish groups, especially by the Qumran sect. In fact, for ordinary Jews outside as well as inside Palestine, the Temple was a remote place, instead synagogue worship was better available elsewhere (Neusner 1975: 34–35; Moore 1954 I: 110–11, 308).

Neusner maintains that there were several answers to the basic question of establishing a new community after the fall of Jerusalem and its Temple. First, the apocalyptic visionaries emphasized future, supernatural redemption, which they believed was soon to come. Second, like the Qumran sect before, the Jesus movement abandoned the Temple and its cult and replaced them with the new community, on the one hand, and the service or pious rites of the new community, on the other. The Pharisees, that is, Judaism, saw the destruction as a calamity, but they also besought the means, in both social forms and religious expression, to provide a new way of atonement and a new form of divine service to constitute a new, symbolic or interim Temple, like the Dead Sea sect and the Christians had been doing for a long time (Neusner 1975: 36, 39–40).

In any case, the synagogue and other religious elements became symbolic ties of a rather dispersed community. The fundamental fact was that the geographical center (the Land of Israel, Jerusalem, and the Temple) obtained symbolic expressions in addition to the synagogue: circumcision, the Sabbath, annual festivals, and public fasts (Neusner 1975: 35–36). Or, as Moore (1954 II: 3) put it, "*cultus*, that is, certain rules, public, domestic, and personal, by which the favor of the deity is cultivated, established and maintained the human association between the Jews." In short, as Neusner (1975: 49) recognizes the destruction of the Temple marked a considerable transformation in the symbolic structures of Judaism: "The ancient symbols were emptied of their old meanings and filled with new ones; they continued formally unchanged but substantively in no way the same" (Neusner 1975: 49; cf. Lightstone 1988: 45).

In short, the sociocultural area and conditions of the Israelite world overran the boundaries of *torah*'s paradigm of the sacred world. The tight concentric model of the ordered (sacred) world, with its relatively impermeable outer boundaries, had come under increasing stress and strain, and therefore was replaced by a more flexible system of the spaceless community. On the other hand, notwithstanding the many changes in the nature of the community, the adaptation process dit not lead to the rejection of the original basis of social relations. On the contrary, *torah* kept its canonical status for virtually all of Israel (Lightstone 1988: 45). *Torah* was not challenged or replaced by something else, it was maintained and strengthened by symbols. These symbols constituted the expanding community of the Jews. Because of the fact that the Jews lost their original geographic center as well as the conventional state boundaries of it, those who shared the belief in *torah* found a new solid community and common identity in that shared belief.

NATIONALISM

The modern concept of nationalism may be problematic to use in the case of ancient history; it is often impossible to find a nation in the modern sense, and even *ethnie* ignores something important in the case of the Jews (cf. Smith 1986, 1991, 1995). Jewish nationalism did not have its origins in ethnic distinctions. The Hebrews were similar to other groups of seminomads who infiltrated the western horn of the Fertile Crescent during the first half of the second millennium B.C.E. (the term "Hebrew" meant caravaner and was applied by the settled folk of Syria-Palestine to landless tribes who came from beyond the boundaries). Furthermore, the Hebrews appeared in history early in the second millennium B.C.E. only to disappear a century or two later. It was only when they reemerged at the beginning of the thirteenth century, that they had a new identity: the *benei Yisrael*, the tribes of Israel. The Hebrews had become the Israelites because various Semitic tribes had to unite in common cause, possibly due to the conquest of Canaan and other practical efforts necessary for settling down. In order to justify this as well as other practical social structures, national identity was carefully formulated in the religious doctrine, especially in the national foundation myth, which established an intimate historical and intellectual relationship between Judaism, Jewish nationalism, and the Land of Israel. It is this myth, not an ethnic nation or *ethnie,* which constitutes Israel's self-conception of its beginning. That is, when *torah* provided the basis for the community of people living in various countries and among foreign populations, *torah* and especially the myth concerning its origin introduced a unique kind of nationalism into the picture (Silver and Martin 1974: 3–6, 34–35; Sicker 1992: ix, 1).

Therefore, Sicker (1992: x) has good reasons to maintain that the idea of Jewish nationalism is probably the oldest nationalist conception known to history:[6] According to Sicker, three essential traits of nationalism originated with the ancient Jews: (1) the idea of the chosen people; (2) the consciousness of national history; and (3) national

Messianism. The two first elements are discussed here; Messianism is related to the politics of exclusion and will be discussed in Chapter 13.

God and the divine law as the basis of human associations is a universal idea, applicable to all humankind. If there is one God there can be only one religion, and the idea of unity in religion carries with it the idea of universality. Therefore, *torah* was not Israel's exclusive possession. In principle, Israel was to hallow God's name by living so that men see and say that the God of Israel is the true God. Israel had to bear a heavier responsibility and its punishment was greater (Cohen 1975: 60–62; Moore 1954 II: 103). However, the doctrine was given, or led to, a more narrow, nationalistic interpretation.

It was true that God was the helper and supporter of all who came into the world, but it was soon maintained that God preferred to help Israel or the Jews. It was also true that world's population proclaimed the praises of God, but it was believed that the Jews' praises were more acceptable than any others' praises (Cohen 1975: 60; Tractate Avot 3: 14c in Neusner 1993a III). For the Jews, right and wrong were not defined by the reason and conscience of men, nor by national custom, but by the revealed will of God, and constituted a distinctive Jewish morality which as a whole was different from that of other peoples (Moore 1954 II: 79).

The covenant was, and is, the major element of national identity for the Jews. *Torah* and the covenant served to emphasize the unity and solidarity of all Jews, wherever they might be, and to separate them from the pagan world (Batho 1945: 116). It is possible that Jewish nationalism was a reaction to external threats to the survival of the nation and national identity (Welch 1935: 281–82). But in any case the doctrine and its application had explicit nationalistic elements. The very editing of *torah* had practical consequences, the men reading and believing in torah had become Jews (Silver and Martin 1974: 415).

The idea of a covenant implied election. God had chosen Abraham, God had initiated his relationship with Israel. Any explanations were inevitably nationalistic in nature however modestly nationalistic feelings were expressed. In a humble way, it was suggested that Israel was chosen precisely because it was the least significant of the nations and the impact and success of such an improbable choice would present to the world impressive evidence of God's power. Another tradition was more openly nationalistic, suggesting that God had not first chosen Israel, but that the more auspicious candidates had disqualified themselves when they found God's stipulations too demanding. Such a doctrine rationalized and justified itself by referring to the heathen's own behavior. *Torah* was made binding on all mankind, but it was not accepted by most of them (Silver and Martin 1974: 29; Cohen 1975: 61; Moore 1954 I: 453; Tractate Avot 5: 2 in Neusner 1993a III).

The basic justification for Jewish nationalism was suggested by the foundation myth that states until mankind generally attains a higher moral state, national diversity is an objective historical necessity. There is no virtue in having a universal society led by morally deficient leaders—the morality of the diverse nations and their leaders must be raised to the desired level. This can be only achieved through the provision of an operating model of a moral society that could be emulated by the nations of the world. Accordingly, the biblical narrative proceeds to describe in some detail the processes by which a new and unique nation—Israel—is fashioned to serve as an instrument of the divine plan for the moral advancement of mankind (Sicker 1992: 3–6).

According to Sicker (1992: 6–12), Abraham, a figure endowed with extraordinary moral qualities, was chosen by God to serve as the human progenitor of the new nation. To prepare him for the task, God first uprooted Abraham from the nation and society into which he was born. Similarly, the nation of Israel had to be constituted in exile and only then brought in to possess its promised land. Such a process could only be carried out in Egypt because only in Egypt would the Israelites be true aliens. In Egypt, the Israelites' awareness of their ethnic-cultural distinctiveness was augmented by a sense of collective historical destiny and a yearning among many of their communal leaders for political freedom and self-determination. All this provided the basis for the two most significant and decisive events in the biblical presentation of the history of the Israelites: the Exodus consummating the national redemption of the Israelites from their bondage in Egypt, followed by the enactment of the covenant between God and Israel, which established the latter's national ethos and mission.

Sicker's analysis maintains that Israel was not a natural social phenomenon but a nation that was deliberately brought into existence as a social construction. The repetition and claimed divine origin made the construction a living power in the life of the people of Israel: "Not the mode of its origin matters, but its operation as a formative, dynamic, seminal force in the history of Israel. The legend of the promise entered so deeply into the experience of the Jews that it acquired its own reality." The myth was justified as a national model of a moral community worthy of emulation by other nations. *Torah*, not the ethnic origin of the nation, provides the guidelines for the operation of such a model community, as well as prepares and disciplines the people of Israel for this divinely assigned task (Sicker 1992: 2, 19; cf. Silver and Martin 1974: 27–28).

The evidence cannot be disputed. The mythology of *torah* strongly implied and openly justified national identity and nationalism among the Jews. However, this does not mean that this nationalism was necessarily violent or even exclusive of other nations. The politics of exclusion emerges in Jewish thought (Chapter 13), but it is a political and intentional choice, not a unavoidable consequence of the doctrine. In the present model of social order, the doctrine has the universal moral society as its goal, the nation of Israel is a means towards this goal.

Indeed, the basic doctrine can be (and was) interpreted in a positive way in accordance with the idea of the present pattern: nationalism and national identity are corollaries of *torah*. National identity does not destroy but supports *torah*. National identity is a fundamental feature of social order among the Jews, but it does not imply hostile or violent relations between the Jews and other nations. In this sense I agree with Boccaccini's (1991: 251) claim that one of the worst stereotypes of the Christian theological tradition is that of a universalistic Christianity emerging from a particularistic Judaism. Boccaccini correctly states that "History instead reveals a great variety of attitudes of middle Judaisms toward Gentiles as well as divisions among and within these Judaisms on the question of the possible salvation of Gentiles."

As Moore states, the unity of mankind was too plainly written in the Scriptures to leave room for any questions. The doctrine implied that all men are descendents from a single pair, to whom God gave the generic name Man, Adam. Accordingly, the Jews also believed that the specific laws given to Adam were binding to all humanity (Moore 1954 I: 274, 445–46). Perhaps the most distinguishing general feature of the covenant is that it commits Israel to constitutional abnormalcy. Israel will always remain unique among the nations of the world, constituted and governed in accordance with divine standards and requirements that are not imposed on other nations. It must be different from the others, and should it fail it will be punished in a way that other nations are not (Sicker 1992: 15; cf. Blau 1966: 119).

It is a fact that when Ezra and Nehemiah presented the return as the second conquest of Canaan (Chapter 13), not all agreed on the interpretation. An alternative tradition had existed and was strengthened during the captivity and consequent Diaspora among many Jews. The issue was openly debated, as reflected in the book of Ruth. This picture stands in sharp contrast to the tales of bloodshed. The heroine of the story is a non-Israelite, a Moabitess; she is also an ancestor of David, the ideal king, and the greatest national hero after Abraham and Moses. Similarly, an anonymous prophet, the second Isaiah, emphasized the duty for Israel to become the missionary of God among the nations and suggested the ideal of freedom from ritual. Jonah received a direct message from God to preach repentance to the Gentiles of Niniveh. Finally, some Psalms show a more generous feeling towards other nations than was officially adopted in post-exilic Judea. Such an alternative doctrine was further elaborated by Ben Sira (Ecclesiasticus) at the beginning of the second century B.C.E. It is Ben Sira's firm conviction that humanity lives in an ordered universe. Such an order is the manifestation of wisdom and the effect of God's creative command over every human being (Batho 1945: 109–12; Blau 1966: 19; Boccaccini 1991: 90–93; Browne 1920: 210–11, 217; Welch 1935: 224).

In fact, Diaspora communities had to maintain intercommunal contacts and solidarity in order to transcend longstanding local modalities and retain meaningful contacts with the Gentile world. According to Lightstone (1988: 69) "boundary-crossers were valued across social, cultic and theological realms." The Jews in the Diaspora attracted to their monotheistic worship a considerable number of those who found no religious satisfaction in paganism (Batho 1945: 111–12). According to Lightstone (1988: 51), "Jews in the Greco-Roman Diaspora took a surprisingly benign attitude to Gentile participation, often with Jews, in Judaic rites."

During and after the Jewish War (66–73) this conciliation process deepened and many figures contributed to it. For example, Boccaccini (1991: 241–42; cf. Farmer 1956) maintains that Josephus contributed to and worked for the survival of the Jewish community and their culture in the Diaspora (Boccaccini 1991: 241–42). More importantly, Eliezer ben Hyrcanus, the first important master of the Jamnian period, made the inevitable conclusions from the new situation of the Diaspora. According to Neusner (1975: 60) Eliezer took measures to improve relationships between Pharisees and other Jews, and between Jews and Samaritans. Similarly, Neusner continues, Yohanan ben Zakkai emphasized the acts of loving kindness as the basis of social order. For him, it was important to follow *torah* in order to contribute to the building of a sacred community. In fact, a new definition of sacrifice was required, the offering now had to be the gift of selfless compassion expressed in the streets and marketplaces (Neusner 1975: 46–47).

As a fundamental conclusion it was maintained that the nation had been awarded the Land of Israel with the specific understanding that it should build its unique society, and not to make the elect people a *nation* like those that surrounded it. According to Sicker (1992: 48–49), the Rabbis emphatically acknowledged that the Land was not theirs to do with as they pleased, it was the special property of God, "who alone would determine who might occupy it at any particular moment in history" (Sicker 1992: 48–49).

In order to complete the picture, I add some varieties of Modern Judaism that take the conclusions even further. It was expected that when the Diaspora continued for centuries a change would occur from thinking about Judaism as religious nationalism to thinking about the Jews as a religious community. The early spokesmen of Reform Judaism and Neo-Orthodoxy stood ready to sacrifice the nationalist element of Judaism to their desire to enter into the emancipated world by seeing a "defensive distinction between civic duty and religion" as fully appropriate (Blau 1966: 128):

Formerly the Jews had striven to create a nation, an independent state, but now their goal was to join other nations and reach for the highest rung of development in human society. It was the task of the new age to form a general human society which would encompass all peoples organically. In the same way, it was the task of the Jews not to create their own nation and their own state or a separate political entity, but rather to obtain from the other nations full acceptance into their society and thereby attain to participation in the general body social. (Blau 1966: 124)

Simon Dubnov's ideas of the spiritual nature of the Jewish nation must be seen in this light as the logical final conclusion. Dubnov participates in the Jewish debate of the twentieth century but derives his ideas logically from the Diaspora Judaism of the ancient world. According to Dubnov, the destruction of the Jewish state forced the Jews to create a social and cultural autonomy in place of political autonomy.[7] For Dubnov, the *Talmud* is the spiritual weapon needed by spiritual people (Pinson 1958: 43–48). Therefore, Jews and non-Jews who deny to the Jews of the Diaspora the right to call themselves a nation, "only because the lack of the specific external marks of a nationality which were taken from them," ignore the factor that kept alive the dispersed nation without state and without territory:

Was it the written law of the Bible, the ordinances of the Talmud and the decisions of the Rabbis, the isolation of the ghetto, inner autonomy, faith in the coming of the Messiah? All of them indeed contributed, but they were only external manifestations of forms of national survival. ... Quite apart from these, the source and vitality of the Jewish people consists in this: that the people, after it had passed through the stages of tribal nationalism, ancient culture and political territory, was able to establish itself and fortify itself in the highest state, the spiritual and historical-cultural, and succeeded in crystallizing itself as a spiritual people that draws the sap of its existence from a natural or intellectual will to live. ... [Israel] has been transformed from a simple nation into the very archetype of a nation, of a nation in the purest and loftiest sense, which has attained the highest stage of nationality. (Dubnov 1958: 84–89)

Therefore, Dubnov concludes that the Jewish nation—because of the special conditions of its existence in the Diaspora—"is not able to aspire anywhere to primacy and dominance." In other words, Dubnov's nationalism, and the nationalism of the present pattern in general, is "purely individualistic and hence completely ethical." His "unsoiled national ideal" fully "combines the visions of the Prophets of truth and justice with the noble dream of the unity of mankind" (Pinson 1958: 44). Whatever the historical truth, Dubnov eloquently formulates the essence of the present model by maintaining that:

There is absolutely no doubt that Jewish nationalism in essence has nothing in common with any tendency toward violence. As of a spiritual or historical-cultural nation, deprived of any possibility of aspiring to political triumphs, of seizing territory by force or of subjecting other nations to cultural domination, it is concerned with only one thing: protecting its national individuality and safeguarding its autonomous development in all states everywhere in the Diaspora. . . . The Jewish nationality is an outstanding example of a collective individuality which protects itself against attacks from the outside but never stops to attack on its own and is not able to do so. (Dubnov 1958: 97).

(DOMESTIC) PEACE

As Ferguson carefully documents, "seek for peace and pursue it" is a central tenet of Judaism. It is a fact that in the literature there are several positive allusions to peace, it "equals to everything, and God's name is peace." Peace finds several pacifistic applications in the written and oral Torah. There is a strong tradition according to which the Lord puts an end to war (Ferguson 1977: 87).

This is not a general theory of international relations, but the moral principle of *torah* as applied to the nation that has accepted the covenant with God. In fact, the moral principle of *torah* establishes the community of the Jews. Therefore, it is expected that major attention is called to social order within that community in everyday life (Batho 1945: 112–13), that is, peace and justice are applied within that covenant to domestic relations between the individuals of that covenant. Without ignoring the preceding discussion on positive relations between Jews and Gentiles, peace and justice in a narrow sense are not issues in international relations but appear closely intertwined within the Jewish community. The words of God were words of peace "to his people and his loyal servants, and to all who turn and trust in him." In praying for the peace of Jerusalem the reference is to peace "within your ramparts and prosperity in your palaces" or "within you." If the Jews practiced idolatry, but peace prevailed among them at the same time, God would say: "I cannot punish them, because peace prevails among them" (Ferguson 1977: 81–89).

This domestic emphasis can be perceived, if not exclusively so, in the very concept of peace, *shalom*. According to Moore (1954 II: 195; cf. Ferguson 1977: 84) the Hebrew word *shalom* has a broader meaning than the English word "peace." It comes from a root meaning wholeness, and indicates a condition of total well-being. *Shalom* concerns health, prosperity, security, contentment, and the like. Without peace no welfare of the individual or the community is possible (Moore 1954 II: 195).

The doctrine and conception of peace is based on a full understanding of the meaning of social life. An individual must belong to a community, human life is always social life. Tractate Avot (2: 4 in Neusner 1993a III) tells man not to "walk out of the community." An isolated life would not be worth living, one must either have companionship or die (cf. Ferguson 1977: 87; Cohen 1975: 184; Moore 1954 I: 445, Moore 1954 II: 196; cf. Moore 1954 I: 116; Moore 1954 II: 151).

Truth is another, similarly domestic, basic element of social order. Truth is the very character of God, the seal of God. Truth belongs to the integrity of a godly man—truth is not only in his speech but in his whole character. Therefore, there is an obligation to speak the truth, for to deceive anybody is a kind of theft. Lie is actually the first of seven kinds of theft, and is as bad as all the rest combined. Therefore, flattery is forbidden if the object is either an Israelite or a foreigner (Moore 1954 II: 188–91, 194–95).

In addition to peace and truth, justice is the third fundamental virtue on which human society is based. It is no less fundamental than the idea of God, and in the definition of what God requires of men. The sword symbolizes the delay and perversion of justice and is used by those who interpret *torah,* not according to its true sense. Justice includes three aspects: (1) fair dealing between man and man, i.e., the distributive justice which gives to each his due; (2) public justice, i.e., the function of the community in defining and enforcing the duties and rights of individuals and classes; and (3) rectitude, or integrity of personal character (Moore 1954 II: 180–97).

Peace, justice, and truth are intertwined. "The world stands fast on three things, on justice, on truth, and on peace." Justice, truth, and peace are really one: "if judgment is executed, truth is vindicated and peace results." Through these pillars, the divine moral code creates the basis of order and meaning for human associations (Cohen 1975: 203, 206; Moore 1954 II: 188).

In conclusion, I note that Neusner expresses the same message of peace, truth, and justice under the conception of virtue, which for him is the third "native category" besides *torah* and learning. Virtue is his "word for the complex of attitudes and actions that in the religious writings of this Judaism govern the social order, transforming individuals into honorable members of Israel, God's holy community" (Neusner 1993a I: 21).

AGAINST POLITICS?

The idea of a *torah*-based community and identity implies and includes the rejection of conventional politics. While this rejection is a rather complex issue, it must be discussed as the final element of the present pattern.

Torah is necessary and sufficient for establishing and maintaining social order; political power is not necessarily required to maintain social order. While this conclusion was produced by practical reasons—full independence was unattainable—the preference of religious ideals was derived from *torah*, not from experience. This is reflected in several well-known situations. For example, the process of national restoration after the return from Babylonia focused principally on the reconstruction of the Temple, or the temple-state, which was impeded by the strong opposition of both internal and external forces. Similarly, the liberation of Judea from the Seleucids' rule for a short period before Rome became the new master was accompanied by an exaltation of the national spirit, but the political aims and worldly policies of the Hasmoneans became highly disliked among serious religious thinkers and the people (Moore 1954 II: 113; Sicker 1992: 34).

The doctrine claimed to be able to establish society which was to be more powerful than the conventional state. *Torah* was thought to be the most efficient way of making a human community; its effects surpass the possibilities of conventional political power. Tractate Avot (3: 5 in Neusner 1993a III) states that *torah* makes the state unnecessay, but if *torah* is rejected, the yoke of the state and hard labor will return (cf. Cohen 1975: 127).

However, the picture is not very clear. The temple-state actually survived as an autonomous structure fully accepted by the foreign masters, and full independence had many supporters. The prophets had decapitated the golden age in idyllic imagery so the Jews in their wide dispersion looked forward to the day when they would be gathered again in their own land and an era of peace and prosperity would follow. While this reflected the question of freedom to live their own life and follow their own religion unhindered by foreign dominion more than the value of independence as such, there was a continuous debate, especially concerning the role of the Holy Land, between the supporters of the religious and the political communities (Moore 1954 I: 117–18; Sicker 1992: 50).

To make either-or claims impossible, religious and social groups were likely to move from one position to another depending on the situation. For example, the Pharisees began as a political party, but toward the end of the Maccabean period they gave up conventional politics by concentrating on what they believed was important in everyday life: the fulfillment of all the laws of *torah*. In a true kingdom everyone was to become a priest, a holy person, a king. Such people might form a community fully comparable to the Temple sanctuary of Jerusalem. However, this challenge to politics did not share the idea of social equality and communality in Jesus's teachings, for the Pharisees the society remained hierarchical.[8] Therefore, it was not unexpected when the Pharisees made a new move. They reconsidered the importance of political life, claiming that *torah* might be effected through political power. So "the party which had abandoned politics for piety now had to recover access to the instruments of power for the sake of piety" (Neusner 1975: 48).

Furthermore, the Jewish texts had a rather open political message: the symbols at hand conveyed religious messages as well as political images. For example, Babylonia, Rome, and Israel constituted political judgments, often giving a basis for the politics of exclusion. On the other hand, openly Zoroastrian elements were rejected by Judaism with all other forms of the heresy of two powers (Moore 1954 I: 115; Neusner 1983: 8).

The dispute was never fully resolved. Both political and apolitical solutions were finally accepted.[9] For example, Tractate Avot (Neusner 1993a III) suggests contending views on the political government. Implying that for moral and religious reasons it is better to be a tail to lions than a head to foxes (Cohen 1975: 190), it claimed to be in favor of politics:

Pray for the welfare of the government, for it were not for fear of it, one man would swallow his fellow alive. (3: 2)
Be quick in service to a superior, efficient in service to the state, and receive everybody with joy. (3: 12).

However, points against politics are much clearer. The text warns individuals not to involve the use of power:

Be wary of the government, for they get friendly with a person only for their own convenience. They took like friends when its is to their benefit, but they do not stand by of a person when he is in need. (2: 3)

NOTES

1. The Judaism covered by the suggested period includes several, even contending, Judaisms. I suggest that the present pattern can be recognized among all of them (Batho 1945; Bocccaccini 1991; Lumb 1937; Maynard 1928; Moore 1954; Neusner 1975, 1983, 1986, 1993a).

2. As to the history and its interpretation, the sources are given in references. Concerning the text and content of *torah*, I use Cohen (1975), Moore (1954), and Neusner (1993a III). Cohen's work is based on the *Babylonian Talmud*, Moore's on the primary sources compiled in the second century C.E. and in the century and a half between the reorganization at Jamnia under Johanan ben Zakkai and his associates after the fall of Jerusalem in the year 70 (Moore 1954 I: vii). Neusner's work (1993a III) includes a translation of Tractate Avot (The Sayings of the Fathers or Founders). Concerning Moore's "normative Judaism," Neusner (1975: 139) states that "today no sophisticated student of Judaism in late antiquity works within the framework of such a synthesis." However, Moore's work is useful as a summary and collection of quotations from the original sources. In delineating the present pattern this is sufficient for my task is not to give a whole view of Judaism in the early centuries of the Common Era.

3. The *Mishnah* is a work of philosophy expressed through laws ("one does this, one does not do that"). Four of the six principal parts deal with the cult and its officers. Two further divisions of the document deal with everyday affairs; the first, Damages, concerns civil law and government, the second, Women, concerns issues of family, home, and personal status (Neusner 1993b: 14–15). As to the present pattern, the existence and role of the *Mishnah* as the expression of *torah* is important, the detailed content we can ignore.

4. The combined idea of *torah* and the covenant has a central place in all the texts of the doctrine, but the Qumran sect perhaps represents an extremity of these ideas. The sect vowed absolute obedience to the particular interpretation of the Law of Moses taught within the sect, and the search for perfection. The sect represented the New Covenant, and supported perfect obedience to the teachings of Moses and the prophets (Vermes 1984: 35).

5. Silver and Martin (1974: 255, 257) state that "the dark night of *galut* settled on" the Jews' world. "*Galut* (exile) signified not only defeat and life in exile, but life in an alien world, an unnatural existence, the amputation of Israel's ability to walk confidently before men and God."

6. The Jewish case was not an exception in its nationalism. Elements of nationalism and religious imagery would be found in many parts of the ancient world, making the politics of exclusion one of the most typical patterns in the ancient world (cf. Chapter 13). I wish to emphasize the relationship between *torah* and the Jews. However, I maintain that there is a conspicuous distinction between ancient Hebrew thought and Judaism. Ancient Hebrew thought emphasized nationalism and the exclusion of the Gentiles from the Holy Land, whereas Judaism gave the common identity a more symbolic and religious meaning.

7. For Dubnov, the difference between the Pharisees and the Sadducees was more than a theological controversy regarding the validity of the oral *torah*. Rather, it was a conflict between the advocates of a "spiritual nation" and those of a "political nation" (Pinson 1958: 44, 47). Dubnov's own ideal is clearly an example of cultural nationalism, a type close to the nationalism I have put forward as an element of the principle-oriented pattern.

8. For example, early Christians gathered for ritual meals but the Pharisees apparently did not. Pharisaic table-fellowship was an ordinary, everyday affair (Neusner 1975: 45), and as such, it did not share the challenge Jesus was making to the hierarchical society of his time (cf. Crossan 1994).

9. Neusner (1991) speaks of the role of politics and political power in Rabbinic political theory. Undeniably, politics can be found in any community, not only within the state. Furthermore, it is true that many elements of Judaism (e.g., the temple-state ideas, and the politics of exclusion) can be included among the power-oriented patterns of social order.

PART III

Power-Oriented Patterns
of Social Order

The discussion on power-oriented patterns of order can be divided into three major approaches. The major approaches of order can be found: (1) in the organization of humankind into the ideal or best community; (2) in the government of such a community; and (3) in relations between the communities.

The three major approaches are not independent of each other. They overlap to the extent that structured discussion is almost impossible. However, for analytical reasons it is not wrong to think that the organizational basis of order (Chapter 7) can be put above the other two approaches—the latter two approaches do not appear independent of the preferred community. On the other hand, it is not possible to imagine that any of the suggested communities would be a sufficient basis for order without due consideration of its government and external relations.

If it is suggested that order can be established and maintained by constituting an ideal political organization, two questions immediately emerge: How to govern it? and How to arrange relations between such organizations? The first question is discussed in the following four chapters. I first deal with the moral basis of the state and politics: the wise king (Chapter 8), and his moral and political education (Chapter 9). Later, another type of ruler is discussed, the heroic king (Chapter 10). Finally, I discuss the politics as politics approach, where the punishing king applies coercive power to maintain law and order (Chapter 11). The heroic king is a bridge between the moral politics of the wise king and the coercive power of law and order, in a sense combining both ideas—high morality and military capacities.

The second question implies that it is not enough to suggest a political organization and discuss its government. Rather, often the organization of humankind, or the actor (e.g., the state) is given. Major attention is then usually called the actor's external relations. Furthermore, discussions on external relations are a derivation from the ideas concerning the ideal organization and the best government within this organization. In fact, both international and domestic order is covered by Chapters 12 through 14. As in the preceding chapters, my point is not to make any artificial distinctions between domestic and international. The international aspect is made more explicit than before, but this does not imply that the final three chapters summarize everything the selected texts, schools, and thinkers have said about international relations. Instead, many such points are discussed in the context of the respective patterns, not detached of them, in the very context where they belong.

In any case, the patterns concerning external or international relations must not be understood as empirical theories of actual interaction. The patterns are collections of ideas that represent preferred approaches to dealing with external or international relations in order to maximize order within and between the respective units. The suggested approaches introduce two major alternatives, once again repeating the basic dimension found in this investigation. The first alternative suggests that interunit or external relations must be based on moral principles (Chapter 12); the second alternative considers power politics, the direct application of (military) force, and violence the keys to international order (Chapter 14). In between these two alternatives, I discuss a general approach called the politics of exclusion (Chapter 13), which is close to power politics but perceives external relations in/a moral light.

When relations between suggested units can be based on moral principles, it is supposed that both partners are more or less equal. The alternative approach excludes "the Other," and justifies its elimination or subordination to "us." This implies that the politics of exclusion and power politics are tightly intertwined. It is also possible, however, that power politics is a rational approach to deal with conflicts of interest between equal contestants, without presupposing any fundamental distinctions between the contending actors, of which both take care of their own interests in a rational way.

This book is not a study of legitimacy but of ideas about social order. However, there are some overlappings and similarities between my concepts of social order and legitimacy. Furthermore, ideas about an ideal government and ideal rulers look like a debate in legitimacy. However, in this book we have no real states, no real ruler nor ruled. The conceptions of legitimacy presuppose all of them.

It is well known that legitimacy is claimed by a political leader, or a group of leaders, on the grounds of one principle or another. It is also acknowledged or rejected by those over whom power is exercised on the same grounds, or on different ones. Where a claim to legitimacy by a regime—"legitimation from above"—coincides with a broad enough acceptance of its title by those subject to its rule—"legitimation from below"—the exercise of political power by the leaders can be regarded as empirically legitimate (Sadenniemi 1995: 13). It is obvious that such a condition is fulfilled when the ruler and the ruled agree upon the best approach(es) to social order.

In fact, if there are contending approaches to social order, one supported by the ruler and the other by the ruled, a crisis is likely to emerge. Such a crisis is not only a question of "the belief in the rightfulness of a state" (cf. Sadenniemi 1995: 18), but something much more. As Ali Sadeghi (1996) correctly suggests, a society questions not only its political system and legitimacy of its leaders but more importantly social order, the basis of its own existence. When the existing social order is not found legitimate, the society either breaks up or finds a new social order. In order to find a new social order, revolution may occur, especially if and when the population shares the belief that the existing leaders represent a degenerated, corrupted, and illegitimate social order. If all, both the population and the leadership, believe in the legitimacy of social order, leaders are removed from their posts by elections or rebellions. The leader is then fully justified in applying normal arguments in legitimizing his position. Interestingly, in international relations it is wide sense of legitimacy as social order that defines relations between the states representing different social orders (cf. Sadenniemi 1995).

Many parts of this book fall outside the academic debate on the concept of legitimacy. In the principle-oriented patterns it is the individual in the first place, who makes moral choices, he or she either controls or does not control him or herself. In addition, the type of the community or the community's external relations are not greatly related to the issue of legitimacy. But there are some cases of leadership (the wise king, the heroic king, and the punishing king) which deserve attention concerning legitimacy. However, it is obvious that the suggested typologies do not apply to the following discussion.

Weber's (1978) three pure types of power-holding are the legal-rational, the traditional, and the charismatic type of domination. These are theoretical, ideal types which could be found among *all* three cases of leadership I discuss in this book, even if some ideal types correlate with some of the cases more than with others. More complex typologies, like the one suggested by Sadenniemi (1995: 78) have the same problem. If there are possibilities for further comparisons, they must be done elsewhere because such attempts fall outside the scope of this book. In Sadeghi's (1996) terms I suggest that when a wise, heroic, or punishing king is determined to be an illegitimate ruler, it will cause a rebellion, not a revolution. The social order will remain but the new leader will be someone who better fulfills the requirements of a wise, heroic, or punishing ruler. It may be likely that both rebellions and revolutions are the most likely to occur in the last case, because "the strongest man is never strong enough to be master all the time" (Sadenniemi 1995: 13). But then the punishing ruler has misunderstood his role in the system, which is not based on force and obedience but right and duty. The punishing ruler has dictatorial power but he cannot misuse it, he must legitimize his power by maintaining social order.

CHAPTER 7

The Ideal Community as the Basis of Social Order

The present pattern of order can be formulated in two ways, the latter consisting of two different types. Each type claims to be the best way of organizing people into a commonwealth thought to be the most appropriate for the establishment and maintenance of peace and order. One alternative is to introduce sovereign territorial associations, which are either small or have distinct territories marked by borders. In ancient history, such sovereign units are often called city-states. Another possibility is to emphasize, at least rhetorically, a world-wide community. Concerning territorial area, none of the ancient empires was a global world state in the modern sense, however, they all were surprisingly large units.

The idea of a world community emerged early in ancient history as the explicit alternative to city-states, actual empires both preceded and existed adjacent to small political units. The idea of the world community claimed that some ancient communities had degenerated into smaller local or regional city-states. This mythology is typical, especially to the Chinese and the Greeks, and has often been taken for granted as historical truth (cf. Starr 1974: 143; Watson 1967). According to this theory new world states and empires (China, Macedonia, and Rome) allegedly reemerged as an answer to the problems and uncertainties caused by the city-state (cf. Fustel de Coulanges 1955).

As a special, actually unique, case among the world community models are non-state organizations established on religious bases. The early church (later, especially the Catholic Church) was the exemplar in openly challenging and replacing the conventional state. The temple-state is somewhere between the conventional state and the pure religious organization, but both can be discussed in the same connection.

When the modern states were beginning in the fifteenth century, they did not introduce a new pattern of social order. The ancient model only was applied on either a wider scale (as a movement from the city-states to bigger units) or a smaller scale (as a movement from the world community to smaller units). The actual movement was from the detested empire to smaller units, later called nation-states. The modern state,

I claim, represented a movement away from the world state or the empire back to the city-state. The modern state was a dialectical synthesis of the city-state and the world-state (cf. Herz 1951). Therefore, the case of the modern state did not deserve a separate discussion if material from later periods were included in the study. The "one nation one state" principle, or nationalism and national identity might perhaps deserve some discussion, but the elements of the idea were known and applied earlier as well (cf. Chapter 6).

SOVEREIGN TERRITORIAL STATES

The idea of sovereign territorial states is typical to the early Greco-Roman world where cities were established around and for the home-gods, in the name of dead fathers and ancestors (Fustel de Coulanges 1955; Ryckwert 1976). However, the idea also appears elsewhere, especially in a lesser known case of Mohism. The case of ancient Hebrew thought—which fully represents the present approach—is discussed mainly in Chapter 13 (cf. Chapter 6).

Undeniably, the doctrine of universal love (Chapter 12) makes Mohism comparable to Daoism and Jesus's teachings (Chapter 3). However, Mo Zi's principle of universal love cannot be detached from the idea of sovereign states preferred by him as the ideal organization of humankind. Universal love is not an independent moral principle, but it is derived from (or suggested as) a justification for the idea of sovereign states.

One might imagine that the Mohists accepted the Confucian question of How to govern? This can be derived from the answers provided by Mo Zi. According to him, the ruler must abstain from military attacks against others but be very careful in preparing to defend himself against any invaders. Mo condemns war, but fondly speaks about war and arms from the point of waging wars and using arms in military battles. Mo Zi accepted defensive action, but strongly condemned offensive warfare.

It is a typical error of translators and other scholars to attempt to explain this inconsistency by citing either of the two opposing elements. Because Mo Zi's pacifism is taken for granted (as in a sense it should be) it has been suggested that perhaps he did not accept any kind of war; his disciples may have added these elements to his work in subsequent compilations (cf. Watson 1967).

I wish to turn the conventional interpretation upside down and suggest that the idea of defensive wars is an essential part of Mo's ideas. If we suppose that the idea of defensive war was seriously put forward by him, it must immediately be noted that he was *not* answering the fundamental questions debated by the Confucians or the Legalists. Mo was not asking how the ruler could establish good government within his state in order to unify the world, that is, in order to extend social order over China. Mo was interested in how to govern a given state in order to produce and maintain order and peace *within* it. He was not interested in the unification of China. Mo put forward the idea of *separate territorial units*, arguing that peaceful relations might be possible between them without any government above them. In this sense, Mo Zi's fundamental problem was a new type of question: How to govern in order to make the existence of sovereign territorial units possible? How to govern in order to produce and maintain order and peace between such units? Therefore, Mo suggested alternatives to the unification of China—whether this was brought about peacefully or through military operations.

Mo's answer to his own question is the suggestion that there can and should be sovereign states that abstain from attacking each other but are always ready to defend themselves against invaders. Strong defense is the key to his approach, to which the condemnation of offensive war adds a complementary element. Mo advised the ruler to govern and cultivate the existing territory instead of trying to expand his territory. According to Mo a war over land is simply to destroy a scarce resource, people, for the sake of what one already has in excess, land (Mo Tzu/Watson: 55).

Mo's solution comes rather close to the Greek idea of city-states, sharing with Plato the idea of peaceful relations between sovereign actors.[1] Neither does Mo's idea differ significantly from the idea of sovereign nation-states. However, in Chinese philosophy Mo Zi was a unique proponent of this idea. Mohism represents a deviant case in Chinese political philosophy, which, excluding Daoism, embraces the unity of the Chinese commonwealth (the *tien-hsia*). The Mohist philosophy was popular until the end of the Warring States period (221 B.C.E.) and successfully contended with Confucianism in the classical period, but lost its status immediately after the establishment of the unified China. After the violent unification, an urgent political need—efficient government of the unified China—invoked a revisited version of Confucianism, but for Mohism there was no space left.

It is clear that Plato discussed the nature of an ideal political unit taking it for granted that all truly civilized men would prefer the *polis,* the city-state. Aristotle has been read in the same light (Starr 1974: 206). However, Aristotle's ideas are problematic because they support, at least indirectly, the world community model, too.

Plato shares the Greek city-state tradition and takes it for granted so that he does not pay much attention to speaking for it explicitly. This is reflected, for example, when Plato maintains that in the ideal system of states not a single country should be too big. A big state, in any case, could not remain a single state but would be soon dissolved. According to Plato, a state must be extended only as long as it can remain a single unit. In fact, it is not a large area but the rule of reason that makes a state great. Under the rule of reason the state does not need many soldiers to be great (*Republic* 423a–c).

According to Plato, social life and development are possible only in the state. The state is founded on needs. Nobody is able to survive alone, but all are dependent on others (*Republic* 369b–d, 415c–e). Therefore, in order to organize and maintain material and social survival, the state must have power over everything. Individuals must do whatever the state orders. Individuals must even die in the name of the common interest in order to guarantee the survival of the state, the precondition of human life (*Crito* 51a–b).

The state has the right to rule over the individual not only because it can create order and guarantee security against enemies (both internal and external), but because the state has a strong effect on the morality of individuals. A good state makes individuals good, evil state makes individuals evil. While a monarchy is based on too much power and democracy on too much freedom, aristocracy can only educate good citizens. Therefore, aristocracy has always been accepted by the people (*Menexenus* 238b–d).

However, the state has no right to oppress individuals or any natural differences between them. It is true that the individual can only achieve his or her best in a unified society, but it is also clear that the wider and more varied a society, the richer the individuals's own development (Stawell 1936: 9). The best way to take advantage of differences is to apply a division of labor in daily activities and production. In a good state, everybody has a place and a task to be carried out. Everybody must be allocated work according to his or her abilities. Only then can man remain whole, and only then, consequently, can the state maintain unity (*Republic* 406c, 421a–c, 423d).[2]

The ideal division of labor is based on the state's happiness, not that of the individual. A state is not established to make one group or class happier than others, but to make the state happy. This can only be achieved if internal disputes can be avoided. These disputes can be avoided in small states where people, and especially leaders, can be morally educated and socially responsible, and where the individual ownership of everything—property, women, and children—can be forbidden because its members form a true community (*Republic* 420a–c; 464d–e; 543a). Furthermore, the existence of several small states is the precondition to a fundamentally pacifying situation where no one is forced to uncritically or unconditionally submit him or herself to the state. An individual must remain able, in principle, to choose otherwise, and be able to leave the state if he or she does not accept its power and laws. Only then can it be claimed that if one continues to live in a state, he or she has made a choice and accepted the power of that state over him or herself. Then the choice is not based on power and violence, but on reason (*Crito* 52e, cf. 53a–e).

Aristotle's ideas shadow Plato's. Aristotle even maintains that a state should be situated far away from others. In fact, Aristotle even maintains that there should be no interaction between the states, nothing that is unnecessary for the maintenance and self-sufficiency of a community (*Politics* 1261b6, 1272b16, 1326a5–b2; Sinclair 1984b: 80, 424).

However, while Aristotle undeniably supports the city-state system, his ideas can be read in a totally different light. He is not so much interested in the eternal existence of city-states, but in finishing wars between city-states. It is likely that this can only be achieved when one state is able to conquer others. In order to do so, a state must be self-sufficient and fundamentally independent of others. Aristotle, therefore, considers the qualities of land required for both economic production and military operations. Economic assets are required to make the state militarily strong for matters of defense as well as of attack. In fact, the ideal configuration of the land helps maintain a strong defense and provides a good military basis for offensive actions (*Politics* 1326b26, b39).

WORLD COMMUNITY

It appears that warlords, feudal masters, and city-states were not an efficient way of establishing order within a limited territory or the expanding and rapidly changing world. In addition to wars, the system of territorial sovereign units tended to encourage domestic struggles and corruption, leading finally to civil wars within both small city-states and the wider nation of which such units were part. A world government was thought to be a powerful device to stopping civil wars. Actually, when warlords, feudal masters, and city-states lost their power rich compensations were offered. Petty wars between neighboring cities with killings and the enslaving of the members of one's own nation became less common. Simultaneously, religious thought encountered dramatic changes when tribal and city-gods either lost their meaning or were transformed into global gods when social development made the world cosmopolitan.

The idea of a world government emerges in several places in the ancient world both preceding the city-states and later correcting the chaos caused by them. In this book the world community model seems to be much more popular than the city-state model, in China both Confucianism and Legalism supported the idea, in Greece many philosophers including Aristotle embraced the model, and in Rome the Stoic philosophers and writers agreed with it as well. Therefore, it is not surprising that the early Christian community adopted the very same Greco-Roman idea.

It is obvious that both Confucianism and Legalism were interested in the proper government of the warring states in order to find a solid basis for the unification of the area now known as China, but then usually referred to as the *tien-hsia*, "all under heaven," or as the area "within the four seas." The ideal of world government was derived from the historical past, which was rather mythical but still represented a kind of reality as the Empire of Zhou. It is true that its existence had degenerated to the mere expression the *tien-hsia*. However, the Empire of Zhou kept the idea of unified empire in the accepted political vocabulary and the minds of men. Therefore, in China the past had a more powerful role than in Greek city-states where writers, historians, philosophers, and orators had to imagine a pan-Hellenistic unity without being able to document its existence. They had to be satisfied with Homer's *Iliad* and other great stories.

The idea of the *tien-hsia* maintained that a world that has achieved order is a world in which *dao* prevails. Such a world is known as the world of Great Harmony. This Confucian world order (*ping*) denotes peace, harmony, evenness, equality, fairness, and the like. All Confucian teaching is aimed at the achievement of this ultimate goal. Such a goal was attainable only if "all under heaven" were united as a single empire. Therefore, a systematic theory of politics was introduced based on the idea that Great Harmony cannot be restricted to a single state in either theory or practice. Concerning the theory, such an idea was a contradiction in terms. In practice, if a king was able to establish such a government in his state, his state would expand to cover the "all under heaven" because men living under bad rulers might dismiss them and join the good ruler (Chen 1991: 33–34).

Legalism shared the idea of a unified China but not the other Confucian assumptions. Instead, the Legalist theory spoke of social order in more practical terms maintaining that unification could only be achieved by law and order within a state and its successful wars of conquest over the others (Chapter 14).

When the anticipated dangers of the Odysseic world came true in the Peloponnesian War between the city-states, the alternative idea of world government claimed to be the only alternative to stop the civil wars. Such an ideal was far removed from contemporary political realities, and it remained expressed in the Olympic games and Euripides's plays, which were well received by the audience but still unable to convince the majority about the dangers of the city-states system. More concrete and practical learning processes were required. It was the Peloponnesian War that became the decisive factor. The practice, not a theory was necessary to give the final blow to the city-state by revealing it the mother of all conflicts, both internal and external.

After the war, no one believed in city-states. Space for alternative ideas became available. As a representative of openly imagined history, Xenophon suggested that peace and order could be achieved if a single state, Sparta, obtained suzerainty over the other Greeks. According to him, the balance of power did not lead to order but to chaos, uncertainty, and confusion in Greece. Xenophon even glorified war in order to find the winner who "would become the dominant power" and make the losers its subjects (*Hellenica* VII.5.26–27).

While earlier representatives of Greek philosophy—the Sceptics, for example—had already challenged the city-state idea, it remained a major task for Aristotle to make a more fundamental contribution to the emerging world view. He thought that the united Greece should be established and governed by one ruler. If required, wars had to be fought to secure peace and establish such a united state (Fustel de Coulanges 1920: 450; Kelsen 1977; Tenkku 1981: 125).

This is not suggested explicitly. On the contrary, Aristotle spoke of and for small city-states. However, Aristotle's ideas were not in favor of the city-state model as uncompromisingly as Plato's ideas. Aristotle recognized correctly that the relations between individual city-states had an inherent inclination towards war. It is not difficult to see that continuous wars between the city-states are not accepted by Aristotle. In a seemingly minor passage Aristotle maintains that the old laws were uncivilized and ancient Greeks themselves had been uncivilized and practiced barbaric and ridiculous manners such as carrying arms against each other and purchasing brides from each other (*Politics* 1268b31). Aristotle's audience knew, of course, that some of these habits were still in practice in Greece—especially wars between the Greeks. Therefore, his criticism of the contemporary—not the past—Greeks was understood but unlikely accepted by the Athenians.

Indeed, the basic question is: Did Aristotle think it possible to attain peace in the city-states system or only under a world state? To find the answer we must understand that it was impossible for Aristotle to make an explicit suggestion in this matter. There were suspicions about him as a foreigner in general and his role as the tutor of Alexander of Macedonia in particular. His approach had to be indirect, but possible to understand.

Aristotle's idea of united Greek rule over the rest of the world is put forward indirectly by his ideas about the fundamental differences between the Greek and the Barbarian, or between the master (free citizens) and the slave. According to Aristotle one of the major functions of the state is to guarantee security against external enemies, therefore it is not impossible to envisage that only a united Greek state could provide a sufficient defense against the Barbarian nations—this was already realized in the struggle against the expanding Persian power (cf. *Politics* 1330b17).

It is also a fact that Aristotle makes some open suggestions in favor of a world government. Indeed, while he says that a large state requires too many manual workers to be sustainable, he does not exclude suzerainty where one king or a state controls the others. For example, Crete was both well placed and naturally suited to dominate the Hellenic world (*Politics* 1265a10, 1271b32). Furthermore, Aristotle suggests the unification of Hellenes as a world-ruling power. According to some interpretations, Aristotle intended it as a formal and theoretical possibility not to be taken seriously. Is it so? Maybe, but not likely. In another passage Aristotle explicitly asks what might be the best state[3] to rule over the Hellenic people, and even the whole inhabited world. His own answer is that both courage and intellect are required for such a task. According to Aristotle the nations that live in cold regions of Europe were full of spirit but lacking in intellect and the political cohesion required for ruling their neighbors. On the other hand, the Asiatic nations were lacking in spirit, and, Aristotle believed, should remain enslaved. The Hellenic race, however, had both capacities. They had only to be united under a *single* constitution in order to become capable of ruling all other people (*Politics* 1327b18).

Where Aristotle was forced to apply indirect speech in favor of the world government by Macedonia, the great orator Isocrates did not hesitate to become, in his last but active years, the orator for the Macedonian expansion. Isocrates condemned the disasters of war between Greek states and spoke for true peace, not for the mere truce or non-war between the cities (Isocrates: 121).

First, Isocrates hoped that Athens would become the suzerain, as it had in ancient times. Athens then had "took charge of the Greeks" when they were living "in a lawless life in scattered communities under the violent control of arbitrary power, or at the mercy of anarchy," and "freed them of these distresses by means either of her own government or of her example, by being the first state to establish law and organize a constitution." But the historical development revealed to Isocrates that Athens was not any more entitled to the suggested task. So thirty-four years after the Panegyricus for the Athenian suzerainty, Isocrates welcomed the Macedonian power and its king, Philip II. Isocrates explicitly stated that he had left Athens alone, but without abandoning his "business" in campaigning for peace among the Greeks (Isocrates: 106–7, 145, 162–63).

The Cynics suggested a new philosophy or a way of life. They advised life to be lived "according to Virtue," and their ideal was "the Wise Man" who lives a simple life "eating food for nourishment only and wearing a single garment; despising wealth and fame and high birth" (Diogenes Laertius VI.103–5).

Furthermore, they denied the idea of a fatherland. They taught that a fatherland could be limited to a city-state but had to be extended over the whole world. Love towards one's city represented nothing more than a prejudice and had to be removed from human feelings. Antisthenes represented cosmopolitanism, which treated the pride of Hellenic birth as vain and poured contempt on the glorious victories of Marathon and Salamis. Diogenes maintained that the only true commonwealth is that which is as wide as the universe. Another Cynic, Crates, did not wish Alexander to rebuild his native city because another Alexander would destroy it again (Arnold

1911: 48; Diogenes Laertius VI.38, 72, 93; Fustel de Coulanges 1920: 450). The Epicureans and the Stoics continued along the same lines.

Both Epicures and Zeno began to teach at Athens about twenty years after the deaths of Alexander the Great and Aristotle (323–322 B.C.E.). Like the Sceptics earlier, both Epicureanism and Stoicism looked for a happiness secure from fortune's changes. They found it in peace of mind, undisturbed by fear and desire. Epicures sought peace in the liberation of man's will from nature's law, Zeno sought peace in submission to nature. To Epicures, man's greatest need was to be rid of fear, especially fear of the gods and fear of death. To Zeno, man's greatest need was to be able to cope with sorrow, disappointment, and misfortune (Rackham 1971: xvii–xviii; Ross 1986: 41).

But while the Cynics and the Epicureans withdrew themselves from political and social life (Epicures advised men not to touch them unless forced by gods!), the Stoics[4] made a strong return to political and social life (Fustel de Coulanges 1920: 451). Therefore, their contributions are much more interesting.

Zeno's ideal was the establishment of the perfect state. This was to be a completion of the work in which Alexander had failed. The ideal state had to embrace the whole world. No one was to call him or herself a citizen of any *polis* (Arnold 1911: 66–67).

The doctrine maintained that the whole world was a living being, endowed with soul and reason, with ether as its ruling principle. Furthermore, the world was said to be ordered by reason and providence and endowed with a common soul, of which individuals are fragments (Diogenes Laertius VII.138–143).

Because there is order in the world, Zeno suggested, the organizing principle behind the world is reason, which governs the other, passive principle. The passive principle is a substance or matter without quality, whereas the active principle is the reason inherent in this substance. Reason is the same as God. In other words, God is one and the same with reason, fate, and Zeus (Diogenes Laertius VII.134–36; cf. VII.87–88).

Stoicism became widely accepted in Rome, especially among the elites who favorably heard the Greek Stoics' message. Among them, Polybius, a Greek who made his career as historian among Romans, maintained that the world had been previously fragmented, but now the world and its history were an organic whole where all local affairs were interlinked with each other (Polybius I.3.1–6).

Roman political needs were nicely served by the Stoic ethics, which were not based on the needs of the individual, but on the demands of the supreme law, the law of nature. The same eternal wisdom through which the material world took shape is, in another function, the right rule which commands and forbids. Right rule and common law are of identical meaning, by which a standard of supreme authority is set up. State law and conventional morality are a reflection of universal law (Arnold 1911: 273–74).

Therefore, the Stoic state is worldwide, a cosmopolis. One is a member not of a clan or city, but of a world-wide society.[5] In this society all distinctions of race, caste, and class are to be subordinated to brotherhood. Only the brute animals are excluded, for they do not possess reason (Arnold 1911: 274–75).

Without forgetting other Roman Stoics—or Livy and Virgil—it can be said that Cicero formulated the idea of the world state into its full maturity. Cicero has a prominent place in Roman political thought and, therefore, we cannot avoid providing an explicit discussion on his ideas, however similar they are to the Greek Stoic views. Furthermore, a more detailed description of Cicero's ideas is justified by the existence of his major works—as for his predecessors only some fragments and secondhand interpretations are available.

Cicero maintains that the whole universe must be conceived as one commonwealth "of which both gods and men are members" (*De Legibus*, hereafter referred to as Legibus I.7.23). According to Cicero, the universe is guided by, and *is*, the god. The sole first cause, the divine mind, realizes itself in the world process. This process proceeds according to a fixed law or formula, effect following cause in an undeviating sequence. Existence repeats itself in an unending series of identical cycles. Man's will is free; but this freedom implies and demands an understanding of the process, and the ability to submit his will to its laws (*De Finibus*, hereafter referred to as Finibus, I.IX. 29–30).

In Cicero's theory, the law of nature has a prominent place. The law of nature is a divine law, governing the whole universe. This law is based on divine reason, which created the whole universe. It is not a product of human thought, but it is "something eternal which rules the whole universe by its wisdom." Natural law is the same as right reason and, therefore, always above the written laws. It is the basic norm to be followed everywhere. Reason commands people to fulfill their obligations and prohibits them from doing wrong. Its validity is universal, it is unchangeable and eternal, it is sinful to supersede this law or to repeal any part of it, and it is entirely impossible to cancel. One cannot be exempted from its demands, and everyone has the right to interpret it (Legibus I.VI., II.IV.8).

This theory has important social and international implications. The law of nature implies that there are no valid national or local laws, but "all nations will be subject all the time to this one changeless and everlasting law." True law, that is, right reason in agreement with nature, is universal, unchanging, and everlasting. Therefore, one eternal and unchangeable law will be valid for "all nations and all times" (*De Re Publica,* hereafter referred to as RePublica, III.XXI.33, III.XXII.33). Indeed, Cicero suggests that there must be one single basic law for everyone because right reason is common to everyone. Also justice is one: "it binds all human society, and is based on one law, which is right reason applied to command and prohibition" (Legibus I.V.16, I.VII.23, I.XV.42).

Reason, when it is full grown and perfected, is called wisdom. Those who share law must also share justice, and those who share law and justice are to be regarded as members of the same commonwealth. They obey the god of transcendent power. Consequently, the whole human race is bound together in unity. The knowledge of the principles of right living is what makes men better. Actually, men can live with one another because they have "a partnership in Justice" (Legibus I.VII.23, I.XI. 32, I.XII.35).

Cicero makes nature the basis of all social associations. His theory is one of social agreement, but Cicero derives the principle of this agreement from the law of nature. The source of social association cannot be found in the weakness of the individual but in one's social spirit, "which nature has implanted in man." Therefore, it is natural for men to seek the company of other men. No resources or wealth can make a man happy if he must live apart from other men. The existence of this natural social spirit explains why a scattered, wandering, and likely warring multitude has become a body of citizens by mutual agreement (RePublica I.XXV.39).

According to Cicero, law, being the highest reason, is implanted in nature (Legibus I.VI.18–19). Nature is the common parent of all people (*On the Good Life*: 72). Nature creates in parents an affection for their children; and this parental affection is the origin of the association of the human race in communities. Although some animals are able to do certain actions for the sake of others, with human beings this bond of mutual aid is far more intimate. Nature has endowed every species with the instinct of self-preservation. Therefore, nature, by the power of reason, associates man with man in the common bonds of speech and life. Nature also prompts men to meet in companies, form public assemblies, and take part in them (Finibus III.XIX.62–63, III.XX.65). To make social life possible, man—uniquely among all animals—has "a feeling for order, for propriety, for moderation in word and deed" (*De Officiis*, hereafter referred to as Officiis I.IV.11–14; cf. I.XVI.55; Legibus X.29–30; *On the Nature of Gods* I.121–22).

To safeguard the universal alliance, affection, friendship and solidarity cover all members of humankind. Because human nature is constituted to possess an innate element of civic and national feeling, solidarity comes into existence immediately upon birth, but its influence spreads beyond the home, "first by blood relationships, then by connections through marriage, later by friendships, afterwards by the bonds of neighborhood, then to fellow-citizens and political allies and friends, and lastly by embracing the whole of the human race" (Finibus III.XX.68–70, V.XXIII. 65–66).

Consequently, everyone ought to identify their interests with the interests of all others. Nature prescribes that every human must help every other human being, whoever he or she is precisely because he or she is a *human being* (Officiis III.IV.20–V.25). In fact, no one must do wrong to another human being. If such a basic moral norm is broken, human society—that is, social order—will soon collapse. Cicero gives human society the widest, universal meaning. Like Mo Zi, Cicero maintains that it is not acceptable to rob and kill strangers, if closer relatives are left in peace. One must reject violence not only towards compatriots but toward foreigners as well (Officiis III.V.26).[6]

THE TEMPLE-STATE AND THE EARLY CHURCH

Religion and religious myths were often the basis of political organizations in the ancient world. Both city-states and empires were often justified by religious doctrines. It was known that political arrangements might not be sufficient alone, no permanent and meaningful social order could be established through the use of mere force. Furthermore, it was also the case that political power and administrative systems were often required to strengthen the social effects of abstract divine and moral precepts.

In addition to this mutual interaction between religion and politics, a third expression of the relationship was well-known in the ancient Near East: the temple-state. The temple-state was a comprehensive social, religious, and especially political system. Like a conventional state, it defined and maintained the cultural, sociological, economical, political, and other bases of the society (Mack 1993: 65). However, the temple-state did not legitimize the king's powers (unless the king was simultaneously the religious leader, as the earliest kings usually were), but the political power of the priests, the clergy, or the church in general.

In the temple-state, the religious leader holds the true and final power. The priest or the church claims to be the embodiment of God's will and so demands unquestionable obedience from the subjects or members of the religious community. In a weaker version, the temple-state represents a sort of duality of power: the king and the religious leader appear and work simultaneously. The religious leader both justifies the king's power and claims a role for himself (cf. Dorraj 1990: 29). In the case of Judaism we encounter this dualistic system, which in early Christianity turns to an open challenge by the church to the state.[7]

Ancient Hebrew thought and practice gave the temple a central role. All that was thought about life, ethics, and human relations assumed the existence of a temple-state, and the perfect society was uncompromisingly based on the temple-state model. After the destruction of the first temple-state by Babylonia, the memory of this wisdom was kept alive by the religious leaders in Babylonian captivity (Mack 1993: 150).

When the long process of rebuilding a safe society was undertaken by Ezra and Nehemiah in the so-called restoration of Jerusalem, it was similarly thought that justification for political power had to be derived from the religious doctrine in order to make political power effective (Cohen 1975: 189–90).

However, the return to Jerusalem did not reestablish the original temple-state under the leadership of priest-kings like Saul and David. The community remained under a foreign rule; first Persian, and later Macedonian and Roman. The existing political machine belonged to and was fully controlled by foreign powers. The second temple-state had a subordinated or even supportive role beside the conventional state power. The central governments held the high priest and the council of elders responsible for the collection and rendering of the tribute, and the maintenance of order. Otherwise the foreign empires gave the Jews a large measure of autonomy in their own affairs and in religion (Moore 1954 II: 112).

The situation was rather complex. On one hand, the second temple-state remained rather weak compared to the first one. Due to continuing foreign occupations and shifting political alliances within the Jewish society, and between many Jews and foreign rulers, the second temple-state never achieved an undisputed role. In the political sense, the second temple-state never reached full maturity (Mack 1993: 171). However, the temple-state became a symbolic social tie connecting the Jews to the shared symbolic community. This, as well as the continuing Diaspora, caused a kind of bifurcation of religious and political powers, both of which had to be obeyed when a Jew lived in a foreign land as a guest. That is, Jewish law had to conform to the law of the state if possible without violating a basic principle of *torah* (Cohen 1975: 189–90).

In any case, distant foreign rule gave space for religious power structures. The high priests and the council of elders had great authority in the maintenance of order. In fact, the class of scribes emerged as the skilled and authorized interpreters of *torah*, and this became even greater in matters of the written word. Once *torah* was recognized as entirely authoritative, the prophet's leadership in matters of religion was replaced by that of the priests. The priests magnified their office and elaborated the system, which they administered. In the process, the old idea and practice of the kingdom of priests and a holy nation passed and what remained was a nation divided by a rigid caste system into priests, Levites, and Israelites.

The process continued after the fall of the second Temple. The Pharisees' successors, the Rabbis led by the patriarch, gained complete control within the Jewish community of Palestine (Batho 1945: 115; Blau 1966: 119–20; Neusner 1975: 48; Welch 1935: 286):

When setting forth its view of power—the legitimate use of violence—and the disposition of power in society, the *Mishnah*'s authorship describes matters in a fundamentally political manner, inventing a political structure and system integral to its plan for the social order. In the *Mishnah*'s system Israel forms a political entity, fully empowered in an entirely secular sense, just as Scripture describes matters. Political institution of the social order—king, priest, and court or civil administration—are assigned the right, each in its jurisdiction, to exercise violence here on earth, corresponding to, and shared with, the same empowerment accorded to institutions of Heaven. Moreover, these institutions are conceived to ration and rationalize the uses of that power permanently. The picture if this-worldly but because it does not distinguish crime from sin, it is not secular. . . . Among prior Judaisms only the scriptural system defined with the closure of the Pentateuch sets forth a politics at all. (Neusner 1992: 83)

In short, during the time of second Temple and to a great degree after that as well, the temple-state structure had strong power over the Jews. As far as the Jewish community was concerned, loyalty to both *torah* and the authority of its interpreters were the undisputed duty of the Jews. This produced a kind of conventional political structure by helping the priests maintain their political power as the masters of the temple-state rules. Later the experts of *torah* occupied the major positions of religious power and authority. The learned would not only teach *torah* but as judges apply it (Alexander 1984: 11; Moore 1954 I: 118–19; Moore 1954 II: 112–13). Such autonomous priestly rule was similar to conventional political power, well deserving a place in the present pattern of social order.

Due to the strong tradition of the temple-state model in the ancient Near East, and especially in Judea, it is logical to think that early Christians had a familiar model to follow. It would have not been outside their imagination to establish or reestablish a new temple-state: the church. However, such development was not inevitable, especially as far as conventional politics was concerned. In fact, Jesus had challenged both conventional political power and the temple-state, as well as conventional social structures in general. However, early Christians (from Jesus's original followers to members of the early church) were involved in politics, not in the alternative sense of Jesus's social radicalism, but in a more conventional sense of the use of power by the ruler over the ruled. That is, there was a widely shared view that early Christians and the early church made a clear-cut distinction between religion and politics; that they were not involved in the conventional, temporary political affairs, is completely wrong.

In fact, early Christians did not exclude conventional politics within their movement. Keeping in mind the openly political nature and the context of the early Christian texts from the *New Testament* to the early Christian writers (Ferguson 1977: 103; Stawell 1936: 40–41), early Christianity represents a consciously political activity, not only a religious innovation. It suggests a new, alternative, type of power structure as the substitute to the preceding, conventional state.

Early Christians challenged, but later reestablished, the Roman state, taking its enormous power into their own hands. They recognized that instead of abolishing the state it was more important to take care of the leader of that state: the leader had to be Christian. The religious alternative was not only able to win the conventional state but to survive as an important political and international actor to the present, and likely to the future as well. In fact, the political function of the church continued unchallenged until the Restoration. Therefore, it is fully justified to include early Christians and the early church as the exemplar of the present pattern of power-oriented social order.

The original Jesus movement was partly responsible for the final acceptance of conventional politics. Jesus's teachings were highly political, and his followers had to continue along the same lines. Unlike individual Cynics, they began forming social structures. According to Mack, signs of social formation can be detected even among the first layer of the Q Gospel. At the second stage of development (Q2), a heightened self-awareness about belonging to a movement is expressed by specific and explicitly argumented social rules required for the maintenance of the established group. At the third stage (Q3), after the Jewish War, the progress towards the organization continued and deepened. A new innovation was introduced by the story of the temptations of Jesus. It was shown that Jesus was the son of God, and that his power was related to neither the state nor the Temple (Mack 1993: 82, 121, 173; Luke 4: 6). Whatever the original purpose of the insert, it gave, or was used to give, the basis for further developments culminating in the establishment of the church.

An additional factor strengthened the change in this same direction. Instead of one Jesus movement there soon were several rival movements, especially after the Jewish War. The movements strongly disagreed on the content and interpretation of the original teachings. All groups tried to establish their own truths by suggesting original and authentic sayings, and later histories of Jesus. The result was a surprisingly rich literature: the three layers of Q, the *Gospel of Thomas*, the NT Gospels, and a high number of other Gospels, and other Bibles in general (Barnstone 1995; Mack 1993; Miller 1994). The historical context itself was fertile ground for the emergence of the rival movements and the rapidly expanding literature, and power struggles within and between movements. The turmoil of first-century Palestine was the setting in which the Christian movement began to grow, just like the turmoil that had been the setting for Jesus's teachings. Knowledge became power, and power struggles emerged both within and between the separate movements. Politicizing and politicking got key roles in the process, especially the use of Satan to represent one's enemies lent to the conflict a specific kind of moral and religious interpretation. Perhaps nowhere in history—either within or without the conventional state—can we find such a period of highly politicized development. Such a terrible and dangerous power struggle had to be stopped in order to save the movement. The single truth had to be established, as well as a single and powerful authority to decide on that truth. Therefore, the establishment of the church was both a logical consequence of earlier developments and the only solution to the problems caused by the religious hostilities within the expanding movement (Crossan 1994: 190–92; Mack 1993; Meyer 1992; Pagels 1995: xviii–xix; cf. Acts 15: 36–41; Gal 2: 11–14; Jam. 3: 1–8; Rom. 12: 10–21).

In the further development of early Christianity such needs were formulated as a new model of social order. In this new model social order was based on two major elements: God's Word and the well-organized church. Early Christians shared the idea that God's Word was able to provide a solid basis for human associations (cf. Mat. 18: 20; 22: 37–40; Luke 1: 33). However, they perceived that this basis to be strengthened by a new social organization, the church. In order to justify the existence and role of the church, the NT Gospels had to imagine a new type of Jesus and tell a narrative supporting the existence, role, and power of the church. Jesus's original teachings were used for that purpose. In fact, the NT Gospels cannot be read without keeping this function in mind (cf. Chapter 3).

Jesus and his teachings were made the cornerstone of the new power struggle. Farmer (1956: 198) maintained that Jesus had not placed his confidence in military power but in God who had promised to win and eliminate the enemy's forces. That is, the Gospels tell us that Jesus did not believe in traditional forms of resistance to Roman power. Instead, it was maintained that Jesus created a much more powerful and less vulnerable way of winning the real war over the minds of men. The purpose was to change the rules of the power struggle, the sword was replaced by the Word (Ferguson 1977: 100).

All of this had to be made open and explicit. It was made clear that Jesus participated in a down-to-earth power struggle where non-resistance was made the chosen weapon, an asset in making Christians unconquerable (Stawell 1936: 34; Farmer 1956: 188, 192, 200–201). Just like the ancient Chinese Daoists, or Socrates—and Jesus, of course—Christians saw that weapons can kill the body but they cannot kill ideas.

The *Old Testament*, as included in the Christian Bible, served the function of making the Word as powerful as possible. To that end, the *Old Testament* documents the power of God; indeed, his omnipotence. The task is to reveal the irresistible power of God and justify the demand for unquestioning submission to his will and power, as in the case of Job. But it was thought insufficient only to demand this unconditional submission and absolute faithfulness (Mat. 12: 30). The demand was made persuasive, constructive, and positive based on "grace and truth." (John 1: 17). Everybody, it was said, was able—of his or her own free will—to transcend all existing social distinctions and become one with other human beings through God (Mat. 16: 24).

Jesus's challenge to politics and the power structures of his time served well the ambitions of his later followers in establishing the church. It was shown that Jesus did not support conventional political power, but referred to the existence of a more important, the divine, ruler. God's rule was not based on force but "grace and truth" (John 1: 17). Jesus also demanded unconditional submission and absolute faithfulness to this authority (Mat. 12: 30; Mark 12: 31). After gaining acceptance of this message, another decisive movement had to be made—it had to be proved that the church was the single legitimate representative of God's power and authority.

Therefore, it had to be shown that Jesus founded the church and authorized its functions. In concrete terms, Mark (6: 7) introduced the twelve apostles, hinting that Jesus's community formed a New Israel in miniature, a new People of God with twelve new patriarchs to replace the twelve sons of Jacob from the *Old Testament*. Matthew's achievement carried the day for the emerging institution. Jesus was always acknowledged as the founder-teacher and thus the great shepherd of the church. Luke's task was to claim the church's rightful place in the Roman world, demonstrate that it was no threat to the Roman order, and make a case for its positive contributions to society (Crossan 1994: 108–9; Mack 1993: 185–86).

Furthermore, the church was required to strengthen the symbolic basis of the new community. The unity of the scattered Christian communities was made dependent on a common faith and a common way of ordering life and worship. Whatever differences there might have been in race, class, or education believers felt bound together by their loyalty to Jesus and his teaching. However, this soon had to be developed into a systematic pattern of rituals: the rite of baptism, the sharing of the sacred meal each Sunday, and so forth (Chadwick 1986: 32). It was witnessed, once again, that Jesus himself wished to give something more concrete than abstract words to make the human association as natural and permanent as possible, he had given rituals to repeat and thus connect men to each other. For example, when it was told that Jesus had taken five thousand men into the countryside, the story gave the audience a lesson in (and justification for) the new Christian community. The Word and the ritual were combined with, and strengthened by, a shared experience. Similarly, it was told that "Jesus took bread, and blessed it, and brake it, and gave it to the disciples, and said, Take, eat; this is my body " (Mat. 26: 26). Among the many convincing narratives, as Farmer (1956: 128 197–98; cf. Crossan 1994: 145, 160ff) suggests, "Jesus's crucifixion gave the most powerful unifying symbol for his followers: while Jesus's arrest scattered the disciples, the Cross began to draw them back together again."

When the idea of the church became generally shared, the new organization had to find specific roles or functions. These were found in the alternative ways of making politics and carrying out the power struggle with the Roman state. The NT Gospels and other early Christian writings repeated that Jesus had applied new rules for the power struggle, but had not remained outside it. Jesus hoped for power capable of replacing and overcoming any conventional political power, including arms. The NT Gospels suggested an alternative way of making politics,[8] but politics in the fundamental sense of challenging the Roman state was not rejected. The church, in fact, took the leadership in the campaign.

In this struggle, the church had to become a united entity. The social dimension of the ethical rules were applied to domestic relations within the new community of Christians. The Christians were to be unanimous and have compassion for one another (1 Pet. 3: 8–11; cf. Pomerius: 155).

Indeed, one of the most conspicuous features in early Christian writings is a concentration on the unity of the Catholic Church. Clement of Rome (pp. 23, 26–

29, 42–43, 50–51), for one, set the tone by referring to the "odious and unholy breach of unity," which must be "quite incompatible with God's chosen people." The writers emphasize the dangers of disunity, which they regard as even more dangerous than persecution. A divine solution to the problem of disunity is suggested time and time again: "In face of heresy and schism, we must recognize that Christ founded the Church on Peter" (Cyprian: 44). This solution made an indirect allusion to the sense of brotherhood, which had linked the early Christian communities together, not in order to reestablish the good old system but to pave the way for the new one (Staniforth 1984: 20–21).

Without going into any details of these well-known narratives on disunity, heresies, and the purists we simply look at the consequence: the increased unity and hierarchy of the church, increased secularization and hastening return to conventional politics (Adeney 1965, Chadwick 1986: 284ff.).

There is no need to suggest that the development was fully intentional, or that the early Christian leaders concentrated their full efforts on increasing their temporary political power. It is more likely that as human beings they felt the responsibility and duty to take the lead and work for the salvation of fellow-Christians. Explicit criticism, best represented by St. Gregory (pp. 21–22, 60; cf. Davis 1950: 4–5), was leveled against those who "aspire to glory and esteem by an outward show of authority within the holy Church." However, even St. Gregory sees that the pastor is called upon to rule. Therefore, he explicitly examines the qualities that are required in a ruler of men for "the government of souls is the art of arts!" St. Gregory's work makes Jesus's refusal of political power explicit, but makes the reasons for the return of politics not less so: "it is necessary that rulers should be feared by subjects, when they see that the latter do not fear God. Lacking fear of God's judgements, these must at least fear sin out of human respect."

Consequently, the Church, which had commenced as a simple brotherhood of Christians, had developed into a highly elaborate hierarchical organization. Genuine Christianity had degenerated into formal membership in the Catholic Church. This membership was secured by baptism, and continued subject to strict orthodoxy in belief and correctness of conduct. Early Christians had to share a fundamental point of departure. There was no recognition of a human being in isolation (Hegbin and Corrigan 1960: 9). It was suggested that the incarnation of God in the human nature of Christ is a union of God with the whole *corpus humanum*. Therefore, the Church soon obtained a magnificent weapon to deter anybody who in practice (sin) or in theoretical debate (heretical interpretations) challenged the role and power of the Church—excommunication. Jesus's message promised union for people across any distinctions—geographical, racial, political, economic, or social—and the Church made this union materialized with a practical and tangible system. The threat to withdraw future salvation was combined with a practical act of expulsion of a member of the new community. Consequently, the Church had become the community outside which there was no meaning for human life. In other words, originally a select community dedicated to a holy life, the Church had become a temporal power center that held authoritative and authoritarian power over its members. In fact, the Church was becoming a new center of social and political power, an alternative to the state.

It is clear that Christians tried to avoid open conflict with the Roman state as long as possible. The Christians took no part in the Jewish nationalists' revolt against the Romans. On the contrary, there were positive deliberations between the Christians and the Romans. Christians were originally treated favorably by the officials of the imperial government, and the NT Gospels make this clear (John 18: 33–38), even by showing that the Roman centurion "saw what was done" and "glorified God, saying, certainly this was a righteous man" (Luke 23: 47). Likewise, St. Paul writes respectfully of the law and authority of Rome, but the Acts already implied that the Empire, under the providence of God, could be an instrument for the furtherance of the Gospel. By the middle of the second century Christians were discerning the hand of God in the fact that Augustus had established the Pax Romana at the very time Christ's gospel of universal peace and goodwill was given to mankind. What was wrong with the state was its old city-religions of the home-gods perceived as paganism by the Christians: change its religion and all would be well. This line was later continued by St. Augustine, who in the *City of God* saw Rome as a vehicle ordained by Providence for the benefit of Christianity in relation to which she would have a new and enduring future (Adeney 1965: 16–17; Chadwick 1986: 24; O'Meara 1986: xxvi).

But the Christians knew that the final battle was still to come. To be as strong as possible they concentrated their efforts on strengthening the basis of their new community. The religious text came from and served this unique historical process. The elements discussed—the Word and the Church—had the function of providing a basis for a new community and making its continuous growth possible. With the resulting unity and hierarchization, the Christians were now ready for the final battle with the state. Justified by the doctrine, martyric death was made the ultimate weapon. It was believed that Roman power was not able to conquer those who were not afraid of death but, on the contrary, were willing to die for the justification of their doctrine.

Therefore, unlike the earlier military challenges to Rome—Macedonia, Carthage, and the Jewish rebels—the well-prepared final battle that waged through the new Christian faith was not hard to win. The persecutions actually raised the Church to the level of social power equal to, and finally above the state. Furthermore, the persecutions influenced the structure of the Church's membership, enhancing the Church's role in temporary politics. The religious idealists—those who perceived that with a growth in numbers, wealth, and general prosperity, the Church was losing its early purity and the fine, heroic enthusiasm of simpler times—were eager to grasp the martyr's crown by provoking the antagonism of the authorities. Consequently, the Church became a serious menace to the state, an *imperium in imperio*, the growth of which threatened to choke civil power.

The Church proved too strong for the state. Christianity became a popularly re-cognized religion. Persecution ceased in 311 and two years later Constantine went over to the winning side, the new (divine) and the old (political) power had become one. It was logical for Constantine to regard himself as a Christian whose imperial duty was to promote the unity of the Church (Chadwick 1986: 126–27).

This also revealed that Rome had not only been an object but a subject in the process. Roman rulers gradually confessed that they had to come to terms with the new power or it would make an end of Rome's: "if the Church conquered the Empire she herself was captured by her captive" (Stawell 1936: 40).

The result was no surprise. Christianity was related to, even indebted to, the Roman Empire. Christianity came to govern and extend the Roman Empire, not to destroy it. As Adeney (1965: 5–6) pointed out, success was based on the existence of the Roman power, and finally led to the adoption of that power back into the Church. The Pax Romana gave the first missionaries the freedom to travel and admitted to an attentive hearing wherever they went. They everywhere appeared as subjects of the vast empire preaching to fellow-subjects of the same empire. They were protected by the strong, just Roman magistracy, and they could travel with ease and safety along the Roman roads. Provincialism was disappearing before expanding cosmopolitan ideas, and in this atmosphere a gospel that overstepped the bounds of national jealousies might most likely receive sympathetic attention. Gradually the genius of Rome in government passed over from the Empire to the Church, and popes came in for the inheritance of the power that had dropped from the enfeebled hands of emperors. In this process the original pacifism of Jesus's teachings had no more practical value. The Church had to dismiss pacifism in order to become a real power in real social life. The Church had conquered the state but simultaneously become a quasi-state itself. Christians' attitudes towards the state had changed. The state had become able to serve the partnership between God and man, therefore both the Church and the state would coexist.

I have emphasized the development towards the increasing power and unity of the Church. This may look like a one-sided picture, for there was a division of Christians into separate churches quite early. According to Adeney (1965: 292ff.), the causes of fragmentation were partly racial and political, partly doctrinal and polemical. The doctrinal and polemical causes of separation were likely more effectual, especially when the Christological controversies combined with national and racial influences to aggravate and perpetuate the severance. But nothing in this more complicated picture requires a change in my interpretation. On the contrary, this development corroborates the suggested picture: the Roman Catholic Church becomes a new center of power and adopts the political functions of the state. The national reaction further combines religious ideas with political ambitions, therefore making the return of politics—in disguise—unavoidable.

The life after the state's death was formulated in terms favorable to the power of the Church, and especially to the power of the Christian rulers of the new state. The idea of hierarchical power, now well-established within the Church, was generalized and extended beyond the walls of the Church. It was now taught that the good Christian had to fear God and honor the king as well: "Servants, be subject to your masters with all fear; not only to the good and gentle, but also to the froward" (1 Pet. 2: 17–18; 1 Cor. 7: 17–24). The change from absolute pacifism to the justification of inevitable violence, and the return to more conventional politics in general, was a logical conclusion:

Let every soul be subject unto the higher power. For there is no power but of God: the powers that be are ordained of God. Whosoever therefore resisteth the power, resisteth the ordinance of God: and they that resist shall receive to themselves damnation. For rulers are not a terror to good works, but to the evil. . . . For he is the minister of God to thee for good . . . for he beareth not the sword in vain: for he is the minister of God, a revenger to execute wrath upon him that doeth evil. (Rom. 13: 1–4; cf. Col. 7: 26–31)

Finally, later historical developments corroborated the Church's new political role. When the Germanic invasions produced chaos in the West, and when the Roman political system was rapidly collapsing, the task of organizing local resistance fell to the bishops. At first, they did not hesitate to use overt armed violence, but when it was found that the invaders had come to stay, the Church slowly took up the task of integrating them into the existing religious power structure. This attempt was as successful as it had been earlier with the Romans (Chadwick 1986: 248).

NOTES

1. Mohism does not speak of cities in the Greek sense of the sacred area where the elders live (Fustel de Coulanges 1920). In Mohism, the city is a secularized concept.

2. Let us note that Plato's idea is much more practical than the castes system in ancient India. Furthermore, Plato's division of labor takes place in the state under the wise king and laws, it was not an alternative to the state.

3. It is not impossible to imagine that for Aristotle the best state was Macedonia (cf. Kelsen 1977).

4. There were three stages of the Stoic school. The Early Stoa appeared between Alexander the Great and the victory of the Roman power and consisted of several thinkers from various parts of the Mediterranean world, with Zeno (336/5–264/3 B.C.E.) as the leading figure. The Middle Stoa (especially Panaetius, 180–110 B.C.E., and Posidonius, 135–51 B.C.E.) made the eclectic Stoicism known in Rome, but M. Terentius Varro (116–27 B.C.E.) and M. Tullius Cicero (106–43 B.C.E.) were the leading Roman Eclectics. The Late Stoa during the first and second centuries (C.E.) consisted of Seneca, Epictetus, and Marcus Aurelius (Tenkku 1981: 127, 139, 146).

5. However, Zeno never did deny that he was a citizen of Citium. On the contrary, he emphasized that fact (Diogenes Laertius VII.12).

6. Cicero writes: "The existence of this natural bond of community between all human beings explains why our ancestors chose to make a distinction between the civil law of the land and the universal law. The law of the land, it is true, ought to be capable of inclusion within the universal law, but they are not synonymous since the latter is more comprehensive" (Officiis III.XVI.68). *Ius gentium*, the law of nations, was considered part of the laws of all civilized people—the sense of "law governing the relations between states" did not exist in antiquity. These rules were applicable to citizens and non-citizens alike. They were explained as being dictated by all men, so that *ius gentium* was often identified with natural law. Arnold (1911: 384–85) suggests that the fundamental ideas expressed by such terms as *ius gentium* and *lex naturae*, are not exclusively Stoic in origin. The former phrase was in common use to indicate the laws generally in force among the peoples that surrounded Rome; the latter is a philosophical term derived from the Greek, denoting an ideal law which ought to exist among men everywhere. The principle of obedience to nature is not peculiar to the Stoic philosophy, but belongs to the common substratum of all philosophical thought.

7. I have earlier discussed the case of the early Church in Harle (1989a).

8. It is interesting to note that Greek Stoicism was able to become Roman Stoicism more than two centuries before Christianity penetrated into Rome. Christianity applied strategy similar

to that of Stoicism in conquering Rome—and with surprisingly similar consequences for its own development (cf. Stawell 1936).

CHAPTER 8

The Wise King as the Basis of Social Order

Excluding Chinese Legalism as the only pure exception, the idea of the wise ruler is found in all the power-oriented patterns of social order. In fact, ancient Indian political thought, Zoroastrianism, and Judaism also imply (or suggest) the same idea. The idea of the wise king claims that there is, or should be, a single ruler,[1] often with the capacities of the sage, the wise man, or the philosopher. Such an idea appears in political theories involving either small sovereign units or a world community. Therefore, this approach is represented by Mo Zi and Plato on the one hand, and by Confucians, Aristotle, the Roman authors, and the temple-state theorists on the other.[2]

It is almost impossible to discuss the idea of the wise king and his education separately, but I will attempt both. Analytically and practically, the wise king and his moral or political education can appear independently of each other. The wise king may be a "given," or mythical figure, and education can be given to any citizens. In this book, however, it is normally education that makes the king wise.

THE WISE KING IN THEORIES OF SOVEREIGN TERRITORIAL STATES

Mo Zi only briefly discusses the nature of the ruler. He simply suggests that people follow the example given by the ruler. Therefore, Mo believes that the ruler must be wise and must fully understand his position. This implies a rather authoritarian position similar to Confucianism.

Plato does not take the king as given but seems to have a practical point of departure. One can accept the post of king not because of a will to power but because of punishment caused by his abstention—the punishment of getting under the rule of less wise men. In order to avoid such a punishment, a kingship must be based on reason and self-restraint. The wise king is an extension of the individual's reason and self-restraint. The final definition of reason is related to a consensus on who has the right to rule. That is, if reason prevails, the worse and the better will agree (voluntarily and in harmony) on which one must rule within the individual and the state (*Republic* 347a–c, 427e–429; Tenkku 1981).

We have already seen (Section 7.1) that the state, for Plato, is a moral entity, the cause and basis of everything is reason. Because reason causes everything, it brings about order and arranges all things best (*Phaedo* 97c–e; cf. *Philebus* 28c, 28e). Consequently, reason is the basis of both society and social order. Therefore, order can be made of chaos if reason rules the state. This implies and demands an ideal ruler, the idea discussed by Plato in the *Republic*, the *Statesman*, and the *Laws*. Plato suggests that a man who understands righteousness will maintain order in society. Therefore, while reason must be extended to all citizens in the state—for wise rule is not the king's exclusive right or responsibility—Plato's theory ends in finding the wise king to rule over the other citizens (*Republic* 428e–429a; *Letters* VII, VIII; Tenkku 1981).

Plato's point of departure is that self-government is the most important goal in reestablishing order. Instead of punishing others, one must learn to restrain oneself. In the seventh *Letter* Plato maintains that civil war can only be stopped by the ruler who is both superior at controlling his desires and more willing than anybody else to subject himself to the law (*Letters* VII.330–33, 337).

Self-restraint is the precondition to moral right, to citizenship, which is based on right-mindedness, deliberation, and piety. These attributes are based on wisdom and reason. Mere knowledge of facts is not enough, virtue and self-restraint are the major elements of wisdom. Wisdom requires that one must not give too much thought to money-making and wealth. According to Plato the soul, the body, and wealth are all separate. When arranged in their proper order, the highest honor is paid to excellence of the soul. The third position (and lowest status) is given to wealth, which should be the servant of the body and the soul (*Letters* VIII.355). The moral maxim is: nothing to excess. One must be satisfied with what one has, for "the half is often greater than the whole" (*Laws* 690e; Tenkku 1981).

In an orderly society younger members do not attack elders because of shame and fear. Shame prevents a son from attacking his father. Furthermore, a potential attacker fears that there are other persons—sons, brothers, or fathers—who will come to the aid of the victim. Conscience, justice, shame, and fear must be distributed widely throughout society. If only a few members have these attributes, there is no society at all. However, a high number of moral individuals is not enough to create an orderly state. In addition, reason—order, the restraint of pleasures and desires—should rule the state in order to maintain harmony between all citizens, between the weak, the strong, and average men (*Protagoras* 322d–323a; *Republic* 431a–432c, 565a–b). Such reason cannot exist without the wise ruler.

According to Plato, it is in accordance with reason that parents rule over their children, the higher born over the lower born, elders over youths, masters over slaves, the strong over the weak, the wise over the less wise. In other words, the state will be wise only to the extent that its smallest—the governing—segment is wise. The number of rulers must remain small because ruling is based on knowledge and wisdom. Nature has limited, Plato argues, the number of those who share the knowledge called wisdom (*Republic* 520d; cf. 347a–d).

According to Plato, the best state is the state whose ruler is the least willing to rule. That is, such a ruler does not use power for his own interests, but recognizes the common interest (*Republic* 520d; cf. 347a–d). Therefore, those who have shown excellence in war *and* philosophy must be elected rulers (*Republic* 543a). In the final analysis, the only remedy for difficulties is the combination of political power and philosophy located in the same person (Hamilton 1985: 111). Justifying his argument by historical and personal experiences in the well-known failures of all earlier or existing governments, Plato concludes that "the troubles of mankind will never cease until either true and genuine philosophers attain political power or the rulers of states by some dispensation of providence become genuine philosophers" (*Letters* VII.326).

However, the philosopher-king's power cannot be left uncontrolled (Hamilton 1985: 151), for absolute power is dangerous for both the ruler and the ruled (*Letters* VII.334). This emphasis on the importance of the rule of law is fully in harmony with the view that a perfectly wise ruler who would dispense with constitutional restraints is a contradiction in terms. A code of laws is an essential part of the king's wisdom (Hamilton 1985: 115).

According to Plato, the purpose of law is to complement and execute self-restraint. It is better to have control through laws than to have full and unlimited freedom. The necessity to submit to laws is required especially when external enemies threaten the state, but submission to laws is a general rule. The rule of laws implies a situation where the people are not in control of laws, but live in a kind of voluntary slavery to them (*Laws* III.700). The law obtains the status of wisdom, even the status of a god. The law is the wise man's only god (*Letters* VIII.354).

THE WISE KING IN THEORIES OF WORLD COMMUNITY

Both the *Mahabharata* and the *Ramayana* emphasize, like ancient Hindu thought in general (Chapter 4), that the king is a crucial figure in maintaining the harmonious realm of *dharma,* that is, social and moral obligations. The *Mahabharata* and the *Ramayana* rarely question the ultimate good involved in the preservation and refinement of the social order and the rituals and religious practices that insure it. In the *Mahabharata* the role of the wise king belongs to Yudhishthira, however he is not praised as an individual but the incarnation of *dharma.* Rama, the hero of the *Ramayana,* is much more an individual, an exemplar of the wise king. Therefore, the idea of the wise king in ancient Hindu thought can be best illustrated by him.

In the Hindu tradition, Rama soon became the archetype of the ideal king. To this day Hindus fondly recall an idealized past by referring to the Rule of Rama (Kinsley 1982: 15, 27). The ancient Hindus generally appreciated the elevating influences of a great man. They not only honored their national heroes but extolled them into divinity. A deep, religious reverence was felt for the character of a man who was an ideal king, an ideal son, an ideal man, an ideal brother, an ideal friend, a devoted husband, a valiant soldier, and above all, a lover of humanity and truth (Sen 1964: ii). The *Ramayana* is written in this light, and Rama is not respected due to his military achievements—which are imagined rather than real—but because of his special character as the king. Rama's personality is highly praised:

The highly beautiful and mighty Rama is supremely intelligent, and of eloquent speech. He is upright, true to his vows, modest and observer of laws. His character is highly pure. He is famous, wise and possesses the knowledge of self. He is the protector of all, defender of religion and caste-system. He is supporter of his kinsmen and friends . . . he is the supporter of all, and the destroyer of his enemies. He always gives shelter to his devoted followers. He is deeply versed in the Vedas and Vedandas. He is highly skilled in archery, and his valor is admitted by his dying foes. He has great fortitude. He is a genius and possesses excellent memory and is profoundly learned in all the sacred lore. He is wise, compassionate and valiant. (*Ramayana* I: 2)

The *Ramayana* (I:8–9, 18) also makes it clear that Rama is the exemplar of the wise king and good government in general, in the future tense:

During his reign his subjects will not suffer from any disease or mental disquietude; they will have no fear of hunger or of thieves; cities will be full of corns and wealth; and the people will live as happily as in the Golden Age. No fire or flood will devastate the land, and women will ever continue to be chaste and they will not suffer from widowhood. He will perform hundred horse sacrifices, give away millions of cows and immense wealth to the famous Brahmins. He will make each of the four castes stick to its own duties.

It is not the person, but the system which is the real thing. "Rama is neither wicked nor stupid, nor under the sway of his senses" and "falsehood never attaches to him." Rama is virtue personified and devoted to truth. Therefore, "as Indra is the king of gods, so he is the king of all." Furthermore, the evil king, Ravana, is established as Rama's opponent. The epics tell Ravana that "a king who is wicked and wileful like you, soon meets with his end and with his kingdom, friends and relations" (*Ramayana* I: 385). Therefore, however great Rama's personal merits, he is not appreciated for them alone. His perfect character is required in order to carry out a great task. A central concern of the epics was to portray Rama as the ideal king who both illustrates and protects *dharma* (Kinsley 1982: 27).

As Kinsley correctly claims, it is Rama's ability to do the right thing in conflicts between contrasting responsibilities, and his ability to perceive a transcendent realm of order that impinges on the social order that make him a great king. Two famous key episodes in the *Ramayana* illustrate the general political aspect of Rama's character: (1) his unquestioned obedience to his father when asked to undertake a fourteen-year exile; and (2) the abandonment of his wife, Sita, in order to stop the gossip of his subjects concerning her chastity while under Ravana's control. Rama had the ability to discern that society is founded on the proper ordering of relations between relatives and citizens and understood that social order can never be simply imposed by laws and punishment, but must flow naturally from the example of the king and his family. The king must provide an example of social order—Rama's exemplary character as king is called into question because of Sita's abduction. Rama demonstrates his proper understanding of the king's role. Social order and the welfare of citizens are foremost; personal happiness and pleasure are secondary. By abandoning Sita, Rama subordinates his personal happiness to the welfare of his people and the orderliness of his kingdom (Kinsley 1982: 27–30). Kinsley (p. 30) ends his pointed analysis of the epics with the following:

To modern readers, Rama may appear inhuman. . . . He may seem to lack individuality. Precisely in this respect, however, he is a model of Hindu dharma. What is crucial in the Hindu vision of the ideal society is the proper definition and functioning of various social roles in relation to each other. An individual *is* his role, as it were, and that role only has significance vis-a-vis other roles in society.

Buddhism fully shared the idea of the wise king. However, the king did not have an explicit responsibility to maintain the caste system, but was more a kshatriya commanding the state and society as a true political leader. Therefore, Buddhism placed the major emphasis on the character of the king, very much like Plato. Indeed, in the Buddha's case reason and self-restraint came from the experiences and traditions of society where all free men were kings or were called kings. In any case, the Buddha himself, and especially his followers, later seemed to think that kingship (i.e., political leadership) was a social necessity for creating order without which no religion might exist. Therefore, it was important that the ruler be a wise king, preferably a Buddhist.

The Buddhist king Ashoka has a central place in the Buddhist doctrine. Ashoka's own edicts reveal the Buddhist logic most openly. Ashoka tells about his military achievements and extreme, even exaggerated cruelty in expanding his kingdom all over India, and praises his consequent Buddhist achievements after his religious awakening. Hirakawa illustrates: "Ashoka led a violent life as a youth and was responsible for the deaths of many people. Later he converted to Buddhism and ruled benevolently." In another similarly revealing sentence he states that after his cruel wars, Ashoka "came to believe that war was wrong, that the only real victory was one based on the truths of Buddhist teachings, not one based on force and violence" (Hirakawa 1990: 96). The suggested model depicts its true political meaning, and reveals the nature of Buddhist political doctrine, when it is recognized that after conquering the world it is not only easy to become a benevolent ruler, it is also a necessity in order to maintain power. However, Ashoka was less successful in this than the Roman Augustus.

In his political theory, Kong Zi gave the major emphasis to the wise ruler, the philosopher-king, usually rendered in English as the sage. The Confucian school maintained that it is not sufficient to teach proper manners to subjects so that they respect the ruler. It is more important that the character of the ruler be perfect, because it is his nature which defines how he will exercise his power. Two major arguments justify the role of the ruler: (1) his function in maintaining order,[3] and (2) the problem of man's nature. Both provide the basis for a certain conservatism imbedded in the Confucian philosophy.

The king's function in maintaining order requires that the wise ruler take care of the common people. He must maintain virtue, for the rule of virtue commands the multitude of people by giving them a solid standard for all social activities (*Analects* II.1, II.2).[4] While the ruler can apply edicts and punishments in order to keep the common people out of trouble or without a sense of shame, it is better to guide them by virtue because then they will have both a sense of shame and a standard for reforming themselves (*Analects* II.3). However, as Xun Zi says in explicit terms, good laws do not prevent disorder, while the wise king always does (Hsün Tzu/Watson: 35).

This focus on the ruler is, according to Confucian political theory, a convenient reduction of the complexity of human behavior which makes it possible to ignore the nature of individuals. Confucians, and Xun Zi in particular, wish to say that even if the common man is evil, the ruler must be good. According to Xun Zi, the government and rulers are required to make life and order possible in spite of the evil nature of ordinary man. The wise king can only establish "ritual principles" required for curbing and training man's desires, and ultimately satisfy them (Hsün Tzu/ Watson: 89).

The argument of human nature is central in Chinese political theory. The various concepts of human nature have different implications for politics. Confucianism implied that "it is man that makes truth great but not truth that makes man great," and although good men can make good laws, laws alone cannot operate themselves (Chan 1960: 158). Therefore, while Confucianism maintained that men should return to the original religious basis of political power, to the comprehensive code of rituals (*li*), or to the five types of social relations, it suggested that man can follow these rules voluntarily because he is, by nature, good. Or more exactly, man can be educated to become good and wise, even to become the sage.

The emergence of man as the most important being took place early in Chinese philosophy, probably even before Kong Zi (551–479 B.C.E.). Originally the major emphasis lay with the spirits and gods. During the Zhou dynasty, due to the breaking up of traditional society and the disappearance of its religious basis, it was suggested that the spirits be kept at a distance. This gave the fundamental moral responsibility to the individual—the individual became responsible for his life and fate. The new emphasis was now on man and his virtue (*te*). The change implied that the destiny of man, or that of a government, no longer depended on the pleasure of the gods or the spirits, but on man himself (Chan 1960: 161–62).

When the old social order began to crumble, individual merit played a greater and greater role. The result expressed itself as humanism, which was mainly represented by Kong Zi and his followers. This mode of thinking suggested that the gods' rewards and punishments depended on whether man obeyed or violated moral principles (*dao*), i.e., through his moral acts man could now control his own destiny. The important basic question emerged as to whether man by nature is capable of accepting this moral responsibility. This raised the key question in the history of Chinese thought: "What is the nature of man? Is he good or bad?" (Chan 1960: 162).

According to Chan (1960: 162, 170ff), the fundamental belief in Chinese thought was that human nature is basically good. However, a number of divergent points of view appeared, some of which even denied the original goodness of man. According to Chan, during the Later Zhou period human nature was considered either originally good (Meng Zi) or originally evil (Xun Zi, and the Legalist thinkers). In addition, there was the doctrine of neutral human nature advanced by Mo Zi.

Kong Zi has been identified as the first Chinese thinker to have formulated a definite proposition regarding human nature. However, he only said that in their original nature people are similar, but through practice they become different from each other, and that only the most intelligent and the most stupid do never change (*Analects* 17.2–3). Therefore, it is obvious that Kong Zi does not advocate the notion that human nature is originally good; he was not interested in the metaphysical problem of what human nature is, but in the practice of learning. In other words, he was interested in molding human nature in order to have men with ability to understand and follow the ancient rules of behavior. Kong Zi was first and foremost an educator (Chan 1960: 166).

A variety of doctrines of human nature were espoused in the period from Kong Zi to Meng Zi. Consequently, Meng Zi felt it necessary to say something more explicit on the question. The doctrine of man's original goodness was introduced by Meng Zi, but his conception did not become orthodox until the neo-Confucianists of the eleventh century advocated and elaborated it (Chan 1960: 166–67).

Meng Zi criticized a contending theory, according to which human nature does not show any preference for either good or bad.[5] He maintained that good human nature is an absolute fact, as natural as all other natural phenomena (*Mencius* VI.A.2). He also suggested that the distinction between man and animal is caused by the fundamental difference in their natures. The central difference between the two lies in the fact that while man is a moral being, animals are not (*Mencius* VI.A.3; cf. Chan 1960: 193; Chan 1963). This can be applied as the definition of man. The *Li Ki* (I.I.I.5/22) maintains that the sages framed the rules of propriety in order to teach men, with their help, to make a distinction between themselves and animals. According to Xun Zi, to pursue learning is to be a man, but to give it up is to become a beast (Hsün Tzu/Watson: 19). Meng Zi emphasized that unless man can distinguish between right and wrong, he is not a man (*Mencius* II.A.6).

What are the attributes of the ideal ruler, the sage? First, he is an extraordinary figure because it is extremely difficult to become a sage. Kong Zi emphasized that he had no hopes of becoming or even meeting a sage. He wrote that he would have been happy to meet a "gentleman" (*Analects* VII.26).

The sage is someone who serves the people. Kong Zi said that a man who helps the common people must not be called benevolent but a sage (*Analects* VI.30). Another type of definition, not contradictory but complementing to the first, is related to learning and teaching. According to Meng Zi (*Mencius* II.A.2) Kong Zi never called himself a sage, but defined himself as a scholar who never tired of learning and teaching. This implies that a sage is somebody who does not "learn" or "teach" any more. A sage has achieved the ultimate knowledge and teaches only through his example, not only his contemporaries but all future generations, too (*Analects* VII.B.14).

The leading characteristic of the ruler is his benevolence, which is directly derived from *dao*, and implies the fulfillment of its demands. Therefore, the ruler had to be benevolent in a special way. The sage was not able to please every individual separately, but he had to create a good government for all in order to maintain *dao*, order (*Analects* IV.8; *Mencius* IV.B.2).

Benevolence is not a question of profits, but is instead an intrinsic moral virtue. Benevolence will make the ruler free from evil. In other words, the gentleman is not invariably for or against something, he is on the side of what is moral (*Analects* IV.2, IV.4, IV.25).

Meng Zi (*Mencius* III.B.3) adds that the wise ruler dislikes the pursuit of power by dishonorable means. There cannot be a true king without benevolence. By forsaking benevolence, no ruler can make himself famous. Therefore the ruler, the gentleman, never deserts benevolence. Everything he does must be in the name of benevolence. According to Kong Zi, there is no point in campaigning for anything that is not benevolent. If the ruler is not benevolent, good rites and proper music do not help. An evil king cannot pursue benevolent policy (*Analects* III.3, IV.5). In fact, the ruler can become a true king, a sage, only by practicing benevolent government. Such a ruler can never be stopped from maintaining order (*Mencius* II.A.1). In fact, under a benevolent government all members of the society are prepared to die for the superiors (*Mencius* I.B.12, IV.A.9, IV.B.3, 5).

In an administration the benevolent ruler takes care of order. The ruler can achieve reverence from his subjects if he provides peace and security. This is a challenging task, which even the mythic sages (Yao and Shun) found demanding. The most important task is the establishment of correct, unambiguous language, "the rectification of names" (*Analects* XIII.3, XIV.42). Consequently, Kong Zi (*Analects* XII.17) said that "to govern is to correct." According to Lau (1982: 115) the concepts "govern" and "correct" in Chinese are written similarly (*cheng*) thus showing their relation to one another.

As mentioned, the existence of the state is based on the trust the common people feel towards their ruler. They must accept biological facts (e.g., death) but without trust, "the common people will have nothing to stand on" (*Analects* XII.7). This theory reflects harmony between the ruler and the subject (*Mencius* I.B.4).

The ruler must guide his subjects by always considering their natural tendencies, which makes it easy to rule even an empire (*Mencius* II.A.6, IV.B.26). The ruler must encourage people to work hard by setting an example. In addition, the ruler must show leniency towards minor offenders and promote men of talent (*Analects* XIII.1–2).

This harmonious relationship between the ruler and his subjects is just another way to emphasize the function of the ruler in the service of the subjects' basic interests in accordance with *dao*. Misrule had to be excluded because "there is no difference between killing somebody with a knife and killing him with misrule" (*Mencius* I.A.49). In short, the benevolent ruler is responsible for the life and happiness of his people (*Mencius* I.A.3).

The wise king can expect solid results, especially under foreign threat. Under attack the ruler must be sure that his subjects would rather die than desert him (*Mencius* I.B.13). Force can be applied to submit only those who are not strong enough to oppose the attempt, whereas the transforming influence of morality makes people submit to power sincerely with admiration in their hearts (*Mencius* II.A.3).

When Aristotle suggested the world state idea, he thought that its government must be given to an individual king. If it cannot be accepted that all must fight against all, one or a limited number of men must govern and all others must be ruled. Aristotle had a preference for the wise king and for kingship, a position that strongly deviated from the prevailing views in Athens. Aristotle maintained that the monarchy was useful from the point of view of the subjects, while tyranny was useful only for the ruler. The same holds true, *mutatis mutandis*, for aristocracy and oligarchy, timocracy and democracy. The best constitution takes the advantage of the ruled into full consideration. Consequently, each of the three forms of constitutional rule can be best applied in varying situations.

Aristotle rejected the typical Athenian idea that the monarchy is appropriate to barbarians. Aristotle's ideal is hereditary monarchy: "good man" and "good citizen" can be combined only in the king, not in the individual citizen. While Aristotle seems to be speaking of any citizen, he actually is discussing the wise ruler. For him, no citizen can exist without the wisdom of the king. Aristotle emphasizes that only in a monarchy is there room for such a king, while in a democracy there is no room for good men. The same idea, similarly implied but not expressed in open terms, is repeated in the case of Cicero (Defourny, P. 1977; Kelsen 1977).

For Aristotle, man is by nature a political animal. This means that men have a desire to live together, even when they have no need to seek each other's help (*Politics* 127b15). Therefore, social order can be based on this nature of men. But while the social nature of man is his point of departure, Aristotle's emphasis lies on the social dimension.

To begin with, man has reason, given to him by nature. Indeed, in the final analysis, the *zoon politikon* means that there is a distinction between man and animal: man can speak. Through speech man can express pleasure and displeasure, appropriate and inappropriate, right and wrong. Indeed, it is his ability to distinguish between good and evil, right and wrong, that distinguishes man from animal. The message in the idea of the *zoon politikon* is that there is no human life outside society. Personal (or individual) and societal belong together. An individual human being can not develop to full perfection outside society. Only in society can man realize his final goal—happiness.

But while man needs to, and is able to, live socially, Aristotle does not suggest that human nature is by nature good. Precisely to the contrary, he emphasizes that men like flattery do everything for their own sake. In fact, self-affection is natural (*Ethics* 1159a, 1168a; *Politics* 1263a40).

According to Aristotle, pleasures are typical to individuals and, therefore, many go astray in excess. However, such natural selfishness and social life are not in contradiction to each other. Self-love is given by nature and therefore it must be the precondition for social life. But to make this possible, man must try to profit himself by performing noble acts that benefit others. On the other hand, the wicked man, in following his evil passions, will not harm his neighbors but only himself (*Ethics* 1118b, 1169a).

In other words, one form of selfishness is accepted, but another is not. Aristotle does not condemn the fact that one is fond of oneself, but he maintains that one must not be excessively so (*Politics* 1263a40).

This leads to an important element in Aristotle's political thought. The avoidance of excess and the emphasis on the mean. According to Aristotle, human nature is inclined to choose the mean, to aim at the mean and reasonableness (*Ethics* 1176a). The mean implies that virtue, as moral virtue, is a central element in establishing social order. Excess and deficiency are deviations from virtue, whereas the mean corresponds with virtue. Aristotle defines moral virtue as "a disposition to choose the mean." Thus, virtue is a disposition to make a preferential choice on the basis of the mean between two vices, one arising from excess and the other from defect. Furthermore, virtue is a mean because it both finds and chooses the intermediate. Virtue is uncompromising, and prefers only the "extreme mean" (*Ethics* 1105b–1109a).

What is moral virtue? Aristotle lists three things that occur in the soul: feelings, faculties, and dispositions. He maintains that because virtues are neither feelings nor faculties, they must be dispositions, that is, states of character. True moral virtue directs man to do morally virtuous deeds, and man will do them voluntarily in the name of the right rule (*Ethics* 1105b–1106a; *Politics* 1114b26). Therefore, Aristotle does not accept the role of shame in the maintenance of order, for shame is more a feeling than a moral disposition. Shame implies fear of dishonor, something similar to fear of danger. Both fears are physical conditions and, therefore, cannot form a basis for moral deeds (*Ethics* 1128b).

Morality or virtue are important to individuals, and morally developed individuals are important to an orderly society. However, orderly social relations presuppose other elements. Among these elements, friendship is one of the most decisive factors. Friendship is a major bridge between individuals—it is living together and partnership. Due to its social role, friendship is a necessary ingredient of meaningful life. Friends, rather than money, make life worth of living. Friendship, then, must be based on virtues. While selfishness and self-love can be a basis for friendship, Aristotle suggests that it is better to give than to receive. In friendship, the altruistic element is definitely present—a man wishes his friends well for their own sake, not because of their utility to him. This does not imply an unrealistic idealism. Aristotle puts forward the view that friendship is ultimately based on a good man's love for himself. Friendship is based on mutuality, but can appear between unequals. True friendship can not be extended beyond a limited number of people, and it is never based on flattery (*Ethics*: xv; 1155a, 1158a–b, 1171b, 1173b).

While friendship delivers morality and virtue to social relations, it does not create a permanent relationship. Friendship can be given up at any moment (*Ethics* 1165b). Friendship creates human associations, but such associations are more important than friendship. Therefore, more permanent, that is, political associations are required. Associations established by friendship can provide a basis for political associations, and they give the experience and knowledge required for the establishment of the political group. In fact, all social associations, including friendship, are predecessors or models for the political group.

The political group, like friendship, is formed for the sake of mutual advantage. However, friendship generally appears between two persons, while the political group joins several persons. To have more general value, the political group must be just, that is, it must benefit the whole community. Furthermore, this benefit must be general not specific. A political group that is just and pursues the most general benefit can be called the state. Below the state we find other associations which seek some advantage such as a ship's crew or fellow soldiers (*Ethics* 1160a).

While we have achieved the highest level of political associations, the state, additional elements are still required in order to achieve a political society.[6] Political society cannot be founded on morality, virtue, friendship, and common interests only. Order must be established consciously, and it must be supported by law. Aristotle maintains that law can be found everywhere, even outside the Greek community. Law is, by nature, a general phenomenon (*Politics* 1285a29).

Aristotle derives the idea of legal order from the moral nature of man. The purpose of life can only be found in man—man's task is to become perfect. Therefore, man must have full sovereignty over himself. Only citizens can follow the law and rule over themselves. By submitting voluntarily to law, in the creation and implementation of which he takes part, the citizen connects his individual deliberations and virtue to the totality, the state.

The law requires positive and negative sanctions, i.e., the use of power and force. This cannot happen without the existence and influence of the state. The birth, the functions and the means of legitimizing the existence of the state occupy a central place in establishing and maintaining order.

The state is a human association created for a specific but comprehensive purpose—namely, good. In other words, the state emerges as the natural end and culmination of other and earlier, similarly natural, associations. The basic form of human association is family. Above the family we find a village, which is the first association established for the satisfaction of something more than daily needs. Finally, the state emerges in order to guarantee the final goal of the process—self-sufficiency, which guarantees not only life itself but the good life (*Politics* 1252a1, 1252a24, 1252b15, 1252b27; *Politics* I.ii).

While all this points to the individual, or the citizen, we can see that Aristotle was more interested in the ruler. We can interject the ruler into the picture by recognizing that the state, which has a central place in Aristotle's ideas, forms a bridge between the citizen and the ruler. For Aristotle, the existence and nature of the state implies the best and most efficient control of violence. Such a control is only possible within the state. Relations between the states remain in state of war (*Politics* 1253a29). In order to stop this terrible war between the Greek city-states, the pan-Hellenist state must be established and then ruled by the wise king.

This emphasis on the state is Aristotle's invitation to the wise king. Because the state now exists, not all men need be virtuous—nor is wisdom required from all men. It is more important and practically possible that the ruler is sound, good, and wise (*Politics* 1276b35). In other words, Aristotle does not pay much attention to the issue of human nature, but walks a rather long road of morality, virtue, friendship, and social associations. With the help of the idea of the state as political association, he reaches the conclusion of the wise king. The conclusion, and its justification, is similar to Confucian political theory, where the idea of human nature provides a similar justification more directly.

Furthermore, we see that Aristotle's theory is based on a kind of division of labor (cf. *Athenian Constitution*, Ch. 7). Aristotle says that manual workers are required to support citizens that do not waste their time on manual work. But this division of labor has a fundamental political sense in Aristotle's mind. He maintained that if and when a single individual is outstanding in virtue, he ought to be made the king. Such a wise king should be given absolute power, even above the law (Saunders 1984b:

229), because the wise ruler has the capacity to control something which does not belong to everybody—wisdom. Like a physicist, the king must have full expert knowledge in order to organize the life of the common man (*Ethics* 1180b).

According to Greek and later Roman Stoicism, men are related to each other by natural law, which is above all laws written by men. This natural law is equated with love. The law of nature reflects reason and this law and reason have existed since the beginning of humankind, uncreated and unwritten. Love and friendship grow naturally between wise men because they partake in the reason of the universe. But society as such cannot function, it must be organized into the state, and the state must have a morally perfect leader or group of leaders (Arnold 1911: 275).

Since the Stoic art of living well was defined as following one's true nature, that is, reason and virtue, the form of government as such was not important. Stoicism maintained that the best form of government is a mixture of democracy, kingship, and aristocracy. In any case, the state needs government, and government must reflect the idea of the wise king who governs in the best interests of his subjects.[7] This is derived from the idea that one must live in accordance with human nature as well as that of the universe, and that one must "refrain from every action forbidden by the law common to all things." Just as reason governs the world, reason must govern within man. Beasts observe natural law due to instincts, but men live in accordance with nature because of their right reason. Because man's reason is part of the world's reason, to follow nature is to live in accordance with both human nature and the nature of the universe (Diogenes Laertius VII.87–88, 131; Ross 1986: 45–46; Tenkku 1981: 128–29).

Self-preservation is a duty, but one must maintain peace of mind and be passionless. Apathy excludes all passions, external and material things are indifferent to the Stoic. The Stoic mind is based on unworried joy, obtained in practical action as a player who enjoys the game but is indifferent about the result. Pleasure is a by-product of the natural life, life according to nature. Such life is virtuous life because virtue is the goal toward which nature guides rational human beings. Virtue is a morally perfect leadership. Under such leadership, life for rational beings becomes the natural life (Diogenes Laertius VII.85–87; Tenkku 1981: 134).

It is in full accordance with Stoic principles that the wise man takes part in politics. The wise man represents virtue and, therefore, the morally perfect leadership. The wise man wishes to restrain vice and promote virtue. The wise man does not live in solitude, he is made for both contemplation and action. The wise man chooses the rational way of life, where both contemplation and action are possible (Diogenes Laertius VII.123, 130, VIII.121).

The wise man alone is free for independent action, therefore, he is entitled to rule. When power is inclined to grow irresponsible, none but the wise man can maintain a true kingship, that is, only he can prevent such a development. Therefore, "knowledge of good and evil is a necessary attribute of the ruler." Consequently, the wise and good alone are fit to be magistrates—they are infallible. The wise do not hurt others or themselves. In short, the Stoic theory claims that the wise possess virtue, and are therefore "at once able to discover and to put into practice what he ought to do" (Diogenes Laertius VII.121–23, 126; cf. VII.33; Tenkku 1981: 134).

Cicero maintained that justice rather than profit is more important to the existence of the state. Men are connected to each other on the basis of law, not personal interests (RePublica I.32). Therefore, the state is the community of law. The state is a legal or true state only so far as it represents and is based on justice. Above the people there is nothing but the law of nature. The king obtains his power from the people and therefore he cannot abrogate the law of nature. The people have no duty to obey laws in conflict with the law of nature. If the king applies his power against the law of nature, he is no longer a true king but a tyrant (Officiis II.31; Tenkku 1981: 155).

For Cicero, politics and political structures are an integral part of the commonwealth. Cicero maintains that every commonwealth must be governed by a deliberative body if it is to be permanent (RePublica I.XXVI.41). Government of the state is completely in accordance with the principles of justice and nature, for without government no association from the smallest to the universe itself can exist. For Cicero, "the universe obeys God; the seas and lands obey the universe, and human life is subject to the decrees of supreme Law" (Legibus III.I.2–3).

Consequently, while an executive authority governs it must give commands that are not only just and beneficial but also conform with the law. Cicero suggests that the laws govern the magistrate, but the magistrate governs the people under their auspices. Therefore, "the magistrate is a speaking law and the law a silent magistrate" (Legibus III.I.2–3).

It does not matter if Cicero preferred the republican government, it is more essential to see that he actually preferred not particular type of government but wise rule in general. If he did not suggest the idea of the wise king directly, he did suggest that only wise and morally good men would be able to save the republic (RePublica I.XXVI.41, I.XXIX.45, I.XXXI.47; Grant 1985: 8; cf. *On the Good Life*: 117).

In explicit terms, Cicero maintained that the greatest number should not have the greatest power. The greatest power must belong to the best, royal element in the state. However, Cicero suggests that a wise rule—by definition—knows that some power ought to be granted to the leading citizens and certain matters should be left to the judgment and desires of the masses. Such an approach provides equality and therefore stability to the system. For Cicero, Romulus was an ideal ruler, for "he saw that the absolute power of the ruler must be strengthened by the influence of the State's most eminent men; and he waged many wars with the greatest good fortune, but brought none of the booty to his own home but enriched his people" (RePublica I.XLV.69, II.IX.15–6, II.XXI.39).

However, while Stoic principles implied or openly spoke for the idea of the wise king and Cicero himself spoke openly in favor of similar things, his position is complicated. On one hand, Cicero maintains that the Persian Cyrus was the wisest of kings, but even then the property of the people (the commonwealth) was administered at the caprice of one man (RePublica I.XXVIII.43, I.XXIX.45). On the other hand, faithfully observing his general principles, Cicero mentions that the whole universe is ruled by a single mind and therefore he presents arguments in favor of the monarchy. For example, when compelled to approve one single unmixed form of government, Cicero chose the kingship, because the king is the father of all citizens, eager to protect them (RePublica I.XXXV.54, I.XXXVI.56).

Cicero is critical of tyranny, not of the wise king. Cicero suggests that the wise king should have almost divine powers to govern, which is not possible for any human, and which would lead to tyranny sooner or later. Therefore, Cicero preferred the republican government of many wise men, and simultaneously gave warnings about persons unfit for wise, kingly government. Cicero's famous *Philippics*, consisting of fourteen speeches and writings against Marcus Antony, can be read in this light. Cicero did not deny the idea of the king, he only saw that not all men were entitled to become kings. Neither did Cicero perceive any such figure among the rivals for power in the civil war (cf. Grant 1985: 337).

Cicero's criticism of tyrants was an important contribution to cultural values in European political thought, therefore, it can be summarized here.

For Cicero, a tyrant is extremely horrible and permanently hateful to gods and men (RePublica II.XXV.47). Cicero maintains that a tyrant is a danger to himself. For example, Dionysus's determination to maintain his tyrannical rule made him lock himself up in the prison of his own home in order to avoid alleged attacks, especially from those who were close to him (*On the Good Life*: 83).

Cicero excludes the tyrant from the commonwealth because the tyrant by definition cannot participate in common property. If a tyrant rules, the commonwealth does not exist at all (RePublica III.XXXI.43). A good man can have nothing in common with a tyrant. Therefore, a good man must kill him:

Indeed, the whole sinful and pestilential gang of dictatorial rulers ought to be cast out from human society. For when limbs have lost their life-blood and vital energy, their amputation may well follow. That is precisely how these ferocious, bestial monsters in human form ought to be severed from the body of mankind. (Officiis III.VI.31–32)

In short, Cicero saw autocracy as general slavery. There was no room for political activities, which were to him the most important of all occupations. When Caesar finally won the civil war and confirmed his own position as dictator, Cicero suggested that there was no longer any scope for manly—political—activities at all. It is well known that Cicero then chose to concentrate on philosophy because there was no space for politics. In a sarcastic tone he explained this move by saying that "the state of the nation was such that the government had of necessity been confided to the case and wisdom of a single man" (*On the Nature of Gods* I.6–9; cf. Grant 1985: 12).

While Cicero's sarcasm was directed against Caesar, it contained a certain truth. Cicero's theory of the rational principle implies that only when reason governs, there can be no room for the passions. Therefore, in a time of danger, when one has something to fear, Cicero supports the old Roman practice to grant all the power to one man. In fact, he adds that "the rule of one man is best, if he be just" (RePublica I.XXXVIII.60, I.XXXIX. 61, I.XL. 63, I.XLI.64).

If Cicero can be seen as an apologist for the wise ruler, another issue emerges— whether or not Cicero advocates the wise king or the heroic king like the two other Roman authors? This is not clear. Considering Cicero's obvious patriotism, it is possible to understand that he cannot avoid accepting the idea that the wise ruler is, almost by definition, the heroic leader. Unbound cleverness is not acceptable for the political leader, therefore, Cicero does not accept Ulysses's stratagem of simulating madness in order to keep his throne and continue living in Ithaca with his parents, wife, and son.

In the case of Regulus, captured by Carthaginians and sent to Rome to collect ransom for himself, Cicero seems to admire military heroism even more. Regulus did not pray for the ransom, but encouraged the Romans to continue the war against Carthage. Afterwards he returned to captivity where he was tortured and killed. Cicero points out that while Regulus seemed willing to stay at home with his wife and children, his fortitude advised him to die for his country. In fact, Regulus had no choice, for if he had stayed in Rome he would have been nothing more than "an aged ex-consul who had fallen into the enemy's hands and then perjured himself" (Officiis III.XXVII.99–100; cf. I.XVIII.61).

Cicero does not stop at this simple level of military heroism. For Cicero, fortitude is much more than simple military heroism, it is one of the most important virtues in his system of moral goodness (Officiis I.XVIII.65, III.XX.80). Therefore, Cicero emphasizes that doing injury is not glorious; only those who prevent injury are considered brave and courageous. Altogether courageous and great souls are marked above all by: (1) indifference to outward circumstances or independence from any man or any passion or any accident of fortune; and (2) willingness to carry out deeds which are extremely arduous and laborious and fraught with danger. Ambition for glory spoils and destroys liberty, in defense of which man must stake everything. Therefore, one should not seek military authority but resign from such a post as soon as possible (Officiis I.XIX.65, I.XX.66–68).

Cicero's Stoic principles provide a basis for social heroism, better called wisdom. For Cicero, such heroism represents an application of moral duties at the social level for social responsibilities. Cicero says that one must contribute to giving and receiving and thus glue human society together (Officiis I.VII.22). Nobody is able to survive alone, real wisdom covers knowledge of the bonds of union between gods and men and the relations of man to man. Therefore, political service in the state to the community in danger is better than mere theoretical knowledge or military heroism in war (Officiis I.XLIII.153; *On the Good Life*: 344).

The wise man should desire to engage in politics and government (RePublica I.II.3). Such true, social heroism reflects real, ultimate courage, which is not typical in war but in politics. Only in politics can one show true heroism in defending the weak who "is evidently the victim of oppression and persecution at the hands of some powerful and formidable personage" (Officiis II.14.51). Courage implies social responsibility to participate in government. It is a duty to endanger private rather than public welfare (Officiis I.XXI.72, I.XXIV.83). Therefore, Cicero says, when "the fate of the whole country . . . will depend on you and you alone . . . it will be your duty to assume the role of dictator, and restore order to our commonwealth" (Finibus III.XX.68; cf. *On the Good Life*: 343; RePublica I.I.1, II.XXV.46).

Social heroism, like military heroism, must be submitted to the strictest control. This is why Cicero maintains that the finest feature of Regulus's action was his sense of responsibility. He subordinated himself and his own judgment to the Senate's

(Officiis XXX.107) and by returning to his captivity and death, Regulus submitted himself to the power of oath, that is, the moral rule which was the solid basis of his own society and its social order:

True, his return to Carthage seems to us admirable but at that epoch he could not have done otherwise, so the merit belongs to the times rather than to the individual for our ancestors believed that no guarantee of good faith was more powerful than an oath. (Officiis XXI.111; cf. Finibus II.XX.65)

RELIGIONS, THE EARLY CHURCH, AND THE WISE KING

The idea of the wise king is actually the paradigm of all religious thought: the god is always wise and good, therefore, his representative on the earth (the priest or the king) must be wise too. If he is not, if his government is tyrannical and evil, he is not the god's representative. The principle-oriented patterns suggest such a ruler in a figurative sense, but similar ideas have been put forward at a more concrete level as legitimation for historically existing rulers.

As to the principle-oriented patterns, we have already seen that a Daoist ruler—if there ever is one—is not indifferent towards his people. He is the wise ruler, who always cares for the life and survival of his peoples (Lao Tzu XXVII.61). In a concrete sense, the Buddha established his monastic order (*samgha*) on the basis of the wise leadership.

In Zoroastrianism, Zoroaster is often described in terms of the wise ruler, even if only as a religious innovator. However, the ideal also appears in Zoroastrian political history. For example, in cases that inevitably arose when a man was accused of breaking his word and denied it, the king had to make the fundamental decision to invoke the gods. The king was able to oblige the accused to an ordeal by water (an oath) or fire (a covenant). The ordeals at which these two mighty beings—Varuna and Mithra—were invoked were highly dangerous and the decision lay with the king of a local community, he had to be a perfect ruler to make it right. This figure of the wise ruler, in ultimate control of the law, seems to have had origins in the concept of the greatest of the lords, Ahura Mazda, the Lord of Wisdom. In another example it is told that Zarathustra's daughter was married to Jamaspa, Vishtaspa's chief counselor, "who is proverbial among Zoroastrians for wisdom." In a third example, Cyrus's actions were described as those of a loyal Mazda-worshipper who sought to govern his vast new empire justly and well in accordance with *asha* (Boyce 1987: 9, 31, 51). Finally, it is a well-known historical fact that the divine principle of kingship rendered the monarchy the second major institution of power, in addition to religious leaders. The king claimed to possess divine glory and be the representative of God on earth, but such legitimacy was dependent on the goodness and righteousness of the kin. Only the good king was considered the symbol of divine sovereignty, Ahura Mazda, on earth, whereas the unjust tyrant represented the evil spirit of darkness (Dorraj 1990: 29).[8]

In ancient Hebrew thought and Judaism the wise king had the prominent role. The kings of ancient Israel, especially Solomon, were praised for their goodness and wisdom but strongly criticized for their moral weaknesses. Indeed, it can be claimed that in whatever form the wise king appears (king, priest, prophet, and *torah* expert), nowhere does the Hebrew or Jewish doctrine justify an arbitrary use of power. The ruler must be wise (for a wise judge will instruct his people) the government of a man of understanding shall be well ordered, and a city can only be established through the understanding of the powerful: "If you value your thrones and screptes, you rulers of the nations, you must honor wisdom, so that you may reign for ever," for "Wise men in plenty are the worlds's salvation and a prudent [wise] king is the sheet-anchor of his people." On the other hand, an uninstructed king will destroy his people, and the wise king will conquer his kingdom: "I shall rule over many peoples. . . . Grim tyrants will be frightened when they hear of me; among my own people I shall show myself a good king and on the battlefield a brave one" (Wisdom of Solomon 6: 21, 25, 8: 14–15 in the *Apocrypha*). In conclusion, the administrators of justice bear a heavy responsibility, since the fate of the entire community depends on them (Cohen 1975: 207).

As a figure of wisdom Jesus belongs to the principle-oriented traditions as a metaphorical figure rather than as a real person. In any case, it is not likely that he tried to establish a leadership for himself among the new community. The Kingdom of God was a principle and a challenge to conventional structure, not a community requiring leadership. But when the community formation continued, the leadership issue naturally emerged. The development can be perceived in the later layers of Q Gospel (Q2 and Q3), but the *Gospel of Thomas* makes it explicit.

In the *Gospel of Thomas* the followers asked Jesus to show them who would be the new leader after his death. Jesus said to them: "No matter where you are, you are to go to James the Just, for whose sake heaven and earth came into being" (GT 12). As Meyer (1992: 73) explains, the saying affirms the leadership of James the Just, the brother of Jesus and the leader of the church in Jerusalem until his death in 62 C.E. Meyer quotes the stories about James to illustrate his reputation, that is, in the tradition of the wise ruler:

He was named Just by all from the times of the master until ours, since many were called James. This one was holy from his mother's womb. He did not drink wine or strong drink. . . . So because of the extraordinary character of his righteousness he was called the Just and Oblias, that is, in Greek, rampart of the people and righteousness, as the prophets point out concerning him.

As the quotation reveals, the question of leadership became a big issue in early Christian writings. However, the idea of wise rule was never limited to an individual. The wise and godly individual was important, but the Church was more important. The Church, not individual bishops, was the representative of wise rule on earth. This, in fact, was the major rhetorical move to justify the all encompassing role and status of the Church.

NOTES

1. In ancient thought the ruler is usually an individual, but may occasionally imply or include a wider group of ministers or a kind of aristocracy.

2. Interestingly enough, the leaders of the schools (Mo Zi, Kong Zi) and the individual thinkers were advisors to politicians. All of them were looking for the wise ruler who might have been willing and capable of following the rules of good government. No one tried to become a king himself, but in practice thought that a philosopher-king would be the final solution to the problems of government (*Mencius* VI.B.6–7).

3. It was typical to Confucianism, Mohism, and Daoism to think that man the basis of all government. The task was, through good government, to improve the everyday life of ordinary people. Even Legalism shared this view by suggesting that coercion and violence can and must be applied for that purpose.

4. It is not surprising that the same idea is made a cornerstone of the political philosophy of Mohism. Mo's authoritarianism was even stronger, but it was complemented by utilitarianism (Fung 1983: 96).

5. According to Meng Zi (VI.A.2), the criticized school maintained: "Human nature is like whirling water. Give it an outlet in the east and it will flow east; give it an outlet in the west and it will flow west." Meng Zi suggested a sort of gravitation theory. According to him, water always flows downwards.

6. In a sense, polity and society in the public sphere were identical for Aristotle and Plato. In making the distinction my approach here is purely analytical.

7. In Stoicism the ruler is most often a wise and morally good individual or a group of wise individuals. This ideal was best observed in politics by Augustus, who's followers were not very successful. Nero was able to observe the Stoic principles only in the beginning. Trajan, Hadrian, Antonius Pius, and Marcus Aurelius returned to the doctrine but their interpretation was no longer consistent with the original doctrines (Tenkku 1981: 157).

8. Similar ideas can be found later in Islamist political theory. For example, Lambton (1974: 422; cf. Lewis 1974) writes: "All assumed the ultimate source of power to be divine, and to come from God through the ruler, be he Caliph or king, which made the problem of the tyrannical ruler insoluble. All identified the state with religion, and disorders in religion with disturbances in the state. . . . The keyword of all these formulations was justice, which medieval Islamic political thought understood to be the harmonious relationship of society in a divinely appointed system, the component parts of which were in perfect equilibrium. The Trojan horse from which abuses invaded the state was arbitrary power. Among its consequences were corruption which fed on insecurity, and the flattery expected and received by the ruler which destroyed the dignity of the citizen."

CHAPTER 9

Education as the Basis of Social Order

It may be that man is considered by nature good, but it is not usually suggested that an individual is morally perfect at birth. Where moral qualities of men or, especially, of the ruler are considered a prerequisite to social order, it is expected that a morally perfect ruler (or individual/citizen) develops only through a systematic moral and political education.

Moral education is highly esteemed in religious traditions from Daoism and ancient Indian thought to Zoroastrianism and early Christianity. This chapter pays attention to the social and political aspects of moral education, both in city-state theories (Plato and Mo Zi) and world community models (Confucianism, Aristotle, and Cicero).[1] Moral and religious education within various religious communities, in the temple-state models, must be recognized as a case in the present pattern.

EDUCATION IN CITY-STATE THEORIES

The ideals and elements of order give political and moral education a central task in Plato's approach to order. For Plato, the emphasis on human nature and political education can be explained in two intertwined ways. First, as we have seen, he makes an analogy between human nature and the political system; second, Plato believes that the evilness of individuals leads to disorder in the city-state and war between them. Human nature is reflected in or reproduced by the state. Human nature disposed to evil leads to chaos, human nature disposed to good leads to order in the state. Quick-tempered and simple human nature prefers war to peace, and values intrigues and plots (*Republic* 545b–c, 547d–548b).

Individual corruption and evilness, and consequently disorder and wars, are caused by the lack of education, or by the wrong kind of education. Without education men must appeal to the law and judges. Men require judges and masters when they are not able to govern themselves (*Republic* 405b).

Socrates and Plato openly participated in the debate on education. Contemporary teaching and education had been, according to them, nothing more than a dream or a figment of the imagination, far away from truth and good. However, Socrates was accused of spoiling youth (*Republic* 414d–e; *Apology*, 23c–e). Consequently, Plato suggested a more indirect criticism by accusing "the Persians" of a womanish education conducted by the royal harem. According to Plato, Cyrus never paid attention to education, for he—like Plato's contemporary Greeks—spent his entire life on military campaigns. Therefore, his sons were educated by women in extreme luxury, that is, they grew up without any proper, correcting instructions from good teachers (*Laws* 694a–d, 695a–b).

For Plato, no free education is considered genuine education. He perceived education as the correct discipline of the feelings of pleasure and pain. That is, education is the route by which virtue first enters the soul of a child (Saunders 1984a: 83). In other words, the idea of order can only be realized through education, which creates all the elements to support it by producing the good man, without which order cannot be possible.

The aim of education is to produce virtue. Plato's (or Socrates's) ideas on virtue can be summarized in three sentences: (1) virtue is knowledge; (2) all virtues can be reduced to one; and (3) nobody does wrong knowing that he is doing wrong. In other words, virtue consists of righteousness, wisdom, and courage. However, in the final analysis, virtue is knowledge. Therefore, teaching virtue is similar to teaching any practical knowledge. Virtue can be learned and taught as long as the method of instruction is proper. Plato insisted that true knowledge was moral knowledge, the knowledge of how to be virtuous. In fact, virtue consists of a knowledge of good and evil (*Laches* 198a–199c; Saunders 1984a: 20; cf. Plato's *Protagoras* 361b–d).

It is not true that children inherit everything from their parents—the son of a good musician can turn out to be a bad musician. However, education has decisive power— even the most unrighteous person educated to respect the law is a master of justice compared to a person who lacks civilization (*Protagoras* 327c–d).

In proper instruction the teacher must give knowledge and share experience on things to be avoided. The teacher's main responsibility is to keep the student away from attractive entertainments and pleasures which otherwise spoil him or her.

One must not tell children about the mistakes made by the gods, because a child cannot distinguish between acceptable and non-acceptable examples. The guards must carefully ensure that education will not be spoiled or corrupted. They must prevent, in physical education and music, all reforms which are against the laws (*Republic* 378d, 424b).

Education must be a continuous process: "a man who intends to be good at a particular occupation must practice it from childhood: both at work and at play he must be surrounded by the special tools of the trade" (*Laws* 635, 643b; cf. *Protagoras* 325c–d). Education can be carried out in anything: sports, the arts, and even drinking parties. Being taught by encouragement and threats to resist temptation when mildly drunk is a valuable exercise in self-control. Education is essentially a training in virtue, not simply in a given trade or vocation (Saunders 1984a: 63).

The arts are important because they reinforce the ability to discipline the feelings of pleasure and pain in adult life. When we enjoy the portrayal of men and their actions in various art forms, we are fired with the desire to imitate them. It is therefore vital that art should portray good men attractively and bad men unattractively, and if a poem or a play accomplishes this, it conforms to good and correct artistic standards (Saunders 1984a: 83).

Concerning the methods of education, Plato believes it possible, and he actually prefers, to transmit knowledge without words—an idea that appears in the Confucian school too. In the *Republic* Plato declares that the supreme idea of good can only be conveyed by analogy. Plato speaks of the ultimate apprehension of the good as something in the nature of a mystical experience, which is incommunicable.

The suggested theory is paradoxical in the light of some other statements and Plato's own prolific production. Elsewhere Plato maintains that language has a powerful impact on the human mind. If somebody hears about sins in a critical light only, one will refrain from them, because he has not learned anything else (*Laws* 838b–c; Hamilton 1985: 131; Pocock 1983). Furthermore, rejecting his own prolific production as futile, Plato maintains that language does not always transmit knowledge—truth and wisdom—in a correct way. He declares that truth and wisdom cannot be put into words like other branches of learning. In short, the suggested non-verbal learning must have been dramatically important during Plato's last years when he had learned that it is not enough to write and lecture in order to contribute to the birth of the wise king.

Instead of spoken or written words, Plato claims, truth and wisdom must be learned in practice through experience. There is no short way to wisdom. One must devote a long life to finding the truth. Only then can the truth "flash upon the soul, like a flame kindled by a leaping spar" (*Letters* VII.341). To provide emphasis Plato says:

If I thought that any adequate spoken or written account could be given to the world at large, what more glorious life-work could I have undertaken than to put into writing what would be of great benefit to mankind and to bring the nature of reality to light for all to see? But I do not think that the attempt to put these matters into words would be to men's advantage, except to those few who can find out the truth for themselves with a little guidance. (*Letters* VII.341)

The problem Plato perceives is related to the fact that written words are dead, they do not provide a basis for fruitful interaction between the teacher and the student:

[Y]ou might suppose that they understand what they are saying, but if you ask them what they mean by anything they simply return the same answer over and over again. Besides, once a thing is committed to writing it circulates equally among those who understand the subject and those who have no business with it; a writing cannot distinguish between suitable and unsuitable readers. And if it is ill-treated or unfairly abused it always needs its parent to come to its rescue; it is quite incapable of defending or helping itself. (*Phaedrus* 275d–e)

In more practical terms, Plato's theory of education gives a decisive role to a long association between teacher and student. Only such a long-standing relationship will make it possible for truth to be received through the direct interaction of one mind and another (*Phaedrus* 278a; Hamilton 1985: 10, 131). Another important point is that only at this point will knowledge maintain itself. Once the truth is truly found, it nourishes itself thereafter. With direct contact, truth emerges as so wonderful that the student "must follow it with all his might if life is to be worth living." Only then is there "no danger of a man forgetting the truth ... since it lies within a very small compass" (*Letters* VII.340–44).

Education creates the wise ruler, but the wise ruler educates his people. Because the self-restraint and reason of the individual are the basis of the good state, the major responsibility in education belongs to the ruler. Plato criticizes those rulers who wish to govern, but lament about the corruption of their people. In explicit terms, Plato concludes that Athens had not given birth to a single statesman who might have been willing and able to educate his people. The true statesman, Plato says, is able to steer his subjects toward wisdom, that is, to social order. The true statesman does not give his subjects whatever they wish (*Gorgias* 516e, 517a, 520a–b).

Plato maintains that a weak and corrupt king cannot change the wrong wishes of his people nor can he prevent his people from attempting to fulfill their one-sided aims. That is, a bad statesman cannot make his people any better. Therefore, one must not praise a king who fattens Athenians and gives them whatever they wish. Plato strongly criticizes the Athenian leaders for providing what they desired rather than needed for becoming better men (*Gorgias* 517b–c, 519a).

In order to fulfill his task in educating his people, the ruler must govern, first and foremost, himself. Only self-restraint produces loyal friends and colleagues. Therefore, the good ruler must first reform his own life, and choose his friends among those who behave in the same way and who are consistent in that behavior. The first major task of the good ruler is to give good laws (*Letters* VII.331–32).

Laws are important in education. Plato suggests that laws do not work without punishments, but unlike the Chinese Legalists, he perceived laws in the conventional sense of crimes and criminal behavior. Even then, punishments are devices in education, laws turn thoughts from vices to virtues and the ordinance that produces this effect should be adopted as an established law since it results in the real happiness of the observers. Therefore, punishments must be accommodated to "the spiritual state of the criminal" not to the degree of the crime. In applying punishments, it must be considered if and how the criminal can be educated to become a better citizen. However, if an educated person commits a crime, he cannot be cured at all and in that case the death penalty is proper punishment (*Letters* VII.355; Saunders 1984b: 361).

All this emphasis on the law reflects Plato's idea that the king has the duty to govern for the happiness of his people, to direct and teach them. The king must not apply physical violence like shepherds which direct their flock by lashes. The king's duty is to reconcile the partners of conflict, not to kill them. It is, therefore, important to provide laws to guide the contenders not only here and now but in the future as well. The true king, as the educator, will ensure that the contenders remain on friendly terms with each other (*Laws* I.627e–628a).

The true king catches the soul of man, because this makes it easiest to direct a living creature and to submit a man's will to the king's power. The ruler must be able to isolate and explain what is good and what is bad in the individual and in his behavior. Therefore, the lawgiver must always explain and justify the laws. The written law, the preamble, must have rhetorical power. It must not only instruct but persuade as well (*Laws* 631d–632a; *Critias* 109c; cf. *Laws* 718ff.; Saunders 1984a).

The king is the educator. His major duty is to educate his people, not to accept what is in their corrupt minds. The king bears in his mind a basic model of what is good and right, and tries to change the wishes of the people to make them better (Saunders 1984a: 38). When Plato says that nobody else as the philosopher-king can prove to everybody that both the state and an individual will be happy under the guidance of righteousness (*Letters* VII.335), he suggests emphatically that the king, then, is not simply a ruler and politician, but a teacher. Anybody could govern and use power over the citizenry, but only the philosopher-king is able to educate them. In that sense the king must be the philosopher, the lover of wisdom, and be capable of teaching this wisdom to his subjects.

In Chinese Mohism education has become a strictly authoritarian idea, which in a sense takes Plato's idea of non-verbal education to its conclusion. According to Mo Zi, the king sets the example followed by everybody. Whatever the king does, all other men will do as well. If the kings decides to burn himself in a fire, all others will do the same. When Mo Zi makes references to heaven, he is not referring to a divine brotherhood of men, but to the supreme example of universal love by heaven towards all peoples. Men should follow the example of heaven.

On the other hand, Mo's theory goes at least partly beyond such pessimistic and authoritarian ideas. It may be more correct to say that Mo applies such visions to support his more positive ideas and prove that it is not impossible for the king to spread the message of universal love. In fact, Mo tries to seek the means by which people can be made to feel universal love towards one another because, he maintains, the capacity for universal love does not derive from the natural goodness of man. According to Mo, man's nature is like pure silk and its goodness or evil is dependent entirely upon how this silk is dyed. Mo emphasized that it is very difficult to make people see the benefits of universal love and substitute these for what is harmful. Therefore, he laid stress on all kinds of sanctions which would induce men to love one another (Fung 1983, 96).

EDUCATION IN WORLD COMMUNITY THEORIES

According to Kong Zi, there is no point to being rich and noble when chaos prevails in the state. In other words, something must to be done in order to get rid of chaos. He suggested that good behavior and love become decisive in the process, for only this guarantees the existence of *dao*, without which any state will collapse. The aim is to establish the world of Great Harmony, the ultimate goal of the *tien-hsia*, a moral world of order. Kong Zi maintains that the creation and maintenance of this order can only be accomplished through political and moral education (*Analects* VIII.13; *Mencius* IV.A.17).

The Confucian theory was based on a specific conception of human nature that maintained human nature is good, or can be made good through education. At the very least, it was maintained that there is an individual, who, after becoming sage through moral education, can guarantee good government, peace, and order for the rest. Even Xun Zi, who maintained that human nature is bad, shared the belief in the power of education.

In the debate on human nature the Confucian school draws attention to education instead of the original nature of man. This can be seen everywhere. For instance, when Meng Zi was asked about the existence of evil in his time, he explained it by the loss of man's originally good mind. In other words, man was the cause of his own downfall. According to Meng Zi, there are people who fail to make the best of their native endowment. Therefore, man keeps his original goodness only if he seeks to find it. But if he lets it go, he will lose it. Meng Zi maintains that man himself is responsible for both his good and bad fortune. In a seemingly fatal tone he emphasizes that since man is fully responsible, there is no hope of escape from this iron law. However, the Confucian position is far from pessimistic. The warning is introduced only to point out that man must become fully aware of his own actions. Only then will he find a way out of jail. He must recognize that he is capable of becoming good. It is this openness to learning and education, not original human nature that makes it possible to speak of the goodness of human nature (*Mencius* VI.A.4, 6).

Meng Zi's idealism was strongly attacked by the great teacher of famous Legalists, Xun Zi, who was the other arch-Confucian in classical Chinese thought. Xun Zi developed a more naturalistic doctrine and interpretation of man. He did not accept the doctrine of an originally good nature in man. On the contrary, he sharply criticized the idea. For him, man's nature is evil. The nature of man is such that he is born with a fondness for profit. Xun Zi said that if there is no authority of the ruler, man will treat others in full selfishness. In the state of anarchy, human nature is revealed when the strong rob and kill the weak, and when the many terrorize the few (Hsün Tzu/Watson: 163).

However, Xun Zi shared the view that goodness is the result of conscious activity. In other words, learning and education can make man good and wise (Chan 1960: 172; Hsün Tzu/Watson: 157). In fact, Xun Zi's strong belief in education, strange as it sounds, was logically derived from his doctrine of man: man wishes to have anything he does not have already. Because he lacks goodness, he strives for it. Xun Zi maintained that "every man who desires to do good does so precisely because his nature is evil." This is so because "whatever a man lacks in himself, he will seek outside." In another statement, Xun Zi claims that man wishes to control his desires to avoid that which is evil. Both claims imply that man knows that his nature is evil and so makes chaos likely. Because no one can survive in chaos, man must control and educate his nature (Hsün Tzu/Watson: 163, 165).

Xun Zi maintains that the human mind selects the acceptable feelings and is able to make the selection on the basis of education. Only without a teacher or rules does man degenerate to his original nature (Hsün Tzu/Watson: 114, 281).

In short, we can refute a traditional explanation according to which the disagreement with Meng Zi and Xun Zi was caused because Meng Zi was concerned only with sages while Xun Zi was concerned only with totally wicked men. From our point of view, this does not matter at all. Both Meng Zi and Xun Zi shared the belief that all men are capable of becoming sages, but only through education (Lau 1983b: 19). Meng Zi and Xun Zi developed the Confucian doctrine in opposing directions, but their common objective was the same as that of Kong Zi, namely, the desirability and possibility of perfection through moral training and social education. The relationship between Xun Zi and Legalist thought is less clear. On one hand, Xun Zi may be included among Legalist thinkers, but on the other hand his lack of faith in the original goodness of human nature was a contributing factor only to the harsh disciplaniarism of the Legalists (Chan 1960: 173; Kao 1974).

As a political philosophy, Confucianism became the philosophy of political and moral education. According to Meng Zi's testimony, Kong Zi said that he can and must be evaluated on the basis of his "major work," in which he had, according to Meng Zi, appropriated his didactic principles[2] (*Mencius* IV.B.21). While this appears to be an invented justification for Meng Zi's emphasis on education, it is true that in his *Analects* (VII.22; cf. 34) Kong Zi gave education a major role: "Even when walking in the company of two other men, I am bound to be able to learn from them. The good points of the one I copy; the bad points of the other I correct in myself."

Similar emphasis on the importance and possibility of education and learning is also suggested also Xun Zi, who said that learning should not cease until death, a program of learning can have an end but its ultimate aim must never be ignored. He claimed that children cry with the same voice at birth, but as they grow older they follow different customs due to socialization processes, including education, which make men differ (Hsün Tzu/Watson: 15, 19). The Confucians regarded the individual human being as the ultimate actor in all community processes. Therefore, they planned to reach their ideal world through the perfection of individuals, and consequently, groups (the family, the state, and the *tien-hsia*). "Ordering" the individual is like the root or beginning for ordering the world. However, in claiming this, the Confucians spoke of the education of the ruler, not the common people.

In Confucian political theory people have the highest value, their welfare the second, and the king the lowest (*Mencius* VII.B.14). This justifies and expresses the idea that the ruler must serve the people in order to make everyday life possible. However, there must be a ruler inclined to good government (i.e., benevolence). Confucianism sees that several ideal characters, of which the highest is the sage. Lower down the scale are the good man and the complete man.

The ideal moral character for Kong Zi is the gentleman, the man in authority, the king.[3] While educated morality and proper manners are applicable to all individuals, the major responsibility belongs to the king. Practically speaking, most of the classical Chinese texts are books on how to govern. The philosopher does not speak—except indirectly—to the common man, but to the ruler. The philosophers told the ruler how to obtain fame and power, how to govern, how to maintain power; in brief, how to become a true king. This occurred in an age of great political instability and ferment, of incessant intrigue and strife (cf. Watson 1967: 3).

In short, while emphasis must be on the moral education of all individual human beings, not all individuals are of equal significance in this process. The ruler is more equal than the others. Therefore, the ordering or education of the king becomes the primary issue:

Things investigated, knowledge became complete: knowledge complete, thoughts were sincere; thoughts sincere, hearts were rectified; hearts rectified, persons were cultivated; persons cultivated, families were regulated; families regulated, States were rightly governed; States rightly governed, the whole world (*tien-hsia*) was made tranquil and happy. (*Great Learning*: 5–7, quoted in Chen 1991: 35)

This emphasis on the ruler was shared by Xun Zi, who believed that with respect to human nature the sage does not surpass the common man, but in his conscious activity—learning—the sage differs from and surpasses all other men. Anybody can be educated to be a sage, but there are some incorrigibly evil men who must be punished rather than reformed. Similarly, people of average capacity can be taught what is right without forcing them into goodness (*Analects* 17.3; Hsün Tzu/Watson: 33).

The role given to the wise king was justified in Confucianism exactly like it was done in Plato's theory: the king is the prominent educator of his subjects and therefore must be educated first. According to Kong Zi, the king loves his subjects and makes them work hard in learning. The king cannot provide any better service to them (*Analects* XIV.7). Similarly, the *Li Ki* (XVI.1–2) maintained that thoughts from the first to the last must be fixed on learning. The king who wishes to transform the people and perfect their manners must start from the lessons of the school. What were the lessons of the school?

One cannot understand the meaning of education in Confucians' thought without paying attention to the content of education.

Education means moral education. Morality is understood as a value pursued for its own sake. Moral education had, however, a wide social meaning. Kong Zi was said to have instructed under four headings—culture, moral conduct, doing one's best, and being trustworthy—all of which were related to the moral development of man towards a member of the society (*Analects* VII.1, 25; Lau 1982: 13).

According to Kong Zi, it might be thought that the best are born with knowledge. In practice, however, no one is born with knowledge. Learning is the only way to become a gentleman (king), or a good citizen. Therefore, learning must be taken seriously. It is insufficient to learn but not to think, and dangerous to think but not to learn (*Analects* II.15, XVI.9). In other words, the goal of learning is not only learning but the achievement of the wisdom of the sage, the gentleman, or the good citizen. Simultaneously, one should not think himself a sage if there is no required learning process involved.

It is argued that the common people are inclined to degenerate to the level of animals if they do not receive education. According to the Confucians, this gave the sage king a cause for concern. He consequently appointed the minister of education to teach proper manners to the common people (*Mencius* III.A.4).

The suggested arguments point towards one direction: it was political education which was given a central role in the maintenance of social order. Meng Zi said that good government is feared by the people but good education is loved by them, or "good government wins the wealth of the people; good education wins their hearts" (*Mencius* VIII.A.14).

The content of education cannot be discussed without a full reference to the comprehensive code of rituals and proper manners (*li*). This doctrine is based on the view that man does not live alone but together with other men. Indeed, the Confucians placed a great emphasis on society. They argued that man is meaningless unless he is involved in actual human relations. Therefore, no man existed in isolation (Chan 1960: 192). To make social life possible, proper manners were required.

In Confucian political theory society is governed by a comprehensive code of rituals; the values and norms of society are contained in the *li*,[4] which came from the mythical past. The Confucians regarded the *li* as products of the ancient sages. The classical rules of good behavior were originally unwritten principles, practiced and learned in rites. The Confucian school gave them a more systematic and written formulation, while Kong Zi still emphasized the role of rituals and music—i.e., nonverbal learning of the sort advocated by Plato.

It was believed that society can be entirely and efficiently controlled by the performance of ritual. If the *li* are carried out, society's disagreements will be resolved, its norms and relationships declared and established. This means that the observance of the *li* equals to—promotes—the maintenance of order. Every deviation from the *li* threatens to destroy the proper social order. Therefore, the highest moral virtue is to live in accord with the rites and proper manners (*Mencius* VII.B.33; Pocock 1973: 43–44). Proper manners are applied in the specific context of the five social relationships: "Love between father and son, duty between ruler and subject, distinction between husband and wife, precedence of the old over the young, and faith between friends" (*Mencius* III.A.4; cf. *Li Ki* III.V.28).

That is, the *li* demand that the weaker or less important partner in the relationship show respect, humility, and submissiveness towards the more important person. The pattern is based on family relationships, and the ruler-ruled relationship had to be an extended father-son relationship. Meng Zi suggested that the relationship between father and son was the most important of those within the family, while the relationship between the king and the subject (or the minister) was the most important of those within society. These two basic relationships are different, the former is based on love, the latter on respect (*Mencius* II.B.2). However, the former gives the basis for the latter: love makes respect possible. Kong Zi emphasized that to be good as a son and obedient as a young man permanently molds a man's character and makes him an obedient citizen (*Analects* I.2; cf. *Mencius* IV.A.11).

According to the *li* there is a definite place for everyone. One must not look, listen, speak, or move unless it is in accordance with the rites and proper manners. The ruler and the subject have different positions and therefore different duties. The ruler rules, the subject is ruled. The ruler uses his mind, the ruled use their muscles. The subjects must support the ruler, who must not do anything but rule or educate his subjects. When a king asked Kong Zi about government, he answered: "Let the ruler be a ruler, the subject a subject, the father a father, the son a son." In the ideal state each one discharges the duty proper to him or her. Any officer who neglects his duty must be severely punished (*Analects* XII.1, 11; *Mencius* IV.A.2, 4; *Li Ki* XII.11).

In conclusion, I repeat Obenchain's (1984) observations. According to Obenchain, Kong Zi gave instruction in the cultivation of moral perfection through the study of the lessons from the former mythical kings. Meng Zi and Xun Zi claimed independent responsibility of moral ministers to preserve the way of former kings. This made Confucian scholars servants of power. Consequently, what developed was an increasingly reflective articulation of the moral ministerial role to instruct rulers as to how former kings demonstrated care and concern for the people. Therefore, the suggested order is strongly hierarchical. The right social order represents the status quo in favor of the privileged and noble classes.[5] The hierarchical nature of the social structure of the *li* is openly expressed in the classical five types of social relations.

Aristotle anticipates and speaks for the coming world ruler. In doing so, he addresses the immediate question as to what would prevent such a suzerain from becoming a tyrant? In a world state, with unlimited power at his disposal, why should the suzerain govern in the interests of his subjects? The answer is that through moral and political education, the ruler has become the wise king, and such a ruler is able to govern his state without selfish motives (*Politics* 1277a12–1277b33; III.iv, xviii).

Aristotle seems to be exclusively interested in the education of the general masses. For example, he maintains that the examination of human nature gives the citizen knowledge—right knowledge—about the state. Note, however, that for Aristotle even the citizen is defined as someone who takes part in the use of political power. Only citizens are able to follow the law in order to rule. This ability is based on nature, the characteristics of the individual, and education.

Therefore, for Aristotle education does not exist outside political society, nor can it be open to everybody. In the widest sense, education becomes a sort of influence from above to those below. In the case of common people, education hopes to abolish *stasis*, civil war, which is caused by real or perceived injury. Therefore, education must influence expectations, the perception of injuries: "it is more necessary to equalize appetites than possessions, and that can only be done by adequate education under the laws" (*Politics* 1266b24).

In fact, Aristotle is explicitly interested in the stability of the state. Aristotle emphasizes that although the wise rule—and therefore, education—applies to both an individual and a city-state, the state is a greater and more complete thing, and must be preserved in the first place: "to secure the good of one man is better than nothing, but it is more noble and godlike to do so for a whole people or for city-states" (*Ethics* 1095a; 1181b12–23).

Education must serve the state and it must be carried out by the king. Because not everybody can be educated wise, and because education requires a soul that is naturally inclined toward the nourishment of the seed of wisdom, all attention must be paid to the education of those who can be educated (*Ethics* 1179b). The ruler must be such a person, and therefore it is the education of the wise king that counts in the issues of the state and social order.

Furthermore, education aims at developing virtue. Virtue is something very important to the citizen but especially to the king. As with Plato and Confucianists, according to Aristotle virtue can be brought about by education. Virtue is, itself, not only moral but intellectual as well. This intellectual element comes from teaching, whereas moral virtue represents habit. Therefore, intellectual virtue takes time to grow to full maturity (*Ethics* 1102a; cf. 1109a–b).

While all this is applicable to anybody, only a citizen is able to take part in governing. Among the citizens the king not only has an opportunity but the duty to do so. Aristotle is obviously speaking to the king when he says that virtue can best be achieved by action, for virtue implies political activity, "dealing with things to be done." Anyone can survey and recognize those virtues at a theoretical level, but the king must also practice them; it is his duty to do so (*Ethics* 1179b).

Even if an individual did become just and temperate merely by doing just and temperate acts, most people *do not* perform such acts. It is more likely that education given to common men will be futile by making them quasi-philosophers who imagine themselves on the road to goodness. Common men remain "philosophers," that is, on the basis of modest studies, they claim to have become philosophers. According to Aristotle, common men perhaps listen to what the teacher has to say, and then immediately and completely ignore his instructions (*Ethics* 1105b).

Therefore, Aristotle maintains, at least one person must perform better. His achievement, then, must go beyond learning to practice of government as well. This person, the king, can combine the theoretical knowledge on the state and practical knowledge (*praxis*) of doing something on the basis of that knowledge. Indeed, the theoretical (ideal) and practical sides of politics support each other. Political practice is tied to the right knowledge of man and society. The right thoughts or the correct understanding of reality produce the right knowledge on which the right action or the art of the state—statesmanship—is based.

There might be no fundamental reason to see any conflicts between the education of the king and that of the common man. The ideals of the wise king and the good citizen support each other. Educated citizens do not make the king obsolete, but without educated citizens no kingship is possible.

It is a fact that the grand theories of education were written in rather hierarchical societies, where education served the interest of state administration. For example in Stoicism, in building up the individual attention must be paid to the virtues which were required for building the true Stoic state. Such a state cannot exist without men and their efforts. One must first "build up the individual, to fill his mind with the conception of reason and love, to strengthen his will to a true independence" (Arnold 1911: 281; Diogenes Laertius VII.92ff).

A broader perspective became gradually known. For example, Zeno was invited to educate King Antigonus on the basis that "whoever instructs the ruler of Macedonia and guides him in the paths of virtue will also be training his subjects to be good men" (Diogenes Laertius VII.7–9). However, in Roman Stoicism we see a return to the old theory of the wise king, now perhaps only applied to a collection of rulers, the republican senate.

Cicero not only repeated the earlier ideas but made a contribution by applying them in practice. He was a practical politician and knew that in politics anybody can become a tyrant. Consequently, Cicero maintained that there may be unacceptable changes in the state led by a wise ruler. There is a danger that if (and when) the king becomes unjust that form of government is immediately at its end. The best and the worst governments are intertwined. The wise "king is easily replaced by a despot, the aristocracy by an oligarchical faction, and the people by a mob and anarchy" (RePublica I.XLI.65, I.XLV.69).

Cicero is aware of the fact that men fall prey to ambitions and lose sight of the claims of justice: "We saw this proved in the effrontery of Gaius Caesar, who, to gain that sovereign power . . . trod underfoot all laws of gods and men." This fact represents a sad truth for "it is in the greatest souls and in the most brilliant geniuses that we usually find ambitions for civil and military authority, for power, and for glory, springing up" (Officiis I.VIII.26).

Therefore, Cicero suggests ways of preventing good and talented men from becoming tyrants. The solution is political (and moral) education. For example, his treatise on the orator[6] deals with a very urgent matter—how to train the men who govern us so that they will be efficient but will refrain from abusing their power. Cicero levels criticism against the lack of political education in his time. In his opinion there had been great interest to train able war leaders, while scarcely a "minimum number of really good public speakers," that is, good political leaders, had been supplied by Rome (*On the Good Life*: 238; Grant 1985: 228).

The aim of political education is to constitute a ruler who will remember two maxims. First, the wise ruler must always keep the good of the people above his private interests; and second, he must uncompromisingly prefer the welfare of the whole body politic to that of any party or faction (Officiis I.XXIV.85, I.XXVI.90).

As to the content of education, Cicero maintains that one must study the science of politics in order to acquire in advance all the knowledge he may require for future political duties. It is important to learn how to rule the state before any emergency threatens it (RePublica I.VI.11). Therefore, it is right to conclude that Cicero's treatise on duties is "a theoretical treatment of the obligations which a citizen should render to the commonwealth, that is, a manual of civic virtue" (Grant 1985: 118).

Cicero maintains that education is not only for rulers. Education must be for everybody with the required abilities (i.e., a member of the ruling elite called citizens), who has a duty to become a ruler if needed. Therefore, in Book IV of *De Re Publica* Cicero speaks of the maintenance of high moral standards in the state, the physical and mental training of the young, and the influence of drama, lyric poetry, and music.

But is education possible? Is there any scope for the wise ruler in real politics? Cicero's answer is strongly positive. In his warnings against incompetent men and their uncontrolled ambitions, he outwardly rejects a common opinion that the government of a state could never be carried on without injustice. Cicero, to the contrary, maintains that no government can be carried on "without the strictest justice." The strictest justice is required for the legal rights of citizens in the same commonwealth to be equal. This is the basic message in the education of the wise ruler, who must have this basic knowledge of social life always in his mind (RePublica I.XXXII.49, II.XLII.70; cf. III.VII.14, III.XIII.23).

EDUCATION IN THE TEMPLE-STATE MODEL

Education and learning have a central place in all religious systems. According to a general image, an individual must use considerable time and suffer considerable pains before being able to establish a religion or to teach others in religious matters. Buddha spent years wandering in forests and Jesus spent years in the wilderness. While they had revealed an exceptional knowledge of the existing scriptures, they had to spend years outside society in order to encounter the Truth or God; that is, in order to create their own systems of religious doctrine.

In the case of the Jews, education has the more conventional meaning of transmitting knowledge from one generation to another. In fact, Judaism presents the most relevant case in political and social education. In the Wisdom of Solomon of the *Apocrypha* (7: 1–6, Chs. 7–8) the author, claiming to be King Solomon himself, suggests a systematic theory of political education and the need for it. Nobody is wise immediately after birth, but one must be educated, "achieve wisdom," in order to become the wise king. The author states that "I too am a mortal man like all the rest." That is, when he was born he "breathed the common air and was laid on the earth that all men tread." He emphasizes that "no king begins life in any other way." Therefore, one must love wisdom to become the king: "Wisdom I lack, I sought her out when I was young." This wisdom can be achieved, like in religious doctrines in general, through loving God.

According to Neusner, the Jewish philosophers, like the Greco-Roman thinkers, rejected prophetic and charismatic leadership and preferred authority governing and governed by rules in an orderly, rational way. Therefore, he claims, the principal political figures—king, high priest, and the disciple of the sage—are carefully nurtured through learning rules, not through the cultivation of gifts of the spirit (Neusner 1992: 84).

In another, more interesting suggestion Neusner points out that in Judaism a sage is someone who has acquired knowledge that is in the status of *torah*, but he has done so only through discipleship to a prior sage. In such a conception, education obtains a fundamental sense where the sage takes his place in a direct line to Moses and *torah* "revealed by God to Moses at Sinai." In other words, the sage himself becomes the embodiment and example of *torah* (Neusner 1993a III: 205).

NOTES

1. In the case of the city-states there is a reason to speak of citizens. An educated citizen may contribute to orderly government and prevent expansion. In the case of the world state, the suzerain remains a single interesting figure. Furthermore, there are no balancing forces so his education and moral being should be perfect.

2. It is not likely that the suggested work is the *Spring and Autumn Annals*, which comes from the Confucian school but was not written by him. Furthermore, it is a boring list of wars. The *Great Learning* might be a more likely candidate, but its origin is similarly disputed (cf. Chen 1991).

3. Education in Confucianism is not a common good, but belongs only to the ruler. In fact, the small man is he who is ruled not educated. Education is a means of power and remaining in power: virtue (*te*), an endowment men get from heaven, is something one cultivates, but also something which enables one to govern the state well (Lau 1982: 11, 14).

4. The Confucians did not distinguish between the *li* and the *fa*, moral and law, but the *li* comprehends both (*Li Ki* I.I.I.5/8 ; Chen 1991: 37; Legge 1966: 10).

5. The authoritarian message has not remained unfamiliar to some Western conservatives. According to Cheadle's (1987) investigation into Ezra Pound's Confucian translations, there was a conspicuous interaction between Pound's fascism and his translations.

6. For Cicero, "oratory is a much more considerable activity, and depends on a far wider range of different arts and branches of study, than people imagine" (*On the Good Life*: 240–41).

CHAPTER 10

Heroism as the Basis of
Social Order

While the idea of the wise king emphasizes the high moral qualifications and wisdom of the ruler, the idea of heroism and the heroic king maintains that the ruler has the right and the duty to rule because he has shown high military talent and success in war. It is thought that when someone has commanded a successful army, he has proved his abilities for political leadership. It is further believed that this person also has the highest moral qualifications and the ability to establish and maintain social order. He is not admired for his individual military glory, but for the services only he can provide for the community.

Therefore, military heroism is not far from social or religious heroism. It is true that the military hero is successful in waging wars, but these wars are not caused by his passions or thirst for glory. He wages the war in order to restore social order for the society (cf. Aho 1981, 1990; Campbell 1988).[1]

Military heroism has a minor role in ancient Indian political thought and ancient Hebrew thought, and a more conspicuous role in Zoroastrianism. However, the idea is given the highest status in Roman Stoicism, especially by Virgil and Livy.

MILITARY HEROISM

The hero appears everywhere during chaos in order to restore order and save life. He is the answer to social problems and disorder, the way of solving them. The hero has accomplished a challenging and dangerous task either in introducing religious, social, and political innovations for the society, or in the military field destroying the enemies of society and social order. The first, social or religious hero, belongs to or is rather similar to the idea of the wise king, and is mainly connected to high moral principles. In the *Mahabharata* and the *Bhagavad Gita,* socioreligious heroism (Yudhishthira) and military heroism (Arjuna) were fully submitted to the moral principle of *dharma*. Similar submission to moral principles is even more conspicuous in ancient Hebrew thought, where the heroic priest-kings from Moses to David are highly admired, but always lack the ultimate and finest rewards. It looks like God is not willing to accept their military victories, which partly challenge God's power in history (cf. Aho 1981).

The idea of military heroism surfaces passingly in Zoroastrianism in its later stage. Zoroastrianism exhibits, as a logical consequence of the military role given to Mithra, undeniable admiration of the warrior. It is told that there is a contrast between the general smell of humanity and the smell of warriors, and it is the latter which has a favorable and positive connotation of victory. "Warrior" is a positive symbol attached to gods and heroes only. The texts combine the beneficent with the warrior. Bahram Yasht speaks of the Genius of Victory, one of the ten incarnations of Ahura Mazda. The warrior represents virility, death, and resurrection, and he alone possesses peace (Bahram Yasht 10–11 in ZA/SBE 23; Farvardin Yasht 12.45–46 in ZA/SBE 23; Sirozah 2.9 in ZA/SBE 28; Gershevitch 1959: 160).

The paradigmatic case of military heroism is reflected in Roman Stoicism,[2] here discussed through Virgil's poems and epics (the *Aeneid*) and Livy's histories. Both authors share a general attempt to explain Roman success and expansion. Such speculation was typical to many other writers too. For instance, Polybius set out for investigating by what means and under what system of policy the Romans in "less than fifty-three years succeeded in subjecting nearly the whole inhabited world to their sole government—a thing unique in history" (Polybius I.I.5; cf. I.I).

Virgil saw the best hope for the future peace and prosperity of the Roman people in the rule of one man. The idea emerges first in the fourth (the so-called Messianic) eclogue (Lee 1984: 20–23, 55). Virgil anticipates the beginning of a new golden age free of chaos and fear launched by the birth of an offspring of a dynastic marriage. The boy in question is not the Christian Messiah, but quite simply Augustus, the hero Virgil gives here and in the *Aeneid* divine capacities (*Eclogues* IV.4–18). The idea is repeated in the *Georgics* (II.167–74), where the idea of unified Italy is connected to brave men and the heroes, who are manly and victoriously fending off "unwarlike Indians" from the Roman strongholds. However, it is finally and eloquently portrayed in the *Aeneid* where Virgil gives full representation to the idea of the great heroic leader. The hero is an imagined figure, actually a poetic expression of Augustus, who in the very ancient past conquers Italy and becomes the ancestor of great Roman heroes from Romulus to Augustus (*Aeneid* VI. 847–53; Jackson Knight 1985: 12–13).

Similarly, Livy's history is a long invitation to the heroic leader. Livy's book is also full of great praise for Augustus, and also for Rome. Reflecting on his own experiences of the civil wars, Livy maintains that a savage storm is a call for a strong pilot (Livy VII.13, XXIV.8). During times of danger, the state needs a strong leader. As in Cicero's time, it was time to return to the tradition of dictators who earlier in Roman history were appointed to lead the state unhampered by any restrictions of authority (Livy XXIV.8.).

In Livy's opinion, the heroic leader was the only right leader for Rome. The peace-loving Numa was required to help Rome to survive but even he "foresaw that in a martial community like Rome future kings were likely to resemble Romulus rather than himself" (Livy 1.20). The nation should follow the heroic leader. In the case of need, Rome should call the heroic leader to save the nation. Without such a leader, the city will be destroyed, as it had been in its early history (Livy V.32, VI.2, 6).

However much Livy emphasizes the idea of the heroic leader, he clearly adds another important element. Unlike Virgil, Livy speaks not only of an individual, heroic leader, but of the city or the Roman nation as well. In fact, the city and its citizens are the true heroes. This is expressed quite often, for example, when Julius Proculus, after Romulus's death, declares: "Go and tell the Romans that by heaven's will my Rome shall be capital of the world" (Livy I.16). Livy is explicit in his admiration of the Roman nation. Its glory is so great that Mars himself must be its first parent. This was agreed upon by all nations of the world who were willing to accept Rome's imperial dominion (Livy I.1). There is also in Livy a sense of pride that Rome had now reached the zenith of her power and achievement, and that all previous history was leading up to this glorious hour. Roman history if full of heroic glory but its culmination point, Livy emphasizes, is in the present, the peace brought to the whole world by Augustus Caesar (Livy I.19.3; Ogilvie 1982: 10; cf. Polybius I.4.1).

But even Rome was not able to become a heroic city without a heroic king. Livy's evaluation of Romulus openly emphasizes the role of heroic leadership. For Livy, Romulus represents heroic vigor and military wisdom that were preconditions for Rome's strength in both war and peace. Therefore, it was to Romulus and no one else that Rome owed the power to establish untroubled tranquillity for herself and the world. Obviously, Livy speaks here of Augustus and Pax Romana (Livy I.16).

THE MILITARY HERO AS THE KING

Livy's hero is a combination of divine and human powers, he proudly speaks of divine birth and the divinity ascribed to Romulus after his death. But Livy (I.4) also agrees with Virgil that man has will to gain political power. It was expected that heroes' capacities must find applications in political matters. The political world does not represent—unlike the idea of the wise ruler had promised—the harmonious co-existence of morally superior persons or that of the ruler and the ruled.

In fact, the political sphere is not waiting for the wise king; a positive action is required to establish his realm. The heroic king must occupy a city or a larger piece of land and make himself the suzerain within its boundaries. The hero does not get power free of charge but must struggle for it, just like Ulysses had to do in his own home, and the Pandavas in their kingdom.

Political struggle for power does not leave any time for rest. It is envisaged that this struggle occurs even between the closest relatives—the struggle for power implies jealousy and conflicts between brothers. In this power struggle it is impossible to find a solution by using a neutral mechanism. There is only one real solution—to kill the opponent (Livy I.6). This basic narrative is told in slightly different versions by the *Mahabharata*, Livy, and Virgil. They all fully agree on the role of war in making the hero. The king must be the hero of the decisive war where the community (the state or the caste) is born. Therefore, it is wrong and forbidden for the hero to hesitate—as Arjuna does—at the decisive point of taking bold action, without which no hero is born (cf. Campbell 1988).

Such hesitation, Livy and Virgil knew, does not belong to the hero. Livy states that Remus was killed by his brother Romulus for the seemingly ridiculous reason of jumping over the symbolic city wall set by Romulus. This challenge to the city's fundamental symbol was not, however, the real reason Romulus killed Remus. It was not an issue of symbols, but a concrete and real power struggle between the brothers. In fact, in Livy's opinion, both brothers knew of this struggle.

Similarly, Virgil knew what the struggle between Rome and Carthage was all about—it was the question of world power, of who was going to govern the world. However, Virgil's main interest lies in the power struggle in Italy. That is, in the nature of politics and its relation to the idea of heroism. Virgil himself explains the major point in his narrative; he makes it explicit that he plans to tell about arms and of a heroic man. Arms, the hero, and political power are interrelated. Aeneas had to endure warfare in order to successfully found the glorious city (*Aeneid* I.1–20).

Divine powers guide and aid the hero (Jackson Knight 1985: 15), making heroism both a duty and a destiny. Indeed, Aeneas is to win a kingdom in Italy as a Prince of Destiny. Aeneas must fulfill his task even against his personal wishes. Even love is submitted to the duty. When Aeneas meets the ghost of his first wife, Creusa, her words come not from a human mouth but from the poet's leading idea. Creusa tells him not to grieve but go to a beautiful and fertile land where men are strong and where a queen waits for Aeneas for marriage (*Aeneid* II.770–804).

This important theme is more fully featured in the Dido episode. The poet knows that there would be no personal need to continue the rivalry between Rome and Carthage, which might better profit in collaborating for a permanent peace. But Virgil cannot accept this solution, for it would violate the fulfillment of heroism, both in his epics and in the real world (*Aeneid* IV.90–119; cf. II.568–634).

As expressed earlier in the *Georgics*, sensual love becomes madness, a sign of a disastrous sickness. Dido's role in the poem is to reveal the consequences of an unmastered love, which lures the hero to forget his duty. Actually, Dido's sin is not to love but to forget her responsibility as the queen. Both Aeneas and Dido are blamed for ignoring their royal duties (*Aeneid* IV.153–216, IV.284–313). Dido was also fully aware of the fundamental sin and mistake that spoiled her only hope of immortality (*Aeneid* IV.314–47). Consequently, the poet does not hesitate to say that neither destiny nor a heroic death finished the life of Dido, who lost her life tragically for nothing (*Aeneid* IV.673–705).

Towards the end of the episode, Aeneas deserves his merit by becoming heartless and denying his own love. He is finally able to hold his eyes steady and master the agony within him. But unlike Rama, who left his wife in the name of *dharma*, Aeneas leaves his beloved for personal glory. This is his duty, but such a duty does not glorify a high moral principle, it simply makes Roman military power possible (*Aeneid* IV. 314–47, VI.688–720).

When the poet writes that the gods intervene in order to steer Aeneas back to his duty, the message becomes pointedly open. Aeneas is criticized for not thinking of the coming glorious cities for which he is responsible. Aeneas has the duty to make Rome a breeding ground of heroic soldiers and to "subject the whole earth to the rule of law." The duty is not based on Aeneas's personal motivation, but on his responsibility towards his own children (*Aeneid* IV.217–83, VI.619–720).

In the final analysis, duty and destiny have become the same. The duty requires a voluntary and unquestionable submission to the destiny. But destiny and its rewards are not automatic; they require heroic actions to reach them (*Aeneid* V.1–27, X.91–121).

To fulfill a duty is not an easy task. The fulfillment requires hard work, especially in military campaigns. To emphasize this, the poet writes of the old empire as totally annihilated to make it seem that no Trojan can escape and to show how the new destiny of the Trojan remnant starts from utter despair. This despair is repeated once again when the Trojans continue on their adventurous way, sometimes inclined to hopeless despondency. Thus, the poet shows that only after immense efforts and through their own strength, as well as divine help and encouragement, the Trojans became successful. Rome grew to greatness after a process which began in weakness and despair. Aeneas himself is more than once ready to abandon hope. But each time he is given some reassurance and fortunately enough he never disregards the voice of destiny (Jackson Knight 1985: 13–14).

A lot of space has been devoted to Dido and the Shades episodes because their messages are convincing and revealing. However, in the epics they are mere introductions to the war in which the hero is finally born. It is a great war between the natives and the immigrants, fought because Aeneas finds the ultimate truth of heroism: he must conquer the land and fight for political power. The duty implies a willingness to fight and to use violent weapons against those who oppose the new political power (*Aeneid* VI.879–901, VIII.715–31).

The Trojans finally arrive in Italy and find their promised land. They are aware of the likelihood of war but they wish to come as friends, suggesting an agreement with the natives. The agreement is made and ratified by generous gifts between the partners (*Aeneid* III.289–323, VII.225–55). However a durable peace, everybody knows, is out of the question. It is not possible to gain power without a military fight. There are conflict of interest between the Trojans and the natives. The natives cannot accept the loss of their interests and power without putting the change of power to the test of war. They are willing to go to war even though they know they are going to lose the battle. Both parties know that power requires its price: "Maid, your dowry shall be blood, Trojan and Rutulian blood. War's Goddess awaits you to be mistress of your wedding" (*Aeneid* III.324–57). Indeed, the major part of the epic, more than two-thirds, is given to the description of the great war. Similarities between the *Aeneid* and the *Mahabharata* are surprisingly striking, as far as the introductions to and the wars themselves are concerned (Sinha 1977). In fact, they tell the same story of heroism and power.

Livy refers to an interesting aspect of heroism by showing that glory respects glory. The heroic leaders admire their enemies, the hero's enemy can and must be another hero. Hannibal and Scipio were great heroes to each other, not just to their nations (Livy XXI.39). War does not divide, but connects heroes.

Therefore, war is the key element of heroism in Livy's system. Without war there is no heroic leader, and without war there is no world government. According to Livy, Julius Proculus said: "Let them [Romans] learn to be soldiers. Let them know, and teach their children, that no power on earth can stand against Roman arms" (Livy I.16).

War makes the man and the nation, military glory and political leadership are intertwined. To have glory is to have the right to command. Military success creates political success, which is why military triumphs became so central in Roman political life, but later degenerated into internal power struggles (Livy I.39, 41, VI.16, VII.13, XXXV.10). Therefore, a great war must be invented—as Virgil did—if one does not exist. For Livy it did exist, because the courage and military talent of both Romans and Carthaginians were sufficient enough to make the great war both possible and decisive (Livy I.22-3, VI.7, VII.29; Polybius I.64.5-6).

Livy praised the hero not only for his courage but for his loyalty to the fathers and the country. The hero is advised to prove that the name of Rome is invincible. Therefore, war glorifies not only commanders and individuals but the whole Roman nation as well (Livy I.32, VII.10, 29).

In conclusion, the heroic king is conceived by war, and war supports him afterwards as well. Livy anticipates a new civil war unless the common fear of invasion keeps Romans together: "Shared danger is the strongest of bonds; it will keep men united in spite of mutual dislike and suspicion" (Livy II.39).

MORAL FITNESS OF THE HERO

The idea of the heroic king does not simply glorify military strength, the ability to win wars, and lead armies and the nation. It is not a justification to ignore everything else. There can be no true heroic king without moral fitness to the role. In ancient Hindu thought this was made the very basis of kingship, and heroism consequently moved into the background by submitting heroism strictly to *dharma*. In Rome the emphasis was explicitly given to military achievements. One can only impose the *Pax Romana* by might and conquest (*Aeneid* VI.847–53; cf. Wilkinson 1982: 11). On the other hand, this did not justify tyranny or glorify war as such—war was a means to make the individual morally perfect or to test his moral fitness for government.

In the *Mahabharata* moral fitness belongs to the wise ruler, Yudhishthira, the leader of the Pandavas. He was born after Karna, but as the son of the divine Yama (*Dharma*) he had the exclusive right to lead his four brothers, among them Arjuna, the great warrior. The five Pandava brothers, unlike Karna—the rejected oldest brother—were great warriors but were never ready for a military contest unlimited by *dharma*. In fact, it is only under Yudhishthira's command and *dharma*'s power that Arjuna, in addition to his military strength, shows perfect moral fitness. Therefore, it is Arjuna, a devoted student of *dharma*, who deserves the major role in the *Gita*. To make the message explicit, Karna, the first boy of Kunti and the son of Indra, while the strongest of all the fighters, is not entitled to kingship or even membership in the kshatriya caste. He lacks *dharma*. He was born outside the society before Yama begat Yudhishthira, i.e., before the *dharma*-caste system was established.

In addition to the epics, the submission of the military hero to moral fitness can be recognized in the historical development of kingship in ancient India. When the political kingship emerged in the small Aryan territories of the Gangetic plains, kings, even hereditary ones, had to consult either a council composed of all the male members of the tribe or an aristocratic tribal council. Some tribes were governed by such councils and did not have kings at all. The early kings, even if they had inherited their rank, always derived their legitimacy from and election by members of the tribe.

A new type of kingship emerged after the transition from nomadic life to settled agriculture, and when the increasing stratification of Aryan society gave rise to both division of labor and the mutual interests of kings (kshatriya) and priests (brahmin) in guaranteeing their respective leading positions. The new kings owed their position to a new ideology. In the late Vedic period the king usually emerged from a struggle for power among the nobility and then derived his legitimacy from the rituals carried out by priests (brahmin). In this system, the king was held responsible for the maintenance of cosmic order and of the fertility of new royal ideology. It is obvious that the relationship between Yudhishthira (a brahmin priest) and Arjuna (a kshatriya) reflects this new constellation and attempts to control the king's power by the religious rules of *dharma* (Drekmeier 1962; Kulke and Rothermund 1986: 43).

According to Polybius, the heroic ruler had to be the wise ruler in the first place. When the Greeks finally succeeded in finding such statesmen "their power at once became manifest, and the League achieved the splendid result of uniting all the Peloponnesian states" (Polybius III.39.11–40.2).

Polybius was interested in the "account of the subsequent policy of the conquerors and their method of universal rule." For Polybius, the end of successful military action was not "merely conquest and the subjection of all to their rule," for no one "goes to war with his neighbors simply for the sake of crushing an adversary." Polybius maintains that the peculiar qualities of the Roman constitution was conducive not only to their victory but also to their conception of a universal empire (Polybius III.4.2–7, III.4.9–10, III.2.5–6).

The evils of modern Rome put the realization of such a project in jeopardy. They had to return to the values of the Golden Age. Therefore historians, especially Livy, took to the task of the curation of character by the study of history. Similarly poets, especially Virgil, believed that the features of good character had made and could keep Rome great. Horace had the same message,[3] and above all Augustus himself attempted by legislation and propaganda to effect a change in Roman character. In 27 B.C.E. he set up a golden shield in the Curia Julia commemorating his *virtus*, *clementia*, *iustia*, and *pietas*. These and other virtues were constantly depicted throughout his reign on coins, public monuments, and other objects (Ogilvie 1982: 10–11).

As Jackson Knight has suggested, the *Aeneid* strongly confirms two important rules of conduct, one principally Greek and the other principally Roman. The Greek rule cautioned all to avoid excess, the Roman rule suggested the importance of being to true, that is, loyal to the gods, Rome, family, and friends. According to Jackson Knight, Virgil regularly calls Aeneas "the True," but only when he is faithful to the socially defined moral demands (Jackson Knight 1985: 14–16).

Furthermore, when Aeneas visits the Shades, he must take with him as his passport a golden bough. Jackson Knight (1985: 18–19) suggests that Virgil follows a Greek poem composed not long before Virgil's time. The poem gives the epithet to Plato's works that are said to contain every virtue. Jackson Knight concludes that Virgil chose this way of saying that moral goodness is necessary for the spiritual discernment, which in turn is necessary for wise and progressive statesmanship.

Livy emphasizes the role of moral factors, which do not refer to personal ethics even if it is an important element in Livy's system (cf. Livy III.44). Morality for Livy is more strongly related to factors such as courage and the military talents of soldiers and commanders. The real meaning of moral fitness can be found in the words by which Livy praises the mythical Roman heroes. According to Livy, these heroes were united in heart, fully able not only to command others but ready to obey moral rules and Roman laws. Furthermore, the true heroic leader distributed glory to the common stock rather than keep it for himself (Livy VI.6).

Morality is a measure of the ruler's true nature and quality; Livy's evaluation shows that Numa fully respected justice, piety, and all the divine and human laws. Naturally, such qualities were born in Rome only. Numa shared "austere discipline of the ancient Sabines, most incorruptible of men" (Livy I.17–18).

In other words, it is necessary but not sufficient to be heroic in warfare in order to become a good political leader. Livy's ideal was a heroic leader with good personal qualities for government and for the service of the society. To be heroic is to be so not only in war but also in peace. In the hands of morally handicapped men, heroism establishes nothing better than tyranny, if and when the hero is willing to use military forces against his own citizens. That is why Julius Caesar became hated and strongly criticized by Livy (Livy I.48; cf. I.52).

In short, to be a heroic leader one must not ignore the highest moral responsibilities. If he does, he is not longer a competent leader. According to Livy, many militarily competent commanders made themselves universally hated. In another case, a dictator fortunately realized that he had to moderate his ways and control his natural severity in order to become victorious in war (Livy I.27, III.42, VIII.36).

Heroism, war, and morality are intertwined at the personal level to form the heroic king. Military success and heroism legitimize the king's power, if he represents high moral qualities too. However, the basic issue does not concern legitimacy but rather social order. The heroic king, if he combines heroism and moral fitness, can stop the chaos of wars, including civil wars. Chaos can not be abolished any other way, neither can social order be established and maintained any other way.

Virgil and Livy were aware of the problems inherent in the heroic kingship. It was obvious that outside poetic and historical mythologies the heroic king must be a human being, and in the real world human beings have more or less selfish interests. In addition, the king has the capacity to fulfill these interests even against others' will. Therefore, it was not enough to find a hero and give him glory in a war. He had to have high moral qualities, extending from personal ethics to the moral qualities required to fulfill the strict social functions of heroism. But this was likely to remain idealistic wishful thinking, much more idealistic than the quest for the wise king. Therefore, both Virgil and Livy paid a lot of attention to moral decline. That is, the fact that democracy could end up in the chaos of civil war, and in the case of the heroic king, in tyranny. Even warnings were not enough, the idea of the heroic king inevitably invites more concrete checks to balance the king's power. If such checks can be connected to the moral fitness of the king, it is all the better.

There were at least two such balancing forces: religion and law. Both were required to maintain good government. Furthermore, it is impossible to imagine a true hero in the Roman sense, if he does not respect both religion and law, which are attributes of both a good society and the heroic king.

For Virgil, the mythological religious basis—the destiny—is the key factor in heroism. Livy suggests, much more explicitly, that traditional religious rites are essential for the well-being of the state (Ogilvie 1982: 14). Livy maintains that the heroic leader *must* carefully follow these religious rites in all behavior, but especially in war and government. There are many heroic figures in Livy's mythology, but all of them fully respect religion. For example, determined not to resign the dictatorship after the celebration of his triumph over the Gauls Camillus revealed both manly and heroic character and acted "with the strictest sense of his religious duties" (Livy V.49–51).

For Livy religious rites are a substitute for war. Livy claims that fear of gods maintain the nation's moral fiber during times of peace. According to Livy, Rome had originally been founded by the force of arms, but Numa gave it a second beginning with a solid bases of law and religious observance (Livy I.19–20).

In addition to the power of religion, Roman law had power over everybody. For example in a controversial case Scipio, the heroic Roman leader during the Punic Wars, was put on trial in 187 B.C.E. Livy admires Scipio as a hero, but says that it was proper to put him on trial for an alleged crime because not even a hero must live above the law (Livy I.9, I.21, XXXVIII.50).

Livy gives an important role to law, because he hates all forms of chaos. Without the standards of law, men exercise free judgment in each individual case, both during war and peace. Livy suggests that Rome must have internal peace in order to have external military success. Furthermore, internal disputes are an invitation to foreign powers to attack Rome. If there is no political dissension, there is no threat of foreign invasion, either (Livy I.7, 17, 33, II.1, IV.7, XXIV.44).

Similarly, Virgil wishes to tell his audience that Aeneas's duty is not only to become a hero or establish a city, but to create and maintain order. All efforts, all military campaigns, everything, are required in order to have the final reward: social order. The bases of order were destroyed by the plots of gods in Troy, therefore, the original empire had to be destroyed. The consequent chaos was not to remain eternal, it ended by establishing a new city. The final battle was required in order to achieve this goal. The imagined Trojan victory over the natives in Italy—as the Roman victories over Macedonia and Carthage—was a precondition for the new order. Heroism was not the ultimate goal, a lawful system of government was the goal (*Aeneid* VI.785–817). In the *Georgics* (IV.560–563, cf. Wilkinson 1982: 24), one could note the pride of bestowing on the world the Roman rule of law, as well as the forecast of immortality as a reward for the man who would bring this about.

NOTES

1. In Homer's *Iliad* Achilles's heroism is individualistic and therefore not the basis of order but a departure to chaos.

2. Concerning the Roman case, Cicero's idea of the wise ruler paved the way for another conclusion made by Livy and Virgil, who supported the heroic king. It can also be said that Virgil represents the climax of the process towards the heroic leader, while Livy takes an intermediary position by supporting both versions of the ideal ruler. However, we cannot divide Livy's ideas into two.

3. See his *Odes* written about 27 B.C.E.

CHAPTER 11

Coercive Power as the Basis of Social Order

Both the wise and the heroic king must possess high moral qualities. In the theory of the wise king, wisdom is achieved through learning. In the theory of the heroic king, his fitness for leadership is revealed in war. Coercive power presents the third basis of leadership and social order. The king is king because he keeps sovereign power to rule his subjects. In order to maintain social order, the king must understand that power is coercive by its very nature; therefore, the king must take and apply politics as nothing else but politics. If he considers any other factors, like his feelings towards his subjects or his responsibility to ethical principles, he is not likely to have order but chaos.

It is another matter if the king wishes to remain the winner of continuous power struggles. In fact, he must know that there are others who hope to replace him and become king in his stead. Therefore, if the king is clever he applies other measures—moral arguments, persuasion, the distribution of positions and other rewards, and so forth—in order to strengthen and maintain his power. If he is clever enough, the distinction between moral and coercive rule will be blurred so that his rule seems legitimized in moral terms. In fact, coercive rule must claim to be representing the true moral rule, where social order is defined by shared basic values, especially the protection of life and property. Because the king's—that is, the state's—coercive power is only able to give sufficient safety to such shared values and to the weak in the first place, it represents the highest morality to maintain that power before anything else.

I start with Aristotle who supports the moral approach, but also suggests some justification for coercive power, or at least the military basis of power. However, the paradigmatic case is represented by Chinese Legalism, which maintains that politics is coercive by nature. This view is also shared by the concept of *danda* in ancient Indian political thought, especially by Kautilya.

ARISTOTLE

Aristotle maintains that individual morality must be strengthened by law. Only then can natural human associations become the state. The power of the state must be above the power of other human associations (friendship, household, and village). Only the state is justified in applying, when required, coercive power. Order is, in the final analysis, based on a certain amount of coercion. Aristotle maintains that those who do not accept the rules of the game based on laws and the state must emigrate (*Athenian Constitution*, Ch. 39).

Compulsion is justified by the nature of the state, which includes its own legitimation. The function of the state is to carry out and protect the general, common good of all citizens. Therefore, the state is an ethical organ and as such, it is more than the sum of its individuals.

In the final analysis, political power is based on military strength. According to Aristotle, military virtue is found in a great number of people. This makes the defensive element the most sovereign body in the state. In other words, those who bear arms must have the highest role in the constitution. Military power and political power go together because it will be necessary to give political power to those who control military power, "for those who are in sovereign control of arms are in a sovereign position to decide whether the constitution is to continue or not" (*Politics* 1287a32, 1329a2; cf. 1268a14, VII.x).

Furthermore, compulsion is required because men are never rendered good by nature, or even by teaching. Human nature is contingent and not always possible to submit to control. Aristotle does not deny that there may be *a* good man or that somebody can be educated to become good. In general, it is possible for one man or a few to be outstanding in virtue, but it is difficult for a large number to reach a high standard of all virtues. In the final analysis, argument and teaching do not have an impact on anybody who lives according to the dictates of passion. Therefore, Aristotle claims, explicitly calling his claim "a general rule," that "passion yields not to argument but to compulsion." Compulsion is required because "most people bow to necessity sooner than to argument, to the threat of punishment rather than to the sense of what is noble" (*Ethics* 1179b).

However, coercive power is not preferred in some abstract instances, but its justification is derived from its function in managing and abolishing social conflicts. This function is represented and executed by the ruler. In fact, as the case of Solon reveals, conflicting actors, in order to get rid of their mutual destruction, appoint someone to rule and so entrust the state—or coercive power—to him (*Athenian Constitution*, Chs. 5–6).

Another justification comes from the assumption that some people are made, by nature, to rule, while other are made to submit. The intelligent rules, the physically strong are ruled. The king must have coercive power and the required military (and other) capacities to control the strong. Therefore, force is derived from and justified by nature. The art of war is a way of acquiring property, but it must only be used against men who are by nature intended to be ruled, but who refuse to be ruled (*Politics* 1256b20).

This argument makes Aristotle's discussion of slavery important. According to Aristotle, as an extreme example of legal power slavery is fully justified because there are human beings that by nature belong not to themselves but to others (*Politics* 1254a9; Saunders 1984b: I.iii–v). However, the use of coercive power over slaves is not justified by an assumption that slaves are not human beings. Aristotle is explicit in classifying slaves as human beings, but maintains that they lack logical reason, which is the only condition of citizenship. The slaves are illogical and emotional and therefore incapable of deliberate actions with forethought. This implies that slaves must not have access to coercive power, the use of which demands the ability to make political decisions.

Similarly, in discussing women Aristotle leaves no doubt about their subordinate role; he clearly states that men are better fitted to command than women. According to Fortenbaugh (1977: 135–38) Aristotle credited women with reason and therefore distinguished them from slaves (who never have reason) and children (who have not yet acquired reason). However, Aristotle assigns women a subordinate role on the same grounds he applied to slaves: women's reason or the logical side of the bipartite soul is subject to emotional or illogical reasoning (*Politics* 1259a37).

The ideal form of state and constitution (Sinclair 1984: 389) is not an academic question for Aristotle. It is related to the fundamental issue of the use of power within the state.

As to the structure of power within the state it is well known that Aristotle preferred a concentration of power. He preferred mild oligarchy but disliked extreme democracy. In fact, he did not prefer any given form of government except for coercive power. This is best revealed when Aristotle recommends that the ruled have no affections between them, in other words wives and children should be common. This lack of affection among the ruled is "necessary in the interests of obedience and absence of revolt" (*Athenian Constitution*: 11; *Politics* 1255b16, 1262a40). This makes clear Aristotle's final conclusion that order is based on coercive power: "Democracy is found chiefly in dwellings that have no master and everyone is on an equal footing; it is found likewise in those where the ruler is weak and everyone can do whatever he likes" (*Ethics* 1161a).

However, it must be emphasized that Aristotle never justifies arbitrary power; coercive power is inevitable, but only in the full interests of the ruled. Aristotle does not trust in the simple existence of coercive force like the Chinese Legalists. Aristotle only maintains that the state needs a master. Such a master must be a commanding but wise king, not a tyrant. Arbitrary power can be avoided if there is space for politics, that is, for debates and discourses for the purposes of finding the common interest. Therefore, the master must respect a division of labor and leave space for politics instead of eliminating it by force (*Politics* 1261a10, 1273b8; Saunders 1984b: II.i–iii).

In other words, coercive power must not eliminate the interests of the subjects but give full attention to the common interest shared by both the ruler and the subjects. This common interest consists of "the purpose of preservation," the survival of citizens (*Politics* 1252a24). A given political structure is justified if it serves its function in the interest of the ruled. The ruled are the members of the society; therefore, what is at stake is not the survival of a given individual but that of the society. When an acceptable political system (kingship, aristocracy, and timocracy) degenerates into an unacceptable form (tyranny, oligarchy, and democracy) power loses its function in establishing and maintaining social order (*Ethics* 1160b; cf. *Politics* 1279a32–b4).

CHINESE LEGALISM AND INDIAN DANDA

The Legalist solution in establishing a new order was, in accordance with the nature of man, to clarify the principles of reward and punishment. Legalism suggested its ideas as the best and only way of establishing a new order. It saw other schools—especially Confucian thought—as the major causes of chaos. The Confucians did not know, the Legalists maintained, the real basis of order, but instead chattered nonsense in order to disturb effective government. The problem, the Legalists claimed, was that the Confucians did not recommend "the use of the commanding position" to "harass the wicked and villainous ministers." The Legalist message was that benevolence may be a significant means of mass control, but not a way of suppressing wickedness and outrage (Han Fei I: 123, 127, 269; Liao 1939: xxxi–ii).

Legalists did not share the concept of man's original goodness (cf. Chapter 8). According to Han Fei, human nature is evil without exception. Even a father and mother happily receive a baby boy but kill a baby girl, because they selfishly think of later conveniences and decreased profits (Han Fei I: 126; Fung 1983: 327).

The Legalists agreed that there may be good men, but this is an exception not the rule. Therefore, the establishment of an orderly government cannot wait for men who are not deceitful. Good government cannot be based on exceptions among human beings, all human beings must be governed. Therefore, a ruler who understands policy does not trust in wishful thinking but prefers the road to certain success (Han Fei/Watson: 109, 126).

While the Confucian school believed that the people of antiquity were morally superior than people of the present, Han Fei saw that this was caused by a mere abundance of supplies. After population increased, the scarcity of resources caused conflict and disorder. Indeed, man's behavior cannot be explained by referring to moral virtue but to material conditions, the scarcity of goods (Han Fei II: 276; Fung 1983: 328–29).

Ancient Indian political thought does not pay explicit attention to the issues of human nature. However, the *danda* tradition and Kautilya imply a similar conception of evil human nature. According to Indian thought, made explicit by Kautilya, men are selfish, they are motivated by material needs, and politics takes place in the world of conflicting interests.

The fact that human nature is evil was made the basis of order by the Legalists. The Legalists suggested that the evilness of man can change from a liability to an asset. The evil nature of human beings does not only make coercive power inevitable but possible as well. According to Legalist thought, men's nature knows only to move toward what is beneficial and avoid what is harmful. Therefore, even kindness or virtue must have its origin in force: "Punishment produces force, force produces strength, strength produces awe, awe produces kindness and virtue" (Shang I.4. 12b–13a). The Legalists maintained that severe penalty is what people fear, heavy punishment is what people hate, and that ministers are afraid of punishment but fond of encouragement and reward. This means that political failures and successes are based on rational principles not emotional factors (Han Fei I: 46, 128, 278; Fung 1983: 327). Furthermore, due to their nature the ruled contribute to the coercive power used over themselves by spying or watching one another in their hidden affairs (Han Fei II: 331).

The Legalists maintained that words and deeds not conforming to laws and decrees must be forbidden and crimes punished, but Legalism has a rather broad and unconventional meaning. In fact, criminal law is not the basic question of Legalist political theory. Legalism generalized law to all human and social relations, similarly to the Zoroastrians. In this sense it is understandable that there are not only negative sanctions for those who break laws, but positive rewards for those who respect them. Furthermore, what is at stake is the promise given by a political actor. In politics, rewards and punishments are distributed to political actors according to the degree that "actualities and their names" correspond with one another. That is, it is the correspondence between the actor's promises—words—and his accomplishments—deeds—that count and is under strict scrutiny (Han Fei I: 46; Han Fei/Watson: 30; Han Fei II: 207).

Chinese Legalist theory is, in fact, a rather unique application of the demand to keep one's promises. In Legalism, one must do what he promises to do. That is, accomplishments should match the promises and goals expressed before the undertaking. Furthermore, the basic proposition of the theory claims that the undertaking must achieve, not surpass what was promised. In explicit terms, those who do more than they have promised must be punished by death. It may sound surprising to deter initiative and lucky achievements, but Legalist theory is not interested in achievements only, it is more interested in social order. By definition, there can not be any great achievements outside social order. Therefore, all discrepancies between "the work" and "the name" are dangerous (Han Fei I: 48–49; Han Fei/Watson: 19). If one reveals achievements *either* below *or* above the stated goal, the promise will only be empty words and, consequently, expressions of disorder.

Another unconventional aspect of Legalist theory concerns the definitions or nature of rewards and punishments. The basic definition is simple, but revealing: mutilation and death is called punishment, honor is called reward. In other words, punishments are always extreme, rewards are both minor and abstract. Order is based on deterrence, not on rewards—on sticks, not carrots. The best rewards and punishments are predictable, and in the Legalist definition, inescapable (Han Fei/Watson: 103–4). Therefore, the reward is and must be extremely small because such rewards are likely to represent empty promises. Using this same logic, severe and inescapable penalties must be applied to the smallest crimes in order to deter everyone from committing more serious crimes.

The essential precondition for the system of rewards and punishment to create order is that everyone must be able to understand the basis of rewards and punishments. Such a basis cannot be found in complex, written laws and words but in the strict correspondence of an individual's own promises and deeds. The individual knows what he promises and what he executes. Both rewards and punishments must be similarly clear and easy to understand, for "subtle and mysterious words are no business of the people" (Han Fei/Watson: 108; cf. Pocock 1973).

Legalists maintain that the power of authority is all that counts. There is, in the human being, the will to obtain power. If one declines the position of king, it occurs not because of moral excellence, but because of the limitations of power. The will to obtain power is corroborated by the will to submission. Legalists maintained that in human nature there is a natural tendency toward submission to authority. In other words, the king can be wise, heroic, or even tyrannical, but everybody acknowledges allegiance even "to the most mediocre ruler" (Han Fei/Watson: 102; Fung 1983: 329).

The suggested concept of human nature, the consequent system of rewards and punishments, and the central role of power give politics a coercive nature. The suggested rational application of power implies "politics as politics," i.e., politics free from any other considerations. Furthermore, because human nature is evil, the power struggle and its harsh methods are justified. The ruler—though he too is evil—struggles against aspirants to power. In order to win them over, he must use efficient methods and leave nothing to chance. Therefore, it is the very power struggle that makes any ruler—good or evil—able to establish and maintain order.

On the other hand, the Legalists emphasized that the weak must be defended against the strong, or as it was expressed in India, "otherwise the big fish eat the small ones" (Manu VII.3; Kinsley 1982: 83). Because man is evil, it is morally right to control him. Indeed, it is the duty of the ruler to do so, for if he "tolerates robbers, he injures good citizens" and creates disorder (Han Fei II: 158). Political order and laws make it impossible for the worthy to violate the unworthy, the strong to violate the weak, and the many to violate the few. A cage enables the weak to subdue the tiger (Han Fei I: 267–68)

The Legalist order must help the weak, and the ruler has the duty to make that possible. The ruler does not serve his own personal interests. Any arbitrary power and capricious use of force and violence would not establish order but disorder. Legalist theory does not wish to add wings to tigers because such monsters would fly into the village and devour the population (Han Fei II: 201). In other words, the ideal Legalist ruler is intelligent and politically prudent. Such a king can make all ministers discard their selfish motives and practice public justice, while the violent sovereign makes ministers cast public justice aside and act on his own selfish motives (Han Fei I: 124).

It is suggested that the ruler must consider the true and best interests of his people. It is his duty to establish an orderly government and society for the benefit of all. He must scrutinize the facts of right and wrong and investigate the conditions of order and chaos (Han Fei I: 167–68). The king's duty to establish and maintain order is fulfilled through power, not love, because compassion makes the law null and void. Indeed, authority, power, rewards, and punishments keep the state in order. The task is carried out by expelling private action and upholding public law. That is, the king must make clear the distinction between public and private interests, forbid private favors, and disperse the partisans of powerful ministers. The king must understand that the name of the statecraft is supremacy, and that the secrets of his successes and failures are caused by the factors of strength and weakness, respectively (Han Fei I: 38, 59, 128–29, 141, 282).

It is due to the evilness of human nature that man must be put under severe control. Men do not understand what is in their best interest. They want order but dislike the path to order. The use of power is required, because "even traitorous ministers would not dare to deceive the king who is able to use force" (Han Fei I: 124; Fung 1983: 318).

All this reveals that according to the Legalist doctrine a harmony of interests exists between the state (the ruler) and the individual. On the other hand, a fundamental conflict of interest exists between the ruler and the ministers. Behind this conflict there is the fundamental tension between public and private interests. The two contenting interests can never prevail at the same time (Han Fei/Watson: 107):

Superior and inferior wage one hundred battles a day. the inferior conceals his tricks which he uses in testing the superior. . . . If the minister does not murder the ruler, it is because his partisans and adherents are not yet powerful enough. (Han Fei I: 59–60)

The central argument is that the interests of the ruler and the ministers interests are based on the zero-sum game: if one wins, the other loses. Therefore, the ministers, if too intimate with the ruler and too powerful, puts the ruler in personal danger and could overturn the position of the sovereign. The state goes to ruin if the ministers are too powerful or are allowed to administer state affairs (Han Fei II: 2, 28, 140; cf. p. 30).

The Legalists see the ruler as being involved in the struggle for power. He is not a non-partisan judge above the quarreling people but a participant in the very same game, interested in the maintenance of his position at the very top of the power pyramid. Similarly, Kautilya shares the view that conflicting interests can be applied to establish and maintain order if the ruler takes care that no interests exist as his own.

It does not matter whether a ruler is good or evil, because all other participants in the game are evil (Han Fei/Watson: 18). Therefore, the ruler cannot avoid the contest. That is why Lord Shang (I.I.1a) declared: "He, who hesitates in action, does not accomplish anything." It is the ruler's duty to play the game without hesitation; he must be tough in order to have peace, and in order to govern his country, he must ruthlessly eliminate any rebellious ministers (Han Fei II: 115).

This is far from the beautiful and harmonious world of the Confucians. In the Legalist world of coercive politics and power struggles many are selfish but only a few serve the ruler by observing the law. Therefore, the sovereign is an extremely lonely figure living in isolation. The ministers conspire and form clicks against the ruler (Han Fei I: 119, cf. 143). In other words, it belongs to the very nature of governing that the ruler, if he is an outstanding Legalist master able to maintain order, is always disapproved of by the outside world, by the ministers, and any others whose interests can only be carried on in disorder. Therefore, the ruler who is concerned about the virtue of order is never "in harmony with popular ideas." In accomplishing the great work of governing, the true ruler "does not take counsel with the multitude" (Shang I.I.1a–b). Furthermore, because situations differ measures must also change. The good ruler must examine the things of his age and be prepared to deal with them (Han Fei II: 276, 279).

Han Fei claims that ministers always try to betray, molest, or murder the ruler. According to him there are eight strategies that ministers customarily employ to work their villainy: the ruler's bedfellows, his attendants, his elders and kin, baleful pursuits, the people, fluent speakers, authority and might, and the surrounding states. Han Fei maintains that unlike the king the leper never suffers choking, shooting, starving to death or similar miseries, therefore, "though the leper feels pity for the king, there is good reason for it" (Han Fei I: 116, 133; Han Fei/Watson: 43–45).

The ministers are never loyal. They do anything the can to damage the ruler and increase their own power. They exhaust public treasuries and armors, serve big powers, and utilize their influence to mislead and destroy the ruler (Han Fei I: 65–66). They disguise their efforts and cheat the ruler in order to accomplish their private interests. For this reason, if the king likes or hates something, the minister deceitfully praises and blames accordingly. Consequently, if the ruler is not beware of such tricks, he will be controlled by the ministers (Han Fei I: 47, 65–66, 116–17; Han Fei II: 3).

This is why the Legalist doctrine justifies the absolute harshness of the power struggle. Instead of practicing benevolence, the ruler must see the necessity of inflicting penalties whenever required. The ideal ruler is prudent and calculating. He must be as selfish or even more so than his inferiors. If there are accomplishments, the ruler must take credit for them. If there are errors, the ministers must be held responsible. The ruler who shows goodness is too stupid a person for his task. During continuous wars between rival states (i.e., the Warring States period) goodness by the ruler increases chaos rather than order. The ruler's benevolence encourages rather than prevents destructive moves by his ministers (Han Fei II: 3–5, 280–81; Han Fei/Watson: 17, 77, 101).

In his politics, the ruler must be sharp and careful, always bearing the power struggle and conflicting interests in his mind. Consequently, it is hazardous for the ruler to trust others and thereby become controlled by others. A ruler must always remember the selfishness of man, and be aware of all the evil tricks used by his inferiors (Han Fei/Watson: 84; Han Fei I: 145; Fung 1983: 327). Therefore, if the ruler reveals the things he hates, likes, or wants, his ministers will conceal their motives and disguise their feelings and attitudes. Therefore, the ruler must never reveal his true preferences. In the logic of rewards and punishments, the ruler makes the ministers reveal their preferences and then keeps his power to distribute rewards or punishments on the basis of accomplishments. The ruler must prevent people from seeing the limits of his own affairs, only then can he keep the safety of his body and maintain possession of his state (Han Fei I: 31, 49–51, 183).

In the world of politics, the ruler must depend on his own position and not the faithfulness of the ministers. On the other hand, the fruits of power are not there to be reaped without efforts. While the king can rely on position and status instead of virtue and wisdom, it can not work alone. The ruler must apply a system of rewards and punishments because he is man and no man is wise enough to prevent all mistakes. In fact, the ruler does not need any extraordinary intellectual capacities to examine the motives and actions of his inferiors. He only needs to use the law of rewards and punishments to select men for him and weigh their merits (Han Fei II: 63 199, 201; Han Fei/Watson: 24).

The Legalists adopted the Daoist doctrine of non-activity but gave a rather peculiar meaning to the doctrine. The Daoists rejected politics and political activity, but the

Legalists gave politics the main role. In Legalism, non-activity maintains that the ruler must not let his power be seen, he must remain actionless (Han Fei/Watson: 35). The system of rewards and punishments is based on the minister's promises and accomplishments, not on the ruler's orders or abstract laws. Ministers must set their own standards, and when they do so they alone are responsible for the required correspondence. The king's single task and duty in the government of the state is, therefore, to do nothing but check to make certain that the stated goals and actual results match. If they do, the king and the ministers achieve harmony (Han Fei/Watson: 37). If they do not, the king punishes the ministers.

Order will be found when the ministers reveal their motivations and match their accomplishments to them. The ruler possesses the power, his ministers try to steal his power. If and when the ministers are forced to set their own goals, they inevitably reveal their motives to the ruler. Therefore, non-action from above makes the ministers below "tremble with fear" (Han Fei/Watson: 17).

There is an important reason to emphasize the activity of the ministers in setting their own goals. The reason is to find a solid basis for common interests. The selfishness of actors gives this a solid basis: if the ministers are allowed to pursue their private interests, molest the ruler, and destroy the state and order, it is not their fault but the ruler's mistake. The intelligent ruler keeps officials in service and thus exhausts their abilities (Han Fei I: 29–30). The ruler makes a major mistake if he does not apply the selfishness of the ministers in order to establish order.

The king must pursue the policy of making the people do good against their will. He can never rely on the people doing good with love. Love is unpredictable and unsure and therefore dangerous. Necessity is predictable and therefore safe. Necessity makes the ruled service the king (the state), whether or not the ruled is good or evil (Han Fei I: 121).

As a result, the ruler and the minister supplement each other as father and son. Not because of love, trust, or compassion the ruled feels or should feel towards the superior, but because politics, or power struggle, establishes a solid tie of true or calculated interests. There is the conflict of interest, which the ruler must never forget, however, this conflict is associative not divisive. The Legalists claim that because everybody has a strong motive for gain, it is easy to reach a balance of interests (Han Fei II: 44–45). It is not harmony but a balance of interests where the partners have a shared understanding of the essence of politics as the struggle for power. Furthermore, balance of interests is not realized automatically, it is established and maintained by the ruler. Therefore, the minister does not necessarily love the ruler, he works for the state and the ruler because of advantages for himself (Han Fei I: 51). Both the king and the ministers work with calculating minds. The ministers never injure their own bodies or interests, nor does the ruler injure the state to benefit the ministers. In rational calculation the ministers regard personal injury as unprofitable, and the ruler regards injury to the state also unprofitable. This rational engine works because the ministers can not avoid the law of rewards and punishments (Han Fei I: 168).

The question in the debate is of the efficiency and certainty—or according to Legalist thought, of inefficiency and uncertainty—of a social order based on the goodness of human nature. Han Fei finds it ridiculous to say that only if ruler and subject become like father and son can there be order, for all parents love their children, but children quite often behave badly. Furthermore, force is efficient in seizing power and the special Legalist righteousness, in the sense of balanced rewards and punishments, is applicable to maintaining it (Han Fei/Watson: 101; Shang II.7.9b–10b).

The Legalist logic is not always easy to understand or describe. The Legalist conception of "politics as politics" can be as valid as any other similar conceptions, and their arguments can be more or less convincing than others. The historical facts are that Legalist theory was able to contribute to the first unification of China, but this China remained short-lived. Furthermore, the Legalist writers were all killed in power struggles. Their doctrines were welcomed, but their personal success was less convincing.

Confucians were aware of the two handles of government (cf. *Analects* 2.3), but whereas they put virtue ahead of punishment, the Legalists put punishment ahead of virtue (Chan 1963: 256). Interestingly enough, the difference between Confucianism and Legalism does not lead to divergent results at the level of social relations. Both sanction authoritarian and hierarchical structures. Even in the Confucian world the ruler exists for transforming—from above—the common people. According to Xun Zi, the ancient sages did not accept equality among the masses because it made it impossible to employ them all. Therefore, the former kings regulated the principles of ritual in order to set up ranks. This was, according to Xun, required for establishing common interests among the higher ranks to maintain their power and status by controlling those in the lower ranks. Therefore, even in the Confucian world "equality is based upon inequality" (Hsün Tzu/Watson: 36, 157).

However, in Confucianism there is a major difference between Xun Zi and the Legalists. Whereas the act of correcting men suggested by Xun Zi consists of ceremonies and music, education, and the so-called rectification of names, similar actions for the Legalists consist of rewards and punishments. Nevertheless, Xun Zi is fully aware that the ruler cannot always be successful in this task. While everyone is capable of becoming a sage, not everyone is willing to become a sage (Chan 1963: 254; Hsün Tzu/Watson: 167).

In ancient Indian political thought *danda* refers to the application of force, violence, and punishments in maintaining power. *Danda* was made the leading principle of government, especially in the Magadha kingdom, which was based on a strict and carefully organized administration (Edwardes 1961: 43–45). The *arthashastras* hold that the institution of kingship originated as a response to hostile pressures from the hostile world, especially from within the society and the evilness of man. It was believed that the original state of nature had been a condition of righteousness and bliss. *Dharma* kept everything in its proper place and there was no need for *danda*. But later things went wrong, anti-social personality traits gradually developed in man due to the law of *karma*. After the fall from absolute *dharma*, men ceased to be guided by wisdom, justice, and righteousness. Therefore, the restraining power of the king became a necessity. The sinful nature of man legitimates compulsion and the state is the instrument for ensuring sufficient order to make decent life possible. Thus, coercion (*danda*) became necessary to maintain order, preserve virtue, and hold men to the duties of their respective castes. Hence, the function of the state in the *danda* tradition was to maintain stability by employing coercive power. *Dharma* cannot exist without *danda* in the world of imperfect man (Drekmeier 1962: 137, 245–48).

Similarities between the Indian *danda* tradition and Chinese Legalists are striking—both share the political role of punishment and rewards. Like Legalism, the *danda* school maintained that in order to safeguard social order for his subjects, the king must apply fear. The principles of *danda* were already formulated in the *Laws of Manu*, which maintained that punishment alone governs all created beings, protects them, and watches over them while they sleep. Punishment is the king, the manager of affairs, the ruler—everything that is required for ensuring obedience to the law. Punishment is a means to achieve that which is not achieved otherwise and to maintain and add that which has been achieved (Manu VII.17–18; Ghoshal 1959: 112, 299).

But unlike Chinese Legalism, ancient Indian thought gave a key role to moral duty: *dharma* and *danda* were not separate but joined. *Danda* maintains social order and guarantees the equilibrium of the social systems, and thus supports *dharma*. Danda does not nullify *dharma*, but strengthens it. According to Manu, "for the king's sake the Lord formerly created his own son, Punishment, the protector of all creatures, an incarnation of the law, formed of Brahman's glory" (Kautilya I.4; Manu VII.14; cf. VII.15–20).

In short, *danda* must not be unlimited. Its use must be based on justice. Only then will *danda* bring happiness. Any unlawful application of *danda* will cause dissatisfaction, as will the non-application of *danda* (Ghoshal 1959: 87, 92, 119, 193, 299, 547): "Having fully considered the time and the place of the offence, the strength and the knowledge of the offender, let him justly inflict that punishment on men who act unjustly." The king must declare punishment to be identical with the law: "If punishment is properly inflicted after due consideration, it makes all people happy; but inflicted without consideration, it destroys everything" (Manu VII.18–19, 218).

Danda itself provides at least a partial explanation for the Kautilyan doctrine of expediency. *Danda* represents a bridge between morality and *Staatsräson*. *Danda* was the nemesis for the king who misused its power, as well as for the subjects who offended the moral order. Punishment, when awarded with due consideration, makes people devoted to righteousness and to works productive of wealth and enjoyment. Punishment, when ill-awarded under the influence of greed and anger or owing to ignorance, excites fury even among hermits and ascetics dwelling in forests, not to speak of participants in economic and political activities (Drekmeier 1962: 202). Even Kautilya maintains that the king who imposes severe punishment becomes repulsive to the people, but he who awards mild punishment becomes contemptible. However, Kautilya shares the Legalist argument by saying that "whoever imposes punishment as deserved becomes respectable" (Kautilya I.4). Kautilya, unlike the Chinese Legalists, places great emphasis on the intellectual and moral discipline of the king, which is essential to the successful functioning of the state. The king must be continent, industrious, and alert—a man of refinement and sound judgment (Drekmeier 1962: 209). Kautilya, in short, saw political disintegration as the major problem. Therefore, politics and especially foreign policy (including military force, violence, and even amoral methods) had to be applied to end political disintegration—in order to find peace for religious pursuits (Ghosal 1966: 94). Kautilya preferred social and moral order (i.e., the society) to the state or use of power hostile to moral principles. This connects Kautilya to the dominating Indian tradition: Brahmanism.

In brief, the Indian *danda* tradition supported the power of the king or the state over the society, but the detachment from the moral norms (*dharma*) was far from absolute. Furthermore, the *danda* tradition admitted, interestingly enough, that the use of *danda*—or politics—is a negative phenomenon with negative consequences. *Danda* requires cruelty, causing the kshatriya to kill and therefore spoil himself. The king must purify himself by making sacrifices, submitting himself to danger, or sacrificing himself on behalf of the society (Aho 1981; Ghoshal 1959: 192).

While the ruler fulfills the virtue and duty of government by applying violence or punishments, is his own behavior based on the law? The Legalists maintained that the ruler does not offer promises like his ministers. This also implies that the ruler must have the power to change laws, even go beyond laws. This implication was made explicit by the Legalists. It was declared that ordinary people and scholars abide by old practices, and are therefore appropriate for "filling offices and for maintaining the law." But those people cannot "take part in a discussion, which goes beyond the law." That is, the king "creates laws, but a foolish man is controlled by them," he "reforms rites, but a worthless man is enslaved by them." Consequently, "with a man, who is controlled by laws, it is not worth while to discuss reform." In short, "a country, where the wicked govern the virtuous, will be orderly, so that it will become strong" (Shang I.I.2a, 1.4.11b).

Ancient Indian political thought did not give similar freedom to the king. The *arthashastra*s were intended as a political guide for the king and his ministers. Their emphasis is on the need for sanctions capable of preventing social disorder. While Kautilya is inclined to share the Legalist position, he still shares the traditional Indian idea that anarchy is considered the greatest catastrophe that can befall mankind. Kautilya does not make the implication of such an idea explicit, but neither does he deny it. The implication is that the need to avoid anarchy can justify a revolution when the king has lost his duty, creating a situation where there is no true king—the servant of the *dharma*-caste system—and where the natural order of the universe is disrupted and destroyed. When the king's power declines, or becomes a tyranny against the needs of his people, and social order is threatened, members of any class may take action to prevent lawlessness, for anarchy is to be avoided at any cost (Drekmeier 1962: 136).

CHAPTER 12

Peaceful External Relations as the Basis of Social Order

It is logical that Plato and Mo Zi, who envisaged the possibility and existence of sovereign units governed by the wise king, consider morality necessary to direct relations between them. Aristotle and Kong Zi, who favored the world community model, are far from Mo Zi's ideas of pacifism, but perhaps closer to Plato's ideas. They condemn war in general, or wars between groups of the same commonwealth, but accept war that establishes such a commonwealth. This specific type of war is the kind that abolishes wars within the community. For Aristotle, morality-based relations within the Greek community was the goal. He hoped Alexander would stop wars between the Greek city-states and govern them as the wise king. For Kong Zi, morality and punitive wars were a means of and first step toward voluntary unification of the *tien-hsia*.

PLATO

Plato's and Aristotle's works can be read too literally, out of context, as pure academic efforts concentrated on the *polis*, the individual, and the relationship between the individual and the *polis*. Such an interpretation makes it appear like they do not discuss or comment on relations between the city-states, and if they did their views were conventionally in favor of war (Donelan 1978). It has even been maintained that Plato's works were an attempt to explain the defeat of Athens in the Peloponnesian War and make it stronger for future campaigns. Plato "felt that Athens' defeat was the defeat of laxity and incompetence by Spartan discipline and good order" (Saunders 1984a: 19).

It is true that Plato's comments on international relations were rather scant. We can observe three short statements. The first concerns the four stages of development of the state: (1) single families; (2) groups of families; (3) the city-state; and (4) the union of city-states (*Laws* 683; cf. *Laws* 681; Saunders 1984a: 128), that is, human associations grow from single families to the international union. Plato maintains that as independent units the city-states are able to have peaceful relations, and even form an orderly union among themselves.

The second statement maintains that non-interaction between the city-states forms the best relationships between them, therefore, the population must concentrate on agriculture, not foreign trade. A state must never be established on the seashore but 80 stadions from the sea (Saunders 1984a: 17, 342; cf. *Laws* 704, 847, 949). This does not, however, justify isolation from the others. In order to achieve a properly advanced level of civilization, a state must come into contact with "all the vices and virtues of mankind" (*Laws* 951a–b).

The third statement concerns some practical rules which are, according to Plato, required to guarantee that people who go to another city will be treated well and properly (*Laws* 750, 848, 941, 950, 953).

Furthermore, Plato did not say in explicit terms that peaceful and orderly relations, instead of war, are possible between the city-states. In fact, he seems to deny such a possibility. Plato's attitude towards war looks extremely positive. He required men to spend a lot of time on military exercises during peace time. Even sports had to be changed for military exercises and carried out with real weapons. Plato suggested that children follow their parents to war in order to learn the skill of war. Women also had to participate in military activities, and a real warrior had the right to be intimate with any female as a reward. Fighting, killing, and dying without hesitation and fear were beautiful things for Plato. He even suggested that "might is right," and that might and knowledge are equal bases for the use of power.[1]

Against such conventional claims I maintain that Plato condemned war between the city-states, and elsewhere. Furthermore, he developed a systematic idea of the city-states system where order both between and within them was based on peaceful coexistence.

Criticism of war is a minor point in Plato's theory of the city-states system, however, its existence can be documented. For example, when Plato praises war, it is obvious that he simply applies the conventional wisdom of his times. Furthermore, in his dialogues most statements in favor of war and might are presented by Glaucon and Calicles, who appear as opponents to Socrates and Plato. Finally, the *Menexenus* can be interpreted as a parodical work conveying ironical criticism of war (Russell 1972; Stawell 1936: 308; cf. Allen 1984: 319–27).

There are many reasons to claim that Plato did not accept war between the city-states, or within them. According to Plato, the wise man comes to war and battle late. To kill people is not a beautiful or permanent solution. The real aim for people is to move away from the sufferings of war into peace. The highest virtue does not consist of war or civil war, but of peace and goodwill among men. In order to be rid of war, one must not imagine that mercenaries ensure their safety. In moral terms, it is better to be an object of injustice than to do wrong to others. The killer damages himself more than the victim, because violence always damages righteousness (*Laws* 628, 678–79, 697; *Republic* 335c, 582d–583d; *Apology* 30c–d, 39d; *Gorgias* 447a, 507e–508e).

There are also more fundamental points suggesting that it is better not to have any knowledge of the art of war. Plato maintains that the many generations that lived in righteousness and harmony "were inevitably unskilled and ignorant of techniques in general, and particularly of the military devices used on land and sea nowadays." Plato concludes that the true statesman "designs his legislation about war as a tool for peace, rather than his legislation for peace as an instrument of war" (*Laws* 628d, 679d–e).

Plato's criticism towards war is in full accordance with his basic, more implicit, message. According to that message, the major approach to achieve social order is education. Evil and uneducated men cause chaos, not order. According to Plato only education brings about the good man and only virtuous individuals will maintain orderly associations. The good, virtuous man, as the statesman, establishes and maintains order within the city-state. Such states are only able to establish and maintain peaceful relations among themselves. That is, an orderly city-state implies harmonious, non-warlike relations between the city-states. Relations between them are based on reason, just like order within the individual and the city-state.

While Plato's real message remains implicit, he makes the ideal model of the city-states system fully explicit in his myth on Atlantis (in *Critias* and *Timaeus*). Plato's story introduces a well-ordered system of states, not as a description of ancient history but as a model for city-states to be realized in the future.

Plato's story states that Atlantis existed nine thousand years ago on a huge island which was bigger than Africa and Asia—two of the three continents known by the ancient Greeks. There were ten states on the island, all of them—conspicuously like the city-states in Greece—belonged to the same, supposedly national origin (*Critias* 108e; *Timaeus* 24e).

The states were populated by good men with a naturally implanted sense of political order. Political order was based on a hereditary monarchy and a strict division of tasks between the regions, as well as the fact that individuals preferred virtue to things like wealth and gold. Furthermore, order was based on the division of labor between the classes: artisans, farmers, and soldiers. Soldiers were god-like heroes living outside the other groups, obtaining anything they needed for support and education from those groups, but having no individual property (*Critias* 109d, 113–19, 121a). It is not difficult to see that all these views are directly derived from Plato's own theories.

Plato maintains that Poseidon provided the rules and laws for relations between the ten states. The kings held a conference every fifth or sixth year in the middle of the island in Poseidon's temple where they discussed common affairs and took an oath of mutual faithfulness. According to the law of Poseidon, a severe punishment was granted to anybody who broke the high oath. According to the shared laws, the ten kings were not allowed to wage war against each other; a king could be sentenced and killed only by the decision of more than five kings. Furthermore, every king had to provide help to any ruler under attack by his citizens. Finally, they had to negotiate and discuss wars against enemies outside their region. During the war the king from Atlantis race was given leadership over all the others (*Critias* 199–120d).

In such an ideal model for the orderly system of states no conventional alliances between the states are accepted. The Atlantis system is not an alliance—where two make an alliance against one breaking the law—but something much more: it is the federalist state consisting of fully autonomous units.[2] Plato does not prefer alliances or leagues because they do not remain permanent and lead to hostilities between the partners, as was often the case with leagues between the Greek city-states (cf. *Laws* 684a–b, 686).[3]

Considering Plato's ideas in general, and the wording of the Atlantis model especially, it is obvious that Plato is inclined to imply and even suggest that peaceful and orderly international relations are only possible between the Greek city-states. In fact, Plato openly accepts war against the Barbarians, but condemns war between the Greeks. A Greek must not make another Greek a slave. Violence between the Greeks, called "a party-strife" rather than war,[4] must be abolished. War represents a relation between the Greeks and the Barbarians, and war in that sense can be approved. This is implied when Plato maintains that party-strifes are extremely bitter and inhuman cases of unlimited violence, and therefore a heroic warrior must never fight against a Greek (*Laws* 629; *Republic* 469b–470b).

However, it must not be understood that peace in Greece is based on war against the Barbarians. Such a war is possible but not inevitable. On the contrary, war against external enemies is one of the causes of ruin in Greek city-states. Plato makes this explicit by referring to the mythical Trojan War during which the domestic affairs of the Greek kings took a turn for the worse. The younger generation took power at home and received many returning kings by exiling and killing them (*Laws* III.682d–e).

While criticism against wars between the city-states became more open after Plato, his belief in the peaceful relations between them was soon lost. Among the rare followers there is actually only a single figure: Demonsthenes. Before he made himself famous by criticizing Macedonia's Philip II, Demonsthenes usually spoke of relations between the Greek city-states. Demonsthenes can be seen as their last apologetist. Demonsthenes suggests that intercity relations can be based on two principles: (1) the balance of power; and (2) non-expansion. These principles govern relations between democratic city-states which, unlike the non-democratic states, duly respect moral principles (Demonsthenes: 195–97).

While Demonsthenes perceived Athens as the defender of Greek freedom, he suggested the balance of power as the basis of intercity relations. In his speech on Megalopolis, Demonsthenes suggests that the most important task for Athens is "not to allow Sparta to rise to a formidable power before the decline of Thebes, not to allow the desired balance of power to alter unperceived so that a Spartan rise exceeds the Theban decline." He continued: "We should not take the other line of wanting Sparta rather than Thebes as opponents, which is not what we require, but that neither shall have the power to injure ourselves" (Demonsthenes: 169–70, 174, 178–89).

In his speech on Rhodes, Demonsthenes adds an important principal component to strengthen the role of the balance of power—any illegitimate use and expansion of power must always be opposed, and any state has the right and duty to do so. Therefore, he says, even Persia has the right to defend itself against, for instance, any Greek interference in its realm, but no right to territorial claims outside its own realm. In fact, Demonsthenes implies that the democratic states do not wage wars between themselves, nor do they attack any other states. When he later called for war against Macedonia, it was justified by these principles (Demonsthenes: 181).

MOHISM

The Mohist school suggests that the system of sovereign units is the best way to overcome chaos, violence, and war and to guarantee security. Mo Zi believed that the greatest harm to both the state and its people is incessant fighting, caused by the fact that men do not love one another. Therefore, Mo Zi maintains, peace and order within and between the sovereign units can be built on universal love. Within the sovereign political units the king provides the example and the ruled follow him in practicing universal love. Concerning external relations, universal love requires the condemnation of offensive wars. Consequently, peaceful coexistence between sovereign states is envisaged feasible by the Mohists.

Indeed, universal love creates major benefits in the world. Approximating an ethical principle of "do unto others as you hope them to do to you," Mo suggested that if everyone regards the states, capitals, and houses of others as he regards his own, there would be no one to attack the other states, no one to seize other capitals, and no one to disturb other houses (Fung 1983: 92).

Mo's analysis of the causes of war, as well as the suggested remedy, goes directly against Confucianism, as well as against more recent applications of patriotism and nationalism. Proper manners in Confucianism demanded that one love a certain person more than somebody else. One must love his own country more than any other country, one's own ruler more than any other, one's own father more than any other, and so on. Mo Zi maintained that there should be no distinctions between one country or another in the mind of its citizens.

In all his conservatism, authoritarianism, and utilitarianism Mo Zi suggested a magnificent condemnation of offensive war. However, we must remember that Mo speaks favorably of defensive war. According to him defense is required to complement the function of universal love, and a strong defense is the basis for interstate moral relations.

Mo Zi, together with his disciples, was always prepared to defend anyone under military attack. When Mo heard of the construction of "cloud-ladders" (ladders for attacking over city walls) in a state that was going to attack its neighbor he tried to persuade with moral arguments (e.g., "to build an offensive weapon equals to kill men by one's own hand") the engineer to cancel the project. Mo failed and had to fight a symbolic contest of arms with the ruler. When the king had used all his offensive weapons, Mo still had decisive resources for defense. He spoke about his heavily armed disciples who were prepared to meet and kill the invaders on the city wall. This finally proved that it was useless for the king to attack. Consequently, the king canceled his war plans (Fung 1983: 81).

Mo speaks of the fortification of towns and their defense against their enemies in rather conventional military terms: any state requires grain, warriors, and fortifications to survive, however, the best defense is moral. The king must not live in joy and leisure while the ruled suffer and die of hunger. If the ruler is immoral, any invader will be able to annihilate the state.

According to Mo Zi, anything can be of profit to a country and its people, and it is the wealth and populousness of a country that constitutes its greatest profit. War is a wasting of scarce resources—material and human. War can never be profitable, because there is nothing useful about a military victory. The possessions obtained through war do "not even make up for what has been lost" (Fung 1983: 87, 95). On the contrary, war wastes scarce resources, otherwise used for civilian production. Mo declared winter too cold and summer too hot for military operations, but to go to war in spring takes people away from sowing and planting; in fall war takes them away from reaping and harvesting. Consequently, war kills an innumerable number of the state's own population of hunger and cold (Fung 1983: 94).

When the fact that some states had been able to increase their areas considerably by means of wars and attacks was mentioned, Mo Zi claimed that such cases can be compared to the situation where a physician gives the same drug to everyone who is sick. It would then be likely that among the ten thousand people who took the drug four or five might benefit. However, Mo Zi pointed out, such a drug might not be called either efficient or good for everybody. Neither should war be accepted if four or five states reap some benefit from war. An innumerable number of states have disappeared through wars (Fung 1983: 95).

Mo Zi suggested that the ruler should turn his attention from the annexation of new areas to the development of existing ones. The ruler should do everything in his power to increase wealth and population in his own state. The ruler should prepare to govern the existing areas in order to make them prosperous, and minimize or eliminate conflicts. It is not reasonable to attack a small country when there are ample fields for agriculture within the existing territory. It is like throwing away one's own possessions and robbing something worthless from another individual. There is no meaning in conflicts over towns—there are too many of them anyway—and killing men in the battles over them—there are not enough people to fill the existing towns (Fung 1983: 87).

Even references to heaven were often made by Mo Zi in economic, utilitarian terms. According to him, all peoples and towns belong to heaven, they are possessed by heaven. Therefore, war implies the destruction of heaven's property. No ruler can accept his subjects destroying each other, or each other's towns—for all of them belong to the ruler.

Finally, Mo Zi referred to the problems of taxation. Wars require heavy taxation, making it impossible for people to satisfy their basic needs. According to Mo, this is not useful to anybody.

However, while Mo Zi's text abounds in utilitarian and economic arguments against offensive war, he applies some strong moral points as well. If some states have reaped benefits from war, they have not then acted in accordance with the *dao*. It is this moral element that makes Mo's pacifism exceptionally fine and well-formulated.

It may be suggested that Mo's moralism is derived from his utilitarianism—the law of universal love demands that people promote useful activity and avoid anything harmful to the world. However, Mo is inclined to present his idea of universal love as a general moral principle, as the major moral goal with intrinsic value of *dao*.

Mo's point of departure is the law of universal love. Universal love implies a high moral standard. The more an individual offends that law, the more serious his or her criminal act. Mo Zi claims that if an individual kills a person, it is a crime punished severely because murder is a deadly sin. Therefore, it is logical to claim that it is a hundred times more criminal to kill a hundred people than to kill one. Offensive war is the highest crime in this very quantitative sense of moral crimes. Therefore, Mo strongly criticizes the rulers for the records of their successful wars. Crimes should be concealed, not praised. If a ruler understood that war is a crime, he would not be willing to leave documentation for future generations to read. But because war and victories are praised, rulers are not able to distinguish right from wrong, or day from night.

Mo Zi himself was the best proof of moral principles. In his own life, he did not pursue benefits. On the contrary, he was willing to sacrifice all to moral principles. For example, when an old friend advised him to give up righteousness because no one else practices it in the world and being the single exception makes him ridiculous and dangers his own life, Mo Zi replied:

Suppose a man has ten sons. Only one cultivates the ground, while the other nine stay at home. Then the one who cultivates must work all the more vigorously. Why? Because many eat and few cultivate. To-day, if no one in the world practices righteousness, you should all the more encourage me. Why do you stop me? (Fung 1983: 85)

When Mo Zi heard of the engineer planning offensive weapons, he marched ten days and ten nights to try and convince him to stop the projects. Mo asked the man to kill an enemy of Mo for a sum of money. The man rejected the proposal as a criminal act inconsistent with his moral principles. The engineer defined himself as a righteous man who would never murder anybody. With this declaration, it was not difficult for Mo Zi to show him that he was responsible for murdering several people in wars. According to Mo, it was a more serious criminal act to plan, develop, and construct offensive weapons than to murder a single person. Furthermore, it was meaningless to speak of righteousness in the case of a single murder and ignore the principles of righteousness in planning war machines.

Mo Zi did not accept the moral justification of war, i.e., the argument that some wars were consistent with the will of heaven when a tyrannical ruler was punished through it. This type of Confucian justification was rejected by Mo, who emphasized that it is not the task of a human being to punish anybody who has offended will of heaven. A father can punish his son, but he does not allow his neighbors or stranger to punish his son.

Finally, there are references to the absolute value of human life in Mo Zi's philosophy. These references, typical of Daoist thinkers, emphasize that a man is unwilling to receive the largest kingdom or all the riches in the world if he is required to sacrifice his life or parts of his body as a precondition.

ARISTOTLE

While Aristotle emphasizes the military capabilities of the state, this does not mean that he admires war. To the contrary, Aristotle rejects war.

Aristotle connects courage to war; he claims that courage can be found in war. However, courage is not an example of military heroism but of moral virtue, for courage is the golden mean between confidence and fear (*Ethics* 1115a–1116a). This is obviously a figurative expression applied to define courage as a moral virtue, or moral virtue itself in conventionally accessible terms. In fact, Aristotle claims that while the courage of the citizen-soldier best resembles moral courage, there is nothing courageous about dying to escape poverty or a painful situation. Because a number of men go to war for morally deficient reasons, dying in war proves nothing but the fact that the soldier has no other good but his life to sell (*Ethics* 1116a, 1117b). More directly, Aristotle repeats Homer's criticism of "the war-mad" man who has rejected family and law. According to Aristotle, such a man becomes unable to cooperate in the ways required for human associations, and therefore becomes isolated from other human beings. Aristotle maintains that war does not refine the man, because war forces men to be just. Such forced justness is arbitrary and disappears in unrestrained leisure in peacetime. There is no point in displaying good qualities during war and beastly ones during peace (*Politics* 1253a1, 1334a11).

This gives us a clue for understanding Aristotle's basic message. To fully understand his message, we must look at another side of Aristotle's ideas on war. We must recognize that according to Aristotle Plato did not pay sufficient attention to war. Due attention, Aristotle maintained, is essential for the state to acquire sufficient strength for war. Aristotle does not speak of defensive capabilities only.

For Aristotle, defense is both a major function of the state and the best approach to peace because no enemy will ever attempt an attack on those who are prepared to meet an external threat (*Politics* 1130b32, 1267a17, 1327a11, 1327a40, 1328b2). But unlike Mo Zi's theory, a strong defense provides a solid basis for offensive actions. Such actions seem to be on Aristotle's mind when he surmises that the state and its territory should have access to the sea and pay sufficient attention to maritime forces in order to be both militarily formidable and able to render aid to its neighbors. Or, for example, when he emphasizes that a good supply of money is required for the military to be successful. However, Aristotle had only one, not all offensive wars, in his mind. He did not attempt to justify war as a way of subjugating neighbors, or to "rule at all costs, not only justly but unjustly" (*Politics* 1324b22).

Aristotle's opinions on the goals of war appear in several contexts to make it more emphatic (*Politics* 1333a30, 1334a11; Saunders 1984b: VII.ii). For example, Aristotle claims that individuals busy themselves in order to have leisure. Similarly, men make war in order to live in peace. War does not represent either leisure or peace, and therefore no one can choose to be at war just to be at war. Similarly, no one makes enemies of his friends just to fight with them, and if he or she does, he or she is called a killer or even murderer (*Ethics* 1177b).

For Aristotle war is not legitimate in itself. The nurture of military institutions is fine, but only as a means to achieve the ideal freedom, the situation of peace. Therefore, Aristotle maintains that a man must be able to stir from his armchair when he is needed on the battlefield, but he must prize peace more highly. Even during a war, devotion to peace should dominate the mind (*Politics* 1325a5–7, 1333a41–b2).

War is not the supreme goal of the state since it must culminate in victory or defeat, and since both options are equally ruinous because they involve both misery and decay. Therefore, war can only play a subordinate role in the state. War can only be justified if its aim is to establish and preserve order, repel aggression, and protect justice. In short, war is just when waged on behalf of a civilized nation, as a justifiable intervention in the affairs of another nation, civilized or not, or to conquer less civilized nations (Defourny, M. 1977: 195–201). This theory requires specific limits for war: it must not be used for the enslavement of Greeks. War can only be used to establish an empire and to enslave those who deserve to be enslaved.[5] Naturally, war can be used to defend one's sovereignty against enslavement (*Politics* 1333b39–1334a2).

In other words, Aristotle did not accept peace at any costs. For him war was—in a specific case—an inevitable means of achieving the right type of peace. This acceptable form of peace has a specific definition: peace is peace only when it makes it possible for the state to fulfill its basic function to promote contemplative life for its citizens (*Ethics* 1177b; Defourny, P. 1977; Kenny 1977).

Aristotle aims at achieving peace to fulfill his ideals of a good life. A good life cannot be based on the pursuit of unlimited wealth, for only a limited amount of wealth is necessary. A good life is based on happiness, attainable in a contemplative life, because happiness is an activity of the soul (*Ethics* 1102a; Saunders 1984b: 76).

A selfish individual wrongly identifies a good life and happiness with pleasure, but the wise man identifies it with honor (*Ethics* 1095b). A contemplative life represents the highest form of happiness—happiness consists of behavior in accordance with virtue, and reason is the highest virtue controlling human activities. Happiness appears together with contemplation. Therefore, happiness is a form of contemplativeness (*Ethics* 1088a, 1178b).

The state must isolate itself from others, not in order to become inactive, but to achieve the full conditions for contemplation. Peace means contemplation, and is, therefore, far from idleness, indolence, and debauch. Only during peace is it possible to give the soul the special form of activity it requires—full interaction of the multiple elements of which it is composed (*Politics* 1325b24–30). One must use the leisure of peace in an intelligent way, consonant with the nature of man, by enriching and expanding intellectual life. Aristotle outlined a program of education to guarantee that the personality, guided by the mind, enjoys a harmonious balance of all the faculties. Only then may men lie in the arms of peace, cultivate their understanding, carry out other activities to dispel any conceivable monotony in the uninterruptedly speculative life, and exercise the lower talents in the service of thought.

Concerning states that are settled at a distance from others and have chosen to live in isolation, there is nothing to oblige them to lead a life of inaction. Aristotle maintains that God himself (and the whole universe) can be in fine condition, even if they have no external activities. On the other hand, happiness is not found in cities that are only concerned with war and neglect the teaching of virtues necessary to enjoy true peace. These cities survive as long as war lasts, but perish with the signing of peace, whether it is a peace of victory or a peace of defeat (*Politics* 1325b23).

Aristotle's acceptance of war and peace form a central element in his philosophy. As Hans Kelsen (1977: 170–94) has suggested one must take Aristotle's views on world government—the united Greece—seriously. According to Kelsen Aristotle believes that the state's aim is not peace at any price. Peace with vassaldom or anarchy is by no means desirable, but a controlled and ordered peace is infinitely precious. Therefore, to achieve an acceptable peace among the Greeks, war is legitimate. This war is the last war between the Greeks to abolish wars among them. The rise of Macedonia fulfilled this program. The doctrines of Aristotle and Isocrates legitimized Macedonia's suzerainty and stopped wars between the city-states (Defourny, M. 1977: 200–201; cf. Airas 1978). However, Alexander the Great directed his attention in the wrong direction, away from the Greek community towards barbarian lands, breaking the distinction between the Greeks and Barbarians by living among them.

CONFUCIANS

It is traditional to interpret the Confucian school in the light of pacifism. For example, Watson suggests that Mo Zi's condemnations of offensive warfare could just as well have come from thinkers of the Confucian school (Watson 1967: 9).

In a sense this is true. It is not difficult to find pacifist statements in the Confucian texts. Kong Zi maintained that there was no need for the king to kill in administering the government. Concerning government, he advised giving up arms, if the king had to give up one of its major bases: food, arms, or trust. Furthermore, Kong Zi maintained that he knew "something about" the rites and proper manners, but knew nothing of commanding troops. He knew—to repeat his understatement—something about important things but nothing about unimportant things. Therefore, among other unimportant things, war and especially warfare had no role in his teachings (*Analects* VII.13, 21, XII.7, 19, XV.1).

Meng Zi's pacifism was more explicit. He believed that the *Spring and Autumn Annals* discussed a multitude of wars, but refused to see any just wars among them. In his opinion, some wars "were only less bad than some others." He said that "a benevolent man would not even take from one man to give to another, let alone seek territory at the cost of human lives." The true king is satisfied with a small state no larger than a village. In his opinion war is simply an occasion for a ruthless king to extend his ruthlessness from his enemies to people in his own state, causing them to be killed. While in the idealized past a border station was set up as a precaution against violence, in Meng Zi's time it was set up to perpetrate violence. On several occasions Meng Zi declared that experts at military formations and war were the worst criminals (*Mencius* II.A.1, VI.B.7–8, VII.B.1–2, 4 , 8).

However, the Confucians, even Kong Zi, accept some wars (*Analects* XIII.29–30). Meng Zi and Xun Zi made their arguments explicit. Even if Meng Zi generally condemns offensive warfare by considering it dangerous to the ruler, he is ready to accept war when the attacked—tyrannical—ruler not the attacker is himself responsible for the operation (*Mencius* IV.A.8). In this sense a justified military operation does not represent war but punishment, a lesson to be taught to the tyrant (*Mencius* I.B.8). The Confucians define war by declaring that the wise king's military operations must never be called war, only punitive expeditions (Hsün Tzu/Watson: 68).

In the Confucian theory of a just war, a punitive expedition rectifies a morally evil king or state. Meng Zi witnesses that "in one outburst of rage King Wen brought peace to the people of the Empire" (*Mencius* I.B.39, VII.B.4; cf. Hsün Tzu/Watson: 68). Logically, a punitive war is based on benevolence, not on the selfish conquer of territories (*Mencius* II.B.8).

The true punitive expedition fulfills the wishes of the suppressed people. Oppressed and exploited people long for the coming of the benevolent ruler and welcome him as their rescuer. In fact, Meng Zi recommends instituting a conquering operation, if people in the attacked state *want* to submit themselves to the new ruler. If an attacking army is met by welcoming people, it is clear that such people are "fleeing from water and fire." Therefore, the attacker himself must not be violent or cruel and if he is, the people in the attacked state must turn elsewhere for help. The people may then even prefer their own cruel ruler (*Mencius* I.B.10–11, II.B.5).

But in order to justify punishing the criminal ruler, the punishing ruler himself must be absolutely and unquestionably good, "a Heaven-appointed officer," otherwise his expedition is just another war (*Mencius* II.B.8).

To give his views more emphasis and general value, Meng Zi not only advises, he threatens the ruler. He states that a benevolent ruler will survive and must carry out punitive expeditions when required. But he also maintains that this applies to the king to whom he is giving this advice. Meng Zi claims that when any ruler endangers the independence of the state, he should and will be replaced by other benevolent kings, and even by his own citizens (*Mencius* VII.B.14; Lau 1983b: 37).

Confucian pacifism, like Aristotle's, should not be called pacifism but rather the politics of unification. In Chinese political philosophy, both the Mohist and Daoist schools condemn not only war but the power struggles between states. However, both the Confucian and Legalist schools accept this very struggle. The distinction between the Confucian school and the Legalist school does not concern the power struggle, but the methods of the struggle. The Confucian school emphasized the moral approach of the good ruler and his punitive expeditions; the Legalist school was not interested in the moral aspects of the approach but in the final results in unifying China. While this difference is important and justifies some claims for Confucian pacifism, its prudent nature requires a brief discussion of its policy of unification.

The Confucians raised the interstate power struggle as the key problem in their political theory. The politics of unification can be based on two approaches: benevolence and overwhelming military force. The Confucians did not believe in the latter. According to them, if one wishes to win the empire, he must apply benevolence, because it will be lost through cruelty. The leading idea in the politics of unification is to ensure that those who are near are pleased and those who are far are attracted towards the unifying emperor (*Mencius* IV.A. 2–3).

Similarly, according to Xun Zi, there are three methods by which one may annex a neighboring state: virtue, military force, and wealth. Xun Zi preferred goodness. He maintained that "he who annexes a state by virtue is a true king," but he who uses force will be "weakened," and he who spends wealth will be "impoverished" (Hsün Tzu/Watson: 76–77).

The Confucians gave their advice to the ruler in order to help him win the struggle over China through the unity of his own nation. In this sense, according to Meng Zi, a small territory is sufficient to enable its ruler to inflict defeat on strong armies, if the king himself practices benevolent government towards his people and supports proper manners (*Mencius* I.A.5).

In fact, internal unity is invaluable because of the external struggle, otherwise it would not count so much. Indeed, Xun Zi is the first thinker to suggest that internal order—obedience to the commands of the ruler—is derived from military practice and interstate war. He maintained that in a war obedience to orders must be preferred to achievements. Xun Zi envisaged or shared the Legalist maxim, according to which advancing without or even against an explicit order is comparable, and punishable, to chaotic retreating (Hsün Tzu/Watson: 56, 60, 67, 78).

While the unity of the state makes military success feasible, a major emphasis in Confucianism lies with more peaceful campaigns. The Confucians suggest that one must try to win the interstate power struggle without the use of arms. If one truly understands how to use force, he does not need to rely on force. In other words, such a ruler gains victory and acquires territory without attack (Hsün Tzu/Watson: 40–41).[6]

Meng Zi does not condemn violent methods because of moral reasons, but because of their effects. He claims that a ruthless man can gain possession of a state, but never of the empire. Benevolence can never be overcome by armies, because people never submit to coercive force willingly but because they are not, for the time being, strong enough to oppose it—but they will, sooner or later. Therefore, unity based on military force is arbitrary and short-lived (*Mencius* I.B.3, II.A.3, 5, 7, VII.B.13).

Xun Zi also condemns the use of mercenaries or paid soldiers because they sometimes win and sometimes lose, but it is never consistent. War, if it must be waged, is a moral undertaking. Therefore, the will of the subjects to serve their ruler during a war must be the basis of all military activities. He explicitly denies the usefulness of rewards and punishments, force, or deception in the context of war. Those means make it meaningless for soldiers to risk their lives for chaos instead of order, which should be the goal of the unity of China (Hsün Tzu/Watson: 57–59, 63–64, 73).

There are cases where benevolence does not work, but this inefficiency is caused by the king, not by benevolence. Meng Zi says that if others do not respond to love with love, the king must look into his own behavior and correct it (*Mencius* IV.A.4).

In conclusion, order is based on the abolishment of litigation. Virtue must be known throughout the world and the observance of *dao* must be universal. Only then can the difference between right and wrong be duly recognized. To carry out this project, a specific war is sometimes required. Unauthorized coercion and violence must be replaced by the authorized, benevolent use of force applied through humanitarian interventions and punitive expeditions. But such cases must remain exceptions. The wise king and his benevolence should normally define relations between the states. This only produces the "maximum order," where the world community, the *tien-hsia*, is "equally shared by all," and therefore voluntarily unified under the leadership of the wise king (Chen 1991: 37–42).

NOTES

1. There are many short references to such phenomena in Plato's works, such as *Apology* 32, 28d–e; *Calicles* 296–97; *Gorgias* 483d; *Ion* 541b; *Laches* 181; *Laws* 625–26, 629, 633, 692–93, 829, 832–35, 921, 943–44; *Menexenus* 240a–242, 247a–b, 234c–235c; *Republic* 338c–339a, 342–44, 347e–348d, 360c, 466e–467a, 468c, 469b–470b; *Statesman* 296d–297b; *Sophist* 219, 222c–d).

2. As to conventional alliances between the Greek city-states, see e.g., Russell 1972.

3. In the same light, criticizing contemporary evils Plato says that the system of colonies must be avoided because in colonies there are people from several states representing different habits and gods (Saunders 1984a: 157).

4. Note that primitive men in Plato's ideal world were innocent of the techniques of warfare called "lawsuits" and "party-strife" (*Laws* 679).

5. Aristotle, like Plato, justifies the politics of exclusion of the Other (cf. Dossa 1987).

6. This Confucian logic was shared by Sun Zi in the *Art of War* (III.3), a collection of both Confucian and Legalist principles. However, it suggests that "to subdue the enemy without fighting is the acme of skill." This gives military, not moral, superiority the decisive role.

CHAPTER 13

The Politics of Exclusion as the Basis of Social Order

There are three cases where the distinction between good and evil is important to both individuals and social life. The first case involves moral values. The second case is political, defined as the opposition of friend and enemy (Schmitt 1993). The third case is religious, the antithesis of God and the devil.

The moral, political, and religious distinctions are not independent of each other. The moral issues are likely to become political and religious, as seen by comparing some principle-oriented and power-oriented patterns (Jesus's teachings and early Christianity, early and late Zoroastrianism, and Judaism and ancient Hebrew thought). The political struggles are likely to become moral campaigns; the religious disputes are likely to become both moral and political.

However, at the theoretical level there is a fundamental difference between the moral distinction on one hand, and the political and religious on the other. Morality is a matter of principles and values, which must be chosen by the individual. This book calls attention to the political and the religious distinctions that often emerge as disputes between human beings, and are therefore directly related to social order. Indeed, it can be maintained that the politics of exclusion, or in general terms, particularism as the opposite of universalism, is one of the most important approaches used to construct social reality and thereby establish social order.

The politics of exclusion appears in two version: the weaker and the stronger. The weaker version is neutral concerning the struggle between good and evil; the stronger perceives "us" as an incarnation of good or the representative of God, whereas the opponent is defined as the representative of evil and the devil. In the weaker version the opponent can be called the Other, in the stronger version the Enemy (Harle 1994). In the weaker version the Other can become a friend, and compromises are always possible. In the stronger version the Enemy never becomes a friend, and any compromises with him are impossible by definition. In politics (and the political) the opponent is usually the Other. In extreme situations—situations outside the political in the world of unlimited violence—the opponent is perceived as the Enemy. Morality is a universal phenomenon even if there are cultural or other differences concerning moral values. Similarly, the distinction between the Self and the Other is universal, and it is almost impossible to imagine politics without weaker form of the politics of exclusion. Politics is always a campaign between us and our opponents. However, there are not many cases where this element is made explicit. It is typical of some political theories, of which we take Cicero's as the paradigmatic case along with Plato and Aristotle (cf. Dossa 1987), Judaism, and Livy and Virgil.

As for the strong version—such as the struggle between good and evil by the human actors representing God and the devil—politics of exclusion is reflected in late Zoroastrianism, ancient Hebrew thought and Jewish nationalism, and early Christianity. They all originate from the Occidental culture, or more exactly, the historical-transcendent religious mythologies (cf. Aho 1981), of which Occidental political thought seems to be partly a diluted derivation. In that tradition, war is an unrestricted effort for the total elimination of the Enemy and any war can be the final battle. Outside the Occidental culture human beings are not identified in similar moral and religious terms as representatives of good or evil.[1] Therefore, war is heavily restricted by ethical rules (e.g., Confucianism and ancient Indian political thought), or justified in other terms, such as "punitive education" (Confucius) or "politics as politics" (Legalism in China and Kautilya in India).

THE EXCLUSION OF THE OTHER IN POLITICS

In its weaker form the politics of exclusion does not inevitably lead to the use of violence for the absolute elimination of the opponent. Exclusion can be absolute, but not openly and unlimitedly violent. At this general level the politics of exclusion occasionally remains both abstract and open to peaceful coexistence or compromises. As shown in Chapter 6, Judaism maintained that it is the duty of Jews to maintain their identity, but the Other can keep his identity.

The politics of exclusion in this weaker form is typical to ancient Greek and Roman political thought. In ancient Greece it was prevalent in the theories of Plato, Aristotle, and Demosthenes; in Rome, this form was expounded by Cicero, Livy, and Virgil. This discussion concentrates on the paradigmatic case of Cicero, but first a brief discussion of the Greek thinkers is required (cf. Dossa 1987).

Plato made a clear-cut distinction between the Greek and the Barbarian. According to him this distinction was real. Plato maintained that there is "pure hate" which is "imbedded in our state against the strange and different" (*Critias* 113a–b; *Laws* 685; *Menexenus* 240c–242a, 245d). Similarly, Aristotle saw the fundamental difference between the Greek and the Barbarian. The Greeks regard themselves as noble everywhere, but allow the nobility of birth of non-Greeks to be valid only outside Greece. In other words, Aristotle suggests two grades of free status and noble birth, one absolute, the other conditional (*Politics* 1255a21). Similar ideas of Greek nationalism were shared by many other writers, including Xenophon (*Hellenica*), hence the term "xenophobia."

While Plato, Aristotle, and others emphasized the distinction between the Greeks and the Barbarians, Demosthenes introduced another permanent and fundamental element to the politics of exclusion, the idea of the ideological struggle, and applied it to struggles among the city-states and between the Greeks and the Macedonians. According to Demonsthenes wars against democracies cannot be accepted, for "against popular governments" war is a "matter of private grievances." But wars against oligarchies are the duty, for it is better that "all the Greeks should be our enemies under democracy than our friends under oligarchy." There cannot be a permanent peace between a democracy and an oligarchy:

In dealing with free states, in my view, there is no difficulty about regaining peace, while with oligarchy even friendship is precarious. There can be no good feeling between oligarchy and democracy, between the desire for power and the aim at life of equality. (Demosthenes: 183)

The first Stoic influence in Rome appeared among the Scipionic circle, and had a central role in social and political life until Cicero's time.[2] Polybius, a Greek from Megalopolis, was the first to suggest the idea of a world government based on the Roman imperium, thereby giving the universalistic cosmopolis a concrete and particularistic name.

Polybius consistently maintained the view that the supremacy of Rome in Greece must be accepted, and that the Greek states must conduct their affairs, whether singly or collectively, and preserve their freedom without giving any offense or cause for complaint, to the Roman republic. Being a Stoic, Polybius believed that the Roman order of things was part of a divine providence that ruled the world (Paton 1975: vii, xiii–xiv).

Polybius was explicit in speaking of Roman power as the world power. In his opinion, Macedonian power left a large part of the inhabited world outside of it. Polybius concluded that the Romans "have subjected to their rule not portions, but nearly the whole of the world" (Polybius I.2.1–7). This justification for using "the world" to describe the region of Roman power became an unquestionable truth both in Rome and in later European traditions.

Cicero's ideas are more difficult to perceive as an application of the present pattern. His ideas look both universalistic and non-religious, in short, far from the ideas discussed here. Undeniably, the Stoic theory of the world community, and Cicero's own views on the same matter, represent a doctrine of universality. One might expect that the universal law of nature, which is expressed by definition, would imply that all its aspects have a universal application. However, one cannot deny that Cicero is speaking of the Roman state, society, and citizens. He suggests a universal theory, but presents a rather narrow, particularistic—even nationalistic—application.

The Stoics, including Cicero, spoke of the universal city or state of which both men and gods are members. Everybody is a part of this universe, and everybody has the duty to prefer a common advantage to his own (Finibus III.XIX.64). However, the universal state obtained a specific, particularistic meaning. The Greek Stoic teachers taught their Roman pupils to see in the nascent Roman empire at least an approximation of the ideal cosmopolis (Arnold 1911: 382). Therefore, it is not a surprise to find that quite early Stoicism became popular among the higher classes of people and leading politicians in Rome.

Cicero—as well as Livy and Virgil—follows the tradition of the politics of exclusion by openly moving from the universal to the particular. Cicero maintains that nature orders man to benefit other men if he can, and sees the protection of the weak as a natural impulse of men protect the human race. However, Cicero concludes that "we are allied by nature in the common society of the state." The existence of the state is very important for Cicero's moral system: if there is no state, "there would be no room either for justice or benevolence" (Finibus III.XX.65–66).

But what is this state or commonwealth? Cicero mentions a conventional theory according to which the state is formed on the basis of smaller human associations preceding it. Therefore, the state is above and includes all associations such as those: (1) between male and female; (2) between parents and their offsprings; and (3) between relatives. However, this technical definition is not enough for Cicero, for him the state, the commonwealth, is a moral and juridical property commonly owned by its members. Indeed, the population of the state does not consist of all the men in the world or a contingent number of them—"the people" is a specific group of men. The people is "an assemblage in large numbers associated in an agreement with respect to justice and a partnership for the common good." That is, some are members of the state but others are not (RePublica I.XXIV.38).

Who is a member of the state and who is not is not an academic question, but the right and the duty of the state to decide. The state decides who is a citizen. Rome was exceptionally strict in this policy of distinguishing between citizens (Romans), allies (other Italians), and foreigners (cf. Schmitt 1993). The issue of citizenship is directly related to private property. Cicero maintains that no principle of justice militates against the possession of private property (Finibus III.XX.67–68). That is, private property is a derivative of the law of nature. But to have private property and keep it safe, friend and enemy must be separated from each other. To do so, men have had to conclude a social agreement to establish the state. The state is required to safeguard private property against both internal chaos and external enemies (Tenkku 1981: 151).

The explicit reason for Cicero to concentrate attention on the state is the effectiveness of social relationships. While human associations at the world level are rather symbolic, they become a concrete reality at the state level. The bond of community links every man in the world with every other man, and this bond is particularly strong as a unifying link between compatriots (Officiis III.XVI.68).

It is not, therefore, difficult to determine that Cicero is actually speaking of a state in which a man is member. For Cicero, common advantage or security is never something above one's country. This is why Cicero gives his highest praise to one who dies for the commonwealth: a man must love his country more than himself (Finibus III.XIX.64). Cicero further maintains that "parents are dear; dear are children . . . but one native land embraces all our loves" (Officiis I.XVII.57).

Cicero's theory includes a short, direct, and explicit path from universalism to particularism. According to him, men "are invested by Nature with two characters: one of these is universal, the other assigned to individuals in particular" (Officiis I.XXX.107). Another justification can be found when Cicero says that happiness is attainable only for the wise man. Such a wise man does not live everywhere in the world, he lives in a specific community and is an active member: man is born for his country and kindred. Therefore, the wise man must engage in politics and government, and that is only possible within the state (Finibus II.XIV.45–46, III.XX.68; cf. RePublica). From the Stoic point of view the world power (Rome) was easier to accept than a limited city-state for the wise man's political activities. Thus, I maintain, the Stoic theory presupposed that a strong power any in theory but Rome in practice, must become a world power in order to govern as great a part of the world community as possible.

Therefore, it is not surprising that some fragments in the third book of *De Re Publica* seem to be part of the argument for the justification of slavery and imperialism. Indeed, it is fully consistent with, or an integral part of, Cicero's system to maintain that certain nations and individuals are naturally fitted for and benefit by subjection to others (III.XXV.37). In fact, this powerful justification for Roman power became the leading philosophy in Rome.

In any case, Cicero speaks like any Roman of his time. For him, Rome was superior to its rivals in every respect. As a non-maritime city Rome was not vulnerable to attacks or the degeneration of its morals like its rivals. Cicero did not have only Carthage in his mind—according to him Carthage had ignored agriculture and the pursuit of arms because of its lust for trafficking and sailing the seas—but he openly detested living Greeks for the same reason (RePublica II.III.5–6, II.IV.7–8, II.V.10; Grant 1985: 29).

Cicero also refers to Cato, who used to say that the Roman constitution was superior to the other states that without exception had been established by one man. Instead, Rome had been founded in a long period of several centuries by many generations of glorious men (RePublica II.I.2). Similarly, in commenting on the origins of Roman law, Cicero claims that the laws of all other countries were incredibly disorderly, even ridiculous (*On the Good Life*: 305; cf. Officiis, Book I).

In the fragmented preface to *De Re Publica* Cicero highly praises patriotism. Cicero claims that without patriotism the native land cannot be delivered from attack or fear of attack (RePublica I.I.1, II.XV.30). Cicero presents his strong patriotic views when he comments on an episode of the Punic Wars, where the Senate did not arrange ransom for eight thousand prisoners in Hannibal's hand because, in Cicero's opinion, Roman soldiers must either conquer or die (Officiis III.XXXII.114).

Cicero makes it a high moral duty to keep the promise—he actually praises the power of the oath when he relates that Regulus returned to his captivity because he had promised to do so. However, Cicero's theory was far from the Zoroastrian ethics. Cicero makes a national reservation when according to him one must not keep a promise against the interests of his country. More recent doctrines of realism reproduce this idea by saying that the national interest is above everything else, including the ethical rules (Officiis III.XXIV.92, III.XXV.94, XXVII.101).

According to national interests, one can and must do anything for his country. In general, it is strictly forbidden to rob or kill anybody, but if that renders great services to one's own state, the action would not be blameworthy. Cicero justifies this inconsistency in morality by claiming that it is unjust and unnatural to neglect the common interest, adding that his common interest applies only to members of the state, most likely Rome. Finally, Cicero maintains that "the means of substance may, if necessary, be transferred from the feeble, useless person to the wise, honest, brave man, whose death would be a grave loss to society." This must hold true in the case of Rome and the weak and uncivilized alien nations (Officiis II.V.27).

In short, it is correct to say that one of the elements in Cicero's lofty motive was a vigorous patriotism, not interest in humankind in general, which helped to direct all his activities (Grant 1985: 15). Cicero's proud patriotism is not surprising to find in a leading Roman politician, but it surely represents particularism, the politics of exclusion, not universalism in the spirit of the original, Greek, Stoicism. Unlike the Greek Stoics, Cicero did not stop at the level of an abstract world community. He was a practical Roman politician who spoke and wrote to his Roman audience.

However, Cicero's particularism did not justify war—especially a religious one— as it did in ancient Hebrew thought and Zoroastrianism. For Cicero, it was politics, not war, that held a central place in his nationalism. However, Cicero's ideas, and Roman Stoicism in general, justified a fundamental distinction between Romans and the Others. These Others were not allowed to become Roman citizens, to which Roman law was exclusively applied.

On the other hand, while the distinction between the Greeks and the Barbarians, and especially between Roman citizens and others, was political—not racial or religious—the role of Greco-Roman religions cannot be totally ignored. The city-state (one of which Rome remained a long time after its extensive conquests, were founded around the domestic heart: the fireside represented the souls of fathers and ancestors who lived as gods among their children. The city around the sacred area was closed by a wall to keep the other gods—not human enemies—out (Fustel de Coulanges 1955).

It is a fact that the Romans were highly religious and waged their wars in openly religious terms. No war could be started without strict religious ceremonies (cf. Russell 1972). Livy makes Camillus speak in the language of the stronger version of the politics of exclusion, when Camillus declares: "Let each man remember that there are gods who help the Roman, the gods who have sent him into battle" (Livy VI.12; cf. Livy V.51, XXV.1). This reveals the distance between the weaker and stronger versions of the politics of exclusion to be short, especially when international relations are concerned.

THE HOLY CENTER AND WAR AGAINST THE FORCES OF CHAOS IN ANCIENT HEBREW THOUGHT

The idealistic principle-oriented approach to the identity of the Jews was not sufficient or appropriate to all Jews. It was challenged by a contending mode of Jewish thought, where peaceful relations between the Jews and the other nations were impossible in practice and never acceptable as a doctrine. Indeed, this alternative view claimed that the Enemy must be eliminated from the Land of Israel, or at least effectively excluded from the community of the Jews. If there are contacts with the Enemy, no compromises can be accepted, at least when the Enemy is found within the sacred area. This can be explained by both ethnic and political factors: the Other is a danger to the race but even more so to the political community established, and continuously reproduced by the covenant. In order to justify his ruthless elimination, the Other is declared the Enemy (Cohn 1994: 86–87; cf. Neusner 1989: 38ff).

This doctrine is referred to as ancient Hebrew thought because it is most strongly connected to the early history of the establishment of Israel. However, this connection was likely made much later in the vocabulary of the suggested model. In any case the idea was represented by the leading early figures of the second Temple, and later by the nationalistic movements preceding and following the beginning of the Common Era. This view has maintained a role much later, especially in the modern Israel. Therefore, ancient Hebrew thought must be understood as a contending, minority view in Judaism.

The majority view, discussed in Chapter 6, is not far from present theories. In fact, when human associations are constructed in the name of God, a community is established in two intertwined ways: through inclusion and exclusion. That is, the relation to God defines us and them. If two or more persons meet without interchanging words of *torah*, no godly man can live with such aliens. However, this claim can be understood as a rather abstract form of the politics of exclusion, and is closer to the weaker version than the stronger version of the politics of exclusion. It seems to emphasize the distinction between the Jews and other nations when the Jews live among foreigners, but must be ready to make the required compromises that do not violate *torah*.

In the stronger version discussed here, the community is formed around the Land of Israel, which is both a powerful symbol and a specific regional area. This geographical center—also called the Holy or Promised Land—occupies a core position in ancient Hebrew thought. The Holy Land appears as a strictly defined area, the center on which the nation has been built. According to Jonathan Z. Smith (1978; 110ff.) the Holy Land has not always existed just waiting for the elect nation to come. The Holy Land was given by God. It is the land which man has established through his rituals, including conquest in the name of God. Simultaneously, it is a heritage from the ancestors, representing a shared history of the generations of the nation it defines.

This sounds so self-evident that—Smith further maintains—another, covert dimension of the idea has often been ignored. The Holy Land, by definition, excludes the wilderness. Smith suggests that the Israelites perceived the wilderness as "sacred in the wrong way." The wilderness is a demonic and dangerous land, the haunt of disgusting and dangerous beasts. It is the land of confusion and chaos:

It is a place of utter desolation, of cosmic and human emptiness. . . . The desert or wilderness is a place of strange, demonic, secret powers. . . . It is not a place which is a homeland, a world where men may dwell. (Smith 1978: 109; based on Isa. 34: 9–15; Deut. 32: 10; Jer. 2: 2; Job 38: 26)

In short, Smith (1978, 110ff.) grasps the full essence of the politics of exclusion by maintaining that the distinction between the Holy Land and the wilderness structures the world, both together define and maintain order. As for social order in the Holy Land, it is not only the wilderness that establishes it, the Enemy has the same function.

But while the wilderness is passive, the Enemy is active. Furthermore, you can find God in the wilderness, but never in the Enemy.

According to ancient Hebrew thought, people within the Holy Land wish to follow *torah*, and it is believed that they will do so unless there is foreign influence tempting men to break it and worship the "wrong gods." Therefore, the Jew must ceaselessly labor to sustain, strengthen, and renew God's blessing, and be alert against the Enemy. Religious rites are sufficient to keep the wilderness out, but against the Enemy war with the help of God is inevitably required (Smith 1978: 111–12, based on Jer. 4: 6–7; 6: 22–23).

The Enemy belongs to the wilderness, not to the Holy Land. This defines the relationship between the Jews and the Gentiles, between those serving God and those serving evil. Therefore, the foreign threat must be removed and foreigners killed. There is always the danger that the Enemy will attack and seduce the believer. Therefore, the relationship must be fundamentally based on violence and war.

The entry into and conquest of the Land of Israel is one of the most well-known myths in the great narrative of the Hebrew people. Aho (1981: 165) maintains that foreigners outside and inside the Holy Land were treated quite differently in ancient Hebrew thought. War was not used as an instrument for the forcible conversion of nonbelievers, it was intended only for expelling the uncircumcised from the villages and farms.

As Aho further documents, there were certain rules to follow before the elect nation was permitted by God to fall upon enemies—outside the Promised Land. Among these rules the enemy city had to be formally offered the choice to either become subjects of God's nation or to fight. Furthermore, those captives residing outside the boundaries of the Promised Land were enslaved, sold, or made concubines. Specific rules gave certain, if limited, responsibilities for the Israelites to respect the rights of captives (Aho 1981: 165–66, based on Deut. 20: 1–14; Num. 10: 1–9 and 31: 19–47).

As for war against those living in the Promised Land before the Israelites arrived and those trying to penetrate the Land of Israel after the Israelites had occupied it, it was God's war against the crimes of unrighteousness. The ancient Hebrew martial ethic placed absolutely no restraints on the use of violence in such a combat. When it came to achieving military victory, no law, even the most sacred, was so binding that it could not be transgressed (Aho 1981: 165–69).

Aho's well-justified conclusion is that an anathema (ban) was applied to all people who did not belong to the Promised Land. God demanded the Israelites to "spare not the life of any living thing" in the towns of those peoples, which God gave the Israelites as their "own inheritance" (Aho 1981: 175–76; Cohn 1994; Dothan and Cohn 1994; Machinist 1994; Silberstein 1994).

The Babylonian captivity and the Diaspora had two different impacts on the Jews. First, it forced the Jews to deal with other nations and find a positive, cultural interpretation for their national identity. Second, while many were willing to give the Land and the Temple a much less important position than before, others strongly believed that the distinction between the Jews and others had to be maintained, or even made an explicit cornerstone of the identity of the Jews. For example, Ezekiel never thought that the Diaspora could serve as a normal mode of existence for the

Jews of God (Batho 1945: 62; Sicker 1992: 6, 30–31, 33, 48, 51–52; cf. Jer. 27: 22; Ps. 137: 5–6).

As part of their effort to affirm the centrality of the Land of Israel some Rabbis produced a series of legends such as the mythic notion of omphalos, the navel of the earth, that focused on the notion that the Land of Israel was the ultimate sacred place in the world of creation. The sacred center of that world was the city of Jerusalem, the place at which the principal interface between the human and the divine occurred, and from which the creation of the world was claimed to have begun. In addition, it was taught that living in the Promised Land was equal to the fulfilment of the entire *Torah* (Sicker 1992: 45–50). Finally, the hope of a miraculous return to the Land and the restoration of its full political independence under the leadership of the Messiah was the main factor in the motivation and mobilization of more hesitant Jews (Blau 1966: 119–20).

As a revealing detail the post-exilic age emphasized the doctrine of redemption: the nation owed its existence to a great deliverance in the past, which was now to be repeated and reproduced. The return from exile was regarded as a second, and even more glorious, Exodus. The Land of Israel had to be conquested again and the covenant reestablished (Batho 1945: 116).

This view justified heated disputes within the Jewish community and especially between orthodox, returning Jews and those who had remained in the Land of Israel and allegedly married foreign daughters, that is, between the Jews and the Samaritans. This dispute was not violent. Samaritan help in the rebuilding of the Temple was excluded by the terms of the decree of Cyrus, and Nehemiah reconstructed Jerusalem's walls as an efficient deterrence to the Samaritan army. Therefore, the dispute remained theological and led to the total exclusion of the Samaritans (Browne 1920). However, the return from the Babylonian captivity was compared and equated with the original conquest of Canaan. Welch suggests that in certain respects the history of the restoration of the Jewish polity after the exile has an interesting resemblance to the history of the conquest of Palestine in the book of Joshua:

There the conquest, instead of being sporadic, effected by the separate clans under different leaders and carried out with very varied success, has been compressed into a single series of campaigns. There, too, the unity of Israel, which was only won after painful effort and with very imperfect success under the kingdom of David, was already present when Israel entered Canaan. The victory was gained under one head by a nation which was already organized for its task under elders who decided and controlled its campaigns. History has been telescoped in both Joshua and Ezra, and what was the outcome of time and much experience has been set down as though it existed from the beginning. (Welch 1935: 158–59; cf. 217–23)

In fact, it seems that the original conquest of Canaan was at least partly imagined during the second conquest[3]:

The leaders of the Jewish thought [Nehemiah and Ezra] went directly counter to [the universalistic] ideals. Instead of welcoming the nations into the religion of Yahweh, they first rejected the Samaritans, and then developed national particularism which manifested itself in the prohibition of intermarriage with foreigners. The limit was reached in . . . the account of the slaughter of the Midianites in Numbers XXXI. The men were all slain in battle, and when the rest were brought in as captives, Moses commanded that all the male children and married women were to be slain in cold blood. There seems to be no historic basis for the story; it only embodies the author's idea of the way in which the Israel of the future will deal with the heathen. (Browne 1920: 210–11)

The importance of the strong version of the politics of exclusion can be explained by its functions. Neusner maintains that once the Jewish group had taken shape around the distinctive doctrine, it also had to introduce the modes of social differentiation, which would ensure the group's continued existence (Neusner 1981: 69). Furthermore,

So long as Israel remained essentially within its own Land. . . the issue of separation from neighbors could be treated casually. Later, due to the troubles, the issue of self-definition clearly would emerge. It would remain on the surface and chronic. And it would persist for the rest of Israelite history. . . . The reason for the persistence is that the social forces which lent urgency to the issue of who is Israel (or, later, who is a Jew) would remain. It is hardly an exaggeration to say that this confusion about the distinctive and ongoing identification to be assigned to Israel would define the very framework of the social and imaginative ecology of the Jewish people. So long as memory remained, the conflicting claims of exclusivist Torah literature and universalist prophecy, of a people living in utopia, in no particular place, while framing its vision to itself in the deeply locative symbols of cult and center—these conflicting claims would make vivid the abiding issue of self-definition. (Neusner 1981: 74–75)

In short, in the world of change experienced by the Jews in and after captivity, "the outsider remained what he had always been, a mere pagan." It is true that Israel was not essentially different from other nations, but Israel alone was guiltless. Therefore, the strict rules affected who might join the community and who might not. "These laws formed a protective boundary, keeping in those who were in, keeping out those who were not" (Neusner 1981: 70; cf. 1983: 8).

The Jewish nationalistic movement during the approximately two hundred years preceding the Jewish war (66–73 CE) fought God's war against the Gentiles who had occupied the Holy Land.[4] War and God's assistance to his people were, again, required in the struggle against foreign enemies in order to cast the new Pharaohs' armies into the sea. It was claimed that the Enemy had human strength, but the Israelites had the Lord to help them fight their battles (Ferguson 1977: 79).

For example, Judith promised that "the Lord will deliver Israel by my hand," as he had given a sword to the hand of her forefather "to take vengeance on those foreigners who had stripped off a virgin's veil." When Judith murdered Holofernes, it was "God who has not withdrawn his mercy from the house of Israel . . . but has crushed our enemies by my hand" (Judith 8: 33; 9: 2, 14–15 in the *Apocrypha*; 2 Macc. 8: 7, 36; 11: 13–38; 13: 1–26 in the *Apocrypha*).

Similarly, in the Maccabean war the Jews believed that their God would defend them. When the Maccabeans saw the army coming to meet them, they became afraid, for they were small in number and weak from having nothing to eat. To this Judas said: "Many can be easily overpowered by a few; it makes no difference to Heaven to save by many or by few. Victory does not depend on numbers. Strength comes from Heaven alone. . . . We are fighting for our lives and our religion" (1 Macc. 3: 18–22).

In another case, Judas told his men not to fear the enemy's multitude, but instead remember how their fathers were saved at the Red Sea. It was now time to ask God to favor the Jews again in the name of the covenant. It was God's task to destroy enemies so that "all the Gentiles will know that there is One who saves and liberates Israel" (1 Macc. 4: 8–11; cf. Farmer 1956: 181). The Jews were ready to play their part, but it was God who was going to kill the enemy "by the sword of those who love thee, and let all who know thy name praise thee with songs of thanksgiving" (1 Macc. 4: 30–33).

This implied that God was Israel's only, but strong, ally. God and Israel were the same, there were mutual responsibilities involved. According to this doctrine, when anyone rises up against Israel, he rises up against God. Consequently, the sword of those who love God is a redemptive instrument. Its zealous use is capable of turning away the wrath of God from his disobedient people, by atoning for the sins of the nation. A zealot is a man who is zealous and active for God in a particular way. He gives himself over to God as an agent of his righteous wrath and renders judgment against anything that excites God's jealousy. This also had a practical dimension. The freedom to live their own lives and follow their own religion unhindered by foreign dominion and to enjoy the favor of God was in the forefront of nationalistic religious thought (Farmer 1956: 178; Moore 1954 I: 118; Aho 1981; cf. Aho1989).

The Maccabean war was successful, but it did not solve the problems permanently. Instead, it led to an increase in Roman power, and later to the direct occupation of the Holy Land by Roman legions. A new nationalistic uprising was mobilized in a extremely nationalistic fervor, but the Jewish War ended in catastrophe when the second Temple was destroyed. As Farmer carefully documented, this unsuccessful fight was directly based on the ideas of God's war against the Enemy. Indeed, the tragic war reveals the essence of such doctrines and their impact on human behavior.

According to Farmer (cf. Josephus' *Jewish War*) the Jews were given an opportunity to surrender but they were uncompromising, nor would they allow their compatriots to surrender. Those Jews who tried to join the Romans were killed by their more zealous brethren. Neither famine (according to Josephus a mother killed her baby and prepared a meal of the body) nor incredible battle casualties could deter the Jews from their refusal to surrender. But when the Temple was set on fire by the Romans, the Jews negotiated with Titus for permission to pass through his lines to the wilderness. The permission was refused them and the last act of the Jews was a suicidal attempt to break through Roman lines. Tragic suicides were deliberately chosen instead of defense from the practically impregnable fortifications in the upper city (Farmer 1956: 111–19).

Farmer explains the process convincingly by the fact that the nationalistic movement looked upon the Maccabean victories as having been made possible through divine assistance. The Zealots had confidence that God would help them in their fight against the Enemy (Farmer 1956: 122, 176).

Furthermore, it was believed that God did not help passive men and that divine assistance had to be combined with the most zealous use of the sword in defense of *torah* and the Temple. An individual had to be actively involved on the side of good, against evil. It was thought that a balance existed between God and the Enemy, but an individual's action could turn the scale to God's advantage. It was fully expected that there would be terrible sufferings, casualties, and unprecedented distress and anguish before the final, divine deliverance. Indeed, heavy casualties and disastrous defeats in battle only served to spur the believing warrior on to greater heights of self–sacrifice and valor. The besieged Jews believed that God dwelt in the Jerusalem sanctuary, and that God would save his own Temple. Therefore, the fanatical resistance to the Romans was grounded in the belief that the result rested with God (Farmer 1956: 109–10, 148, 177, 183–84; Ferguson 1977: 95–96).

However, there was no reason to continue the fight after the final act of blasphemy, the burning of the Temple. The event showed that God had abandoned His house and His people. Therefore, the people had to return to the wilderness where Yahweh had earlier spoken to Moses. It was time to find God again and renew the covenant. The Enemy had not won, but the Jews had lost their God. He had to be won back (Farmer 1956: 115–19, 184).

The destruction of Jerusalem and the second Temple was a terrible blow to the Jews, but not to their theory of the struggle between God and the Enemy. They still believed that the Enemy must and could be abolished. Therefore, according to Neusner, the destruction of the Temple in 70 and the catastrophic failure of the rebellion against Rome led by Bar Kokhba in 132–35 formed a single historical moment: the first set in motion the expectations that led to the second:

When the Temple was destroyed, Jews naturally looked to Scripture to find the meaning of what had happened and, more important, to learn what to expect. There they discovered that when the Temple had been destroyed earlier, a period of three generations—seventy years—intervened. Then, in aftermath of atonement and reconciliation with God, Israel was restored to its Land, the Temple to Jerusalem, the priests to the service of the altar. So, many surmised, in three generations the same pattern will be reenacted, now with the Messiah at the head of the restoration. So people waited patiently and hopefully. But whether or not Bar Kokhba said he was the Messiah, he was to disappoint the hopes placed in him. Jerusalem was closed to the Jews, except on special occasions, much Jewish settlement in the southern part of the country was wiped out. (Neusner 1993b: 14)

The transcendent-historical mythologies see war and conflict as absolute, related to some fundamental differences between the participants. "Every animal loves its like, and every man his neighbor," but it can be asked, "What has a wolf in common with a lamb, or a sinner with a man of piety? What peace can there be between hyena and dog?" While this quotation (Eccl. 13: 15–23) is related to the conflict between the rich and the poor,[5] the same argument applies to the fundamental conflict between the Jews and the foreign nations. Any war related to that kind of conflict may have only one aim: "to destroy and to exterminate" as it was expressed by the Qumran sect (Yadin 1962: 19).

The Qumran sect was not alone in claiming that there is an absolute difference between the Jews and the Gentiles, between us and them. The Jews were not to let their children marry foreign daughters, nor seek peace with foreigners forever. Otherwise, the Jews could not remain strong enough to leave the Land of Israel as an inheritance to their children (1 Esd. 8: 65–9: 4 in the *Apocrypha*).

The Qumran scroll of the *War of the Sons of Light against the Sons of Darkness* (Vermes 1984; Yadin 1962) makes it clear that the sect's "patriotism grows out of their religion, their nationalism out of their piety, and the sword with which they fight is a consecrated weapon" (Farmer 1956: 169). Indeed, according to the scroll the war will be fought not only by men but also by the cosmic powers of light and darkness. The war will take place "when the exiles of the Sons of Light return from the wilderness of the nations to encamp in the wilderness of Jerusalem," between the Sons of Light and the Sons of Darkness. The Sons of Light are assisted by the powers of light and justice and the angels appointed over them, while the Sons of Darkness are assisted by Belial and the powers of darkness and evil under his authority (Yadin 1962: 4–7).

The scroll repeats the themes discussed above: the exact fulfillment of the law is an essential condition for the war; there is no contradiction resulting from the difficulties created by the exact fulfillment of both the laws of *torah* and of warfare, the result is preordained. God himself cares for the welfare of Israel when his people observe *torah*, and for victory over their enemies. God's intervention will take place only after a series of real battles in which the Sons of Darkness are alternately defeated and victorious. The opposing forces are equally matched and only by the intervention of the mighty hand of God is the balance between them to be disturbed when He deals an everlasting blow to Satan and all the hosts of his kingdom. The war provides a crucible in which God tests the members of the sect and causes Himself to be hallowed among them (Vermes 1984: 124; Yadin 1962: 4–5, 12, 234–35).

There are certain similarities between the Qumran and Zoroastrian beliefs but the Qumran doctrine is strictly monotheistic. There is no evil power comparable to the Evil Spirit of Zoroastrianism. Belial is the angel of wickedness, the ruler of this world, but he is powerless to harm those who observe *torah*. In the final analysis, because God created Belial, God is able to get rid of him anytime. The Lord himself has created Belial to carry out a specific function: to reveal the wicked so that God can destroy them "with the assistance of the angels appointed for that task" (Yadin 1962: 232–33).

The victory implies the triumph of righteousness: "wickedness shall then be banished by righteousness as darkness is banished by the light." Wickedness will perish for ever, and the evil kingdom shall be brought low by Israel, its wives and his children shall go into captivity, its mighty men shall perish by the sword (Vermes 1984: 209–10, 234).

There is no need to discuss the details of the Qumran scroll, but we must note that its specific function is to give meaning and order to all events and problems by defining the Sons of Light and the Sons of Darkness at the time the document was written (Yadin 1962: 242). Ideas of God's war and the need for social meaning, order, and security are fully intertwined. This reveals that violence and war fulfill an important function in the society- and state-building processes through the elimination of both internal and external enemies.

Furthermore, the Qumran scroll promises a solid hope for men. Its main purpose is to give courage to the Sons of Light by explaining that the defeats and victories have been determined from time immemorial. The scroll was written for the purpose of consolation, to describe the splendid future following the last war (Yadin 1962: 8–15).

WAR AGAINST THE FORCES OF THE EVIL SPIRIT IN ZOROASTRIANISM

Historically, Zoroastrianism precedes the doctrines called ancient Hebrew thought. However, the latter was discussed first because ancient Hebrew thought shares national particularism typical to the political doctrines in the weaker version of the pattern. Neither is Zoroastrianism fully unaware of national divisions. According to Zoroastrianism, Ahura Mazda made "the Aryan Glory" to withstand enemies and destroy "the non-Aryan nations" (Astad Yasht in ZA/SBE 23). However, the land of Iranians (or Aryans) represents a dynamic conception. The "Aryan land" is a continuously expanding group of believers, not a geographical region given to Zoroastrians by Ahura Mazda. Zoroaster's doctrine was proclaimed for the whole of mankind (Mills, 1887: xxv, 37).

In the final analysis, geographical area remains unimportant in Zoroaster's system, where the moral principle, due to its social interpretation and social function, divides men into two groups—those who respect the contract and those who break it. This division holds a central place in the doctrine, which instead of monotheism develops toward dualism. Among Zoroastrians or the believers and among those who have received the law of Mazda, no representatives of the Evil Spirit are allowed to live. Both figuratively and geographically, the evil ones must remain elsewhere, in the world of chaos waiting for a conversion to become a believer or to die at the hands of the growing number of believers.

In Chapter 5, I interpreted the Zoroastrian system of *asha* and contract as a principle-oriented approach to social order. I described the struggle between good and evil in details as a moral issue. However, it is a fact that the moral distinction between the followers of Ahura Mazda and those of Angra Mainyu soon becomes the real historical battle because the believer has the duty and responsibility to carry out the god's will, to help Ahura Mazda fight against the Angra Mainyu.

Such a confrontation can easily be given a historical interpretation when the struggle concerns two groups: the representatives of Ahura Mazda and Angra Mainyu. Furthermore, in such a confrontation the relationship is extremely violent: the good must kill the representatives of the Evil Spirit. In fact the difference between the principle-oriented pattern and the present power-oriented patterns in the case of Zoroastrianism is a matter of interpretation. In the first interpretation, the struggle is seen in figurative terms, as my duty to keep my promises uncompromisingly. In the latter interpretation the confrontation between us and them obtains a historical and concrete sense of armed violence.

There is not much new to add to the discussion, however, two details can be briefly discussed: the doctrines of just wars and the final battle.

Mithra—Mazda's personification for the control of international contracts—represents an overwhelming military power that makes him able to conquer all of his opponents. The defensive ability of Mithra is not stressed in the Avesta, since there are no forces that have even the remotest chance of prevailing against the strongest of the strong gods (Gershevitch 1959: 158).

Mithra is not only a moral being, he is also a violent master. Mithra is both extremely good to friends and extremely wicked to enemies. Mithra protects countries if they abide by the contract, and destroys them if they are defiant. Mithra is the punisher of wrong and brings the Enemy terror and fear. He even "hurls off the wicked heads of men false to the covenant" (*Avestan Hymn to Mithra*, hereafter referred to as Mithra 8.29; 9.36–37, 41, 43, 18.72, 19.78; Boyce 1984: 28–29).[6]

Typical to religious war rituals (where men think themselves the god's representatives in armed battle) Zoroaster links the weakness of benign cattle, helpless before raiders, with that of himself, weak materially but strong if aided by Ahura Mazda (Boyce 1984: 41). Therefore, Zoroastrians ask Mithra to give them strength. People ask Mithra for help, "so that we . . . may overcome all opponents, so that we . . . may overcome all enemies, so that we . . . may overcome all hostilities of evil gods and men, sorcerers and witches, tyrants, hymn-mongers, and mumblers" (Mithra 8.34, 20.94). The god is asked to help the believer smite bad nations (Ashi Yasht 9.51 in ZA/SBE 23).

Mithra is just, but violent, he carries out justice himself while Ahura Mazda, equally good, does not personally seek out the wicked for punishment, but lets them run to their self-appointed doom. Mithra is not only accompanied by the embodiment of justice, he has the necessary insight to pass judgment and the physical skill to execute it. Mithra's justice is militant with an enduring affection for the unjustly oppressed (Gershevitch 1959: 53–54).

However symbolic it may look, Mithra has a military function: the rhetoric represents justifications for an armed battle and a means of making real warriors strong and fearless. Indeed, the "word" is not alone sufficient. The weapons against evil are not only spiritual. The death of an armed religious enemy was devoutly desired for moral, political, and personal reasons (Mithra 3.10–11; Darmesteter 1880: lxxviii, 203).

Violence is justified because the Zoroastrian believers are weak compared to the contract breakers. Furthermore, the believers are oppressed because of their adherence to *asha*. Indeed, it may be that their challenge to the earlier religious establishment originally led to opposition, persecution, and exile. Similarly, arch-enemy Alexander the Great and his generals tried to destroy the believers. The Zoroastrians often lament: "Fury and raiding hold me captive, cruelty and might," or "To what land shall I go for refuge? Where am I to turn my steps? I am thrust out from family and from tribe. I find no support in my home-village, none from my country's evil rulers" (Yasna 29, 46.1 in Boyce 1984).

This is fully developed in the doctrine of the last battle, concluding with the application of war and violence as the negative sanction against those who break the contract. The Zoroastrians were particularly interested in—and worried about—an important basic question: Will the just man ever conquer the wicked one? (Yasna 48 in Boyce 1984: 39). The doctrine answered that when the appointed time comes, the son of Ahura Mazda will appear, Angra Mainyu and hell will be destroyed and everlasting happiness will reign over the world. This will start when a maid bathing in Lake Kasava is impregnated by it and brings forth the victorious Saoshyant (Savior), "who will come from the region of the dawn to free the world from death and decay, from corruption and rottenness" (Darmesteter 1880: lxxix, lvi).

The final battle is not easy. The apocalypse is full of violence and chaos, and begins with an invasion by a foreign enemy, then "ten thousand kinds of devs [*daevas*] with disheveled hair will arrive." The devils will burn the villages, and destroy the pure religion among many other valuable things. The bases of order will disappear, the small will become large, and the large will become small. Even the uncompromising ethics of the contract will break into pieces. The covenants will be changed at caprice, everybody will become the deceiver. No treaties will be made, for they will not be kept. There will be great changes in the natural world and the physical structure of men, but most importantly "all people will worship greed and be of false religion." But with the help of Saoshyant, just men will finally win; the dark powers will be overthrown, and meaningful life will be renewed in unending youth and incorruption (The Zand of Vahman Yasht, Ch. 4 in Boyce 1884: 92; Ferguson 1977: 21).

In considering the function of the apocalyptic vision, it is clear that Zoroaster's doctrine had to give a certain promise to those who were willing to fight against the enemy and perhaps be killed in the fight (Greater Bundahishn, Ch.3 in Boyce 1984: 50). We have already seen that the antagonism between Ahura Mazda and Spenta Mainyu cannot be resolved in any rational way through a compromise. Ahura Mazda knows that if he does not set a time for the battle, the Evil Spirit would eternally create strife and a state of confusion. Therefore, the believer must know for sure that Saoshyant will arrive and evil destroyed; it is clear that he need not fight eternally or in vain (cf. Fargard 19.5 in ZA/SBE 4; Yasna 30.5 in Boyce 1984: 35; Darmesteter 1880: lxxv).

The destiny of the Evil Spirit (and his supporters) is to be reduced to nothingness, he is to be kicked out of the cosmic order. He will stay in absolute nothingness, alone in total chaos. Ahura Mazda and his supporters, instead, will have reached the absolute order. It is absolute because there is now no longer any place for the Evil Spirit. History has ended. It has not returned to any cyclical beginning. Instead, it has reached the final goal of the plot of history (Sharif 1963: 67–72). The realism of the suggested image can be disputed, but it is rather unimportant. What is important is the ultimate definition of social order preferred in Zoroastrianism.

I have claimed that there are no other cases of the stronger version of the politics of exclusion, in addition to late Zoroastrianism, ancient Hebrew thought, and early Christianity. Therefore, I discuss a potential candidate, which I have excluded on the basis that exclusively moral issues are of no concern. In Carl Schmitt's (1993) terms the moral distinction of good and evil defines the special nature of ethics. Only when one speaks of social relations between the friend and enemy do we have the political in our hands.

Due to the same roots, similarities between ancient Indian and Zoroastrian thought are not difficult to recognize, even if the heroes and villains have opposite roles in the two systems: Indian gods are Zoroastrian demons, and Indian evil spirits have become the god in Zoroastrianism (Parpola 1994). However, there is a fundamental difference. In ancient Indian thought the issues of good and evil remain moral; the social world must not be divided into the two. In the Indian doctrines anyone can be born either good or evil depending on his or her *karma*. Similarly, everyone must be able to reach *nirvana*. It does not matter that the Buddha reaches it sooner, all others will eventually follow. Furthermore, real life is too complex for the dualistic distinction. For example, in the *Mahabharata* we cannot always be sure if the Pandavas are good and the Kauravas bad—the latter have committed the original crime but the Pandavas commit many crimes during the battle.

I maintain that in India the dualistic doctrine did not have much value. It was used as a linguistic, figurative device to provide dramatic emphasis to more important basic messages. This is revealed in the *Ramayana*, where the epic story seems to be close to the Zoroastrianistic world.

The *Ramayana* narrative concerns a cosmic battle between Rama, from a city in north India, and Ravana, the king of the south (the island of Lanka). Rama's task is to subdue the south by defeating its powerful leader, Ravana. The battle is presented as a typical example of Lord Vishnu's ongoing struggle with the forces of disorder, *adharma*. Rama is Vishnu's incarnation; Ravana the king of *ashuras*.

However, the fight is more symbolic than real. The ultimate issue concerns Rama's commitment to *dharma*. Will he be able to follow *dharma* and take social responsibility as king, forgetting his personal comforts, including his beloved wife? The campaign and Rama's decisions prove his ability to become the true king, the servant of the common good (*dharma*-caste system), not somebody interested in his own feelings and needs. Both Rama and Ravana are mythical figures. Furthermore, the epic is interested in Rama's personality, not in the battle or Ravana. Therefore, no one has suggested that the epic justifies or might be used as a justification for a real war against a real enemy (cf. Kinsley 1982: 26).

In India, no justifications for real wars were required, because there were no wars where such doctrines might have been applied. As far as historical reality is concerned, it is unlikely that military excursions were undertaken by the north against the south. Aryan domination was established primarily through small settlements and the increasing influence of the brahmin elite. In fact, the Aryans themselves came to accept into their own traditions many indigenous traditions and cultural forms wherever they went in India, including the south. There was no need to distinguish between us and them, the coexistence of both was the preferred ideal (Kinsley 1982: 26).

EARLY CHRISTIANITY AND THE CHURCH

Early Christianity emerges as an explicit challenge to exclusion and particularism. While ancient Hebrew thought and early Judaism tried to solve the problem of human associations at the domestic level between individual Jews, early Christians, adopting Jesus's teachings put the goal into a much a wider perspective, recognizing the need to transcend a number of new divisions—according to Paul, the national distinction between Greek and Barbarian, the social distinction between rich and poor, and the political distinction between freeman and slave. Something good was included in everyone, so Paul became a debtor to both the Greeks and the Barbarians, to both the wise and the unwise (Rom. 1: 14). The message was to eliminate the differences: "There is neither Greek nor Jew, circumcision nor uncircumcision, Barbarian, Scythian, bond nor free." Instead, a common denominator was found: "Christ is all, and in all." The new idea was made universalistic (Col. 3: 11).

This reflected the contemporary social change, due to active and extensive trade relations, free and forced movement of people, and the Roman power a mixture of several nationalities had emerged. Everyday life had irreversibly become internationalized, the distinction between native and foreign populations was disappearing everywhere. There was a quest for doctrines transcending the old distinctions, to make orderly social life possible among men of different nationalities and social positions. There was an urgent need to feel that everybody had something in common. They only had to find a common language (Acts 2: 4, 8–11).

As an open challenge to the Judaic tradition, Christians were willing to include the Gentiles among the would-be elect in order to gain new allies in the struggle against the Roman state. From the Judaic perspective, universalism simply represented the danger of changing an enemy into a friend. This meant blurring the line between friend and foe, good and evil, thereby causing a threat to the statehood and independence of the Jews. In order to overcome this criticism, the *New Testament* had to make the Gentiles entitled to God's Word.

Positive references to the Gentiles were written into the Gospels. It was said that in the very beginning, "there came wise men from the east to Jerusalem" (Mat. 2: 1–2; Mat. 12: 21). The new attitude was made a duty, justified once again through an allusion to Jesus's example: "Go ye therefore, and teach all nations, baptizing them in the name of the Father, and of the Son, and of the Holy Ghost." It was pointed out that Jesus himself did not avoid associating with foreigners (John 4: 9; Mark 16: 15–17; Mat. 8: 10, 28:19; Luke 2: 32, 47).

However, Jesus had been a Jew and his attitude towards the Gentiles had to be left unclear. In an indirect way his followers needed to prove themselves better than Jesus in this respect. Therefore Jesus was sometimes presented as a passive or reluctant object for foreigners to approach, the latter were given the more active role in reconciliation. Jesus's followers wrote the final justification into a direct divine message to Peter, who was urged to eat unclean meat and told that "What God hath cleansed, that call not thou common." The importance of this process and change is emphasized by the ample space given to the narrative. Consequently, the traditional distinction was eliminated (Acts 10: 1–11:24, 15: 9; Mark 7:24–30).[7]

The narrative aimed to eliminate the traditional distinction between us and them in both directions: it made the Gentiles acceptable to Christianity, but it also made Christianity acceptable to the Gentiles. Subsequent texts continued to make the idea more and more accessible to new members. Christians were advised to extend brotherly love and to entertain strangers (Acts 17: 23; Heb. 13: 1–2; Rom. 10: 12; cf. Gal. 3: 28).

However, early Christians were not uncompromising followers of Jesus's truly universalistic doctrine, they used his teachings for their own power political pursuits. Therefore, the original universalistic idea was actually applied in full contradiction to its own spirit. Furthermore, a new application of the earlier modes of exclusion was introduced. The old distinction was eliminated and the Gentiles became entitled to receive Jesus's Word in order to make Christianity acceptable to the Romans.[8]

Simultaneously, new enemies were created, mainly to tell the Romans that the Christians deviated from those responsible for the Jewish War.[9] The Gentile became the hero, while the Jew was made the villain. This was generalized, in order to provide a new religious basis to the distinction of the Christian from the Pagan, as well as between the elect and the lost. The NT Gospels had the major role in the process, therefore we discuss them by briefly summarizing Pagels's (1995)[10] salient contribution.

Pagels's (1995: xvi–xvii) point of departure is the fact that while angels often appear in the Hebrew Bible, Satan is virtually absent. Then, among certain first-century Jewish groups, including the Essenes and later followers of Jesus, the figure began to take on central importance, and finally,

Such visions have been incorporated into Christian tradition and have served, among other things, to confirm for Christians their own identification with God and to demonize their opponents—first other Jews, then pagans, and later dissident Christians called heretics.

Pagels maintains that Mark introduced the devil into the crucial opening scene of his Gospel, and characterized Jesus's ministry as involving the continual struggle between God's spirit and the demons of Satan's kingdom. However, Satan is not a hostile power assailing Israel from outside the community, but the source and representation of conflict within the community (Pagels 1995: 12, 17, 34, 38; based on Mark 3: 23–27, 16: 5–7).

Pagels claims that Matthew's Jesus interprets *torah* so that Gentiles can fulfill it as well as Jews. Matthew, in effect, encourages Christians to abandon their identification with Israel. Furthermore, he now gives the Pharaoh's role to Herod, the Jewish king. Through this device he turns the alien enemies of Israel's antiquity into the *intimate* enemy within the same community. In fact, Egypt, traditionally the land of slavery, becomes a sanctuary for Jesus (Pagels 1995: 76, 79).

In Luke, Pagels continues, Jesus himself suggests that the arresting party of chief priests, scribes, and elders is allied with "the power of darkness." Satan has now returned to challenge Jesus. In general, spiritual warfare between God and Satan—as the historical conflict between the Jesus movement and the Jewish leaders—intensifies throughout Luke's gospel (Pagels 1995: 89–91). Finally in John,

Jesus accuses the Jews of trying to kill him, saying, "You are of your father, the devil!" and "the Jews" retaliate by accusing Jesus of being a Samaritan—that is, not a real Jew—and himself "demon-possessed," or insane. (Pagels 1995: 98; cf. 99, 103–5, 106–7, 111)

Pagels (1995: 111) ends her analysis of the four gospels[11] by correctly emphasizing the correlation between the depictions of Satan and the history of increasing conflict between groups representing Jesus's followers and their opposition. This was made in order to increase group solidarity within Christians. Furthermore, it can be added that there was another obvious reason: hostility towards the traditional Judaic doctrine and the Jews had the function of separating the new religion from its predecessor. It was emphasized that Israel, which followed the law of righteousness, had not attained it, but had finally killed Jesus (Rom. 2: 17–3: 1, 9: 31–2; 1 Thess 2: 14–16; Chadwick 1986: 21).

Another new enemy was found in the pagan. Prosper (p. 58) put it succinctly: "One section of mankind attains salvation, the other perishes." Arnobius of Sicca (pp. 115, 403) wrote an extensive volume against the pagans dealing with features of pagan cults, centering its polemic first upon the deification of abstractions, the sinister gods, and multiple deities, and concluding with a vigorous onslaught on the myths that impute lustful characters to both gods and goddesses, and even to the great Jupiter himself. Hence he spoke of the "truth of the Christian religion and falsity of the pagan." He further suggested that the pagans hate Christ because he "has driven religions from the earth, because He has prevented access to the worship of the gods." The pagans were guilty of mistakes: "Is He then charged with being a destroyer of religion and a promoter of impiety, who brought true religion into the world, who opened the doors of piety to men blind and truly living in impiety, and pointed out to whom they should be submissive?"

The new distinction between Christians and pagans was based on, or logically derived from, the concept of man and ideas related to good and evil. The dark side of man was introduced as a threat to both his fellowmen and God. This starts in the NT Gospels, but develops to full maturity in the Book of Revelations and Augustine's thought.

The apocalyptic vision in the Book of Revelation, just like many similar apocryphic texts, gave a central role for good and evil in the conception of man, leading to the distinction between good people and evil people. It may be true that the suggested conception of man, here as elsewhere, implied internal war within the human being: "the spirit indeed is willing, but the flesh is weak" (Mat. 26: 41; cf. Aho 1981: 146).

However, this had social consequences. It also had a great influence on the *Weltanschauung* and social relations, finding applications in social life. Here, as in Zoroastrianism and the Qumran sect, some people are defined as good, others as evil—with the responsibility for the good to fight against the evil. There was no place to hide, everybody had to participate. The admonition was to beware of evil men: "for the children of this world are in their generation wiser than the children of light" (Luke 16:8; cf. 22: 53).

It was Augustine who had the greatest influence on the introduction of dualistic conceptions into Christianity, in addition to connecting the pagans and the Jews. There was an important background to his major contribution: St. Augustine is a direct link between Manicheism, a version of Zoroastrianism, and Christianity. In accordance with that tradition, Augustine (*The First Catechetical Instruction*: 23, 61) made the distinction between carnal men and spiritual men, and later suggested that "there are two cities, one of the wicked, the other of the just, which endure from the beginning of the human race even to the end of time." According to Augustine, the two cities are "now intermingled in body, but separated in will, and which, moreover, are to be separated in body also on the day of judgement," representing a threat and a duty to eliminate it. "From this world's city there arise enemies against whom the City of God has to be defended" (Augustine, *The City of God*: 6).[12]

Consequently, human beings, both living and dead, are divided into two clear-cut groups: the God-worshippers and the devil-worshippers. The God-worshippers will be saved, while the devil-worshippers will fall prey to death, violence, and war. The message is clear, evil must be destroyed. There are no possibilities for a compromise. There was also a clear international dimension in the vision introduced by the Book of Revelation. The Book was written after the fall of Jerusalem, reflecting disappointment in the military effort and a belief that there had to be some reason for God to abandon his people. Therefore, it could be interpreted to prophesy the final destruction of Rome—and the devil-worshippers in general—the fundamental wish of the Jewish people, a wish adopted by Christians as well.

DISCUSSION

The present pattern is, more than the others, built on a pure, imagined reality. While all the patterns discussed in this book are examples of the social construction of reality, they have something real to give: a shared moral principle, an ideal organization, an ideal ruler. They reflect facts, social and shared experiences, and can stand a test of observable consequences. The politics of exclusion is a pure example of social imagination, therefore, it is more powerful than others and is able to resist attempts to prove it wrong.

The power of the dualistic views is also based on the fact that challengers—both within and without—can and must be ruthlessly killed. If an individual violates a moral principle, he or she must be educated. If an individual does not think the existing social organization ideal, he or she can suggest another one or move elsewhere. If an individual thinks that his or her ruler is not wise or heroic enough, he or she can prove to be better. But if an individual challenges the structures of exclusion, he or she is likely threatening the basic, shared meaning of human life, the very social order itself. In fact, the present basis of social order is weaker than any other basis: one can kill the god by a simple story, by arousing the first sign of disbelief.

Exclusion and particularism create order within a certain community by stating *who do not belong* to the community, and who must be excluded as a danger to internal order and cohesion. Indeed, because the distinction between us and them does not really exist it must be established by doctrinal maneuvers, by creating a powerful social reality to direct and control man's behavior. The universal doctrine of God and his children is made to be a particularistic doctrine in favor of a single nation, or the "good." Consequently, man can serve his god by fighting a real war against real enemies. If one wishes to satisfy Lord Mazda continually with rightful acts (Boyce 1984: 35), he must find opportunities for doing so. Perhaps, then, it would be better for an individual to create enemies if there are not any available, than to become a heretic by remaining passive and thinking or perhaps also saying something against the doctrine. Similar social pressures are typical to politics, that is, in the weaker form of exclusion. For example, Cicero, or the nationalists in general, does not leave any opportunities to escape the social pressure towards nationalistic values. Any deviation will cause the accusation of high treason.

NOTES

1. This claim is shared by postmodernists who reject the contrast of the west and the rest as a Western view (Nederveen Pieterse 1994), and by other scholars like Ali Mazrui (1990).

2. As a student, Cicero heard the heads of the three chief schools of Athens (the Epicurean, the Stoic, and the Academic). Furthermore, at the age of 27 he retired from politics to devote two more years to philosophy and rhetoric. Six months were spent at Athens, where he attended the lectures of the Epicurean Zeno and the Academic Antiochus. In Rhodes he met Posidonius, the most renowned Stoic of the day. In Rome, the Stoic Diodotus was an inmate of his house (Rackham 1971: xii–xiii).

3. Cohn (1994: 86) suggests that "the names of no-longer-surviving peoples . . . served as signifiers to carry the image of the Other that defined Israel's cultural boundary."

4. Both heirs of ancient Hebrew thought, i.e., Judaism and early Christianity, wished to ignore such ideas in order to maintain peaceful relations with the people among which they lived. Consequently, while nationalistic ideas can be found in the *Old Testament*, the movement and the nationalistic debate is fully represented elsewhere, especially in the apocryphic literature and the Qumran scrolls (cf. Farmer 1956).

5. The quotation continues: "What peace can there be between rich man and pauper?" for "as lions prey on the wild asses of the desert, so the rich man on the poor."

6. There are other figures with similar destructive capacities (Srosh Yasht 5.19 in ZA/SBE 23; cf. Sirozah II in ZA/SBE 23; Zamyad Yasht 2.9 in ZA/SBE 23).

7. This doctrinal change was not easy to make. Indeed, the problem of the Christian attitude towards the Gentiles was rather delicate, causing a deep division of opinion within the Church. The problem of the salvation of Gentiles became one of the major issues among the early Christian writers, who created several justifications for spreading the divine message among the Gentiles (Acts 6–7; Chadwick 1986: 16; Prosper of Aquitaine: 31; Augustine, *Sermons for Christmas and Epiphany*: 41).

8. Here and elsewhere concerning attempts to please the Romans: see e.g., Crossan (1994) on the NT Gospels, and Farmer (1958) and Boccaccini (1991) on Josephus's strategy.

9. Here as elsewhere in similar situations Jews were singled out for primarily political reasons, not because of anti-Judaism.

10. Among the other sources I omitted here I must mention Cohn (1975), who in addition to discussing the origin of Satan in the *Old Testament* books and early Christian texts, continues the story until the persecution of the witches in the Middle Ages.

11. Pagels (1995: 179–80) continues her social history of Satan by discussing the cases of pagans and heretics. Islam adopted the same heritage from Zoroastrianism, Judaism, and Christianity; therefore Christians have not been alone in reproducing the tradition.

12. The Manichean image of Augustine and others is discussed by Chydenius (1985).

CHAPTER 14

Power Politics as the Basis of Social Order

Violence and war appear in several patterns of peace and order. Only Daoism, Jesus's teachings, and Buddhism rule them out altogether and without reservations. Furthermore, early Christians excluded them by preferring non-military ways of gaining power. Another element that can be eliminated from the present discussion is that of defense. Defense can be a moral duty, but it is never the first means of resisting attack. Furthermore, war and violence alone do not usually promise to bring about social order. They may do so only if submitted to serve other, more primary approaches to social order. Thus, war contributes to the perfection of the individual warrior and the fulfillment of religious duties in ancient Indian thought, offers a test of heroism in Rome[1]; and separates us from them in the politics of exclusion.

There are just two cases which maintain that only war establishes social order. Chinese Legalism and the *danda* tradition in ancient India.[2] Recent history would add the theorists of political realism, the Machiavellians (Meinecke 1984). However, none of them add anything new to the two cases.[3]

The Legalists' explicit aim was to stop chaos not only within states but to establish order in the whole empire. Legalism shared with Confucianism the goal of Chinese unification, the ideal of the *tien-hsia*. But Legalism did not believe it possible to achieve a comprehensive order through persuasion. Suggesting that the name of the political game was power struggle, Legalism maintained that the government of the unified China had to be based on coercive methods such as the application of rewards and punishments. After ordering the state, the king became able to attack and conquer the others and unify China, or as it was expressed, the whole world, the *tien-hsia*.

The Legalists generalized the issue of intrastate order to include order in all China. It was not enough to establish order between the king and the minister. Feudal lords were an even bigger problem. It was a mistake to accept the feudal lords' existence because they represented private interests in the *tien-hsia*. Therefore, like the ministers, the feudal lords had to be submitted under the power of the king. This was thought possible not through benevolence and persuasion but through conquest. One cannot win by means of benevolence and righteousness, but by taking advantage of opportunities (Han Fei I: 159–60; Hsün Tzu/Watson: 70).

Therefore, the state (Qin) had to be capable of conquering the world and attaining supremacy (Shang I.3.8a). The Legalists promised that the king, who had loyal ministers, need not to worry about outside enemy states; that he would enjoy permanent peace in "all-under-Heaven" (Han Fei I: 130). The Legalist ruler never fails to win attacks on rivals; his country is doomed to conquer wide lands (Han Fei I: 4).

Kautilya's *Arthashastra* suggests a similar goal. Indeed, Kautilya gave a systematic plan to the king—the conqueror—for unifying India through the only efficient way: military conquest. The system is based on the circle of states (*mandala*), where each state has place and task. The conqueror is the "fountain of policy." In front of him are the enemy, the friend, the enemy's friend, the conqueror's friend, and finally, the enemy's friend's friend. To the rear of the conqueror we find the rearward enemy, the rearward friend, the ally of the rearward enemy, and the ally of the rearward friend. In addition, the system includes the Mayadama king, who is able to help or resist either the conqueror or his enemy, united or disunited. There is also the Udasina king, who is very powerful and capable of resisting the conqueror, the enemy, and the Mayadama king. Because the conqueror is the fountain of policy—the actor who unifies the whole area—the two powerful kings do not have any role in the unification, therefore they seem to remain outside the system, and are not expected to get involved (Kautilya VI.II.260–61).

Furthermore, in Kautilya's system the conqueror, his friend, and his friend's friend are the three primary kings constituting one circle of states. Three other circles consist of the enemy, the Mayadama king, and the Udasina king at the center of their respective circles, but only the circles of the conqueror and his enemy are relevant (Kautilya VI.II.261).

Kautilya's task is to formulate politics and foreign policy for the conqueror to make it possible for him to establish the unified state. For that purpose, Kautilya speaks of the sixfold policy (VII.I.263):

Agreement with pledges is peace; offensive operation is war; indifference is neutrality; making preparations is marching; seeking the protection of another is alliance; and making peace with one and waging war with another, is termed a double policy.

War was considered a necessity for establishing world order. If the ruler does not follow *dao*, he will be responsible for constant warfare. Lord Shang thought war permissible "if by war one wishes to abolish war," and killing acceptable, "if by killing one wants to abolish killing." This reflected the Legalist assumptions that stated heavy punishments were expected to abolish crimes, and therefore make punishments unnecessary (Han Fei I: 207; Shang IV.18.8a).

War was not recommended lightly. If the sovereign is easily provoked and fond of resorting to arms but neglects agricultural and military training, his state will be ruined. This can be fully understood in a period where states waged wars against each other in order to annex the opponent and eliminate its king. In such a situation warfare is always a life-or-death question to the ruler: the king may wage several victorious wars successively, but if he loses a single one, his state will disappear (Han Fei I: 5, 135, 138).

Concerning explicit statements about international relations, it is not difficult to find that they are an extension of the Legalist political theory and its functions to serve the unification process. The point of departure is an alleged natural inclination to serve one's own state instead of that of another king's (Liao 1939: xxviii–xxix, xxxiii). Any means during unification can be justified as long as they guarantee the two basic elements of foreign policy: the state's survival and its geographical growth.

Survival is the basic task, without which other duties become impossible by definition. Therefore, the Legalists advise the ruler if his country is small to serve big powers. Similarly, Kautilya advises negotiation if the opponent cannot be beat. If the state's survival is not in danger, it must extend its area by annexing other states to itself. The ruler must then never disapprove of the measures of deception in engaging enemies on the battlefield. Deception is justified because the everlasting advantage rests with the present victory. War is to be won, because only then can the ruler safeguard his country and stabilize his position, while his army becomes strong and his prestige is enhanced. In foreign policy only strength and purpose count. The king must accomplish anything the enemy is unable or dares not to accomplish. The king must undertake affairs the enemy is ashamed to perform (Han Fei I: 65; Han Fei II: 139–41; Han Fei/Watson: 77; Kautilya VII.I.263ff.; Shang I.4.11a).

Kautilya maintains that a king shall always endeavor to augment his power and elevate his happiness. According to Han Fei Zi, the ruler, in order to be a true king, must develop the military strength of his state, thus ensuring that any other ruler would gain little profit seizing his lands, and that during wars it will be able to beat the enemy. A true king is one who is in a position to attack others, and a ruler whose state is secure cannot be attacked. But once this wisdom of foreign policy "is exhausted and its internal government has fallen into disorder, no state can be saved from ruin" (Han Fei/Watson: 113–15; Kautilya VI.II.261).

In addition to the goal of foreign policy—the survival and growth of the state—and the prudence of the king in his foreign policy, Legalist theory calls attention to the correspondence of the goals and capacities of the state to pursue these goals. At the general level, the Legalists maintained that disorderly and weak states go to ruin, but orderly and strong states attain supremacy. In more practical terms, the Legalist theory of international relations is based on the strict analysis of capacities. The king must know in advance—before engaging in a war—who will and who will not lose. He can accomplish this by applying an analysis of capacities, and carefully estimating his capacities and those of his opponent (Han Fei I: 159; Shang I.4.11a). Similarly, Kautilya maintains that "whoever is inferior to another shall make peace with him; whoever is superior in power shall wage war." Therefore, "a king in the circle of sovereign states shall, by adopting the sixfold policy, endeavor to pass from the state of deterioration to that of stagnation, and from the latter to that of progress" (Kautilya VI.I.266 and VII.I.263).

The capacities are both material and moral. If the state's topographical features are not advantageous, its population is heterogenous and hard to rule, and if the rewards and punishments are of no faith, it will not be successful in the power struggle (Han

Fei I: 2, 7–8). Kautilya also lists both material and human capacities in his system: "The king, the minister, the country, the fort, the treasury, the army and the friend, and the enemy are the elements of sovereignty" (Kautilya VI.1.257).

Concerning material capacities, the Legalists mention treasuries, armors, granaries, and storehouses. Lord Shang suggested that "a state that has to fight on four fronts values defense, and a state that rests against the sea values attack." He formulated a theory according to which a country is made prosperous by agriculture and war. Indeed, Lord Shang admits no occupations for the people other than agriculture and warfare by prohibiting all merchants, artisans, and scholars (Shang I.3.6b, III.12.6a; cf. Duyvendak 1963: 48). Han Fei (I: 2, 134, 138) maintains that the king makes a lethal mistake if he attacks while he lacks the required resources for offensive operations—he and his state will be wiped out in the ruthless game.

Lord Shang wished to revert the entire economic life of the country from money to production, from the means of exchange to true, material commodities. According to Lord Shang, a state that imports material products is strong, but one that exports material commodities in order to collect money is weak. The ultimate aim of hoarding grain in the state is military strength: grain had to be ready for the army. Finally, colonists should be attracted to the country by freedom from taxes and military service, so that the old population of the expanding state can be free to devote themselves entirely to warfare (Duyvendak 1963: 49–50).

However, human resources are more important than material ones. The ruler must win the hearts of the people, otherwise he will fail in war. Without support of the masses, no king is able to win the game of unification (Han Fei I: 259, 275). This is not a simple element of quantitative capacity, but has a much more fundamental aspect of motivation. It implies the fact that a man resolved to die a courageous death can overcome any enemies who are afraid of death—a single brave man can overcome ten cowardly enemies (Han Fei I: 3).

The Legalists suggest, once again, a peculiar solution to the problem of motivating men to fight and even die: the king must make men unable to do anything but fight. In other words, he must establish a uniformity of purpose. That is, men must fight in order to collect rewards; if they try to avoid their duties, they are punished because "if the warriors neglect their duties at the camps, the army becomes weak." The uniformity of purpose actually means that all citizens belong to the garrison state, where everybody, not only warriors but the farmers as well, contribute to the strength of the state, and where everyone is punished if the goals—the duties—are not accomplished. In other words, the warriors are not forced to fight because they have nothing else to do. If their accomplishment in fighting deviates from their duty, they are punished (Han Fei II: 53, 114; Shang I.3.9b).

It is also clear that the king must not distribute rewards unless the soldiers have achieved clear merits in battle. In addition to causing a decrease in motivation, such a policy would "provide space for private interest and public profit would come to nothing" (Han Fei II: 332; cf. Han Fei/Watson: 104–5).

In short, the Legalist theory trusts measures, not the individual preferences of soldiers. That is, if reward and punishment are of no faith, no one would ever fight to the death (Han Fei I: 3). Rewards and punishments make even a small state strong. If rewards and punishments follow clear and predictable rules, the state will have strong soldiers. The people will then risk their lives for their state. The law makes the king strong, and when the king is strong, the state will be strong (Han Fei I: 160, 168; Han Fei/Watson: 22; cf. Shang I.4.11a, II.5.1a).

Therefore, Confucian thinking may be dangerous to the internal unity of the state. The wrong ideals and values tend to weaken the state: "a man who is a filial son to his farther may be a traitorous subject to his lord" (Han Fei/Watson: 106). The Legalists thought that a nation at peace may apply benevolence and patronize philosophers, but "the nation in danger must call upon its fighting men." They further thought that private scholars never exert physical strength, and are inclined to neglect the work of farming and fighting, therefore injuring the law of the sovereign. The Legalists declared sarcastically that mere talk about political order will be useless if no one takes care of plowing and fighting. In such a case the state would only become poorer and poorer and unable to fight. In short, the Confucian measures—odes, rites, music, virtue, benevolence, and intelligence—make it impossible for the ruler to find individuals whom he can employ for defense and warfare (Han Fei I: 30; Han Fei II: 287, 290; Han Fei/Watson: 107; Shang I.3.8a).

NOTES

1. Virgil and Livy imply that war is the only natural relationship between Rome and the Other. However, war provides the opportunity for heroism and keeps men uncorrupted and strong (Chapter 11). Actually, Virgil and Livy do not give any explicit role to power politics in their views.

2. Drekmeier (1962: 266) notes that it was in the administration of foreign policy and in war that the king was least restrained in his actions. He maintains that only in recent history has the doctrine of *ahimsa* been interpreted to include outlawing war: "Although Ashoka renounced war in the name of the Buddhist ideal, he did not disband his army." Furthermore, Drekmeier claims that the Shantiparva in the *Mahabharata*, the *Laws of Manu*, and Kautilya "insist that foreign must be dominated not by ethical considerations but by self-interest, even if this should involve attacking a friendly power." However, this does not increase the number of cases in the present pattern. Ashoka's case and the Shantiparva only reveal that the *danda* tradition had wide support in ancient India, therefore Kautilya did not represent it alone. Similarly, several sections of the Manu's book belong to the same tradition. Another reason not to include such cases in the present pattern is that, unlike Drekmeier's claims, the *dharma* ethics did restrain the king's action in war (Aho 1981).

3. There is a fundamental difference between the two ancient schools and the modern Realist School of International Relations. They all maintain that power politics alone guarantees law and order in international relations under an anarchical international system. Although the ancient schools explicitly pursue the world state, the modern theory aims at preventing its realization. The modern realists prefer and justify balance-of-power politics, which actually stops anybody in an attempt to establish a world government.

Conclusions: Comparison of the Ideas of Social Order

Criticism of the existing conditions, i.e., the description and explanation of chaos, is the central point of departure for all suggestions to establishing order. Theories of chaos can be divided into four major groups:

1. *Immanentist-cosmologic religious theories.* Confucianism, Daoism, and ancient Indian political thought, including the *danda* tradition and Buddhism, can be put in this category without hesitation. In Mohism this idea is subordinated, and even more so in Legalism, which shares the immanentist-cosmological background, but speaks of political factors and aspects of chaos rather than religious factors.

2. *Transcendent-historical religious theories.* Ancient Hebrew thought, Jesus's teachings, and early Christianity belong in this category. So does Judaism, which, due to specific historical reasons, does not pay much attention to the analysis of chaos, but takes the Diaspora as a given.

3. *Dualistic religious theories.* Zoroastrianism is a single case in this category. However, ancient Hebrew thought and early Christianity indirectly share the same view, while they otherwise belong to the second category.

4. *Individualistic political theories.* Plato and Mohism represent the pure cases in this category. In other cases, the moral problems of individuals are discussed more as a subordinated factor. However, ancient Indian political thought, Buddhism, Zoroastrianism, and the Roman writers give this factor some attention.

5. *Societal political theories.* Legalism, Daoism, Judaism, Jesus's teachings, and Aristotle tend to see the major problem in the moral decline of societies. Plato also gives it a high emphasis, while ancient Indian political thought gives it a more subordinated role.

On the basis of the preceding discussions I suggest the following hypothetical relationships between the images of chaos and the ideas of social order:

1. It is clear that the immanentist-cosmological images of chaos are related to principle-oriented approaches to social order. Even when power-oriented patterns are suggested, world community and morality are preferred as the basis of social order.

2. The transcendent-historical images of chaos put the major emphasis on the contractual moral basis (the contract between man and God) and the exclusion of those who do not share the contract. The dualistic image suggests similar approach to social order that shares the idea of the contract and implies the exclusion of the other. However, the transcendent-historical theory speaks of a national or territorial center of the ordered world, while the dualistic theory goes beyond territorial boundaries.

3. Political images of chaos suggest two connections. The individualistic version (Plato) emphasizes the wise king and the improvement of individual morality through education. It comes close to Mohism, i.e., an immanentist-cosmological theory. The societal version (Aristotle and the Roman authors) shares the moral condition, but gives more emphasis to the national identity, implying exclusion of the Other. The societal version comes close to the transcendent-historical theories.

The suggested connections look promising, but I must emphasize that my suggestion is rather tentative and is presented mainly to serve as a comparison of the ideas of social order. A more systematic analysis would require a detailed analysis of the images of chaos, and a number of detailed case studies to reveal relationships between the images of chaos and the ideas of social order in the specific case. My tentative suggestion is insufficient to prove the existence of such relationships, and in any case is unable to elaborate them further. My main point in rejecting such an attempt is the fact that there does not exist any exclusive one-on-one relationship between an image of chaos and an approach to social order. A given image of chaos may lead to several different ideas of social order, and a given idea of social order can be derived from different images of chaos.

Turning now to more direct comparisons, I summarize the major findings of this book by applying two dimensions: (1) the units of comparison; and (2) the *tertium comparationis* variables.

In the first case, we will see if a given school or thinker concentrates on a single approach to social order or deals with several of them. In the second case we will find out if a given approach has been shared by one or more cases. The required information is summarized in Table 1 where I have tried to estimate—both on the basis of the preceding discussion and more subjective or intuitive comprehension of the cases I have reached during the long research process—what variables the cases are connected to and to what degree. A very strong connection is marked with a "3," a strong connection with a "2," and a recognizable connection with a "1." A "0" means that the variable is not relevant in the respective case, and a "−1" reveals that the respective case has expressed or strongly implied total rejection of the approach. The row totals reveal the number of ideas to which the case is related either positively or negatively; and the column totals reveal how many cases share or reject the respective idea.

All the cases—the schools, texts, or thinkers—share or support several approaches to social order. In other words, the ideas of social order are not exclusive but at least

Table 1
The Cases and Approaches to Social Order

APPROACHES TO SOCIAL ORDER

CASES	Moral Principle Alone	With	Ideal Organization Sovereign Units	World Comm.	Church	Moral Rule Wise King	Educa-tion	Use of Power Heroic King	Coercive Politics	External Relations Peaceful Relations	Exclu-sion	Power Politics	TOTAL
Confucianism	0	0	-1	3	0	3	3	0	1	2	0	0	5-1
Legalism	-1	0	-1	3	0	0	0	0	3	-1	0	3	3-3
Mohism	0	0	3	-1	0	3	1	0	-1	3	0	-1	4-3
Daoism	3	0	-1	-1	0	0	0	-1	-1	0	0	-1	1-5
Indian thought	0	3	1	0	0	3	3	2	1	2	-1	0	7-1
Kautilya	-1	0	-1	3	0	3	2	2	3	-1	0	3	6-3
Buddhism	3	0	1	0	2	3	2	0	0	3	-1	-1	6-2
Zoroastrianism	0	2	0	3	0	2	0	2	1	2	3	0	7-0
Hebrew thought	0	0	3	-1	2	3	1	2	0	-1	3	2	5-2
Judaism	2	3	1	0	2	2	2	0	0	2	2	-1	8-1
Jesus	3	0	-1	-1	0	0	0	0	-1	0	-1	-1	1-5
Church	0	0	-1	-1	3	3	3	0	2	2	3	0	6-2
Plato	0	0	3	-1	0	3	3	0	0	3	2	0	5-1
Aristotle	0	0	1	2	0	3	3	1	2	2	2	2	9-0
Cicero	0	0	0	3	0	3	3	0	0	2	2	0	5-0
Livy	0	0	0	3	0	3	1	3	0	0	2	1	6-0
Virgil	0	0	0	3	0	3	1	3	0	2	2	1	6-0
TOTAL	4-2	3	7-6	8-6	4	14	12	7-1	7-3	10-3	9-3	6-5	

partly overlap. In fact, the application of *tertium comparationis* variables has already emphasized that a given school, text, or author is a rather eclectic collection of various ideas rather than a watertight and exclusive system of thought. A text may have several unknown authors. Furthermore, even when we know for sure that a single author has written all parts of the specific text, the author has written several texts throughout his life and in various political and social contexts, each time doing a different political act (cf. Skinner 1978/1980; Tully 1984). There is no point in reconstructing a system where the original author never imagined or constructed it as such.

As to the substantive findings, my comparison suggests two major groups of approaches to social order:

1. *Comprehensive or diffused schools* maintaining more than four patterns of social order. Ancient Indian thought, Kautilya, Buddhism, Zoroastrianism, Judaism, early Christianity, Aristotle, Livy, and Virgil are the best examples in this group. Confucianism, ancient Hebrew thought, Plato, and Cicero can also be included here.

2. *Selective schools*, which concentrate on 1–3 patterns only (Legalism, Mohism, Daoism, and Jesus's teachings). While these are unique cases, Mohism, Daoism, and Jesus' s teachings are not far from each other; Legalism is their antonym.

From the table (columns) we can see that a given image of chaos or a pattern of social order is shared to a great extent by many schools, if not all of them. Indeed, there seems to be only two unique approaches to social order: moral principles as the basis of social order, and the organization of humankind as temple-states. However, the idea of moral principles in its various applications is shared by six cases altogether, and the idea of the temple-state by four.

The most popular approach to social order is the pattern of the wise king, as is the education of the wise king. The idea is shared by fourteen cases with no explicit criticism by any of the schools. Other generally shared patterns are morality-based external relations and the politics of exclusion, both of which both are explicitly rejected by three schools.

Among power-oriented patterns those of sovereign units and the world community have a rather even distribution in Table 1, but my intuitive classification likely exaggerates the popularity of sovereign units. Much attention is paid to the moral rule in the form of the wise king, and his moral and political education. The heroic king and the use of coercive power are clearly less popular. As for external relations, there is almost equal support for theories of peaceful international relations and the politics of exclusion. Power politics is the least popular in external relations, and it is explicitly rejected by several cases.

I unhesitantly claim that my work and this summary have provided a strong answer to the question presented in Chapter 1. It has become obvious that *there are alternatives to war for establishing and maintaining social order*. There are alternatives to war as "a shield against terror" (cf. Aho 1981). The approaches that provide a major emphasis to war are much less popular than various principle-oriented and morality-inclined power-oriented approaches. It is not only that "politics as politics" in an open and uncompromising form is not a generally supported approach to social order

(Chapters 11 and 13), it is more important to see that if and when war is accepted, it is never war in general, but a specific war serving fundamental principles like *dharma, asha, torah,* the ideal political organization, the wise or heroic rule, and the politics of exclusion. It is then not war but the respective factor that reestablishes social order. On the other hand, this fully confirms Aho's findings that suggest war is often justified by religious mythologies, that is, principles, values, and ideals that are thought decisive to social order in the respective society. Therefore, the important message in this book is that other factors of social order have often been thought sufficient and possible *without* war, and that war is therefore given a modest role in the discussed ideas of social order.

Finally, let me suggest an extension to the typology of social order applied in the preceding discussion, where the approaches to social order were divided into principle-oriented and power-oriented (Table 2). The extension is rather tentative because there can be no full agreement on the variables and their measurement in the case of ideas, and because much more research is required before a solid and parsimonious list of *tertium comparationis* variables can be found. For this, and for other substantive reasons as well, I present alternative typologies constructed in other ways.

My typology starts with the basic categorization of the principle-oriented and power-oriented patterns. The cases among the first type can be called the *principalist*. The cases among the latter group must be divided into two major types: the *sovereigntist* and the *cosmopolisist*, depending on the type of ideal organization they prefer, sovereign units, or the world community, respectively.

The principalists can be divided into two major categories. The first is called the *pure principalist*. It maintains that nothing else but the given principle is required for establishing and maintaining social order. The category includes Daoism, Jesus's teachings, and Buddhism. The second is called the *social principalist*. It maintains that the given principle must be connected to a social structure in order to maintain the principle and make it efficient in establishing social order. The category includes ancient Indian thought, Zoroastrianism, and Judaism.

Among the power-oriented patterns, the sovereigntists maintain that social order must be built on sovereign political units, which are governed by the wise king, who has obtained a perfect moral and political education. Furthermore, sovereign units can and must have peaceful relations with other similar units. The category includes two variants: the *moral sovereigntist* (Mohism) as a pure type, and the *exclusive sovereigntist* (Plato) that adds the politics of exclusion to the pure moral sovereigntist system. Because the latter is otherwise similar to the moral sovereigntist, it can be used as a sub type.

The second major category in the power-oriented patterns, the cosmopolisist, emphasizes a world community approach both in the sense of the world community and the temple-state. This category is divided into the *moral cosmopolisist,* the *exclusive cosmopolisist,* and the *coercive unificationist.*

The moral cosmopolisist suggests a world community, emphasizes its wise rule and the political education of the ruler, and prefers morality-based international relations as a realistic option until full, but voluntary, unification is achieved. Confucianism is included in this category.

Table 2
A Typology of the Ideas of Social Order in Civilizational Thought

BASIS OF SOCIAL ORDER

POWER USED IN

PRINCIPLE	SOVEREIGN UNITS	WORLD COMMUNITY
PRINCIPALIST (A)	SOVEREIGNTIST (B)	COSMOPOLISIST (C)
A.1. **Pure principalist**	B.1. **Moral sovereigntist**	C.1. **Moral cosmopolisist**
A.2. **Social principalist**	B.2. **Exclusive sovereigntist**	C.2. **Exclusive cosmopolisist**
		—Moral exclusionist
		—Heroic exclusionist
		—Warring exclusionist
		C.3. **Coercive unificationist**
		—Moral powerist
		—Pure powerist

The exclusive cosmopolisist category is inclined to emphasize military power, heroism, and especially the politics of exclusion, usually in addition to the ideas of the wise kingship. The group can be divided into three categories.

For the first group, the *moral exclusionist* takes the politics of exclusion as a principal matter, a political choice without much attention. The group does not give heroism or military elements important role. The case is best illustrated by Aristotle and Cicero. For the *heroic exclusionist,* heroism is an important additional element, as illustrated by Livy and Virgil. For the *warring exclusionist* the politics of exclusion takes place, or can take place, in a war for the god. While there are some differences between the cases, Zoroastrianism, ancient Hebrew thought, and early Christianity can be included in this category.

The third category of the cosmopolisists, coercive unificationist, emphasizes that the world state can only be achieved through military force. The category includes two variations. The *moral powerist,* illustrated by Kautilya, justifies the use of power and force in moral terms, as a means of achieving a morally perfect world. Furthermore, Kautilya supposes that the king is the key figure. He must share traditional Brahmanist values and be clever in power campaign. The *coercive powerist* does not suggest any justifications but takes politics as politics. This final case is illustrated by Chinese Legalism.

The suggested typology can be criticized due to problems caused by the two-dimensional figure in which it was presented. In the world of ideas, the model should be multidimensional because there are obvious connections not only between adjacent cases but between cases separated by one or more cases. In other words, a typology of ideas can never be a perfect taxonomical construction. Furthermore, in the world of ideas, it is not fully justified to claim that all empirical examples can be reduced into or categorized as a parsimonious number of ideal types. As Martin Wight's typology shows, it is possible to construct ideal types, but it will remain an eternal issue, whether or not his ideal types are the best ones, and if any author can be undisputedly included in a given category. For example, does Machiavelli belong to the Machiavellians or elsewhere, perhaps among many other schools of thought? My typology is based on the discussed cases, and does not claim to describe any others. Even so, there are other bases to construct such a typology. I briefly note three of them.

First, it is possible to reject the distinction between the principle-oriented and the power-oriented approaches to social order. During the course of this book we have encountered a conventional but dominating distinction between morality and power several times. In addition to the presented findings, this alternative distinction might be justified by earlier suggestions. For example, Eckhardt (1972) has similarly distinguished between compassion and compulsion. I have explicitly rejected this idea in my work, but it can be presented here without potential subcases. According to this idea, there are two major patterns of social order:

1. *Morality-oriented patterns* of social order consisting of three elements: (a) order emerges as spontaneous social harmony between individuals or groups if men follow strict moral principles; (b) the wise, morally perfect king guarantees order; and (c) morality must direct international relations. The cases include: Confucianism, Mohism, Daoism, ancient Indian thought, Buddhism, early Zoroastrianism, Judaism, Jesus's teachings, early Christianity, Plato, Aristotle, and the Roman authors.

2. *"Politics as politics" -oriented patterns*, where national identity and the exclusion of the Other, sometimes combined with open or structural violence and coercive power, establish social order. The cases include: Legalism, Kautilya, and ancient Hebrew thought.

Second, rejecting all *a priori* distinctions or qualitatively derived basic categories, and dealing with all the *tertium comparationis* variables without any assumptions, I applied a multivariate statistical technique called factor analysis to the data in Table 1.[1] The analysis provided six independent factors, in some of them schools strongly opposed each other. Keeping this in mind, I developed eight groupings of approaches to social order.

The first group consists of supporters of sovereign territorial units (Mohism and Plato), and the second—the opposite of the first group—prefers the world state (Kautilya and Legalism). The third group sees moral principle and pacifism as the basis of social order (Daoism, Jesus's teachings, Buddhism). As the opposite of this group I located the fourth group that speaks for the last war in the unification of the world state (Legalism, Kautilya, and Aristotle). The fifth group suggests peaceful unification of the world state (Confucianism, Aristotle, and Cicero) and is opposed by the sixth group which strongly prefers the idea of the Holy Land (ancient Hebrew thought). The seventh group sees heroism as the solution (Livy and Virgil) while the eighth group prefers a religious government of humankind (early Christianity). The ninth group gives the major emphasis to the contract (Zoroastrianism and Judaism). Ancient Indian thought has not found a place in this system, but comes close to being the opposite of the eighth group (early Christianity). Similarly, Judaism is located in several places by sharing views with Mohism and Plato, Daoism and others, and also Zoroastrianism.

Third, hierarchical cluster analysis provides a typology where statistical distances between groups are higher than within groups. That is, within a cluster the included cases are statistically similar to each other (if more than one school is included in the cluster). The first step of the operation divides the case into two groups; further steps divide them into subgroups, if required by the statistical criteria.

The fist attempt involving all the cases did not provide logical results because the cases preferring moral principles as a basis of social order cannot be compared to any other cases. Therefore, I omitted Daoism and Jesus's teachings from the analysis, thereby partly maintaining the original distinction between the principle-oriented and power-oriented approaches. Furthermore, in order to emphasize the social and political aspects of Indian political thought, Buddhism, Zoroastrianism, and Judaism value "0" was given to them on the principle-oriented variables. That is, as principle-oriented patterns they are similar to Daoism and Jesus's teachings, but as power-oriented patterns they find their place among others on a statistical basis.

Therefore, before the cluster analysis we have two basic groups: *moral principles* as the basis of social order (Daoism, Jesus, Buddhism, ancient Indian political thought, Zoroastrianism, and Judaism) and *social and political constructions of social order* (all other cases, including the power aspects of the four principle-oriented cases). This, however, is the given point of departure for clustering the latter group into smaller groups.

The clustering process was continued until the clusters remained more or less logical. Many cases remained alone suggesting that they tend to be unique, though they may share some views within a given approach to social order. This is both a logical and obvious compromise between the two theories of cultures: according to one theory, cultures or civilizations are unique, according to the other theory they are not.

At the conclusion of the statistical process I had the following groups: (1) ancient Hebrew thought; (2) early Christianity; (3) ancient Indian political thought; (4) Judaism, Buddhism, Mohism, and Plato; (5) Legalism and Kautilya; (6) Zoroastrianism, Livy, and Virgil; and (7) Confucianism, Aristotle, and Cicero. In addition to these groups were the two versions of the principle-oriented group, left out from the statistical analysis.

The statistical analysis does not give any substantive reasons for the emergence of the seven groups. Therefore, it remains subjective on where to place them on a continuum from absolute moral principle to the most clear-cut power politics. However, it is logical to suggest the following groups: (1) Daoism, Jesus's teachings, and Buddhism; (1.b) ancient Indian political thought, Zoroastrianism, and Judaism; (2) Judaism and Buddhism; (3) Mohism and Plato; (4) ancient Indian political thought; (5) early Christianity; (6) ancient Hebrew thought; (7) Confucianism, Aristotle, and Cicero; (8) Zoroastrianism, Livy, and Virgil; (9) Legalism and Kautilya.

Even this listing creates a rather neutral result, and must therefore be regrouped, by summarizing all information in this book, as follows:

1. *Pure principalists* (Daoism, Jesus's teachings)

2. *Social principalists and sovereigntists* (Buddhism, Mohism, Judaism, Zoroastrianism, Plato, and ancient Indian political thought)

3. *Temple-statists* (early Christianity, and ancient Hebrew thought)

4. *World- statists* (all other cases)

The last group, the world-statists, includes many cases that can be further divided into three variations: *peaceful unificationists* (Confucianism, Aristotle, and Cicero); *exclusive unificationists* (Zoroastrianism, Livy, and Virgil); and *coercive unificationists* (Legalism and Kautilya). The similarities with the first typology are, naturally, striking. Both typologies, like the two typologies between them, are based on the same data. Further research is needed to determine the best way of typologizing the cases, and what, if any, typology might contain value outside the presented data.

NOTE

1. This is a heuristic experiment with rather weak, nominal data (cluster analysis is not similarly vulnerable to this problem, but the suggestive and subjective nature of the data matrix can not be ignored). In the analysis, the *tertium comparationis* variables (the wise king and education combined) were cases whereby correlations between the schools were calculated. This technique (q) provides factors where the schools have factor loadings. Six factors with an eigenvalue over 1.0 were rotated (varimax). The factors explain 92 per cent of the total variation, but this is expected in the matrix where the number of variables is higher than that of cases. Due to the low number of cases, factor loadings above .65 were taken into consideration in the interpretation.

Appendix: Notes on the Primary and Secondary Sources

The academic debates on the origin, author, translations, and contending interpretations of a text are easily available. This is particularly true with the secondary sources, and introductions or commentaries of the primary texts. I have paid due attention to such views in reading the texts, but I have nothing to add to the debates.

My investigation is concentrated on a limited number of the basic texts from each civilization. Before I was able to select the material and essential issues needed for my research, I had to read a high number of texts. I list some of them in this appendix as consulted sources. They were not used for writing the book, therefore, I will give the bibliographical data here, not in the bibliography. In addition to the English editions of the primary sources, I consulted, wherever possible, the German and French editions. Furthermore, being Finnish, it is natural that a lot of my readings were based on Finnish translations.

This Appendix explicitly identifies, where necessary, the texts of a given school, or the works used to describe a specific school. I also briefly list the important secondary sources, which I found to be important, even if these sources can be recognized in the high number of references I make to them.

During the research process I usually wrote extensive interim reports on each civilization or schools on the basis of the sources available, sometimes including the consulted works. However, in this book I decided to quote from and refer to more easily accessible editions, where available. In any case, I have constructed rather general pictures, where minute details and contending translations of single words are unimportant.

The editions referred to in the study are listed in the bibliography under the primary sources section. Furthermore, I list works on the texts, historical figures, and historical context under the secondary sources section. However, in most cases I intentionally constructed patterns of social order on the basis of my reading and understanding of the texts; therefore, the number of secondary sources (and other interpretations) remains lower than would otherwise be expected.

CHINA

Consulted Works

Chan, W. T. 1963. *A Source Book in Chinese Philosophy*. Translated and compiled by W. T. Chan. Princeton: Princeton University Press.

Chinese Classics in Five Volumes. Translated and edited by J. Legge. Hong Kong: Hong Kong University Press (1970).

Chuang Tzu (Zhuang Zi). In Wieger (1984).

Lao Tzu (Lao Zi). In L. Wieger (1984).

The Li Chi. Book of Rites. An Encyclopedia of Ancient Ceremonial Usages. 2 Vols. Translated by J. Legge. Edited by Ch'u Chai and Wingberg Chai. New Hyde Park, NY: University Books (1967). See the original *Li Ki* in the primary sources.

Lieh Tzu (Lie Zi). In L. Wieger (1984).

The Sacred Books of China. In *The Sacred Books of the East*. Vols. 3, 16, 27, 28, 39, and 40. Translated and edited by J. Legge, Delhi: Motilal Banarsidass (various years).

Wieger, L. 1984. *The Wisdom of the Daoist Masters*. Translated by D. Bryce. Cambrian News, Aberystwyth, Great Britain: Llanerch Enterprises.

Texts of the Schools

Confucianism: *Confucius (The Analects)*, Hsün Tzu, Hsün Tzu/Watson, *The Li Ki*, and *Mencius*.
Daoism: Chuang Tzu, and Lao Tzu.
Legalism: Han Fei Tzu, Han Fei Tzu/Watson, and Shang Yang.
Mohism: Fung (1983), and Mo Tzu/Watson.

Important Secondary Sources

Chan (1960), Chen (1991), Fung (1983), and Wu (1978).

INDIA

In order to concentrate my attention on ancient Hindu political thought I mainly refer to literature from the Epic period—400 B. C. E. through 400 C. E. In this, secular, literature—the *Mahabharata*, the *Ramayana*, the *Laws of Manu*, and Kautilya's *Arthashastra*—politics is explicit. I do not discuss the religious differences between Brahmanism, Buddhism, and Jainism, which all at least partly share the basic elements of Hindu political thought (*dharma*, caste, wise king). However, I have inserted a brief discussion on the Buddhist alternative in Chapter 4 due to its similarities with Daoism and Jesus's teachings.

Consulted Works

All books on India published in the *Sacred Books of the East* (SBE), that is, Vols. 1, 2, 7, 8, 10–15, 17, 20–22, 26, 29–30, 34–36, 38, 41–45, 48, and 49. I also consulted one complete translation of the *Mahabharata* (in 18 volumes) translated by K. M. Ganguli (also known as the P. C. Roy translation)—the *Mahabharata* referred to in my work is exclusively P. Lal's work (1980). Finally, I must mention the *Edicts of Ashoka* (translated by N. A. Nikam, and R. McKeon. Chicago: University of Chicago Press, 1957); and B. Walker's *Hindu World: An Encyclopedic Survey of Hinduism* (London: Allen & Unwin, 1968).

Texts of the Schools

Ancient Indian political thought: *The Mahabharata, The Laws of Manu, The Bhagavad Gita, The Ramayana*, and *Rig Veda*.
Buddhism: *Buddhist Scriptures*, and *The Dhammapada*.
Kautilya: *Arthashastra*, and *The Laws of Manu*.

Important Secondary Sources

Drekmeier (1962), Ghoshal (1959), Kinsley (1982), Radhakrishnan (1929), Raju (1960), and Tahtinen (1976, 1979, 1983).

ZOROASTRIANISM

Consulted Works

Humbach, H. 1991. *The Gathas of Zarathustra*. Part I: Text and Translation. Heidelberg: Carl Winter Universitätsverlag.

Texts of the Schools

See Moulton (1913).

Important Secondary Sources

Boyce (1984), Gershevitch (1959), Moulton (1913), and Sharif (1963).

ANCIENT HEBREW THOUGHT AND JUDAISM

Consulted Works

The Apocrypha. Authorized version. London: Eyre and Spottiswoode. (N.d.).
The Babylonian Talmud. 34 volumes. Translated under the editorship of I. Epstein. London: Soncino (1935–48; reissued 1961).
The Books of Moses. Translation with introductions, commentary, and notes by E. Fox. New York: Schocken Books (1995).
Maimonides. *The Code of Maimonides (Mishneh Torah)*. Yale Judaica Series. Various translators. New Haven: Yale University Press (1956).
Mishnah. Translated by H. Danby. Oxford: Oxford University Press (1933/1977).

JESUS'S TEACHINGS AND EARLY CHRISTIANITY

Consulted Works

All volumes in the *Ancient Christian Writers: The Works of the Fathers in Translation* (ACW). Edited by J. Quasten and J. C. Plumpe. Westminister: Newman Press and London: Longmans, Green & Co. (1946).
Barnstone, W., ed. 1984. *The Other Bible*. San Francisco: HarperSanFrancisco.
Miller, R. J., ed. 1994. *The Complete Gospels*. Sonoma, CA: Polebridge Press.

Texts of the Schools

Early Christianity: *The New Testament*, Arnobius (ACW), Athenagoras (ACW), Augustine, several works (ACW), Augustine, *The City of God*, Iohannes Chrysostomus (ACW), Clement of Rome (*Early Christian Writings*), Cyprian (ACW), Gregory the Great (ACW), Gregory of Nyssa (ACW), Iganatius of Antioch (ACW), Maximus the Confessor (ACW), Pomerius (ACW), Prosper of Aquitaine (ACW), and Tertullian, two works (ACW).

Jesus's teachings: Mack (1993), *The Gospel of Thomas*, and *The New Testament* (King James version).

Important Secondary Sources

Crossan (1994), Pagels (1995), Räisänen (1984, 1986, 1990), and Adeney's (1965) and Chadwick's (1986) histories.

GREECE

Consulted Works

All the Greek writers in the *Loeb Classical Library*.

Homer. *Iliad*, and *Odyssey* (in several translations).

Plato. *The Collected Dialogues of Plato, including the Letters*. Edited by E. Hamilton and H. Cairns. Princeton, NJ: Princeton University Press (1973).

Plato. *The Early Socratic Dialogues*. Edited by T. J. Saunders. Harmondsworth, Great Britain: Penguin (1987).

Thucydides's *History of the Peloponnesian War* (translated by R. Warnes. Harmondsworth, Great Britain: Penguin 1986).

Important Secondary Sources

Baldry (1965), Caldwell (1919), Fustel de Coulanges (1920/1955), Stawell (1929/1936), and Tenkku (1981).

ROME

Consulted Works

All the Roman texts published in the *Loeb Classical Library*, and J. A. C. Thomas, *The Institutes of Justinian: Text, Translation and Commentary* (Amsterdam: North-Holland 1975).

Important Secondary Sources

Arnold (1911), and Tenkku (1981).

Bibliography

PRIMARY SOURCES BY CIVILIZATIONS

China

Chuang Tzu. *Mystic, Moralist, and Social Reformer*. Translated by H. A. Giles. Second revised edition. Shanghai: Kelly & Walsh (1926).

Confucius. *The Analects* (Lun yü). Translated by D. C. Lau. Harmondsworth, Great Britain: Penguin (1982).

Fung, Yu-lan. 1983. *A History of Chinese Philosophy*. 2 Vols. Translated by D. Bodde. Princeton: Princeton University Press.

Han Fei Tzu. *The Basic Writings of Mo Tzu, Hsün Tzu, and Han Fei Tzu*. Translated by B. Watson. New York: Columbia University Press (1967).

Han Fei Tzu. *The Complete Works of Han Fei Tzu*. 2 Vols. Edited and translated by A. K. Liao. London: Arthur Probsthain (1939 and 1959).

Hsün Tzu. *The Basic Writings of Mo Tzu, Hsün Tzu, and Han Fei Tzu*. Translated by B. Watson. New York: Columbia University Press (1967).

Hsün Tzu. *The Works of Hsüntze*. Edited and translated by H. H. Dubs. London: Arthur Probsthain (1928).

Lao Tzu. *Tao Te Ching*. Translated by D. C. Lau. Harmondsworth, Great Britain: Penguin (1983).

The Li Ki. In *The Sacred Books of the East*, Vols. 27 and 28. Translated and edited by J. Legge (*The Sacred Books of China: The Texts of Confucianism*. Parts 3 and 4, 1885/1966).

Mencius. Translated by D. C. Lau. Harmondsworth, Great Britain: Penguin (1983).

Mo Tzu. *The Basic Writings of Mo Tzu, Hsün Tzu and Han Fei Tzu*. Translated by B. Watson, New York: Columbia University Press (1967).

Shang Yang. *The Book of Lord Shang*. Edited and translated by J. J. L. Duyvendak. London: Arthur Probsthain (1928/1963).

Sun Tzu. *The Art of War*. Translated by T. Cleary. London: Shambhala (1991).

India

The Bhagavad Gita. Translated by E. Easwaran. London: Arkana (1986).
Buddhist Scriptures. Selected and translated by E. Conze. Harmondsworth, Great Britain: Penguin (1982).
The Dhammapada. Translated by J. Mascaró. Harmondsworth, Great Britain: Penguin (1987).
Kautilya. *Arthashastra.* Translated by R. Shamasastry. Mysore, India: Mysore Printing and Publishing House (1915/1961).
The Mahabharata of Vyasa. Condensed and translated by P. Lal. Delhi: Vikas (1980).
Manu. *The Laws of Manu.* Translated with extracts from seven commentaries by G. Bühler. *The Sacred Books of the East,* Vol. 25. Delhi: Motilal Banarsidass 1967. (1886).
The Ramayana. A modernized version in English prose by M. L. Sen. 3 Vols. Calcutta: Oriental Publishing Co. (1964).
Rig Veda. Translated by W. D. O'Flaherty. Harmondsworth, Great Britain: Penguin (1984).

Zoroastrianism

The Avestan Hymns to Mithra. Translated by I. Gershevitch. Cambridge: Cambridge University Press (1959).
Boyce, M. 1984. *Textual Sources for the Study of Zoroastrianism.* Manchester: Manchester University Press.
The Zend-Avesta. In *The Sacred Books of the East.* Vol. 4 (Part 1), Vol. 23 (Part 2), and Vol. 31 (Part 3). Parts 1 & 2 translated by J. Darmesteter. Part 3 translated by L. H. Mills. Delhi: Motilal Banarsidass 1969. (1880, 1883, 1887).

Ancient Hebrew Thought and Judaism

Alexander, P. S. 1984. *Textual Sources for the Study of Judaism.* Manchester: Manchester University Press.
The Apocrypha. In the *New English Bible with the Apocrypha.* Oxford Study Edition. Edited by S. Sandmel. New York: Oxford University Press (1976).
Cohen, A. 1975. *Everyman's Talmud.* New York: Schocken Books.
The Holy Bible. King James Version.
The Jerusalem Bible. Edited by A. Jones. Garden City, NY: Doubleday & Co. (1966).
Tractate Avot. In Neusner, J. 1993. *Classical Judaism. Torah, Learning, Virtue.* Vol. 3. Frankfurt am Main: Peter Lang.
Vermes, G. 1984. *The Dead Sea Scrolls in English.* Harmondsworth, Great Britain: Penguin.
Yadin, Y. 1962. *The Scroll of the War of the Sons of Light against the Sons of the Darkness.* Oxford: Oxford University Press.

Jesus's Teachings and Early Christianity

Arnobius. *The Case against the Pagans.* Translated and annotated by G. E. McCracken. *Ancient Christian Writers* (ACW), Vols. 7–8, Westminster, MD: Newman Press, and London: Longmans, Green & Co. (1949).
Athenagoras. *Embassy for the Christians/The Resurrection of the Dead.* Translated and annotated by J. H. Crehan. ACW, Vol. 23. (1956).
Augustine. *The City of God.* Translated by H. Bettenson. Harmondsworth, Great Britain: Penguin (1986).

Augustine. *The First Catechetical Instruction.* Translated and annotated by J. P. Christopher. ACW, Vol. 2. (1946).

Augustine. *The Lord's Sermon on the Mount.* Translated and annotated by J. J. Jepson. ACW, Vol. 5. (1948).

Augustine. *Sermons for Christmas and Epiphany.* Translated and annotated by T. C. Lawler. ACW, Vol. 15. (1952).

Clement of Rome. *The First Epistle of Clement to the Corinthians.* In *Early Christian Writings* (1984).

Cyprian. *The Lapsed/The Unity of the Catholic Church.* Translated and annotated by M. Bévenot. ACW, Vol. 25. (1957).

Early Christian Writings. 1984. Translated by M. Staniforth. Harmondsworth, Great Britain: Penguin.

The Gospel of Thomas. Translated by M. Meyer. San Fransisco: HarperSanFransisco (1992).

Gregory the Great. *Pastoral Care.* Translated and annotated by H. Davis. ACW, Vol. 11. (1950).

Gregory of Nyssa. *The Lord's Prayer/The Beatitudes.* Translated and annotated by H. C. Graef. ACW, Vol. 18. (1954).

The Holy Bible. King James Version.

Ignatius of Antioch. *The Epistles of Ignatius.* In *Early Christian Writings* (1984).

Iohannes, Chrysostomus. *Baptismal Instructions.* Translated and annotated by P. W. Harkins. ACW, Vol. 31. (1963).

Julian (Julianus Pomerius). *The Contemplative Life.* Translated and annotated by M. J. Suelzer. ACW, Vol. 4. (1947).

Mack, B. L. 1993. *The Lost Gospel.* Shaftesbury, Great Britain: Element.

Maximus. *The Ascetic Life/The Four Centuries on Charity.* Translated and annotated by P. Sherwood. ACW, Vol. 21. (1955).

Origen. *Prayer/Exhortation to Martyrdom.* Translated and annotated by J. J. O'Meara. ACW, Vol. 19. (1954).

Origen. *The Song of Songs/Commentary/Homilie.* Translated and annotated by R. P. Lawson. ACW, Vol. 26. (1957).

Prosper of Aquitaine. *The Call of All Nations.* Translated and annotated by P. de Letter. ACW, Vol. 14. (1952).

Tertullianus. *The Treatise against Hermogenes.* Translated and annotated by J. H. Waszink. ACW, Vol. 24. (1956).

Tertullianus. *Treatises on Penance.* Translated and annotated by W. P. le Saint. ACW, Vol. 28. (1959).

Greece

Aristotle. *The Athenian Constitution.* Translated by P. J. Rhodes. Harmondsworth, Great Britain: Penguin (1984).

Aristotle. *Ethics (The Nichomachean Ethics).* Edited and translated by J. Warrington. London: Dent (Everyman's Library) (1963).

Aristotle. *The Politics.* Translated by T. A. Saunders, revised by T. J. Saunders. Harmondsworth, Great Britain: Penguin (1984).

Demonsthenes. *For Megalopolis, On the Liberty of Rhodes, Philippic I–III, Olynthiac I–III, On the Peace & On the Chersonese.* In *Greek Political Oratory* (1985).

Diogenes Laertius. *Lives of Eminent Philosophers.* English translation by R. D. Hicks. Cambridge, MA: Harvard University Press (1980).

Greek Political Oratory. Selected and translated by A. N. W. Saunders. Harmondsworth, Great Britain: Penguin (1985).

Isocrates. *Panegyricus & Philip.* In *Greek Political Oratory* (1985).

Plato. *The Apology.* In the *Dialogues of Plato,* and the *Works of Plato in Five Volumes.*

Plato. *Calicles.* In the *Dialogues of Plato,* and the *Works of Plato in Five Volumes.*

Plato. *Critias.* In the *Dialogues of Plato,* and the *Works of Plato in Five Volumes.*

Plato. *Crito.* In the *Dialogues of Plato,* and the *Works of Plato in Five Volumes.*

Plato. *The Dialogues of Plato.* Translated with analysis by R. E. Allen. New Haven: Yale University Press (1984).

Plato. *Gorgias.* In the *Dialogues of Plato,* and the *Works of Plato in Five Volumes.*

Plato. *Laches.* In the *Dialogues of Plato,* and the *Works of Plato in Five Volumes.*

Plato. *The Laws.* Translated by T. J. Saunders. Harmondsworth, Great Britain: Penguin (1984).

Plato. *Menexenus.* In the *Dialogues of Plato,* and the *Works of Plato in Five Volumes.*

Plato. *The Phaedo.* Translated and edited by D. Gallop. Oxford: Oxford University Press (1993).

Plato. *Phaedrus & Letters VII and VIII.* Translated by W. Hamilton. Harmondsworth, Great Britain: Penguin (1985).

Plato. *Philebus.* In the *Dialogues of Plato,* and the *Works of Plato in Five Volumes.*

Plato. *Protagoras.* Translated with notes by C. C. W. Taylor. Oxford: Clarendon Press (1976).

Plato. *The Republic.* Translated by D. Lee. Harmondsworth, Great Britain: Penguin (1955).

Plato. *Sophist.* In the *Dialogues of Plato,* and the *Works of Plato in Five Volumes.*

Plato. *The Statesman.* Translated by R. Waterfield, edited by J. Annas and R. Waterfield. Cambridge: Cambridge University Press (1995).

Plato. *Timaeus.* In the *Dialogues of Plato,* and the *Works of Plato in Five Volumes.*

Plato. *The Works of Plato in Five Volumes.* Vol. 1 Translated by T. Taylor and F. Sydenham. Frome, Great Britain: The Prometheus Trust.

Xenophon. *A History of My Times* (Hellenica). Translated by R. Warner. Harmondsworth, Great Britain: Penguin (1986).

Xenophon. *The Persian Expedition* (Anabasis). Translated by R. Warner. Harmondsworth, Great Britain: Penguin (1984).

Rome

Cicero. *De Finibus.* In *Cicero in Twenty-Eight Volumes.* Vol. 17. With an English translation by H. Rackham. London: Heinemann (1971).

Cicero. *On the Good Life.* Translated by M. Grant. Harmondsworth, Great Britain: Penguin (1985).

Cicero. *De Legibus.* In *Cicero in Twenty-Eight Volumes.* Vol. 16. With an English translation by C. W. Keyes. London: Heinemann (1970).

Cicero. *The Nature of the Gods.* Translated by H. C. P. McGregor. Harmondsworth, Great Britain: Penguin (1986).

Cicero. *De Officiis.* In *Cicero in Twenty-Eight Volumes.* Vol. 21. With an English translation by W. Miller. London: Heinemann (1968).

Cicero. *De Re Publica.* In *Cicero in Twenty-Eight Volumes.* Vol. 17. With an English translation by H. Rackham. London: Heinemann (1971).

Diogenes Laertius. *Lives of Eminent Philosophers.* English translation by R. D. Hicks. Loeb Classical Library. Cambridge, MA: Harvard University Press (1979).

Horace. *The Odes of Horace.* Translated by J. Michie. Harmondsworth, Great Britain: Penguin (1976).

Livy. *The History of Rome from Its Foundation.* Translated by B. Radice. Introduction by R. M. Ogilvie. Harmondsworth, Great Britain: Penguin (1982).

Polybius. *The Histories.* English translation by W. R. Paton. Loeb Classical Library. Cambridge, MA: Harvard University Press (1975).

Virgil. *The Aeneid.* Translated by W. F. Jackson Knight. Harmondsworth, Great Britain: Penguin (1985).
Virgil. *The Eclogues.* Translated by G. Lee. Harmondsworth, Great Britain: Penguin (1984).
Virgil. *The Georgics.* Translated by L. P. Wilkinson. Harmondsworth, Great Britain: Penguin (1982).

SECONDARY SOURCES

Adeney, W. F. 1965. *The Greek and Eastern Churches.* Clifton, NJ: Reference Book Publishers.
Aho, J. A. 1981. *Religious Mythology and the Art of War.* London: Aldwych Press, and Westport, CT: Greenwood Press.
Aho, J. A. 1989. "I Am Death . . . Who Shatters Worlds: The Emerging Nuclear Death Cult." In I. Chernus and E. T. Linenthal, eds., *A Shuddering Dawn: Religious Studies and the Nuclear Age.* Albany: State University of New York Press.
Aho, J. A. 1990. "Heroism, the Construction of Evil, and Violence." In V. Harle, ed.
Airaksinen, T., and M. A. Bertman, eds. 1989. *Hobbes: War among Nations.* Aldershot, Great Britain: Avebury.
Airas, P. 1978. *Die Geschichtlichen Wertungen, Krieg und Friede von Friedrich dem Grossen bis Engels.* Rovaniemi, Finland: Pohjois-Suomen Historiallinen Yhdistys.
Ajami, F. 1993. "On the Clash of Civilizations." *Foreign Affairs* 72 (4): 2–27.
Alestalo, M. 1992. "European Integration and Comparative Research." In P. Kosonen, ed., *Changing Europe and Comparative Research.* Helsinki: Academy of Finland.
Alexander, P. S. 1984. *Textual Sources for the Study of Judaism.* Manchester: Manchester University Press.
Alker, H. 1987. "Fairy Tales, Tragedies and World Histories." *Behaviometrika,* No. 21: 1–28.
Allen, J. W. 1957. *Political Thought in the Sixteenth Century.* London: Macmillian.
Allen, R. E. 1984. Introductions to Plato's *Dialogues of Plato.*
Archibugi, D. 1989. "Peace and Democracy: Why Such an Unhappy Marriage?" In V. Harle, ed.
Armer, J. M., and R. M. Marsh, eds. 1982. *Comparative Sociological Research in the 1960s and 1970s.* Leiden, the Netherlands: E. J. Brill.
Arnold, E. V. 1911. *Roman Stoicism.* Cambridge: Cambridge University Press.
Baldry, H. C. 1965. *The Unity of Mankind in Greek Thought.* Cambridge: Cambridge University Press.
Banks, M. 1973. "Charles Manning, the Concept of 'Order,' and Contemporary International Theory." In A. James, ed.
Barnes, J., M. Schofield, and R. Sorabji, eds. 1977. *Articles on Aristotle.* Vol 2. London: Duckworth.
Barnstone, W., ed. 1984. *The Other Bible.* San Francisco: HarperSanFrancisco.
Basham, A. L. 1982. *The Wonder That Was India.* Third revised edition. London: Sidgwick & Jackson.
Basu, S. K. 1983. "The Two Interpretations of the Gita: Tilak's Karmayoga and Gandhi's Anasaktiyoga." *Gandhi Marq* 5 (6): 315–29.
Batho, D. 1945. *The Birth of Judaism.* London: National Society for the Promotion of Christian Knowledge.
Bederman, D. J. 1991. "Religion and the Sources of International Law in Antiquity." In M. W. Janis, ed.
Bereday, G. 1966. *Comparative Method in Education.* New York: Holt, Rinehart and Winston.

Bereday G. 1969. "Reflections on Comparative Methodology in Education 1964–1966." In M. Eckstein, and H. Noah, eds., *Scientific Investigations in Comparative Education*. London: Macmillan.

Berger, P., and T. Luckmann, 1966. *The Social Construction of Reality*. Garden City, NY: Doubleday-Anchor.

Bernal, M. 1987. *Black Athena*. Vol. 1. London: Free Association Books.

Bernal, M. 1991. *Black Athena*. Vol. 2. London: Free Association Books.

Bhattacharyya, N. N. 1990. *A Glossary of Indian Religious Terms and Concepts*. New Delhi: Manohar.

Bilimoria, P. 1982. "Mahatma Gandhi and Rabindranath Tagore on the Authority of 'Sruti' (Vedas)." *Gandhi Marq* 4 (8): 734–40.

Blau, J. L. 1966. *Modern Varieties of Judaism*. New York: Columbia University Press.

Boccaccini, G. 1991. *Middle Judaism*. Minneapolis, MN: Fortress Press.

Borg, M. J. 1993. *Jesus, a New Vision*. London: Society for Promotion of Christian Knowledge.

Boucher, D. 1985. *Texts in Context*. Dordrecht, the Netherlands: Martinus Nijhoff.

Boyce, M. 1984. *Textual Sources for the Study of Zoroastrianism*. Manchester: Manchester University Press.

Boyce, M. 1987. *Zoroastrians—Their Religious Beliefs and Practices*. London: Routledge & Kegan Paul.

Brayton, A. A., and S. J. Landwehr, 1981. *The Politics of War and Peace*. Washington, DC: University Press of America.

Brock, P. 1968. *Pacifism in the United States*. Princeton, NJ: Princeton University Press.

Brock, P. 1970. *Twentieth-Century Pacifism*. New York: Van Nostrand Reinhold Company.

Brock, P. 1972. *Pacifism in Europe to 1914*. Princeton, NJ: Princeton University Press.

Brown, S. 1984. *Origins of Christianity*. Oxford: Oxford University Press.

Browne, L. E. 1920. *Early Judaism*. London: Cambridge University Press.

Bühler, G. 1886. Introduction to the *Laws of Manu*.

Bull, H. 1976. "Martin Wight and the Theory of International Relations." *British Journal of International Studies* 2 (1): 101–16

Bull, H. 1977a. *The Anarchical Society*. London: Macmillan.

Bull, H. 1977b. "Introduction: Martin Wight and the Study of International Relations." In M. Wight, *Systems of States*. Leicester: Leicester University Press.

Burn, A. R. 1968. *The Warring States of Greece*. London: Thames and Hudson.

Burress, L. 1988. "A Comparison of Selected Old Testament Prophets and Gandhi." *Gandhi Marq* 10 (3): 135–48.

Burtt, E. A. 1951. "The Problem of a World Philosophy." In W. R. Inge et al.

Butchvarov, P. 1966. *Resemblance and Identity*. Bloomington: Indiana University Press.

Buzan, B. 1984. "Peace, Power, and Security." *Journal of Peace Research* 21 (4): 109–26.

Buzan, B. 1991. *People, States & Fear: The National Security Problem in International Relations*. Second edition. Brighton, Great Britain: Wheatsheaf Books

Caldwell, W. E. 1919. *Hellenic Conceptions of Peace*. New York: Columbia University Press.

The Cambridge History of Iran. Vol. 1. Edited by W. B. Fisher. London: Cambridge University Press 1968.

The Cambridge History of Iran. Vol. 2. Edited by I. Gershevitch. Cambridge: Cambridge University Press 1985

The Cambridge History of Iran. Vol. 3. (3 Parts). Edited by E. Yarshater. Cambridge: Cambridge University Press 1983.

The Cambridge History of Judaism. Vols. 1 and 2. Edited by W. D. Davies and L. Finkelstein. Cambridge: Cambridge University Press 1984/1989.

Campbell, J. 1986. *The Masks of God: Oriental Mythology*. Harmondsworth, Great Britain: Penguin.

Campbell, J. 1988. *The Hero with a Thousand Faces*. London: Paladin Books. (1949).

Carr, E. H. 1981. *The Twenty Years's Crisis 1919–1939*. London: Macmillan. (1939).

Carroll, B. A., ed. 1969. Special Issue on "Peace Research in History." *Journal of Peace Research* 6 (4): 287–400.

Cawkwell, G. 1986. Introduction to Xenophon's *A History of My Times*.

Chadwick, H. 1986. *The Early Church*. Harmondsworth, Great Britain: Penguin.

Chan, S. 1996. *Towards a Multicultural Roshamon Paradigm in International Relations*. Tampere, Finland: Tampere Peace Research Institute.

Chan, W. T. 1960. "The Concept of Man in Chinese Thought." In S. Radhakrishnan, and P.T. Raju, eds.

Chaturverdi, L. N. 1991. *The Teachings of Bhagavad Gita*. New Delhi: Sterling Publishers.

Cheadle, M. P. 1987. *Ezra Pound's Confucian Translations*. Ph.D. diss. University of California, Berkeley.

Chen, F. T. 1991. "The Confucian View of World Order." In M. W. Janis, ed.

Chernus, I. 1987. *Dr Strangegod: On the Symbolic Meaning of Nuclear Weapons*. Columbia, SC: University of South Carolina Press.

Chernus, I. 1991. "War and the Enemy in the Thought of Mircea Eliade." *History of European Ideas* 13 (4): 335–44.

Christopher, J. P. 1946. Introduction to Augustine's *First Catechetical Instruction*.

Chydenius, J. 1985. *Humanism in Medieval Concepts of Man and Society*. Helsinki: Societas Scientiarum Fennica.

Cohn, N. 1976. *Europe's Inner Demons*. St. Albans, Great Britain: Paladin.

Cohn, N. 1993. *Cosmos, Chaos, and the World to Come*. New Haven: Yale University Press.

Cohn, R. L. 1994. "Before Israel: The Canaanites as Other in Biblical Tradition." In L. J. Silberstein, and Cohn, eds.

Collingwood, R. G. 1980. *The Idea of History*. Oxford: Oxford University Press.

Constantinescu-Bagdat, E. 1924/1925. *Etudes d'historie pacifiste*. 2 Vols. Paris: Les Presses Universitaires de France.

Crehan, J. H. 1956. Introduction to Athenagoras's *Embassy for the Christians/The Resurrection of the Dead*.

Crossan, J. D. 1994. *Jesus, a Revolutionary Biography*. San Fransisco: HarperSanFransisco.

Darmesteter, J. 1880. Introduction and summaries to the *Zend-Avesta*/SBE 4.

Darmesteter, J. 1883. Introduction and summaries to the *Zend-Avesta*/SBE 23.

Davis, H. 1950. Introduction to Gregory the Great's *Pastoral Care*.

Defourny, M. 1977. "The Aim of the State: Peace." In J. Barnes et al., eds.

Defourny, P. 1977. "Contemplation in Aristotle's Ethics." In J. Barnes et al., eds.

Dhar, M. K., and R. L. Mehta, 1991. *Social and Economic History of Ancient India*. Delhi: S. S. Publishers.

Dhawan, N. 1990. *Brahmanism. A Political Concept*. New Delhi: R. K. Gupta & Co.

Donelan, M., ed. 1978. *The Reason of States*. London: Allen & Unwin.

Dorraj, M. 1990. *From Zarathustra to Khomeini*. Boulder, CO: Lynne Riennier Publishers.

Dossa, S. 1987. "Political Philosophy and Orientalism: The Classical Origins of a Discourse." *Alternatives* 12 (3): 343–57.

Dossa, S. 1988. "Auschwitz and the Palestinians: Christian Conscience and the Politics of Victimization." *Alternatives* 13 (4): 515–28.

Dossa, S. 1990. "In Europe's Shadow: Zionism and the Palestinian Fate." In V. Harle, ed.

Dothan, T., and R. L. Cohn, 1994. "The Philistine as Other." In L. J. Silberstein, and R. L. Cohn, eds.

Drekmeier, C. 1962. *Kingship and Community in Early India*. Stanford, CA: Stanford University Press.

Dubnov, S. 1958. *Nationalism and History*. Cleveland: Meridian Books.

Dubs, H. H. 1927. *Hsüntze: The Moulder of Ancient Confucianism*. London: Arthur Probsthain.

Dubs, H. H. 1928. "A Sketch of Chinese History." In Hsün Tzu.

Dutt, R. C. 1991. *A History of Civilisation in Ancient India*. 2 Vols. Delhi: Ankit Book Centre. (1888/1889).

Duyvendak, J. J. L. 1963. Introduction to ShangYang's *Book of Lord Shang*.

Easwaran, E. 1986. Introduction to the *Bhagavad Gita*.

Eckhardt, W. 1972. *Compassion: Toward a Science of Value*. Oakville: Canadian Peace Research Institute Press.

Eckstein, H., and D. E. Apter, eds. 1965. *Comparative Politics*. Glencoe, IL: Free Press.

The Economist, November 9th, 1966: 25–30. "Cultural Explanations."

Edwardes, M. 1961. *A History of India*. London: Thames and Hudson.

Edwards, R. 1970. "The Dimensions of Comparison and of Comparative Education." *Comparative Education Review* 14 (3): 239–54.

Eliade, M. 1971. *Cosmos and History. The Myth of the Eternal Return*. Translated by W. T. Trask. New York: Princeton University Press. (1954).

Farmer, W. R. 1956. *Maccabees, Zealots, and Josephus*. New York: Columbia University Press.

Ferguson, J. 1977. *War and Peace in the World's Religions*. London: Sheldon Press.

Fitzgerald, R., ed. 1980. *Comparing Political Thinkers*. Sydney: Pergamon Press.

Ford, C. S. 1977. "On the Analysis of Behavior for Cross-Cultural Comparisons." In C. S. Ford, ed.

Ford, C. S., ed. 1977. *Cross-Cultural Approaches*. New Haven, CT: Hraf Press.

Fortenbaugh, W. W. 1977. "Aristotle on Slaves and Women." In J. Barnes et al., eds.

Fukuyama, F. 1992. *The End of History and the Last Man*. London: Hamish Hamilton.

Fung, Yu-lan 1983. *A History of Chinese Philosophy*. 2 Vols. Translated by D. Bodde. Princeton: Princeton University Press.

Fustel de Coulanges, N. D. 1955. *The Ancient City*. Garden City, NY: Doubleday. (Page references to the Finnish translation by J. V. Lehtonen, Helsinki: Otava 1920).

Gallie, W. B. 1978. *Philosophers of Peace and War*. Cambridge: Cambridge University Press.

Galtung, J. 1975. "Peace Research: Past Experiences and Future Perspectives." In J. Galtung, *Essays in Peace Research*. Vol. 1. Copenhagen: Christian Ejlers.

Galtung, J. 1981. "Social Cosmology and the Concept of Peace." *Journal of Peace Research* 18 (2): 183–99.

Germino, D. 1975. "The Contemporary Relevance of the Classics of Political Philosophy." In F. I. Greenstein, and N. W. Polsby, eds., *Handbook of Political Science*, Vol. 1. Reading, MA: Addison-Wesley Publishing Company.

Gershevitch, I. 1959. Introduction and commentary to the *Avestan Hymn to Mithra*.

Ghosal, H. R. 1966. *An Outline History of the Indian People*. Delhi: Government of India, Ministry of Information.

Ghoshal, U. N. 1959. *A History of Indian Political Ideas*. Oxford: Oxford University Press.

Golding, M. P. 1989. "Agreements with Hostage-Takers." In M. A. Bertman, and T. Airaksinen, eds.

Gorny, Y. 1994. *The State of Israel in Jewish Public Thought*. London: Macmillan.

Graef, H. C. 1954. Introduction to Gregory of Nyssa's *Lords Prayer/The Beatitudes*.

Grant, M. 1985. Introduction to Cicero's *On the Good Life*.

Greenleaf, W. H. 1964. *Order, Empiricism and Politics*. Oxford: Oxford University Press.

Gurr, T. R., ed. 1980. *The Handbook of Political Conflict*. New York: Free Press.

Halliday, F. 1994. *Rethinking International Relations*. London: Macmillan.

Halliday, F. 1995. *Islam and the Myth of Confrontation*. London: I. B. Tauris.

Halliday, F. 1996. "Culture and International Relations." Paper presented at the Millenium 25th Anniversary Conference, London School of Economics and Political Science, October, 17–19.

Hamilton, W. 1985. Introduction to Plato's *Phaedrus and Letters VII and VIII*.

Hardie, W. F. R. 1977. "Aristotle's Doctrine that Virtue is a 'Mean.' " In J. Barnes et al., eds.

Harle, V. 1987a. "Has Peace Research Obligations to its Traditions." In V. Harle, ed., *Essays in Peace Studies*. Aldershot, Great Britain: Avebury.

Harle, V. 1987b. "Ideas of Peace and Order in Chinese Mohism and Daoism." In V. Harle, ed., *Essays in Peace Studies*. Aldershot, Great Britain: Avebury.

Harle, V. 1987c. "On the Alternatives to War and its Functions." *Current Research on Peace and Violence* 9 (3): 131–43.

Harle, V. 1989a. "From the Word to the Church." In V. Harle, ed.

Harle, V. 1989b. "Towards a Comparative Study of Peace Ideas." *Journal of Peace Research*, 26 (4): 341–51.

Harle, V. 1991. *Hyva, paha, ystava, vihollinen*. Jyväskylä, Finland: Rauhankirjallisuuden edistamisseura.

Harle, V. 1994. "On the Concepts of the 'Other' and the 'Enemy.' " *History of European Ideas* 19 (1–3): 27–34.

Harle, V. 1995. "The Ancient Daoist Alternative." *Peace Review* 7 (2): 205–10.

Harle, V., ed. 1989. *Studies in the History of European Peace Ideas*. Tampere, Finland: Tampere Peace Research Institute.

Harle, V., ed., 1990. *European Values in International Relations*. London: Pinter.

Hayashi, C., T. Suzuki, and M. Sasaki, 1992. *Data Analysis for Comparative Research*. Amsterdam: North-Holland.

Hegbin, and Corrigan. 1960. Introduction to Augustine's *On the Psalms*. Translated and annotated by Hebgin, and Corrigan. ACW, Vol. 29.

Herz, J. H. 1951. *Political Realism and Political Idealism*. Chicago: The University of Chicago Press.

Hirakawa, A. 1990. *A History of Indian Buddhism*. Honolulu: University of Hawaii Press.

Hiriyanna, M. 1967. *Outlines of Indian Philosophy*. London: Allen & Unwin.

Hoffmann, F. 1970. "Arms Debates—a 'Positional' Interpretation." *Journal of Peace Research*, 7 (3): 219–28.

Horowitz, I. L. 1973. *War and Peace in Contemporary Social and Philosophical Theory*. London: Souvenir Press.

Huntington, S. P. 1993. "The Clash of Civilizations?" *Foreign Affairs* 72 (3): 22–49.

Huntington, S. P. 1996. *The Clash of Civilizations and the Remaking of World Order*. New York: Simon & Schuster.

Hyslop, T. 1984. "The Buddha and the Mahatma." *Gandhi Marq* 6 (3): 131–42.

Inge, W. R. et al. 1951. *Radhakrishnan: Comparative Studies in Philosophy Presented in Honour of his Sixtieth Birthday*. London: Allen & Unwin.

Ishida, T. 1969. "Beyond the Traditional Concept of Peace in Different Cultures." *Journal of Peace Research* 6 (2): 133–46.

Jackson Knight, W. F. 1985. Introduction to Virgil's *Aeneid*.

James, A. 1973. "Preface," and "Law and Order in International Society." In A. James, ed.

James, A., ed. 1973. *The Bases of International Order*. London: Oxford University Press.

Janis, M. W., ed. 1991. *The Influence of Religion on the Development of International Law*. Dordrecht, the Netherlands: Martinus Nijhoff.

Jha, N. K. 1989. "Cultural and Philosophical Roots of India's Foreign Policy." *International Studies* 26 (1): 45–67.

Jha, R. 1983. "Gandhi's Encounter with Western Thought." *Gandhi Marq* 5 (4): 209–21.

Josephus. *The Jewish War*. Translated by G. A. Williamson, revised by E. M. Smallwood. Harmondsworth, Great Britain: Penguin (1985).

Joxe, A. 1991. *Voyage aux sources de la guerre*. Paris: Presses Universitaires de France.

Kao Heng. 1974. "Western Chou Slavery Upheld by Confucius." In *Selected Articles Criticizing Lin Piao and Confucius*. Vol.1. Peking: Foreign Languages Press.

Kelsen, H. 1977. "Aristotle and Hellenic-Macedonian Policy." In J. Barnes et al., eds.

Kende, I. 1989. "The History of Peace: Concept and Organizations from the Late Middle Ages to the 1870s." *Journal of Peace Research* 26 (3): 233–47.

Kende, I. 1990. "History of Peace." Unpublished English translation. Tampere Peace Research Institute, Finland.

Kenny, A. 1977. "Aristotle on Happiness." In J. Barnes et al., eds.

Khanna, S. 1983. " 'Of Faith': A Comparative Study of Gandhi and Marcel." *Gandhi Marq*, 5 (2): 88–108.

Kinsley, D. R. 1982. *Hinduism*. Englewood Cliffs, NJ: Prentice-Hall.

Kirkpatrick, J. J. 1993. "On the Clash of Civilizations." *Foreign Affairs* 72 (4): 2–27.

Klaassen, W. 1978. "The Just War: A Summary." *Peace Research Reviews* 7 (6): 1–70.

Knutsen, T. L. 1992. *The History of International Relations Theory*. Manchester: Manchester University Press.

Koskenniemi, M. 1989. "The Hobbesian Structure of International Legal Discourse." In M. A. Bertman, and T. Airaksinen, eds.

Kulke, H., and D. Rothermund, 1986. *A History of India*. London: Croom Helm.

Lal, P. 1980. Introduction to the *Mahabharata of Vyasa*.

Lakoff. G. 1991. "Metaphor and War." Manuscript. Linguistics Department, University of California, Berkeley.

Lambton, A. K. S. 1974. "Islamic Political Thought." In J. Schacht, and C. E. Bosworth, eds.

Lange, C. L. 1919. *Histoire de l'internationalisme I: Jusgu'a la paix de Westphalie 1648*. Kristiania, Oslo: H. Aschehoug & Co.

Lange, C. L., and A. Schou, 1954. *Histoire de l'internationalisme II: De la paix de Westphalie jusgu'a congres de Vienne 1815*. Kristiania, Oslo: H. Aschehoug & Co.

Lau, D. C. 1982. Introduction to Confucius's *Analects*.

Lau, D. C. 1983a. Introduction to Lao Tzu's *Tao Te Ching*.

Lau, D. C. 1983b. Introduction to *Mencius*.

Law, B. C. 1987. *Kshatriya Clans in Buddhist India*. Delhi: Indian Bibliographies Bureau. (1922).

Lee, G. 1984. Introduction to Virgil's *Eclogues*.

Legge, J. 1966. Introduction to the *Li Ki*.

Levine, R. 1963. *The Arms Debate*. Cambridge, MA: Harvard University Press.

Lewis, B. 1974. "Politics and War." In J. Schacht, and C. E. Bosworth, eds.

Liao, W. K. 1939. "Methodological Introduction." In *The Complete Works of Han Fei Tzu*, Vol. 1.

Lightstone, J. N. 1988. *Society, the Sacred and Scripture in Ancient Judaism*. Waterloo, Canada: Wilfrid Laurier University Press.

Liu Xiaogam. 1988. "Sartre's and Zhuang Zi's Views on Freedom." *Social Sciences in China* 9 (3): 93–111.

Lumb, W.,1937. *Later Judaism*. London: Society for Promoting Christian Knowledge.

Lyon, P. 1973. "New States and International Order." In A. James, ed.

MacFarlane, R. T. 1991. *The Narrative of Politics: Julius Caesar and the "Bellum Civile."* Ph.D. diss. University of Michigan.

Machinist, P. 1994. "Outsiders and Insiders." In L. J. Silberstein, and R. L. Cohn, eds.

Maitra, S. K. 1951. "The Gita's Conception of Freedom as Compared with that of Kant." In W. R. Inge et al.

Manning, C. A. W. 1962. *The Nature of International Society.* London: Bell.

Mascaró, J. 1987. Introduction to the *Dhammapada.*

Maurseth, P. 1964. "Balance-of-Power Thinking from the Renaissance to the French Revolution." *Journal of Peace Research* 1 (2): 120–35.

Maynard, J. A. 1928. *The Birth of Judaism.* London: Lucaz & Co.

Mazrui, A. 1990. *Cultural Forces in World Politics.* London: Currey.

McKinlay, R. D, and R. Little, 1986. *Global Problems and World Order.* London: Pinter.

Meinecke, F. 1984. *Machiavellism: The Doctrine of Raison d'Etat and its Place in Modern History.* Translated by D. Scott. Boulder, CO: Westview Press.

Merritt, R. L., and S. Rokkan, eds. 1966. *Comparing Nations.* New Haven: Yale University Press.

Meyer, M. 1992. Introduction to the *Gospel of Thomas.*

Miller, R. J., ed. 1994. *The Complete Gospels.* Sonoma, CA: Polebridge Press.

Mills, L.H. 1887. Introduction and summaries to the *Zend-Avesta*/SBE 31.

Mookerji, R. K. 1957. *Nationalism in Hindu Culture.* Delhi: S. Chand & Co.

Moore, G. F. 1954. *Judaism in the First Centuries of the Christian Era: The Age of the Tannaim.* 3 Vols. Cambridge, MA: Harvard University Press.

Morrison, D. 1986. Chapter introductions to the *Bhagavad Gita.*

Moulton, J. H. 1913. *Early Zoroastrianism.* London: Williams and Norgate.

Nadel, S. F. 1967. "Witchcraft in Four African Societies." In C. S. Ford, ed.

Nargolkar, V. 1981. "Vinoba and Satyargha." *Gandhi Marq* 2 (12): 661–72.

Nederveen Pieterse, J. 1994. "Unpacking the West: How European is Europe?" In A. Rattansi, and S. Westwood, eds., *Racism, Modernity, Identity.* Cambridge: Polity Press.

Neumann, I. B., and J. M. Welsh, 1991. "The Other in European Self-definition: An Addendum to the Literature on International Society." *Review of International Studies* 17 (4): 327–48.

Neusner, J. 1975. *Early Rabbinic Judaism.* Leiden, the Netherlands: E. J. Brill.

Neusner, J. 1981. *Judaism The Evidence of the Mishnah.* Chicago: University of Chicago Press.

Neusner, J. 1983. *Major Trends in Formative Judaism: Society and Symbol in Political Crisis.* Chico, CA: Scholars Press

Neusner, J. 1985. *Major Trends in Formative Judaism. Third Series: The Three Stages in the Formation of Judaism.* Chico, CA: Scholars Press.

Neusner, J. 1986. *Ancient Judaism and Modern Category-Formation.* Lanham, MN: University Press of America.

Neusner, J. 1989. *Judaism and Its Social Metaphors.* Cambridge: Cambridge University Press.

Neusner, J. 1990. *Torah through the Ages.* London: SCM Press

Neusner, J. 1991. *Rabbinic Political Theory.* Chicago: University of Chicago Press.

Neusner, J. 1992. *The Transformation of Judaism from Philosophy to Religion.* Urbana: University of Illinois Press.

Neusner, J. 1993a. *Classical Judaism. Torah, Learning, Virtue.* Vols. 1 and 3. Frankfurt am Main: Peter Lang.

Neusner, J. 1993b. *How Judaism Reads the Torah.* Frankfurt am Main: Peter Lang

Niebuhr, R. 1944. *The Children of Light and the Children of Darkness.* New York: Charles Scribner's Sons.

Niessen, M., J. Peschar, and C. Kourilsky, C. 1984. *International Comparative Research.* Oxford: Pergamon Press.

Northedge, F. S. 1973. "Order and Change in International Society." In A. James, ed.

Northrop, F. S. C. 1951. "The Relation between Eastern and Western Philosophy." In W. R. Inge et al.

O'Flaherty, W. D. 1984. Introduction and annotations to the *Rig Veda.*

O'Meara, J. 1986. Introduction to Augustine's *City of God.*

Obenchain, D. B. 1984. " *Ministers of the Moral Order: Innovations of the Early Chou Kings, the Duke of Chou, Chung-ni and Ju.*" Ph.D. diss., Harvard University.

Ogilvie, R. M. 1982. Introduction to Livy's *History of Rome from Its Foundation.*

Pagels, E. 1995. *The Origin of Satan.* New York: Random House.

Panayiotou, G. 1984. *"Consistence and Variation in Cicero's Oratorical Style."* Ph.D. diss., University of Illinois at Urbana-Champaign.

Parekh, B., and T. Pantham, 1987. *Political Discourse: Explorations in Indian and Western Political Thought.* New Delhi: Sage.

Parkinson, F. 1977. *The Philosophy of International Relations.* London: Sage.

Parpola, A. 1994. *Deciphering the Indus Script.* Cambridge: Cambridge University Press.

Patomäki, H. 1992. *Critical Realism and World Politics.* Turku, Finland: University of Turku.

Paton, W. R. 1975. Introduction to Polybius's *Histories.*

Pinson, K. S. 1958. "Simon Dubnov: Historian and Political Philosopher." In Dubnov's *Nationalism and History.*

Pocock, J. G. A. 1973. *Politics Language and Time: Essays on Political Thought and History.* New York: Atheneum.

Przeworski, A., and H. Teune, 1985. *The Logic of Comparative Social Inquiry.* Malabar, FL: Robert E. Krieger.

Purnell , R. 1978. "Theoretical Approaches to International Relations: The Contribution of the Greco-Roman World." In T. Taylor, ed., *Approaches and Theory in International Relations.* London: Longman.

Rackham, H. 1971. Introduction to *De Finibus.* In *Cicero in Twenty-Eight Volumes.* Vol. 17. With an English translation by H. Rackham. London: Heinermann.

Radhakrishnan, S. 1929. *Indian Philosophy.* London: Allen & Unwin.

Radhakrishnan, S., and P. T. Raju, eds. 1960. *The Concept of Man.* London: Allen & Unwin.

Ragin, C. C. 1987. *The Comparative Method.* Berkely, CA: University of California Press.

Ragin, C. C., ed. 1991. *Issues and Alternatives in Comparative Social Research.* Leiden, the Netherlands: E. J. Brill.

Räisänen, H. 1984. *Raamattunäkemystä etsimässä.* Helsinki: Gaudeamus.

Räisänen, H. 1986. *The Torah and Christ.* Helsinki: The Finnish Exegetical Society.

Räisänen, H. 1990. *Beyond New Testament Theology.* London: SCM Press.

Raivola, R. 1984. *Vertaileva kasvatustiede.* Tampere, Finland: Tampereen yliopiston kasvatustieteen laitos.

Raju, P. T. 1960. "Introduction," and "Comparison and Reflections." In S. Radhakrishnan, and P. T. Raju, eds.

Ramsey, P. 1983. *The Just War.* Langham, MN: University Press of America.

Raumer, K. von 1953. *Ewiger Friede.* München, Germany: Alber.

Rhodes, P. J. 1984. Introduction and notes to in Aristotle's *Athenian Constitution.*

Roberts, J. M. 1967. "Oaths, Autonomic Ordeals, and Power." In C. S. Ford, ed.

Rokkan, S. 1968. *Comparative Research across Cultures and Nations.* Paris: Mouton.

Rosenau, J. N. 1990. *Turbulence in World Politics.* New York: Harvester Wehatsheaf.

Ross, J. M. 1986. Introduction to Cicero's *Nature of the Gods.*

Russell, F. M. 1972. *Theories of International Relations.* New York: Arno Press (1936).

Ryder, T. T. B. 1965. *Koine Eirene. General Peace and Local Independence in Ancient Greece.* London: Oxford University Press.

Rykwert, J. 1976. *The Idea of a Town.* Princeton, NJ: Princeton University Press.

Sadeghi, A. 1996. "The Theory of Revolution: Towards a Fifth Generation." Paper presented at the Millennium 25th Anniversary Conference, London School of Economics and Political Science, October 17–19.

Sadenniemi, P. 1995. *Principles of Legitimacy and International Relations.* Helsinki: University of Helsinki, Department of Political Science.

Sanders, E. P. 1993. *The Historical Figure of Jesus.* London: Allen Lane, Penguin Press.

Sartori, G. 1994. *Comparative Constitutional Engineering.* London: Macmillan.

Saunders, A. N. W. 1985. Introduction to *Greek Political Oratory.*

Saunders, T. J. 1984a. Introduction to Plato's *Laws.*

Saunders, T. J. 1984b. Reviewer's introduction to Aristotle's *Politics.*

Schacht, J., and C. E. Bosworth, eds. 1974. *The Legacy of Islam.* Second Edition. Oxford: Clarendon Press.

Schmitt, C. 1993. *The Concept of the Political.* Translated by J. H. Lomax. Chicago: University of Chicago Press.

Schou, A. 1963. *Histoire de l'internationalsme III: Du congres de Vienne jusqu'a la premiere guerre mondiale.* Kristiania, Oslo: H. Aschehoug & Co.

Schürer, E. 1986. *The History of the Jewish People in the Age of Jesus Christ.* Translated and revised by G. Vermes et al. Edinburgh: T. &. T. Clark.

Selected Articles Criticizing Lin Piao and Confucius I. Peking: Foreign Languages Press 1974.

Sen, M. L. 1964. Introduction to the *Ramayana.*

Shaffer, E. S. ed. 1981. *Comparative Criticism.* Vol. 1. Cambridge: Cambridge University Press.

Shaffer, E. S. ed. 1984. *Comparative Criticism.* Vol. 6. Cambridge: Cambridge University Press.

Sharif, M. M. 1963. *A History of Muslim Philosophy.* Wiesbaden: Otto Harrassowitz.

Sicker, M. 1992. *Judaism, Nationalism, and the Land of Israel.* Boulder, CO: Westview Press.

Silberstein, L. J. 1994. "Others within and Others without." In L. J. Silberstein, and R. L. Cohn, eds.

Silberstein, L. J., and R. L. Cohn, eds. 1994. *The Other in Jewish Thought and History.* New York: New York University Press.

Silver, D. J., and B. Martin, 1974. *A History of Judaism.* Vol. 1. New York: Basic Books.

Sinclair, T. A. 1961. *A History of Greek Political Thought.* London: Routledge.

Sinclair, T. A. 1984. Introduction to Aristotle's *Politics.*

Singh, M. 1986. "Gandhi and Schweitzer: How Alike?" In *Gandhi Marg* 8 (1): 23–31.

Sinha, J. P. 1977. *The Mahabharata: A Literary Study.* New Delhi: Meharch and Lachhmandas.

Skinner, Q. 1978/1980. *The Foundations of Modern Political Thought.* 2 Vols. Cambridge: Cambridge University Press.

Smith, A. D. 1986. *The Ethnic Origin of Nations.* Oxford: Basil Blackwell.

Smith, A. D. 1991. *National Identity.* Harmondswort, Great Britain: Penguin.

Smith, A. D. 1995. *Nations and Nationalism in a Global Era.* Cambridge, MA: Polity Press.

Smith, J. Z. 1978. *Map is Not Territory.* Studies in the History of Religions. Leiden, the Netherlands: E.J. Brill.

Smith, J. Z. 1982. *Imagining Religion.* From Babylon to Jonestown. Chicago: University of Chicago Press.

Smith, M. 1987. *Palestinian Parties and Politics that Shaped the Old Testament.* London: SCM Press.

Smith, V. A. 1984. *The Oxford History of India*. Third Edition. Eited by P. Spear (Part I revised by Sir Mortimer Wheeler and A. L. Basham).

Spiro, M.E., and R. G. d'Andrade. 1967. "A Cross-Cultural Study of Some Supernatural Beliefs." In C. S. Ford, ed.

Srivastava, G. 1982. "Mazzini and Gandhi." *Gandhi Marq* 3 (12): 734–41.

Staniforth, M. 1984. Commentaries to *Early Christian Writings*.

Starr, C. G. 1974. *A History of the Ancient World*. Second Edition. New York: Oxford University Press.

Stawell, F. M. 1936. *The Growth of International Thought*. London: Thornton Butterworth (1929).

Stern, G. 1973. "Morality and International Order." In A. James, ed.

Strauss, D. F. 1973. *The Life of Jesus Critically Examined*. Edited by P. C. Hodgson, translated by George Eliot. London: SCM Press.

Taheri, A. 1985. *The Spirit of Allah*. London: Hutchinson.

Tahtinen, U. 1976. *Ahimsa*. London: Rider and Company.

Tahtinen, U. 1979. *The Core of Gandhi's Philosophy*. New Delhi: Abhinav Publications.

Tahtinen, U. 1983. *Indian Traditional Values*. New Delhi: Abhinav Publications.

Tandon, V. 1980. "Vinoba and Satyagraha." In *Gandhi Marq* 2 (7): 385–94.

Tang Yung-Tung. 1951. "On 'Ko-yi,' the Earliest Method by which Indian Buddhism and Chinese Thought were Synthesized." In W. R. Inge et al.

Targ, H. R. 1974. "Violence and Social Change: The Contemporary Relevance of Camus and Merleau-Ponty." *Peace and Change* 2 (3): 10–16.

Tenkku, J. 1981. *Vanhan- ja keskiajan moraalifilosofian historia*. Helsinki: Gaudeamus.

Ter Meulen, J. 1917, 1929, and 1940. *Der Gedanke der Internationalen Organisation in seiner Entwicklung*, Vols. 1–3. Haag, Holland: Martinus Nijhoff.

Tomasson, R. F. 1978. Introduction to *Comparative Studies in Sociology*. Vol. 1. Greenwich, CT: Jai Press.

Tucker, R. W. 1978. *The Just War*. Westport, CT: Greenwood Press.

Tully, J. H. 1984. "Review Article: The Pen is a Mighty Sword—Quentin Skinner's Analysis of Politics." *British Journal of Political Science* 13 (4): 489–509.

Ulich, R. 1967. *The Education Of Nations*. Cambridge: Harvard University Press.

Vagts, A., and D. F. Vagts. 1979. "The Balance of Power in International Law: A History of an Idea." *The American Journal of International Law* 73 (4): 555–80.

Vaux, R. de. 1961. *Ancient Israel*. Translated by J. McHugh. New York: McGraw-Hill.

Vermes, G. 1984. Introduction and notes on the text in *The Dead Sea Scrolls in English*.

Wallach, J. L. 1986. *The Dogma of the Battle of Annihilation: The Theories of Clausewitz and Schlieffen and Their Impact on the German Conduct of Two World Wars*. Westport, CT: Greenwood Press.

Waltz, K. N. 1970. *Man, the State and War*. New York: Columbia University Press (1959).

Walzer, M. 1992. *Just and Unjust Wars*. New York: Basic Books.

Watson, A. 1992. *The Evolution of International Society*. London: Routledge.

Watson, B. 1967. Introductions to the *Basic Writings of Mo Tzu, Hsun Tzu, and Han Fei Tzu*.

Weber, M. 1952. *Ancient Judaism*. Translated by H. H. Gerth. New York: Free Press.

Weber, M. 1964. *The Religion of China: Confucianism and Taoism*. Translated by H. G. Gerth. New York: Macmillan.

Weber, M. 1978. *Economy and Society*. Berkeley: University of California Press.

Weiler, G. 1990. "Violence—An Israeli Perspective." In V. Harle, ed.

Welch, A. C. 1935. *Post-Exilic Judaism*. Edinburgh: William Blackwood & Sons.

Wheeler, M. 1977. "Aristotle's Analysis of the Nature of Political Struggle." In Barnes et al., eds.

Whiting, J. W. M. 1967. "Sorcery, Sin, and the Superego." In C. S. Ford, ed.

Wight, M. 1966. "Why is there no International Theory?." In H. Butterfield, H., and M. Wight, eds., *Diplomatic Investigations*. London: Allen & Unwin.

Wight, M. 1991. *International Theory: The Three Traditions*. Leicester: Leicester University Press.

Wilkinson, L. P. 1982. Introduction and notes to Virgil's *Georgics*.

Willms, B. 1991. "Politics as Politics: Carl Schmitt's 'Concept of the Political' and the Tradition of European Political Thought." *History of European Ideas* 13 (4): 371–84.

Wu, G. 1978. *Die Staatslehre des Han Fei*. Wien, Österreich: Springer-Verlag.

Yadin. Y. 1963. *The Art of War in Biblical Lands*. 2 Vols. Translated by M. Pearlman. Jerusalem: International Publishing Company.

Zinnes, D. 1980. "Why War? Evidence on the Outbreak of International Conflict." In T. R. Gurr, ed., *Handbook of Political Conflict*. New York: Free Press.

Index

Achilles, 24

Adharma (chaos), 53, 63, 194. *See also*
dharma

Aeneas, 146–47

The Aeneid (Virgil), 144, 146–49, 151

Ahimsa, 45, 48, 63, 204 n.2

Aho, James A.: comparative method,
30–31; definition of order, 4, 6, 40,
208–9; *dharma* and caste, 40, 54,
56–57, 59–61, 63, 64 n.2; heroism,
143–44, 164; images of chaos, 27;
king's action in war, 204 n.2, 208;
politics of exclusion, 179, 185, 197.
Work: *The Religious Mythology and
the Art of War,* 12, 14, 21

Ahura Mazda, 19–20, 65–70, 126, 144,
191–93

Alexander the Great, 17–18, 20, 98,
109 n.4, 174, 192

Alliance, 19, 62, 100, 167, 181, 195,
201

The Analects (Kong Zi), 115–18, 133,
135–37, 162, 174

Analogy, 129, 131

Anarchy, 7, 54, 97, 134, 164, 174

Anarya, 18

Ancient Hebrew thought: compared to
the other schools, 208, 211–13;
heroism, 143; historical context,
20–21; images of chaos, 27, 205;
nationalism, 84 n.6, 199 n.4; politics

of exclusion, 178–79, 183–85,
191,193–94; temple-state, 101;
territorial state, 92; wise king, 126.
See also evil; Gentiles; God; *torah*;
war; wisdom

Ancient Hindu thought. *See* ancient
Indian political thought

Ancient Indian political thought: caste
system, 52, 56; compared to the other
schools, 207–9, 212–13; *danda*, 153,
162–63; *dharma*, 38, 50 n.4, 53, 163;
education, 129; historical context,
17; human nature, 156; images of
chaos, 205; king, 16, 52, 111, 113,
164; military heroism, 143, 200; the
state, 60; struggle between good and
evil, 63, 193; war, 179. *See also*
happiness; hero; *karma*; kshatriya;
peace; ruler; wisdom; wise king

Angra Mainyu: 19–20, 65, 68, 70, 126,
190–93

The Apocrypha, 127, 141, 187, 190

Arbitrary power, 97, 128, 155, 158

Aristocracy, 93–94, 119, 122, 128 n.1,
155

Aristotle: city-state, 93–94, 96;
coercive power, 153–55; compared
to the other schools, 207–8, 211–13;
education, 29, 138–39; exclusion of
the Other, 179; human nature, 119,
121; images of chaos, 205–6; law,

About the Author

VILHO HARLE is Professor of International Relations at University of Lapland in Finland. He was a Visiting Fellow at the Centre for International Studies, the London School of Economics in 1996–1997. He has published and edited more than ten books and journal issues as well as a number of articles in scientific journals.

ISBN 0-313-30582-X

90000>

HARDCOVER BAR CODE